Praise for *Agile Testing*

"As Agile methods have entered the mainstream, we've learned a lot about how the testing discipline fits into Agile projects. Lisa and Janet give us a solid look at what to do, and what to avoid, in Agile testing."

—Ron Jeffries, www.XProgramming.com

"An excellent introduction to agile and how it affects the software test community!"

—Gerard Meszaros, Agile Practice Lead and Chief Test Strategist at Solution Frameworks, Inc., an agile coaching and lean software development consultancy

"In sports and music, people know the importance of practicing technique until it becomes a part of the way they do things. This book is about some of the most fundamental techniques in software development—how to build quality into code—techniques that should become second nature to every development team. The book provides both broad and in-depth coverage of how to move testing to the front of the development process, along with a liberal sprinkling of real-life examples that bring the book to life."

—Mary Poppendieck, Author of *Lean Software Development* and *Implementing Lean Software Development*

"Refreshingly pragmatic. Chock-full of wisdom. Absent of dogma. This book is a game-changer. Every software professional should read it."

—Uncle Bob Martin, Object Mentor, Inc.

"With *Agile Testing*, Lisa and Janet have used their holistic sensibility of testing to describe a culture shift for testers and teams willing to elevate their test effectiveness. The combination of real-life project experiences and specific techniques provide an excellent way to learn and adapt to continually changing project needs."

—Adam Geras, M.Sc. Developer-Tester, Ideaca Knowledge Services

"On Agile projects, everyone seems to ask, 'But, what about testing?' Is it the development team's responsibility entirely, the testing team, or a collaborative effort between developers and testers? Or, 'How much testing should we automate?' Lisa and Janet have written a book that finally answers these types of questions and more! Whether you're a tester, developer, or manager, you'll learn many great examples and stories from the real-world work experiences they've shared in this excellent book."

—Paul Duvall, CTO of Stelligent and co-author of *Continuous Integration: Improving Software Quality and Reducing Risk*

"Finally a book for testers on Agile teams that acknowledges there is not just one right way! *Agile Testing* provides comprehensive coverage of the issues testers face when they move to Agile: from tools and metrics to roles and process. Illustrated with numerous stories and examples from many contributors, it gives a clear picture of what successful Agile testers are doing today."

—Bret Pettichord, Chief Technical Officer of WatirCraft and Lead Developer of Watir

AGILE TESTING

AGILE TESTING

A PRACTICAL GUIDE FOR TESTERS AND AGILE TEAMS

Lisa Crispin
Janet Gregory

♦ Addison-Wesley

Upper Saddle River, NJ • Boston • Indianapolis • San Francisco
New York • Toronto • Montreal • London • Munich • Paris • Madrid
Capetown • Sydney • Tokyo • Singapore • Mexico City

The publisher offers excellent discounts on this book when ordered in quantity for bulk purchases or special sales, which may include electronic versions and/or custom covers and content particular to your business, training goals, marketing focus, and branding interests. For more information, please contact:

U.S. Corporate and Government Sales
(800) 382-3419
corpsales@pearsontechgroup.com

For sales outside the United States, please contact:

International Sales
international@pearson.com

Visit us on the Web: informit.com/aw

Library of Congress Cataloging-in-Publication Data:

Crispin, Lisa.
  Agile testing : a practical guide for testers and agile teams /
Lisa Crispin, Janet Gregory. — 1st ed.
      p.   cm.
  Includes bibliographical references and index.
  ISBN-13: 978-0-321-53446-0 (pbk. : alk. paper)
  ISBN-10: 0-321-53446-8 (pbk. : alk. paper)   1. Computer software—
Testing.   2. Agile software development.   I. Gregory, Janet.   II. Title.

  QA76.76.T48C75 2009
  005.1—dc22

                                        2008042444

ISBN-13: 978-0-321-53446-0
ISBN-10:   0-321-53446-8
Text printed in the United States on recycled paper at LSC Communications in Crawfordsville, Indiana.
13   17

To my husband, Bob Downing—you're the bee's knees!
—Lisa

To Jack, Dana, and Susan, and to all the writers in my family.
—Janet

And to all our favorite donkeys and dragons.
—Lisa and Janet

CONTENTS

FOREWORD

By Mike Cohn

"Quality is baked in," the programmers kept telling me. As part of a proposed acquisition, my boss had asked me to perform some final due diligence on the development team and its product. We'd already established that the company's recently launched product was doing well in the market, but I was to make sure we were not about to buy more trouble than benefit. So I spent my time with the development team. I was looking for problems that might arise from having rushed the product into release. I wondered, "Was the code clean? Were there modules that could only be worked on by one developer? Were there hundreds or thousands of defects waiting to be discovered?" And when I asked about the team's approach to testing, "Quality is baked in" was the answer I got.

Because this rather unusual colloquialism could have meant just about anything, I pressed further. What I found was that this was the company founder's shorthand for expressing one of quality pioneer W. Edwards Deming's famous fourteen points: Build quality into the product rather than trying to test it in later.

The idea of building quality into their products is at the heart of how agile teams work. Agile teams work in short iterations in part to ensure that the application remains at a known state of quality. Agile teams are highly cross-functional, with programmers, testers, and others working side by side throughout each iteration so that quality can be baked into products through techniques such as acceptance-test driven development, a heavy emphasis on automated testing, and whole-team thinking. Good agile teams bake quality in by building their products continuously, integrating new work within minutes of its being completed. Agile teams utilize techniques such as refactoring and a preference for simplicity in order to prevent technical debt from accumulating.

Learning how to do these things is difficult, and especially so for testers, whose role has been given scant attention in previous books. Fortunately, the book you now hold in your hands answers questions on the mind of every tester who's beginning to work on an agile project, such as:

- What are my roles and responsibilities?
- How do I work more closely with programmers?
- How much do we automate, and how do we start automating?

The experience of Lisa and Janet shines through on every page of the book. However, this book is not just their story. Within this book, they incorporate dozens of stories from real-world agile testers. These stories form the heart of the book and are what makes it so unique. It's one thing to shout from the ivory tower, "Here's how to do agile testing." It's another to tell the stories of the teams that have struggled and then emerged agile and victorious over challenges such as usability testing, legacy code that resists automation, transitioning testers used to traditional phase-gate development, testing that "keeps up" with short iterations, and knowing when a feature is "done."

Lisa and Janet were there at the beginning, learning how to do agile testing back when the prevailing wisdom was that agile teams didn't need testers and that programmers could bake quality in by themselves. Over the years and through articles, conference presentations, and working with their clients and teams, Lisa and Janet have helped us see the rich role to be filled by testers on agile projects. In this book, Lisa and Janet use a test automation pyramid, the agile testing quadrants of Brian Marick (himself another world-class agile tester), and other techniques to show how much was missing from a mind-set that said testing is necessary but testers aren't.

If you want to learn how to bake quality into your products or are an aspiring agile tester seeking to understand your role, I can think of no better guides than Lisa and Janet.

FOREWORD

By Brian Marick

Imagine yourself skimming over a landscape thousands of years ago, looking at the people below. They're barely scraping out a living in a hostile territory, doing some hunting, some fishing, and a little planting. Off in the distance, you see the glitter of a glacier. Moving closer, you see that it's melting fast and that it's barely damming a huge lake. As you watch, the lake breaks through, sweeping down a riverbed, carving it deeper, splashing up against cliffs on the far side of the landscape—some of which collapse.

As you watch, the dazed inhabitants begin to explore the opening. On the other side, there's a lush landscape, teaming with bigger animals than they've ever seen before, some grazing on grass with huge seed heads, some squabbling over mounds of fallen fruit.

People move in. Almost immediately, they begin to live better. But as the years fly past, you see them adapt. They begin to use nets to fish in the fast-running streams. They learn the teamwork needed to bring down the larger animals, though not without a few deaths along the way. They find ever-better ways to cultivate this new grass they've come to call "wheat."

As you watch, the mad burst of innovation gives way to a stable solution, a good way to live in this new land, a way that's taught to each new generation. Although just over there, you spy someone inventing the wheel . . .

■ ■ ■

In the early years of this century, the adoption of Agile methods sometimes seemed like a vast dam breaking, opening up a way to a better—more productive, more joyful—way of developing software. Many early adopters saw benefits right away, even though they barely knew what they were doing.

Some had an easier time of it than others. Programmers were like the hunters in the fable above. Yes, they had to learn new skills in order to hunt bison, but they knew how to hunt rabbits, more or less, and there were plenty of rabbits around. Testers were more like spear-fishers in a land where spear-fishing wouldn't work. Going from spear-fishing to net-fishing is a much bigger conceptual jump than going from rabbit to bison. And, while some of the skills— cleaning fish, for example—were the same in the new land, the testers had to invent new skills of net-weaving before they could truly pull their weight.

So testing lagged behind. Fortunately, we had early adopters like Lisa and Janet, people who dove right in alongside the programmers, testers who were not jealous of their role or their independence, downright *pleasant* people who could figure out the biggest change of all in Agile testing: the tester's new social role.

As a result, we have this book. It's the stable solution, the good way for testers to live in this new Agile land of ours. It's not the final word—we *could* use the wheel, and I myself am eager for someone to invent antibiotics—but what's taught here will serve you well until someone, perhaps Lisa and Janet, brings the next big change.

PREFACE

We were early adopters of Extreme Programming (XP), testing on XP teams that weren't at all sure where testers or their brand of testing fit in. At the time, there wasn't much in the agile (which wasn't called agile yet) literature about acceptance testing, or how professional testers might contribute. We learned not only from our own experiences but from others in the small agile community. In 2002, Lisa co-wrote *Testing Extreme Programming* with Tip House, with lots of help from Janet. Since then, agile development has evolved, and the agile testing community has flourished. With so many people contributing ideas, we've learned a whole lot more about agile testing.

Individually and together, we've helped teams transition to agile, helped testers learn how to contribute on agile teams, and worked with others in the agile community to explore ways that agile teams can be more successful at testing. Our experiences differ. Lisa has spent most of her time as an agile tester on stable teams working for years at a time on web applications in the retail, telephony, and financial industries. Janet has worked with software organizations developing enterprise systems in a variety of industries. These agile projects have included developing a message-handling system, an environmental-tracking system, a remote data management system (including an embedded application, with a communication network as well as the application), an oil and gas production accounting application, and applications in the airline transportation industry. She has played different roles—sometimes tester, sometimes coach—but has always worked to better integrate the testers with the rest of the team. She has been with teams from as little as six months to as long as one-and-a-half years.

With these different points of view, we have learned to work together and complement each other's skill sets, and we have given many presentations and tutorials together.

WHY WE WROTE THIS BOOK

Several excellent books oriented toward agile development on testing and test patterns have been published (see our bibliography). These books are generally focused on helping the developer. We decided to write a book aimed at helping agile teams be more successful at delivering business value using tests that the business can understand. We want to help testers and quality assurance (QA) professionals who have worked in more traditional development methodologies make the transition to agile development.

We've figured out how to apply—on a practical, day-to-day level—the fruits of our own experience working with teams of all sizes and a variety of ideas from other agile practitioners. We've put all this together in this book to help testers, quality assurance managers, developers, development managers, product owners, and anyone else with a stake in effective testing on agile projects to deliver the software their customers need. However, we've focused on the role of the tester, a role that may be adopted by a variety of professionals.

Agile testing practices aren't limited to members of agile teams. They can be used to improve testing on projects using traditional development methodologies as well. This book is also intended to help testers working on projects using any type of development methodology.

Agile development isn't the only way to successfully deliver software. However, all of the successful teams we've been on, agile or waterfall, have had several critical commonalities. The programmers write and automate unit and integration tests that provide good code coverage. They are disciplined in the use of source code control and code integration. Skilled testers are involved from the start of the development cycle and are given time and resources to do an adequate job of all necessary forms of testing. An automated regression suite that covers the system functionality at a higher level is run and checked regularly. The development team understands the customers' jobs and their needs, and works closely together with the business experts.

People, not methodologies or tools, make projects successful. We enjoy agile development because its values, principles, and core practices enable people to do their best work, and testing and quality are central to agile development. In this book, we explain how to apply agile values and principles to your unique testing situation and enable your teams to succeed. We have more about that in Chapter 1, "What Is Agile Testing, Anyway?" and in Chapter 2, "Ten Principles for Agile Testers."

HOW WE WROTE THIS BOOK

Having experienced the benefits of agile development, we used agile practices to produce this book. As we began work on the book, we talked to agile testers and teams from around the globe to find out what problems they encountered and how they addressed them. We planned how we would cover these areas in the book.

We made a release plan based on two-week iterations. Every two weeks, we delivered two rough-draft chapters to our book website. Because we aren't co-located, we found tools to use to communicate, provide "source code control" for our chapters, deliver the product to our customers, and get their feedback. We couldn't "pair" much real-time, but we traded chapters back and forth for review and revision, and had informal "stand-ups" daily via instant message.

Our "customers" were the generous people in the agile community who volunteered to review draft chapters. They provided feedback by email or (if we were lucky) in person. We used the feedback to guide us as we continued writing and revising. After all the rough drafts were done, we made a new plan to complete the revisions, incorporating all the helpful ideas from our "customers."

Our most important tool was mind maps. We started out by creating a mind map of how we envisioned the whole book. We then created mind maps for each section of the book. Before writing each chapter, we brainstormed with a mind map. As we revised, we revisited the mind maps, which helped us think of ideas we may have missed.

Because we think the mind maps added so much value, we've included the mind map as part of the opening of each chapter. We hope they'll help you get an overview of all the information included in the chapter, and inspire you to try using mind maps yourself.

OUR AUDIENCE

This book will help you if you've ever asked any of the following excellent questions, which we've heard many times:

- If developers are writing tests, what do the testers do?
- I'm a QA manager, and our company is implementing agile development (Scrum, XP, DSDM, name your flavor). What's my role now?

- I've worked as a tester on a traditional waterfall team, and I'm really excited by what I've read about agile. What do I need to know to work on an agile team?
- What's an "agile tester"?
- I'm a developer on an agile team. We're writing code test-first, but our customers still aren't happy with what we deliver. What are we missing?
- I'm a developer on an agile team. We're writing our code test-first. We make sure we have tests for all our code. Why do we need testers?
- I coach an agile development team. Our QA team can't keep up with us, and testing always lags behind. Should we just plan to test an iteration behind development?
- I'm a software development manager. We recently transitioned to agile, but all our testers quit. Why?
- I'm a tester on a team that's going agile. I don't have any programming or automation skills. Is there any place for me on an agile team?
- How can testing possibly keep up with two-week iterations?
- What about load testing, performance testing, usability testing, all the other "ilities"? Where do these fit in?
- We have audit requirements. How does agile development and testing address these?

If you have similar questions and you're looking for practical advice about how testers contribute to agile teams and how agile teams can do an effective job of testing, you've picked up the right book.

There are many "flavors" of agile development, but they all have much in common. We support the Agile Manifesto, which we explain in Chapter 1, "What Is Agile Testing, Anyway?" Whether you're practicing Scrum, Extreme Programming, Crystal, DSDM, or your own variation of agile development, you'll find information here to help with your testing efforts.

A User Story for an Agile Testing Book

When Robin Dymond, a managing consultant and trainer who has helped many teams adopt lean and agile, heard we were writing this book, he sent us the user story he'd like to have fulfilled. It encapsulates many of the requirements we planned to deliver.

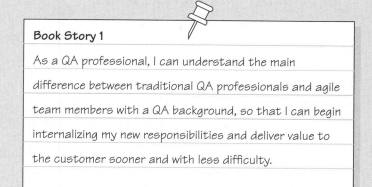

Book Story 1

As a QA professional, I can understand the main difference between traditional QA professionals and agile team members with a QA background, so that I can begin internalizing my new responsibilities and deliver value to the customer sooner and with less difficulty.

Acceptance conditions:

- My concerns and fears about losing control of testing are addressed.
- My concerns and fears about having to write code (never done it) are addressed.
- As a tester I understand my new value to the team.
- As a tester new to Agile, I can easily read about things that are most important to my new role.
- As a tester new to Agile, I can easily ignore things that are less important to my new role.
- As a tester new to Agile, I can easily get further detail about agile testing that is important to MY context.

Were I to suggest a solution to this problem, I think of Scrum versus XP. With Scrum you get a simple view that enables people to quickly adopt Agile. However, Scrum is the tip of the iceberg for successful agile teams. For testers who are new, I would love to see agile testing ideas expressed in layers of detail. What do I need to know today, what should I know tomorrow, and what context-sensitive things should I consider for continuous improvement?

We've tried to provide these layers of detail in this book. We'll approach agile testing from a few different perspectives: transitioning into agile development, using an agile testing matrix to guide testing efforts, and explaining all the different testing activities that take place throughout the agile development cycle.

HOW TO USE THIS BOOK

If you aren't sure where to start in this book, or you just want a quick over-view, we suggest you read the last chapter, Chapter 21, "Key Success Factors," and follow wherever it leads you.

Part I: Introduction

If you want quick answers to questions such as "Is agile testing different than testing on waterfall projects?" or "What's the difference between a tester on a traditional team and an agile tester?," start with Part I, which includes the following chapters:

- Chapter 1: What Is Agile Testing, Anyway?
- Chapter 2: Ten Principles for Agile Testers

These chapters are the "tip of the iceberg" that Robin requested in his user story. They include an overview of how agile differs from a traditional phased approach and explore the "whole team" approach to quality and testing.

In this part of the book we define the "agile testing mind-set" and what makes testers successful on agile teams. We explain how testers apply agile values and principles to contribute their particular expertise.

Part II: Organizational Challenges

If you're a tester or manager on a traditional QA team, or you're coaching a team that's moving to agile, Part II will help you with the organizational chal-lenges faced by teams in transition. The "whole team" attitude represents a lot of cultural changes to team members, but it helps overcome the fear testers have when they wonder how much control they'll have or whether they'll be expected to write code.

Some of the questions answered in Part II are:

- How can we engage the QA team?
- What about management's expectations?
- How should we structure our agile team, and where do the testers fit?
- What do we look for when hiring an agile tester?
- How do we cope with a team distributed across the globe?

Part II also introduces some topics we don't always enjoy talking about. We explore ideas about how to transition processes and models, such as audits or SOX compliance, that are common in traditional environments.

Metrics and how they're applied can be a controversial issue, but there are positive ways to use them to benefit the team. Defect tracking easily becomes a point of contention for teams, with questions such as "Do we use a defect-tracking system?" or "When do we log bugs?"

Two common questions about agile testing from people with traditional test team experience are "What about test plans?" and "Is it true there's no documentation on agile projects?" Part II clears up these mysteries.

The chapters in Part II are as follows:

- Chapter 3: Cultural Challenges
- Chapter 4: Team Logistics
- Chapter 5: Transitioning Typical Processes

Part III: The Agile Testing Quadrants

Do you want more details on what types of testing are done on agile projects? Are you wondering who does what testing? How do you know whether you've done all the testing that's needed? How do you decide what practices, techniques, and tools fit your particular situation? If these are your concerns, check out Part III.

We use Brian Marick's Agile Testing Quadrants to explain the purpose of testing. The quadrants help you define all the different areas your testing should address, from unit level tests to reliability and other "ilities," and everything in between. This is where we get down into the nitty-gritty of how to deliver a high-quality product. We explain techniques that can help you to communicate well with your customers and better understand their requirements. This part of the book shows how tests drive development at multiple levels. It also provides tools for your toolkit that can help you to effectively define, design, and execute tests that support the team and critique the product. The chapters include the following:

- Chapter 6: The Purpose of Testing
- Chapter 7: Technology-Facing Tests that Support the Team

- Chapter 8: Business-Facing Tests that Support the Team
- Chapter 9: Toolkit for Business-Facing Tests that Support the Team
- Chapter 10: Business-Facing Tests that Critique the Product
- Chapter 11: Critiquing the Product Using Technology-Facing Tests
- Chapter 12: Summary of Testing Quadrants

Part IV: Automation

Test automation is a central focus of successful agile teams, and it's a scary topic for lots of people (we know, because it's had us running scared before!). How do you squeeze test automation into short iterations and still get all the stories completed?

Part IV gets into the details of when and why to automate, how to overcome barriers to test automation, and how to develop and implement a test automation strategy that works for your team. Because test automation tools change and evolve so rapidly, our aim is not to explain how to use specific tools, but to help you select and use the right tools for your situation. Our agile test automation tips will help you with difficult challenges such as testing legacy code.

The chapters are as follows:

- Chapter 13: Why We Want to Automate Tests and What Holds Us Back
- Chapter 14: An Agile Test Automation Strategy

Part V: An Iteration in the Life of a Tester

If you just want to get a feel for what testers do throughout the agile development cycle, or you need help putting together all the information in this book, go to Part V. Here we chronicle an iteration, and more, in the life of an agile tester. Testers contribute enormous value throughout the agile software development cycles. In Part V, we explain the activities that testers do on a daily basis. We start with planning releases and iterations to get each iteration off to a good start, and move through the iteration—collaborating with the customer and development teams, testing, and writing code. We end the iteration by delivering new features and finding ways for the team to improve the process.

The chapters break down this way:

- Chapter 15: Tester Activities in Release or Theme Planning
- Chapter 16: Hit the Ground Running

- Chapter 17: Iteration Kickoff
- Chapter 18: Coding and Testing
- Chapter 19: Wrap Up the Iteration
- Chapter 20: Successful Delivery

Part VI: Summary

In Chapter 21, "Key Success Factors," we present seven key factors agile teams can use for successful testing. If you're having trouble deciding where to start with agile testing, or how to work on improving what you're doing now, these success factors will give you some direction.

Other Elements

We've also included a glossary we hope you will find useful, as well as references to books, articles, websites, and blogs in the bibliography.

JUST START DOING IT—TODAY!

Agile development is all about doing your best work. Every team has unique challenges. We've tried to present all the information that we think may help agile testers, their teams, managers, and customers. Apply the techniques that you think are appropriate for your situation. Experiment constantly, evaluate the results, and come back to this book to see what might help you improve. Our goal is to help testers and agile teams enjoy delivering the best and most valuable product they can.

When we asked Dierk König, founder and project manager of Canoo Web-Test, what he thought was the number one success factor for agile testing, he answered: "Start doing it—today!" You can take a baby step to improve your team's testing right now. Go get started!

ACKNOWLEDGMENTS

So many people have helped us with this book that it's hard to know whom to thank first. Chris Guzikowski gave us the opportunity to write this book and kept encouraging us along the way. When we were deciding whether to take on such a mammoth task, Mike Cohn gave us the sage advice that the best reason to write a book is that you have something to say. We sure have lots to say about agile testing. Fortunately, so do lots of other people who were willing to lend us a hand.

Many thanks to Brian Marick and Mike Cohn for writing such kind forewords. We're honored that Mike selected our book for his signature series. We're grateful for the many ideas and observations of his that are included in this book.

Brian Marick's "Agile Testing Matrix" has guided both of us in our agile projects for several years, and it provides the core of Part III. Thank you, Brian, for thinking up the quadrants (and so many other contributions to agile testing) and letting us use them here.

We made constant use of the agile value of feedback. Many thanks to our official reviewers: Jennitta Andrea, Gerard Meszaros, Ron Jeffries, and Paul Duvall. Each one had unique and insightful comments that helped us greatly improve the book. Gerard also helped us be more consistent and correct in our testing terminology, and contributed some agile testing success stories.

Special thanks to two reviewers and top-notch agile testers who read every word we wrote and spent hours discussing the draft chapters with us in person: Pierre Veragen and Paul Rogers. Many of the good ideas in this book are theirs.

We interviewed several teams to learn what advice they would give new agile teams and testers, and solicited success stories and "lessons learned" from colleagues in the agile testing community. Heartfelt thanks to our many contributors of sidebars and quotes, as well as providers of helpful feedback, including (in no particular order) Robin Dymond, Bret Pettichord, Tae Chang, Bob Galen, Erika Boyer, Grig Gheorghiu, Erik Bos, Mark Benander, Jonathan Rasmusson, Andy Pols, Dierk König, Rafael Santos, Jason Holzer, Christophe Louvion, David Reed, John Voris, Chris McMahon, Declan Whelan, Michael Bolton, Elisabeth Hendrickson, Joe Yakich, Andrew Glover, Alessandro Collino, Coni Tartaglia, Markus Gärtner, Megan Sumrell, Nathan Silberman, Mike Thomas, Mike Busse, Steve Perkins, Joseph King, Jakub Oleszkiewicz, Pierre Veragen (again), Paul Rogers (again), Jon Hagar, Antony Marcano, Patrick Wilson-Welsh, Patrick Fleisch, Apurva Chandra, Ken De Souza, and Carol Vaage.

Many thanks also to the rest of our community of unofficial reviewers who read chapters, gave feedback and ideas, and let us bounce ideas off of them, including Tom Poppendieck, Jun Bueno, Kevin Lawrence, Hannu Kokko, Titus Brown, Wim van de Goor, Lucas Campos, Kay Johansen, Adrian Howard, Henrik Kniberg, Shelly Park, Robert Small, Senaka Suriyaachchi, and Erik Petersen. And if we've neglected to list you here, it's not that we value your contribution any less, it's just that we didn't keep good enough notes! We hope you will see how your time and effort paid off in the finished book.

We appreciate the groundwork laid by the agile pioneers who have helped us and our teams succeed with agile. You'll find some of their works in the bibliography. We are grateful for the agile teams that have given us so many open source test tools that help all of our teams deliver so much value. Some of those tools are also listed in the bibliography.

Thanks to Mike Thomas for taking many of the action photos of an agile team that appear in this book. We hope these photos show those of you new to agile testing and development that there's no big mystery—it's just good people getting together to discuss, demo, and draw pictures.

Thanks so much to our Addison-Wesley editorial and production team who patiently answered many questions and turned this into the professional-looking book you see here, including Raina Chrobak, Chris Zahn, John Fuller, Sally Gregg, Bonnie Granat, Diane Freed, Jack Lewis, and Kim Arney.

Lisa's Story

I'm eternally grateful to Janet for agreeing to write this book with me. She kept us organized and on track so we could juggle book writing with our full-time jobs and personal lives. I'm fortunate to have a writing partner whose experience is complementary to mine. Like any successful agile project, this is a true team effort. This has been hard work, but thanks to Janet it has been a lot of fun, too.

I'd like to thank the members of my current team at ePlan Services Inc. (formerly known as Fast401k), which I joined (thanks to Mike Cohn, our first leader) in 2003. All of us learned so much working for Mike that first year, and it's a testament to his leadership that we continue to improve and help the business grow. Thanks to my awesome teammates who have each helped me become a better tester and agile team member, and who were all good sports while Mike Thomas took action photos of us: Nanda Lankapalli, Tony Sweets, Jeff Thuss, Lisa Owens, Mike Thomas, Vince Palumbo, Mike Busse, Nehru Kaja, Trevor Sterritt, Steve Kives, and former but still beloved team members Joe Yakich, Jason Kay, Jennifer Riefenberg, Matt Tierney, and Charles LeRose. I also have been lucky enough to work with the best customer team anywhere. They are too numerous to mention here, but many thanks to them, and in particular to Steve Perkins, Anne Olguin, and Zachary Shannon, who help us focus on delivering value. Thanks also to Mark and Dan Gutrich, founders and leaders of ePlan Services, for giving us all the opportunity to succeed with agile development.

Thanks to Kay and Zhon Johansen for teaching me about mind maps at Agile 2006. I hope we have put this skill to good use in creating this book.

Much gratitude to all my friends and family, whom I neglected terribly during the many months spent writing this book, and who nevertheless supported me constantly. There are too many to mention, but I must specially thank Anna Blake for her constant understanding and provision of donkey therapy. Chester and Ernest, the donkeys of my heart, have kept pulling me along. Dodger didn't make the whole book-writing journey in this world, but his memory continues to lift me up. My little poodle and muse Tango was by my side every minute that I worked on this book at home, joined occasionally by Bruno, Bubba, Olive, Squiggy, Starsky, Bobcat, and Patty. Thanks to my parents for being proud of me and not complaining about my neglect of them during this book-writing time.

I know that my husband, Bob Downing, took a deep breath when I exclaimed, "I have the chance to write another book about agile testing," but he nevertheless encouraged me constantly and made it possible for me to find the time to write. He kept the "no-kill shelter" running, kept our lives rolling, kept my spirits up, and sustained me with many fabulous meals. He is the light of my life.

—Lisa

Janet's Story

Lisa and I made a great team; each of us had our own strengths. When one of us faltered and took some time to recoup, the other picked up the slack. I learned so much from Lisa (thanks go to her for giving me this opportunity), but I also found I learned a lot from myself. Just the process of articulating my thoughts helped to clarify things that had been rumbling around in my brain for a long time. The mindmaps helped immensely, so thanks to Kenji Hiranabe, who gave a workshop at Agile 2007 and made me realize what a powerful yet simple tool mind maps can be.

This book-writing journey was an amazing experience. Thanks to the people on all the teams I worked with who provided so many of the examples in this book.

It's been a pretty special year all the way around. During the year (or so) it took to write this book, my family increased in size. My two daughters, Dana and Susan, each gave me a grandson—those were some of the times Lisa picked up the slack. I would like to thank my granddaughter Lauren (currently three) for making me leave my computer and play. It kept me sane. Thanks to my sister Colleen who gave me long-distance encouragement many mornings using instant messenger when I was feeling overwhelmed with the sheer number of hours I was putting in.

And a very special thanks to Jack, my husband, who moved his office downstairs when I took over the existing one. There were times when I am sure he felt neglected and wondered if he even had a wife as he spend many long hours alone. However, he was there with me the whole way, encouraging and supporting me in this endeavor.

—Janet

ABOUT THE AUTHORS

Lisa Crispin is an agile testing practitioner and coach. She specializes in showing testers and agile teams how testers can add value and how to guide development with business-facing tests. Her mission is to bring agile joy to the software testing world and testing joy to the agile development world. Lisa joined her first agile team in 2000, having enjoyed many years working as a programmer, analyst, tester, and QA director. Since 2003, she's been a tester on a Scrum/XP team at ePlan Services, Inc. She frequently leads tutorials and workshops on agile testing at conferences in North America and Europe. Lisa regularly contributes articles about agile testing to publications such as *Better Software* magazine, *IEEE Software*, and *Methods and Tools*. Lisa also co-authored *Testing Extreme Programming* (Addison-Wesley, 2002) with Tip House.

For more about Lisa's work, visit her websites, www.lisacrispin.com and www.agiletester.ca, or email her at lisa@agiletester.ca.

Janet Gregory is the founder of DragonFire Inc., an agile quality process consultancy and training firm. Her passion is helping teams build quality systems. For the past ten years, she has worked as a coach and tester, introducing agile practices into both large and small companies. Her focus is working with business users and testers to understand their role in agile projects. Janet's programming background is a definite plus when she partners with developers on her agile teams to implement innovative agile test automation solutions. Janet is a frequent speaker at agile and testing software conferences, and she is a major contributor to the North American agile testing community.

For more about Janet's work, visit her websites at www.janetgregory.ca, www.janetgregory.blogspot.com, and www.agiletester.ca, or you can email her at janet@agiletester.ca.

Part I

INTRODUCTION

In the first two chapters, we provide an overview of agile testing, highlighting how agile testing differs from testing in a traditional phased or "waterfall" approach. We explore the "whole team" approach to quality and testing.

Chapter 1

WHAT IS AGILE TESTING, ANYWAY?

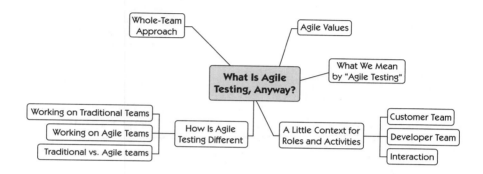

Like a lot of terminology, "agile development" and "agile testing" mean different things to different people. In this chapter, we explain our view of agile, which reflects the Agile Manifesto and general principles and values shared by different agile methods. We want to share a common language with you, the reader, so we'll go over some of our vocabulary. We compare and contrast agile development and testing with the more traditional phased approach. The "whole team" approach promoted by agile development is central to our attitude toward quality and testing, so we also talk about that here.

AGILE VALUES

"Agile" is a buzzword that will probably fall out of use someday and make this book seem obsolete. It's loaded with different meanings that apply in different circumstances. One way to define "agile development" is to look at the Agile Manifesto (see Figure 1-1).

Using the values from the Manifesto to guide us, we strive to deliver small chunks of business value in extremely short release cycles.

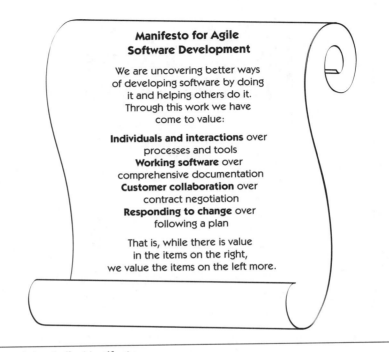

Figure 1-1   Agile Manifesto

Chapter 21, "Key
Success Factors,"
lists key success
factors for agile
testing.

We use the word "agile" in this book in a broad sense. Whether your team is
practicing a particular agile method, such as Scrum, XP, Crystal, DSDM, or
FDD, to name a few, or just adopting whatever principles and practices make
sense for your situation, you should be able to apply the ideas in this book. If
you're delivering value to the business in a timely manner with high-quality
software, and your team continually strives to improve, you'll find useful information here. At the same time, there are particular agile practices we feel
are crucial to any team's success. We'll talk about these throughout the book.

WHAT DO WE MEAN BY "AGILE TESTING"?

You might have noticed that we use the term "tester" to describe a person
whose main activities revolve around testing and quality assurance. You'll
also see that we often use the word "programmer" to describe a person whose
main activities revolve around writing production code. We don't intend that
these terms sound narrow or insignificant. Programmers do more than turn
a specification into a program. We don't call them "developers," because ev-

eryone involved in delivering software is a developer. Testers do more than perform "testing tasks." Each agile team member is focused on delivering a high-quality product that provides business value. Agile testers work to ensure that their team delivers the quality their customers need. We use the terms "programmer" and "tester" for convenience.

Several core practices used by agile teams relate to testing. Agile programmers use test-driven development (TDD), also called test-driven design, to write quality production code. With TDD, the programmer writes a test for a tiny bit of functionality, sees it fail, writes the code that makes it pass, and then moves on to the next tiny bit of functionality. Programmers also write code integration tests to make sure the small units of code work together as intended. This essential practice has been adopted by many teams, even those that don't call themselves "agile," because it's just a smart way to think through your software design and prevent defects. Figure 1-2 shows a sample unit test result that a programmer might see.

This book isn't about unit-level or component-level testing, but these types of tests are critical to a successful project. Brian Marick [2003] describes these types of tests as "supporting the team," helping the programmers know what code to write next. Brian also coined the term "technology-facing tests," tests that fall into the programmer's domain and are described using programmer terms and jargon. In Part II, we introduce the Agile Testing Quadrants and examine the different categories of agile testing. If you want to learn more about writing unit and component tests, and TDD, the bibliography will steer you to some good resources.

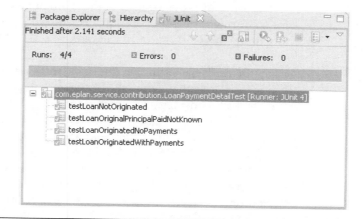

Figure 1-2 Sample unit test output

If you want to know how agile values, principles, and practices applied to testing can help you, as a tester, do your best work, and help your team deliver more business value, please keep reading. If you've bothered to pick up this book, you're probably the kind of professional who continually strives to grow and learn. You're likely to have the mind-set that a good agile team needs to succeed. This book will show you ways to improve your organization's product, provide the most value possible to your team, and enjoy your job.

Lisa's Story

During a break from working on this chapter, I talked to a friend who works in quality assurance for a large company. It was a busy time of year, and management expected everyone to work extra hours. He said, "If I thought working 100 extra hours would solve our problems, I'd work 'til 7 every night until that was done. But the truth was, it might take 4,000 extra hours to solve our problems, so working extra feels pointless." Does this sound familiar?

—Lisa

If you've worked in the software industry long, you've probably had the opportunity to feel like Lisa's friend. Working harder and longer doesn't help when your task is impossible to achieve. Agile development acknowledges the reality that we only have so many good productive hours in a day or week, and that we can't plan away the inevitability of change.

Agile development encourages us to solve our problems as a team. Business people, programmers, testers, analysts—everyone involved in software development—decides together how best to improve their product. Best of all, as testers, we're working together with a team of people who all feel responsible for delivering the best possible quality, and who are all focused on testing. We love doing this work, and you will too.

When we say "agile testing" in this book, we're usually talking about business-facing tests, tests that define the business experts' desired features and functionality. We consider "customer-facing" a synonym for "business-facing." "Testing" in this book also includes tests that critique the product and focus on discovering what might be lacking in the finished product so that we can improve it. It includes just about everything beyond unit and component level testing: functional, system, load, performance, security, stress, usability, exploratory, end-to-end, and user acceptance. All these types of tests might be appropriate to any given project, whether it's an agile project or one using more traditional methodologies.

Agile testing doesn't just mean testing on an agile project. Some testing approaches, such as exploratory testing, are inherently agile, whether it's done an agile project or not. Testing an application with a plan to learn about it as you go, and letting that information guide your testing, is in line with valuing working software and responding to change. Later chapters discuss agile forms of testing as well as "agile testing" practices.

A LITTLE CONTEXT FOR ROLES AND ACTIVITIES ON AN AGILE TEAM

We'll talk a lot in this book about the "customer team" and the "developer team." The difference between them is the skills they bring to delivering a product.

Customer Team

The customer team includes business experts, product owners, domain experts, product managers, business analysts, subject matter experts—everyone on the "business" side of a project. The customer team writes the stories or feature sets that the developer team delivers. They provide the examples that will drive coding in the form of business-facing tests. They communicate and collaborate with the developer team throughout each iteration, answering questions, drawing examples on the whiteboard, and reviewing finished stories or parts of stories.

Testers are integral members of the customer team, helping elicit requirements and examples and helping the customers express their requirements as tests.

Developer Team

Everyone involved with delivering code is a developer, and is part of the developer team. Agile principles encourage team members to take on multiple activities; any team member can take on any type of task. Many agile practitioners discourage specialized roles on teams and encourage all team members to transfer their skills to others as much as possible. Nevertheless, each team needs to decide what expertise their projects require. Programmers, system administrators, architects, database administrators, technical writers, security specialists, and people who wear more than one of these hats might be part of the team, physically or virtually.

Testers are also on the developer team, because testing is a central component of agile software development. Testers advocate for quality on behalf of the customer and assist the development team in delivering the maximum business value.

Interaction between Customer and Developer Teams

The customer and developer teams work closely together at all times. Ideally, they're just one team with a common goal. That goal is to deliver value to the organization. Agile projects progress in iterations, which are small development cycles that typically last from one to four weeks. The customer team, with input from the developers, will prioritize stories to be developed, and the developer team will determine how much work they can take on. They'll work together to define requirements with tests and examples, and write the code that makes the tests pass. Testers have a foot in each world, understanding the customer viewpoint as well as the complexities of the technical implementation (see Figure 1-3).

Some agile teams don't have any members who define themselves as "testers." However, they all need someone to help the customer team write business-facing tests for the iteration's stories, make sure the tests pass, and make sure that adequate regression tests are automated. Even if a team does have testers, the entire agile team is responsible for these testing tasks. Our experience with agile teams has shown that testing skills and experience are vital to project success and that testers do add value to agile teams.

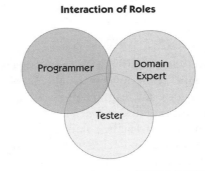

Figure 1-3 Interaction of roles

HOW IS AGILE TESTING DIFFERENT?

We both started working on agile teams at the turn of the millennium. Like a lot of testers who are new to agile, we didn't know what to expect at first. Together with our respective agile teams, we've worked on we've learned a lot about testing on agile projects. We've also implemented ideas and practices suggested by other agile testers and teams. Over the years, we've shared our experiences with other agile testers as well. We've facilitated workshops and led tutorials at agile and testing conferences, talked with local user groups, and joined countless discussions on agile testing mailing lists. Through these experiences, we've identified differences between testing on agile teams and testing on traditional waterfall development projects. Agile development has transformed the testing profession in many ways.

Working on Traditional Teams

Neither working closely with programmers nor getting involved with a project from the earliest phases was new to us. However, we were used to strictly enforced gated phases of a narrowly defined software development life cycle, starting with release planning and requirements definition and usually ending with a rushed testing phase and a delayed release. In fact, we often were thrust into a gatekeeper role, telling business managers, "Sorry, the requirements are frozen; we can add that feature in the next release."

As leaders of quality assurance teams, we were also often expected to act as gatekeepers of quality. We couldn't control how the code was written, or even if any programmers tested their code, other than by our personal efforts at collaboration. Our post-development testing phases were expected to boost quality after code was complete. We had the illusion of control. We usually had the keys to production, and sometimes we had the power to postpone releases or stop them from going forward. Lisa even had the title of "Quality Boss," when in fact she was merely the manager of the QA team.

Our development cycles were generally long. Projects at a company that produced database software might last for a year. The six-month release cycles Lisa experienced at an Internet start-up seemed short at the time, although it was still a long time to have frozen requirements. In spite of much process and discipline, diligently completing one phase before moving on to the next, it was plenty of time for the competition to come out ahead, and the applications were not always what the customers expected.

Traditional teams are focused on making sure all the specified requirements are delivered in the final product. If everything isn't ready by the original target release date, the release is usually postponed. The development teams don't usually have input about what features are in the release, or how they should work. Individual programmers tend to specialize in a particular area of the code. Testers study the requirements documents to write their test plans, and then they wait for work to be delivered to them for testing.

Working on Agile Teams

Transitioning to the short iterations of an agile project might produce initial shock and awe. How can we possibly define requirements and then test and deliver production-ready code in one, two, three, or four weeks? This is particularly tough for larger organizations with separate teams for different functions and even harder for teams that are geographically dispersed. Where do all these various programmers, testers, analysts, project managers, and countless specialties fit in a new agile project? How can we possibly code and test so quickly? Where would we find time for difficult efforts such as automating tests? What control do we have over bad code getting delivered to production?

We'll share our stories from our first agile experiences to show you that everyone has to start somewhere.

Lisa's Story

My first agile team embraced Extreme Programming (XP), not without some "learning experiences." Serving as the only professional tester on a team of eight programmers who hadn't learned how to automate unit tests was disheartening. The first two-week iteration felt like jumping off a cliff.

Fortunately, we had a good coach, excellent training, a supportive community of agile practitioners with ideas to share, and time to learn. Together we figured out some ins and outs of how to integrate testing into an agile project—indeed, how to drive the project with tests. I learned how I could use my testing skills and experience to add real value to an agile team.

The toughest thing for me (the former Quality Boss) to learn was that the customers, not I, decided on quality criteria for the product. I was horrified after the first iteration to find that the code crashed easily when two users logged in concurrently. My coach patiently explained, over my strident objections, that our customer, a start-up company, wanted to be able to show features to potential customers. Reliability and robustness were not yet the issue.

I learned that my job was to help the customers tell us what was valuable to them during each iteration, and to write tests to ensure that's what they got.

—Lisa

Janet's Story

My first foray into the agile world was also an Extreme Programming (XP) engagement. I had just come from an organization that practiced waterfall with some extremely bad practices, including giving the test team a day or so to test six months of code. In my next job as QA manager, the development manager and I were both learning what XP really meant. We successfully created a team that worked well together and managed to automate most of the tests for the functionality. When the organization downsized during the dot-com bust, I found myself in a new position at another organization as the lone tester with about ten developers on an XP project.

On my first day of the project, Jonathan Rasmusson, one of the developers, came up to me and asked me why I was there. The team was practicing XP, and the programmers were practicing test-first and automating all their own tests. Participating in that was a challenge I couldn't resist. The team didn't know what value I could add, but I knew I had unique abilities that could help the team. That experience changed my life forever, because I gained an understanding of the nuances of an agile project and determined then that my life's work was to make the tester role a more fulfilling one.

—Janet

Read Jonathan's Story

Jonathan Rasmusson, now an Agile Coach at Rasmusson Software Consulting, but Janet's coworker on her second agile team, explains how he learned how agile testers add value.

So there I was, a young hotshot J2EE developer excited and pumped to be developing software the way it should be developed—using XP. Until one day, in walks a new team member—a tester. It seems management thought it would be good to have a QA resource on the team.

That's fine. Then it occurred to me that this poor tester would have nothing to do. I mean, as a developer on an XP project, I was writing the tests. There was no role for QA here as far as I could see.

So of course I went up and introduced myself and asked quite pointedly what she was going to do on the project, because the developers were writing all the tests. While I can't remember exactly how Janet responded, the next six months made it very clear what testers can do on agile projects.

With the automation of the tedious, low-level boundary condition test cases, Janet as a tester was now free to focus on much greater value-add areas like exploratory testing, usability, and testing the app in ways developers hadn't originally anticipated. She worked with the

customer to help write test cases that defined success for upcoming stories. She paired with developers looking for gaps in tests.

But perhaps most importantly, she helped reinforce an ethos of quality
and culture, dispensing happy-face stickers to those developers who
had done an exceptional job (these became much sought-after badges
of honor displayed prominently on laptops).

Working with Janet taught me a great deal about the role testers play on
agile projects, and their importance to the team.

Agile teams work closely with the business and have a detailed understanding
of the requirements. They're focused on the value they can deliver, and they
might have a great deal of input into prioritizing features. Testers don't sit
and wait for work; they get up and look for ways to contribute throughout
the development cycle and beyond.

If testing on an agile project felt just like testing on a traditional project, we
wouldn't feel the need to write a book. Let's compare and contrast these testing methods.

Traditional vs. Agile Testing

It helps to start by looking at similarities between agile testing and testing in
traditional software development. Consider Figure 1-4.

In the phased approach diagram, it is clear that testing happens at the end,
right before release. The diagram is idealistic, because it gives the impression
there is as much time for testing as there is for coding. In many projects, this
is not the case. The testing gets "squished" because coding takes longer than
expected, and because teams get into a code-and-fix cycle at the end.

Agile is iterative and incremental. This means that the testers test each increment of coding as soon as it is finished. An iteration might be as short as one
week, or as long as a month. The team builds and tests a little bit of code,
making sure it works correctly, and then moves on to next piece that needs to
be built. Programmers never get ahead of the testers, because a story is not
"done" until it has been tested. We'll talk much more about this throughout
the book.

There's tremendous variety in the approaches to projects that agile teams take.
One team might be dedicated to a single project or might be part of another

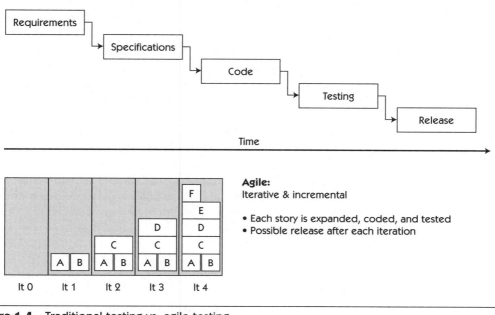

Figure 1-4 Traditional testing vs. agile testing

bigger project. No matter how big your project is, you still have to start some-where. Your team might take on an epic or feature, a set of related stories at an estimating meeting, or you might meet to plan the release. Regardless of how a project or subset of a project gets started, you'll need to get a high-level un-derstanding of it. You might come up with a plan or strategy for testing as you prepare for a release, but it will probably look quite different from any test plan you've done before.

Every project, every team, and sometimes every iteration is different. How your team solves problems should depend on the problem, the people, and the tools you have available. As an agile team member, you will need to be adaptive to the team's needs.

Rather than creating tests from a requirements document that was created by business analysts before anyone ever thought of writing a line of code, some-one will need to write tests that illustrate the requirements for each story days or hours before coding begins. This is often a collaborative effort between a business or domain expert and a tester, analyst, or some other development team member. Detailed functional test cases, ideally based on examples provided by business experts, flesh out the requirements. Testers will conduct manual exploratory testing to find important bugs that defined test cases might miss. Testers might pair with other developers to automate and execute test cases as coding on each story proceeds. Automated functional tests are added to the regression test suite. When tests demonstrating minimum functionality are complete, the team can consider the story finished.

If you attended agile conferences and seminars in the early part of this decade, you heard a lot about TDD and acceptance testing but not so much about other critical types of testing, such as load, performance, security, usability, and other "ility" testing. As testers, we thought that was a little weird, because all these types of testing are just as vital on agile projects as they are on projects using any other development methodology. The real difference is that we like to do these tests as early in the development process as we can so that they can also drive design and coding.

If the team actually releases each iteration, as Lisa's team does, the last day or two of each iteration is the "end game," the time when user acceptance testing, training, bug fixing, and deployments to staging environments can occur. Other teams, such as Janet's, release every few iterations, and might even have an entire iteration's worth of "end game" activities to verify release readiness. The difference here is that all the testing is not left until the end.

As a tester on an agile team, you're a key player in releasing code to production, just as you might have been in a more traditional environment. You might run scripts or do manual testing to verify all elements of a release, such as database update scripts, are in place. All team members participate in retrospectives or other process improvement activities that might occur for every iteration or every release. The whole team brainstorms ways to solve problems and improve processes and practices.

Agile projects have a variety of flavors. Is your team starting with a clean slate, in a greenfield (new) development project? If so, you might have fewer challenges than a team faced with rewriting or building on a legacy system that has no automated regression suite. Working with a third party brings additional testing challenges to any team.

Whatever flavor of development you're using, pretty much the same elements of a software development life cycle need to happen. The difference with agile is that time frames are greatly shortened, and activities happen concurrently. Participants, tests, and tools need to be adaptive.

The most critical difference for testers in an agile project is the quick feedback from testing. It drives the project forward, and there are no gatekeepers ready to block project progress if certain milestones aren't met.

We've encountered testers who resist the transition to agile development, fearing that "agile development" equates with chaos, lack of discipline, lack of documentation, and an environment that is hostile to testers. While some teams do seem to use the "agile" buzzword to justify simply doing whatever they want, true agile teams are all about repeatable quality as well as efficiency. In our experience, an agile team is a wonderful place to be a tester.

WHOLE-TEAM APPROACH

One of the biggest differences in agile development versus traditional development is the agile "whole-team" approach. With agile, it's not only the testers or a quality assurance team who feel responsible for quality. We don't think of "departments," we just think of the skills and resources we need to deliver the best possible product. The focus of agile development is producing high-quality software in a time frame that maximizes its value to the business. This is the job of the whole team, not just testers or designated quality assurance professionals. Everyone on an agile team gets "test-infected." Tests, from the unit level on up, drive the coding, help the team learn how the application should work, and let us know when we're "done" with a task or story.

An agile team must possess all the skills needed to produce quality code that delivers the features required by the organization. While this might mean including specialists on the team, such as expert testers, it doesn't limit particular tasks to particular team members. Any task might be completed by any team member, or a pair of team members. This means that the team takes responsibility for all kinds of testing tasks, such as automating tests and manual exploratory testing. It also means that the whole team thinks constantly about designing code for testability.

The whole-team approach involves constant collaboration. Testers collaborate with programmers, the customer team, and other team specialists—and not just for testing tasks, but other tasks related to testing, such as building infrastructure and designing for testability. Figure 1-5 shows a developer reviewing reports with two customers and a tester (not pictured).

Figure 1-5   A developer discusses an issue with customers

The whole-team approach means everyone takes responsibility for testing tasks. It means team members have a range of skill sets and experience to employ in attacking challenges such as designing for testability by turning examples into tests and into code to make those tests pass. These diverse viewpoints can only mean better tests and test coverage.

Most importantly, on an agile team, anyone can ask for and receive help. The team commits to providing the highest possible business value as a team, and the team does whatever is needed to deliver it. Some folks who are new to agile perceive it as all about speed. The fact is, it's all about quality—and if it's not, we question whether it's really an "agile" team.

Your situation is unique. That's why you need to be aware of the potential testing obstacles your team might face and how you can apply agile values and principles to overcome them.

SUMMARY

Understanding the activities that testers perform on agile teams helps you show your own team the value that testers can add. Learning the core practices of agile testing will help your team deliver software that delights your customers.

In this chapter, we've explained what we mean when we use the term "agile testing."

- We showed how the Agile Manifesto relates to testing, with its emphasis on individuals and interactions, working software, customer collaboration, and responding to change.
- We provided some context for this book, including some other terms we use such as "tester," "programmer," "customer," and related terms so that we can speak a common language.
- We explained how agile testing, with its focus on business value and delivering the quality customers require, is different from traditional testing, which focuses on conformance to requirements.
- We introduced the "whole-team" approach to agile testing, which means that everyone involved with delivering software is responsible for delivering high-quality software.
- We advised taking a practical approach by applying agile values and principles to overcome agile testing obstacles that arise in your unique situation.

Chapter 2

TEN PRINCIPLES FOR AGILE TESTERS

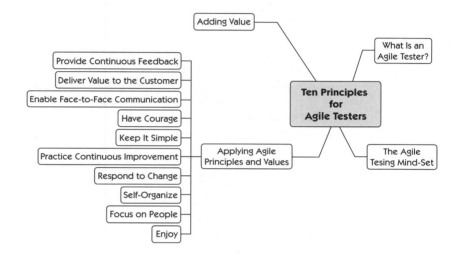

Everyone on an agile team is a tester. Anyone can pick up testing tasks. If that's true, then what is special about an agile tester? If I define myself as a tester on an agile team, what does that really mean? Do agile testers need different skill sets than testers on traditional teams? What guides them in their daily activities?

In this chapter, we talk about the agile testing mind-set, show how agile values and principles guide testing, and give an overview of how testers add value on agile teams.

WHAT'S AN AGILE TESTER?

We define an agile tester this way: a professional tester who embraces change, collaborates well with both technical and business people, and understands the concept of using tests to document requirements and drive development. Agile testers tend to have good technical skills, know how to collaborate with others to automate tests, and are also experienced exploratory testers. They're willing to learn what customers do so that they can better understand the customers' software requirements.

Who's an agile tester? She's a team member who drives agile testing. We know many agile testers who started out in some other specialization. A developer becomes test-infected and branches out beyond unit testing. An exploratory tester, accustomed to working in an agile manner, is attracted to the idea of an agile team. Professionals in other roles, such as business or functional analysts, might share the same traits and do much of the same work.

Skills are important, but attitude counts more. Janet likes to say, "Without the attitude, the skill is nothing." Having had to hire numerous testers for our agile teams, we've put a lot of thought into this and discussed it with others in the agile community. Testers tend to see the big picture. They look at the application more from a user or customer point of view, which means they're generally customer-focused.

THE AGILE TESTING MIND-SET

What makes a team "agile"? To us, an agile team is one that continually focuses on doing its best work and delivering the best possible product. In our experience, this involves a ton of discipline, learning, time, experimentation, and working together. It's not for everyone, but it's ideal for those of us who like the team dynamic and focus on continual improvement.

Successful projects are a result of good people allowed to do good work. The characteristics that make someone succeed as a tester on an agile team are probably the same characteristics that make a highly valued tester on any team.

An agile tester doesn't see herself as a quality police officer, protecting her customers from inadequate code. She's ready to gather and share information, to work with the customer or product owner in order to help them express their requirements adequately so that they can get the features they need, and to provide feedback on project progress to everyone.

Agile testers, and maybe any tester with the right skills and mind-set, are continually looking for ways the team can do a better job of producing high-quality software. On a personal level, that might mean attending local user group meetings or roundtables to find out what other teams are doing. It also means trying out new tools to help the team do a better job of specifying, executing, and automating customer requirements as tests.

The bottom line is that agile testers, like their agile teammates, enjoy learning new skills and taking on new challenges, and they don't limit themselves to solving only testing issues. This isn't just a trait of testers; we see it in all agile team members. Agile testers help the developer and customer teams address any kind of issue that might arise. Testers can provide information that helps the team look back and learn what's working and what isn't.

Creativity, openness to ideas, willingness to take on any task or role, focus on the customer, and a constant view of the big picture are just some components of the agile testing mind-set. Good testers have an instinct and understanding for where and how software might fail, and how to track down failures.

Testers might have special expertise and experience in testing, but a good agile tester isn't afraid to jump into a design discussion with suggestions that will help testability or create a more elegant solution. An agile testing mind-set is one that is results-oriented, craftsman-like, collaborative, eager to learn, and passionate about delivering business value in a timely manner.

APPLYING AGILE PRINCIPLES AND VALUES

Individuals can have a big impact on a project's success. We'd expect a team with more experienced and higher-skilled members to outperform a less talented team. But a team is more than just its individual members. Agile values and principles promote a focus on the people involved in a project and how they interact and communicate. A team that guides itself with agile values and principles will have higher team morale and better velocity than a poorly functioning team of talented individuals.

The four value statements in the Agile Manifesto, which we presented at the start of the first chapter, show preferences, not ultimatums, and make no statements about what to do or not to do. The Agile Manifesto also includes a list of principles that define how we approach software development. Our list of agile "testing" principles is partially derived from those principles. Because we both come from the Extreme Programming culture, we've adopted many of its values and underlying principles. We've also incorporated guidelines and principles that have worked for our teams. Your team's own values and principles will guide you as you choose practices and make decisions about how you want to work.

The principles we think are important for an agile tester are:

- Provide continuous feedback.
- Deliver value to the customer.
- Enable face-to-face communication.
- Have courage.
- Keep it simple.
- Practice continuous improvement.
- Respond to change.
- Self-organize.
- Focus on people.
- Enjoy.

Provide Continuous Feedback

Given that tests drive agile projects, it's no surprise that feedback plays a big part in any agile team. The tester's traditional role of "information provider" makes her inherently valuable to an agile team. One of the agile tester's most important contributions is helping the product owner or customer articulate requirements for each story in the form of examples and tests. The tester then works together with teammates to turn those requirements into executable tests. Testers, programmers, and other team members work to run these tests early and often so they're continually guided by meaningful feedback. We'll spend a lot of time in this book explaining ways to do this.

When the team encounters obstacles, feedback is one way to help remove them. Did we deliver a user interface that didn't quite meet customer expectations? Let's write a task card reminding us to collaborate with the customer on paper prototypes of the next UI story.

Is management worried about how work is progressing? Display a big visible chart of tests written, run, and passing every day. Display big-picture functionality coverage such as test matrices. Having trouble getting the build stable? Lisa's team displayed the number of days remaining until time to tag the build for release in order to keep everyone focused on finishing stories in time. After that became a habit, they didn't need the visual cue anymore.

Deliver Value to the Customer

Agile development is about delivering value in small releases that provide exactly the functionality that the customer has most recently prioritized. This usually means limiting scope. It's easy to get caught up in the customer team's desire for cool features. Anyone can question these additions, but a tester often recognizes the impact to the story, because they need to think about the testing repercussions.

Lisa's Story

Our product owner participates in planning meetings before each iteration. Nevertheless, after the iteration has started and we discuss more details about the stories and how to test them, he often brings up an idea that didn't come out during the planning, such as, "Well, it would really be nice if the selection on this report could include X, Y, and Z and be sorted on A as well." An innocent request can add a lot of complexity to a story. I often bring in one of the programmers to talk about whether this addition can be handled within the scope of the story we had planned. If not, we ask the product owner to write a card for the next iteration.

—Lisa

Agile testers stay focused on the big picture. We can deliver the most critical functionality in this iteration and add to it later. If we let new features creep in, we risk delivering nothing on time. If we get too caught up with edge cases and miss core functionality on the happy path, we won't provide the value the business needs.

Lisa's Story

To ensure that we deliver some value in each iteration, our team looks at each story to identify the "critical path" or "thin slice" of necessary functionality. We complete those tasks first and then go back and flesh out the rest of the features. The worst-case scenario is that only the core functionality gets released. That's better than delivering nothing or something that works only halfway.

—Lisa

Agile testers take the same approach as that identified in Lisa's story. While one of our skills is to identify test cases beyond the "happy path," we still need to start by making sure the happy path works. We can automate tests for the happy path, and add negative and boundary tests later. Always consider what adds the most value to the customer, and understand your context. If an application is safety-critical, adding negative tests is absolutely required. The testing time needs to be considered during the estimation process to make sure that enough time is allotted in the iteration to deliver a "safe" feature.

Enable Face-to-Face Communication

No team works well without good communication. Today, when so many teams are distributed in multiple geographical locations, communication is even more vital and more of a challenge. The agile tester should look for unique ways to facilitate communication. It is a critical aspect to doing her job well.

Janet's Story

When I was working with one team, we had a real problem with programmers talking with the product owner and leaving the testers out of the discussion. They often found out about changes after the fact. Part of the problem was that the developers were not sitting with the testers due to logistical problems. Another problem was history. The test team was new, and the product owner was used to going straight to the programmers.

I took the problem to the team, and we created a rule. We found great success with the "Power of Three." This meant that all discussions about a feature needed a programmer, a tester, and the product owner. It was each person's responsibility to make sure there was always a representative from each group. If someone saw two people talking, they had the right to butt into the conversation. It didn't take very long before it was just routine and no one would consider leaving the tester out of a discussion. This worked for us because the team bought into the solution.

—Janet

Any time there is a question about how a feature should work or what an interface should look like, the tester can pull in a programmer and a business expert to talk about it. Testers should never get in the way of any direct customer-developer communication, but they can often help to make sure that communication happens.

Agile testers see each story or theme from the customer's point of view but also understand technical aspects and limitations related to implementing features. They can help customers and developers achieve a common language. Business people and software people often speak different languages. They have to find some common ground in order to work together successfully. Testers can help them develop a shared language, a project dialect, or team jargon.

Brian Marick (2003) recommends that we use examples to develop this language. When Lisa's team digresses into a philosophical discussion during a sprint planning meeting, Lisa asks the product owner for an example or usage scenario. Testers can encourage whiteboard discussions to work through more examples. These help the customers envision their requirements more clearly. They also help the developers to produce well-designed code to meet those requirements.

Face-to-face communication has no substitute. Agile development depends on constant collaboration. Like other agile team members, the people doing testing tasks will continually seek out customer and technical team members to discuss and collaborate. When an agile tester suspects a hidden assumption or a misunderstood requirement, she'll get a customer and a developer talking about it. If people in a different building or continent need to talk, they look for creative ways to replace face-to-face, real-time conversations.

Have Courage

Courage is a core value in XP, and practices such as test automation and continuous integration allow the team to practice this value. The developers have the courage to make changes and refactor the code because they have the safety net of an automated regression suite. In this section, we talk about the emotional courage that is needed when transitioning to an agile team.

Have you worked in an organization where testers were stuck in their own silo, unable to talk to either business stakeholders or other members of the technical team? While you might jump at the chance to join a collaborative agile environment, you might feel uncomfortable having to go ask the customer for examples, or ask a programmer to help automate a test or bring up a roadblock during the daily stand-up.

When you first join an agile team, or when your current team firsts transitions to agile development, it's normal to experience fear and have a list of questions that need to be answered. How in the world are we going to be able to complete testing tasks for each story in such a short time? How will testing "keep up" with development? How do you know how much testing is enough? Or maybe you're a functional testing manager or a quality process manager and it's not clear to you where that role fits on an agile team, and nobody has the answers. Agile testers need courage to find the answers to those questions, but there are other reasons as well for having courage.

We need courage to let ourselves fail, knowing that at least we'll fail fast and be able to learn from that failure. After we've blown an iteration because we didn't get a stable build, we'll start thinking of ways to ensure it doesn't happen again.

We need courage to allow others to make mistakes, because that's the only way to learn the lesson.

I worked on a project where the agile coach insisted that I be on a separate test-ing team (often a team of one!) whose work wasn't included in the programmers' tracking and velocity. I had to just go along and try this. After the release ran into trouble because testing wasn't finished, I asked the coach if we could try things my way for an iteration or two. The whole-team approach worked much better. Each story was tested and "done" by the end of the iteration, and the customers were much happier with the results.

—Lisa

We need courage to ask for help, especially when the person who could pro-vide that help looks pretty busy and stressed-out himself. Climbing out of your old silo and joining in a team responsibility for success or failure takes courage. Asking a question or pointing out what you think is a flaw requires courage, even in a team supported by agile values and principles. Don't be afraid! Agile teams are open and generally accepting of new ideas.

Keep It Simple

Kent Beck's *Extreme Programming Explained* advised us to do the simplest thing that could possibly work. That doesn't mean the first thing you try will actually work, but it ought to be simple.

Agile testers and their teams are challenged to not only produce the simplest possible software implementation but to take a simple approach to ensuring that software meets the customer requirements. This doesn't mean that the team shouldn't take some time to analyze themes and stories and think through the appropriate architecture and design. It does mean that the team might need to push back to the business side of the team when their re-quirements might be a bit elaborate and a simpler solution will deliver the same value.

Some of us worked in software organizations where we, as testers and quality assurance staff, were asked to set quality standards. We believe this is back-wards, because it's up to the customer team to decide what level of quality they want to pay for. Testers and other team members should provide information to customers and help them consider all aspects of quality, including nonfunc-tional requirements such as performance and security. The ultimate decisions are up to the customer. The team can help the customer make good decisions by its taking a simple, step-by-step approach to its work. Agile testing means

Chapter 9, "Toolkit for Business-Facing Tests that Support the Team," and Chapter 11, "Critiquing the Product using Technology-Facing Tests," give examples of test tools.

Part IV, "Test Automation," explains how to build a "doable" test automation strategy.

doing the simplest tests possible to verify that a piece of functionality exists or that the customer's quality standard (e.g., performance) has been met.

Simple doesn't mean easy. For testers, it means testing "just enough" with the lightest-weight tools and techniques we can find that will do the job. Tools can be as simple as a spreadsheet or a checklist. We need to automate regression tests, but we should push them down to the lowest level possible in order to encourage fast feedback. Even simple smoke tests might be enough for business-facing test automation.

Exploratory testing can be used to learn about your application and ferret out hard-to-find bugs, but start with the basics, time-boxing side trips and evaluating how far to go with edge cases. Simplicity helps us keep our focus on risk, return on investment, and improving in the areas of greatest pain.

Practice Continuous Improvement

Looking for ways to do a better job is part of an agile tester's mind-set. Of course, the whole team should be thinking this way, because the central core of agile is that the team always tries to do better work. Testers participate in team retrospectives, evaluating what's working well and what needs to be added or tweaked. Testers bring testing issues up for the whole team to address. Teams have achieved their greatest improvements in testing and all other areas through the use of process improvement practices such as retrospectives and impediment backlogs. Some improvement ideas might become task cards. For larger problems, teams focus on one or two issues at a time to make sure they solve the real problem and not just the symptom.

Agile testers and their teams are always on the lookout for tools, skills, or practices that might help them add more value or get a better return on the customer's investment. The short iterations of agile development make it easier to try something new for a few iterations and see whether it's worth adopting for the long term.

Learning new skills and growing professionally are important to agile testers. They take advantage of the many available free resources to improve their specialized skills, such as exploratory testing. They go to meetings and conferences, join mailing lists, and read articles, blogs, and books to get new ideas. They look for ways to automate (or get help from their coworkers to automate) mundane or repetitive tasks so they have more time to contribute their valuable expertise.

Pierre Veragren, an SQA Lead at iLevel by Weyerhaeuser, identified a quality we often see in agile teams ourselves: "AADD," Agile Attention Deficit Disorder. Anything not learned quickly might be deemed useless. Agile team members look for return on investment, and if they don't see it quickly, they move on. This isn't a negative characteristic when you're delivering production-ready software every two weeks or even more often.

Retrospectives are a key agile practice that lets the team use yesterday's experience to do a better job tomorrow. Agile testers use this opportunity to raise testing-related issues and ask the team to brainstorm ways to address them. This is a way for the team to provide feedback to itself for continual improvement.

Lisa's Story

We'll talk more about retrospectives and how they can help your team practice continuous improvement in Chapter 19, "Wrap Up the Iteration."

Our team had used retrospectives to great benefit, but we felt we needed something new to help us focus on doing a better job. I suggested keeping an "impediment backlog" of items that were keeping us from being as productive as we'd like to be. The first thing I wrote in the impediment backlog was our test environment's slow response time. Our system administrator scrounged a couple of bargain machines and turned them into new, faster servers for our test environments. Our DBA analyzed the test database performance, found that the one-disk system was the impediment, and our manager gave the go-ahead to install a RAID for better disk access. Soon we were able to deploy builds and conduct our exploratory testing much faster.

—Lisa

Respond to Change

When we worked in a waterfall environment, we got used to saying, "Sorry, we can't make this change now; the requirements are frozen. We'll have to put that in the first patch release." It was frustrating for customers because they realized that they didn't do a great job on defining all their requirements up front.

In a two-week agile iteration, we might have to say, "OK, write a card for that and we'll do it in the next iteration or next release," but customers know they can get their change when they want it because they control the priority.

Responding to change is a key value for agile practitioners, but we've found that it's one of the most difficult concepts for testers. Stability is what testers crave so that they can say, "I've tested that; it's done." Continuously changing requirements are a tester's nightmare. However, as agile testers, we have to welcome change. On Wednesday, we might expect to start stories A and B and then C the next Friday. By Friday, the customer could have re-prioritized and now wants stories A, X, and Y. As long as we keep talking to the customer, we can handle changes like that because we are working at the same pace with the rest of team.

Some agile teams try to prepare in advance of the next iteration, perhaps by writing high-level test cases, capturing business satisfaction conditions, or documenting examples. It's a tricky business that might result in wasted time if stories are re-prioritized or greatly changed. However, distributed teams in particular need extra feedback cycles to get ready for the iteration.

Lisa's Story

Our remote team member used to be our on-site manager. He's a key player in helping the business write and prioritize stories. He has in-depth knowledge of both the code and the business, which helps him come up with creative solutions to business needs. When he moved to India, we looked for ways to retain the benefit of his expertise. Meetings are scheduled at times when he can participate, and he has regular conference calls with the product owner to talk about upcoming stories. We've had to switch from low-tech tools such as index cards to online tools that we can all use.

Because the team was willing to make changes in the way we worked, and looked for tools that helped keep him in the loop with ongoing changes, we were able to retain the benefit of his expertise.

—Lisa

Some teams have analysts who can spend more time with the business experts to do some advance planning. Each team has to strike a balance between brainstorming solutions ahead of time and starting from scratch on the first day of each iteration. Agile testers go with the flow and work with the team to accommodate changes.

Automated testing is one key to the solution. One thing we know for sure: No agile team will succeed doing only manual testing. We need robust automation in order to deliver business value in a time frame that makes it valuable.

Self-Organize

The agile tester is part of a self-organizing agile team. The team culture imbues the agile testing philosophy. When programmers, system administrators, analysts, database experts, and the customer team think continually about testing and test automation, testers enjoy a whole new perspective. Automating tests is hard, but it is much easier when you have the whole team working together. Any testing issue is easier to address when you have people with multiple skill sets and multiple perspectives attacking it.

My team is a good example of a self-organizing team. When we implemented Scrum, we had a buggy legacy system and no automated tests. Making any changes to the code was risky at best. Our manager probably had some excellent solutions to the problem, but he didn't suggest them. Instead, we explored the issues and came up with a plan.

The programmers would start implementing new stories in a new, testable architecture, using test-driven development. The testers would write manual regression test scripts, and the entire team—programmers, testers, the system administrator, and the DBA—would execute them on the last two days of every iteration. The testers (at the time, this meant me) would work on an automated regression smoke test suite through the user interface. Eventually, the architecture of the new code would let us automate functional tests with a tool such as FitNesse.

We implemented this plan in baby steps, refining our approach in each iteration. Using the skills of every member of the team was a much better approach than my going off and deciding the automation strategy on my own.

—Lisa

When an agile team faces a big problem, perhaps a production showstopper or a broken build, it's everyone's problem. The highest-priority issues are problems for the whole team to solve. Team members discuss the issue right away and decide how to and who will fix it.

There's no doubt that Lisa's manager could have mandated that the team take this approach to solving its automation problems, but the team itself can come up with the most workable plan. When the team creates its own approach and commits to it, its members adopt a new attitude toward testing.

Focus on People

Projects succeed when good people are allowed to do their best work. Agile values and principles were created with the aim of enabling individual and team success. Agile team members should feel safe and not have to worry about being blamed for mistakes or losing their jobs. Agile team members respect each other and recognize individual accomplishments. Everyone on an agile team should have opportunities to grow and develop their skills. Agile teams work at a sustainable pace that lets them follow disciplined practices and keep a fresh perspective. As the Agile Manifesto states, we value individuals and interactions over processes and tools.

In the history of software development, testers haven't always enjoyed parity with other roles on the development team. Some people saw testers as failed programmers or second-class citizens in the world of software development. Testers who don't bother to learn new skills and grow professionally contribute to the perception that testing is low-skilled work. Even the term "tester" has been avoided, with job titles such as "Quality Assurance Engineer" or "Quality Analyst" and team names such as "QA Department" given preference.

Agile teams that adhere to the true agile philosophy give all team members equal weight. Agile testers know they contribute unique value to their teams, and development teams have found they are more successful when their team includes people with specific testing skills and background. For example, a skilled exploratory tester may discover issues in the system that couldn't be detected by automated functional tests. Someone with deep testing experience might ask important questions that didn't occur to team members without testing experience. Testing knowledge is one component of any team's ability to deliver value.

Enjoy

Working on a team where everyone collaborates, where you are engaged in the project from start to finish, where business stakeholders work together with the development team, where the whole team takes responsibility for quality and testing, in our opinion, is nothing short of a tester's Utopia. We're not alone in believing that everyone should find joy in their work. Agile development rewards the agile tester's passion for her work.

Our jobs as agile testers are particularly satisfying because our viewpoint and skills let us add real value to our teams. In the next section, we'll explore how.

ADDING VALUE

What do these principles bring to the team? Together, they bring business value. In agile development, the whole team takes responsibility for delivering high-quality software that delights customers and makes the business more profitable. This, in turn, brings new advantages for the business.

Team members wear many hats, and agile development tends to avoid classifying people by specialty. Even with short iterations and frequent releases, it's easy to develop a gap between what the customer team expects and what the team delivers. Using tests to drive development helps to prevent this, but you still need the right tests.

Agile testers not only think about the system from the viewpoint of stakeholders who will live with the solution but they also have a grasp of technical constraints and implementation details that face the development team. Programmers focus on making things work. If they're coding to the right requirements, customers will be happy. Unfortunately, customers aren't generally good at articulating their requirements. Driving development with the wrong tests won't deliver the desired outcome. Agile testers ask questions of both customers and developers early and often, and help shape the answers into the right tests.

Agile testers take a much more integrated, team-oriented approach than testers on traditional waterfall projects. They adapt their skills and experience to the team and project. A tester who views programmers as adversaries, or sits and waits for work to come to her, or expects to spend more time planning than doing, is likely to cling to skills she learned on traditional projects and won't last long on an agile team.

Peril: You're Not "Really" Part of the Team

If you're a tester, and you're not invited to attend planning sessions, stand-ups, or design meetings, you might be in a situation where testers are viewed as somehow apart from the development team. If you are invited to these meetings but you're not speaking up, then you're probably creating a perception that you aren't really part of the team. If business experts are writing stories and defining requirements all by themselves, you aren't participating as a tester who's a member of an agile team.

If this is your situation, your team is at risk. Hidden assumptions are likely to go undetected until late in the release cycle. Ripple effects of a story on other parts of the system aren't identified until it's too late. The team isn't making the best use of every team member's skills, so it's not going to be able to produce the best possible software. Communication might break down, and it'll be hard to keep up with what the programmers and customers are doing. The team risks being divided in an unhealthy way between developers and testers, and there's more potential that the development team will become isolated from the customer team.

How can you avoid this peril? See if you can arrange to be located near the developers. If you can't, at least come to their area to talk and pair test. Ask them to show you what they're working on. Ask them to look at the test cases you've written. Invite yourself to meetings if nobody else has invited you. Make yourself useful by testing and providing feedback, and become a necessity to the team.

> Help customers develop their stories and acceptance tests. Push the "whole team" attitude, and ask the team to work on testing problems. If your team is having trouble adapting to agile development, suggest experimenting with some new ideas for an iteration or two. Propose adopting the "Power of Three" rule to promote good communication. Use the information in this book to show that testers can help agile teams succeed beyond their wildest expectations.

During story estimating and planning sessions, agile testers look at each feature from multiple perspectives: business, end user, production support, and programmer. They consider the problems faced by the business and how the software might address them. They raise questions that flush out assumptions made by the customer and developer teams. At the start of each iteration, they help to make sure the customer provides clear requirements and examples, and they help the development team turn those into tests. The tests drive development, and test results provide feedback on the team's progress. Testers help to raise issues so that no testing is overlooked; it's more than functional testing. Customers don't always know that they should mention their performance and reliability needs or security concerns, but testers think to ask about those. Testers also keep the testing approach and tools as simple and lightweight as possible. By the end of the iteration, testers verify that the minimum testing was completed.

Lines between roles on an agile team are blurred. Other team members might be skilled at the same activities that testers perform. For example, analysts and programmers also write business-facing tests. As long as all testing activities are performed, an agile team doesn't necessarily require members who identify themselves primarily as testers. However, we have found that teams benefit from the skills that professional testers have developed. The agile principles and values we've discussed will help any team do a good job of testing and delivering value.

SUMMARY

In this chapter, we covered principles for agile testers and the values we think an agile tester needs to possess in order to contribute effectively to an agile team.

- An "agile testing mind-set" is customer-focused, results-oriented, craftsman-like, collaborative, creative, eager to learn, and passionate about delivering business value in a timely manner.
- Attitude is important, and it blurs the lines between testers, programmers, and other roles on an agile team.

- Agile testers apply agile values and principles such as feedback, communication, courage, simplicity, enjoyment, and delivering value in order to help the team identify and deliver the customer requirements for each story.
- Agile testers add value to their teams and their organizations with their unique viewpoint and team-oriented approach.

Part II
ORGANIZATIONAL CHALLENGES

When software development organizations implement agile development, the testing or QA team often takes the longest to make the transition. Independent QA teams have become entrenched in many organizations. When they start to adapt to a new agile organization, they encounter cultural differences that are difficult for them to accept. In Part II, we talk about introducing change and some of the barriers you might encounter when transitioning to agile. Training is a big part of what organizations making the transition need, and it's often forgotten. It's also hard to see how existing processes such as audits and process improvement frameworks will work in the agile environment. Going from an independent QA team to an integrated agile team is a huge change.

Chapter 4, "Team Logistics," talks about the team structure, such as where a tester actually fits into the team, and the never-ending question about tester-developer ratio. We'll also talk about hiring testers and what to look for in a successful agile tester.

Traditional testing activities, such as logging bugs, keeping track of metrics, and writing test plans, might not seem like a good fit in an agile project. We introduce some of the typical processes that might need special care and attention and discuss how to adapt existing quality processes.

You can expect to find ways that testers and test teams accustomed to a traditional waterfall type of development environment can change their organizational structure and culture to benefit from and add value to agile development.

Chapter 3

CULTURAL CHALLENGES

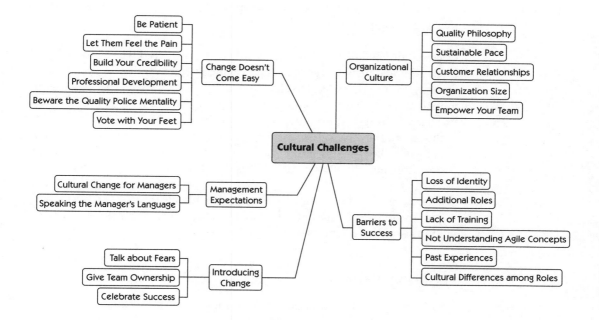

Many organizational influences can impact a project, whether it uses an agile or a traditional phased or gated approach. Organizational and team culture can block a smooth transition to an agile approach. In this chapter, we discuss factors that can directly affect a tester's role on an agile team.

ORGANIZATIONAL CULTURE

An organizational culture is defined by its values, norms, and assumptions. An organization's culture governs how people communicate, interrelate, and make decisions, and it is easily seen by observing employee behavior.

The culture of an organization can impact the success of an agile team. Agile teams are best suited for organizations that allow independent thinking. For example, if a company has a hierarchical structure and encourages a directive management style for all its projects, agile teams will probably struggle. Past experiences of the organization will also affect the success of a new agile team. If a company tried agile and had poor results, people will be suspicious of trying it again, citing examples of why it didn't work. They might even actively campaign against it.

Organizational culture is too frequently not considered when attempts are made to implement an agile process, leaving people wondering why it didn't work as promised. It's hard to change established processes, especially if individuals feel they have a stake in the status quo. Each functional group develops a subculture and processes that meet their needs. They're comfortable with the way they work. Fear is a powerful emotion, and if it is not addressed, it can jeopardize the transition to agile. If team members feel that a new agile process threatens their jobs, they'll resist the change.

We'll talk specifically about how organizational culture affects testers working in an agile environment. The bibliography contains resources that deal with other cultural aspects that may affect teams.

Quality Philosophy

Consider an organization's quality philosophy in terms of how it determines the acceptable level of software quality. Does it tolerate poor quality? Does it take customers' quality requirements into account, or is it just concerned with getting the product into the customers' hands as fast as it can?

When an organization lacks an overall quality philosophy and pressures teams to get the product out without regard to quality, testers feel the pinch. A team that tries to use agile development in such an environment faces an uphill battle.

Some organizations have strong, independent test teams that wield a lot of power. These teams, and their managers, might perceive that agile development will take that power away. They might fear that agile runs contrary to their quality philosophy. Evaluate your organization's quality philosophy and the philosophy of the teams that enforce it.

Peril: Quality Police Mentality

If an existing QA team has assumed the role of "Quality Police," its members usually enforce quality by making sure code reviews are completed and bugs are religiously entered into the defect-tracking systems. They keep metrics about the number of bugs found, and then are charged with making the final decision as to whether to release the product.

We've talked to testers who brag about accomplishments such as going over a development manager's head to force a programmer to follow coding standards. We've even heard of testers who spend their time writing bugs about requirements that aren't up to their standards. This kind of attitude won't fly on a collaborative agile team. It fosters antagonistic behavior.

Another risk of the "Quality Police" role is that the team doesn't buy into the concept of building quality in, and the programmers start using testers as a safety net. The team starts communicating through the bug-tracking system, which isn't a very effective means of communicating, so the team never "jells."

Read on for ways to help avoid this peril.

Companies in which everyone values quality will have an easier time transitioning to agile. If any one group has assumed ownership of quality, they'll have to learn to share that with everyone else on the team in order to succeed.

Whole-Team Ownership of Quality

In Chapter 1, "What Is Agile Testing, Anyway?," we talked about the whole-team approach to quality. For many testers and QA teams, this means a mind shift from owning quality to having a participatory role in defining and maintaining quality. Such a drastic shift in attitude is difficult for many testers and QA teams.

Testers who have been working in a traditional setting might have a hard time adjusting to their new roles and activities. If they've come from an organization where development and QA have an adversarial relationship, it may be difficult to change from being an afterthought (if thought of at all) to being an integral part of the team. It can be difficult for both programmers and testers to learn to trust each other.

Skills and Adaptability

Much has been observed about programmers who can't adapt to agile practices—but what about testers who are used to building test scripts according to a requirements document? Can they learn to ask the questions as the code is being built? Testers who don't change their approach to testing have a hard time working closely with the rest of the development team.

Testers who are used to doing only manual testing through the user interface might not understand the automated approach that is intrinsic to agile development. These testers need a lot of courage in order to face their changing roles, because changing means developing new skill sets outside their comfort zones.

Factors that Help

Although there are many cultural issues to consider, most QA teams have a focus on process improvement, and agile projects encourage continuous improvements and adaptability through the use of tools like retrospectives. Most quality assurance professionals are eager to take what they've learned and make it better. These people are adaptable enough to not only survive, but to thrive in an agile project.

If your organization focuses on learning, it will encourage continual process improvement. It will likely adopt agile much more quickly than organizations that put more value on how they react to crises than on improving their processes.

If you are a tester in an organization that has no effective quality philosophy, you probably struggle to get quality practices accepted. The agile approach will provide you with a mechanism for introducing good quality-oriented practices.

Testers need time and training, just like everyone else who is learning to work on an agile project. If you're managing a team that includes testers, be sure to give them plenty of support. Testers are often not brought in at the beginning of a greenfield project and are then expected to just fit into a team that has been working together for months. To help testers adjust, you may need to bring in an experienced agile testing coach. Hiring someone who has previously worked on an agile team and can serve as a mentor and teacher will help testers integrate with the new agile culture, whether they're transitioning to agile along with an existing team or joining a new agile development team.

Sustainable Pace

Traditional test teams are accustomed to fast and furious testing at the end of a project, which translates into working weekends and evenings. During this end-of-project testing phase, some organizations regularly ask their teams to put in 50, 60, or more hours each week to try to meet a deadline. Organizations often look at overtime as a measure of an individual's commitment. This conflicts with agile values that revolve around enabling people to do their best work all the time.

In agile projects, you are encouraged to work at a sustainable pace. This means that teams work at a consistent pace that sustains a constant velocity that permits maintaining a high-quality standard. New agile teams tend be overly optimistic about what they can accomplish and sign up for too much work. After an iteration or two, they learn to sign up for just enough work so no overtime is needed to complete their tasks. A 40-hour week is the normal sustainable pace for XP teams; it is the amount of effort that, if put in week in and week out, allows people to accomplish the most work over the long haul while delivering good value.

Teams might need to work for short bursts of unsustainable pace now and then, but it should be the exception, not the norm. If overtime is required for short periods, the whole team should be working extra hours. If it's the last day of the sprint and some stories aren't tested, the whole team should stay late to finish the testing, not just the testers. Use the practices and techniques recommended throughout this book to learn how to plan testing along with development and allow testing to "keep up" with coding. Until your team gets better at managing its workload and velocity, budget in extra time to help even out the pace.

Customer Relationships

In traditional software development, the relationship between the development teams and their customers is more like a vendor-supplier relationship. Even if the customer is internal, it can feel more like two separate companies than two teams working on a common goal of producing business value.

Agile development depends on close involvement from customers or, at the very least, their proxies. Agile teams have invited customers to collaborate, work in the same locations if possible, and be intimately involved with the development process. Both sides learn each other's strengths and weaknesses.

This change in the relationships needs to be recognized by both sides, and it doesn't matter whether the customer is internal or external. An open relationship is critical to the success of an agile project, where the relationship between the customer team and the development team is more like a partnership than a vendor-supplier relationship.

Janet's Story In a large project I was on recently, the customer was actually a consortium of five companies, with one of them being the software company creating the software. Each of the companies supplied three of their best domain experts to represent their needs. There was regular communication between these on-site users and their own organizations, and they were also an integral part of the team they worked with on a daily basis.

A steering committee with representatives from all five companies was kept in the loop on progress and was brought in when decisions needed to be made at a higher level.

—Janet

Having a few representative domain experts, while keeping all stakeholders continually informed, is one approach to successful developer-customer collaboration. We'll talk about others in Part V. Customers are critical to the success of your agile project. They prioritize what will be built and have the final say in the quality of the product. Testers work closely with customers to learn requirements and define acceptance tests that will prove that conditions of satisfaction are met. Testing activities are key to the development team-customer team relationship. That's why testing expertise is so essential to agile teams.

Organization Size

The size of an organization can have great impact on how projects are run and how the structure of a company matures. The larger the organization, the more hierarchical the structure tends to be. As top-down communication channels are developed, the reporting structures become directive and less compatible with collaboration between technology and business.

Communication Challenges

Some agile processes provide ways to facilitate inter-team communication. For example, Scrum has the "Scrum of Scrums," where representatives from multiple teams coordinate on a daily basis.

If you work in a large organization where the test teams or other specialized resources are separate from the programming teams, work to find ways to keep in constant touch. For example, if your database team is completely separate, you need to find a way to work closely with the database specialists in order to get what you need in a timely manner.

Chapter 16, "Hit the Ground Running," describes how one large organization uses functional analysts to mitigate problems due to remote customers.

Another problem that tends to be more common in large companies is that customers might not be as accessible as they are in smaller companies. This is a big obstacle when you try to gather requirements and examples and seek to get customer involvement throughout the development cycle. One solution is to have testers or analysts with domain expertise act as customer proxies. Communication tools can help deal with such situations as well. Look for creative ways to overcome the problems inherent in big companies.

Conflicting Cultures within the Organization

With large software development shops, agile development is often first implemented in one team or just a few teams. If your agile team has to coordinate with other teams using other approaches such as phased or gated development, you have an extra set of challenges. If some of the external teams tend to be dysfunctional, it's even harder. Even when an entire company adopts agile, some teams make the transition more successfully than others.

Your team might also run into resistance from specialist teams that are feeling protective of their particular silos. Lisa talked to a team whose members could not get any help from their company's configuration management team, which was obviously a major obstacle. Some development teams are barred from talking directly to customers.

If third parties are working on the same system your team is working on, their cultures can also cause conflicts. Perhaps your team is the third party, and you're developing software for a client. You will need to think about how to mitigate culture-based differences. Part V goes into more detail about working with other teams and third parties, but here are a few ideas to get you started.

Chapter 15, "Tester Activities in Release or Theme Planning," and Chapter 16, "Hit the Ground Running," talk about what testers can do to help with planning and coordinating with other teams.

Advanced Planning If you have to coordinate with other teams, you will need to spend time during release planning, or before the start of an iteration, to work with them. You need time to adapt your own processes to work with others' processes, and they might need to change their processes to accommodate your requests. Consider arranging access to shared resources such as performance test specialists or load test environments, and plan your own work around others' schedules. Your stakeholders might expect certain deliverables, such as formal test plans, that your own agile process doesn't include. Some extra planning will help you to work through these cultural differences.

Act Now, Apologize Later We hesitate to make suggestions that might cause trouble, but often in a large organization, the bureaucratic wheels turn so slowly that your team might have to figure out and implement its own solutions. For example, the team that couldn't get cooperation from the configuration management team simply implemented its own internal build process and kept working on getting it integrated with the officially sanctioned process.

If there aren't official channels to get what you need, it's time to get creative. Maybe testers have never talked directly to customers before. Try to arrange a meeting yourself, or find someone who can act as a customer proxy or go-between.

Empower Your Team

Chapter 4, "Team Logistics," talks more about separate functional teams and how they affect the agile tester.

In an agile project, it is important for each development team to feel empowered to make decisions. If you're a manager and you want your agile teams to succeed, set them free to act and react creatively. The culture of an organization must adapt to this change for an agile project to be successful.

BARRIERS TO SUCCESSFUL AGILE ADOPTION BY TEST/QA TEAMS

Any change faces barriers to success. Organizational culture, as we discussed in the previous section, might be the largest obstacle to overcome. Once organizational culture has become well established, it's very hard to change. It took time for it to form, and once in place, employees become committed to the culture, which makes it extremely resistant to alteration.

This section discusses specific barriers to adoption of agile development methods that can be encountered by your testers and QA teams.

Loss of Identity

Testers cling to the concept of an independent QA team for many reasons, but the main reason is fear, specifically:

- Fear that they will lose their QA identity
- Fear that if they report to a development manager, they will lose support and programmers will get priority
- Fear that they lack the skills to work in an agile team and will lose their jobs
- Fear that when they're dispersed into development teams they won't get the support they need
- Fear that they, and their managers, will get lost in the new organization

Chapter 4, "Team Logistics," covers ideas that can be used to help people adapt.

We often hear of QA managers asking questions such as, "My company is implementing agile development. How does my role fit in?" This is directly related to the "loss of identity" fears.

Additional Roles

We know from experience that new teams are often missing specialists or expertise that might be key to their success. Lisa's team has run into obstacles so large that the only thing to do was sit back and ask, "What role are we missing on our team that is holding us back? What do we need? Another developer, another tester, a database designer?" We all know that testing is a vast field. Maybe you need someone experienced in testing on an agile team. Or maybe you need a performance testing specialist. It's critical that you take the time to analyze what roles your product needs to be successful, and if you need to fill them from outside the team, do it.

It's critical that everyone already on the product team understand their role or figure out what their role is now that they're part of a new agile team. Doing this requires time and training.

Lack of Training

We hosted a session in the "Conference within a Conference" at Agile 2007 that asked people what testing-related problems they were having on their agile teams. One of the attendees told us that they split up their test organization as advocated by the agile literature. However, they put the testers into development units without any training; within three months, all of the testers had quit because they didn't understand their new roles. Problems like these can be prevented with the right training and coaching.

When we started working with our first agile teams, there weren't many resources available to help us learn what agile testers should do or how we should work together with our teams. Today, you can find many practitioners who can help train testers to adapt to an agile environment and help test teams make the agile transition. Local user groups, conferences, seminars, online instruction, and mailing lists all provide valuable resources to testers and managers wanting to learn. Don't be afraid to seek help when you need it. Good coaching gives a good return on your investment.

Not Understanding Agile Concepts

Not all agile teams are the same. There are lots of different approaches to agile development, such as XP, Scrum, Crystal, FDD, DSDM, OpenUP, and various mixes of those. Some self-titled "agile" teams are not, in our opinion, really practicing agile. Plenty of teams simply adopt practices that work for them regardless of the original source, or they invent their own. That's fine, but if they don't follow any of the core agile values and principles, we question giving them an agile label. Releasing every month and dispensing with documentation does not equate to agile development!

If different team members have opposing notions of what constitutes "agile," which practices they should use, or how those practices are supposed to be practiced, there's going to be trouble. For example, if you're a tester who is pushing for the team to implement continuous integration, but the programmers simply refuse to try, you're in a bad spot. If you're a programmer who is unsuccessful at getting involved in some practices, such as driving development with business-facing tests, you're also in for conflict.

The team must reach consensus on how to proceed in order to make a successful transition to agile. Many of the agile development practices are synergistic, so if they are used in isolation, they might not provide the benefits that teams are looking for. Perhaps the team can agree to experiment with certain practices for a given number of iterations and evaluate the results. It could decide to seek external input to help them understand the practices and how they fit together. Diverse viewpoints are good for a team, but everyone needs to be headed in the same direction.

Several people we've talked to described the "mini-waterfall" phenomenon that often occurs when a traditional software development organization implements an agile development process. The organization replaces a six-month or year-long development cycle with a two- or four-week one, and just tries to squeeze all of the traditional SDLC phases into that short period. Naturally, they keep having the same problems as they had before. Figure 3-1 shows an "ideal" version of the mini-waterfall where there is a code-and-fix phase and then testing—the testing comes after coding is completed but before the next iteration starts. However, what really happens is that testing gets squeezed into the end of the iteration and usually drags over into the next iteration. The programmers don't have much to fix yet, so they start working on the next iteration. Before long, some teams are always an iteration "behind" with their testing, and release dates get postponed just as they always did.

Everyone involved with delivering the product needs time and training to understand the concepts behind agile as well as the core practices. Experienced coaches can be used to give hands-on training in practices new to the team, such as test-driven development. In larger organizations, functional

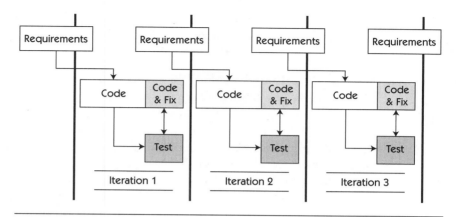

Figure 3-1 A mini-waterfall process

test managers can become practice leads and can provide support and resources so that testers learn how to communicate and collaborate with their new teams. Programmers and other team members need similar help from their functional managers. Strong leadership will help teams find ways to migrate away from "mini-waterfall" to true collaborative development, where coding and testing are integrated into one process.

See the bibliography for a link to more information about XP Radar charts.

XP has developed a radar chart to help teams determine their level of adaptation to key XP practices. They measure five different key practices: team, programming, planning, customer, and pairing, and they show the level of adaptation to practices by teams. Figure 3-2 shows two such charts. The chart

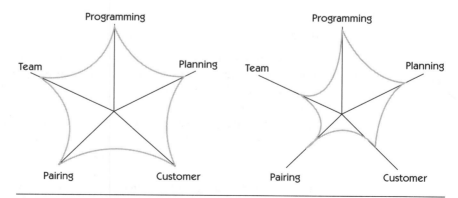

Figure 3-2 XP Radar charts

on the left shows successful adaptation, while the chart on the right shows that there are some problem areas.

Past Experience/Attitude

Lots of people have been through changes that didn't stick. Some development organizations have lived through a succession of the "methodology du jour." They throw up their hands and wonder, "Why should we do it again?" People get stuck in their old, unsuccessful patterns. Even when they try something new, they might revert to bad old habits when under stress. The following are just a few examples of people resisting change due to past experience and their perception of "the way things are":

- A tester sat in his cube and wouldn't talk with the programmers about problems he was having. He complained that programmers didn't understand what he wanted.
- A tester couldn't shake his existing attitude that programmers didn't know how to write good code, or how to test it. His condescending attitude was clear to all, and his credibility as a tester was challenged.
- A customer threw up his hands when the programmers did something he didn't like, because they "always" do what they want anyhow.

When faced with a transition to agile development, people like this often leave without giving the new process a chance. Agile development isn't for everyone, but training and time to experiment can help adjust attitudes. Ask everyone to be part of the solution, and work together to find out what processes and practices work best for their particular situations. The self-organizing team can be a powerful tool to use to reassure all members of the development team that they're in control of their own destiny.

Cultural Differences among Roles

Each new agile team member is making the transition from a different perspective. Programmers are often used to writing production code and getting it released as quickly as possible. System administrators and database experts might be accustomed to working in their own silo, performing requests on their own schedule. Customers may never have talked directly with development team members. Testers might be used to coming in at the end of the project and not interacting much at all with programmers.

It's no wonder a transition to agile can be scary. Teams can come up with rules and guidelines to help them communicate and work well together. For example, Lisa joined a new agile team whose rule was that if someone asked you to pair with her, you had to agree. You might not be able to do it right that minute, but as soon as you could free yourself up, you had to go help your teammate.

Identify what people doing different activities need, and find ways to provide it. Customers need some way to know how development is progressing and whether their conditions of satisfaction are being met. Developers need to know business priorities and requirements. Testers need ways to capture examples and turn them into tests. All team members want to feel they are valued, first-class team members. Each team member also needs to feel safe and to feel free to raise issues and try new ideas. Understanding the viewpoint of each role helps teams through the transition.

INTRODUCING CHANGE

When implementing any change, be aware of the side effects. The first stage may be chaos; your team isn't sure what the new processes are, some groups are loyal to old ways, and some people are unsure and disruptive. People mistake this chaotic stage for the new status quo. To avoid this, explain the change model up front and set expectations. Expect and accept perceived chaos as you implement agile processes. Find the areas of the most pain, and determine what practices will solve the problem so that you can get some immediate progress out of the chaos.

Talk about Fears

When you start iterative development, use retrospectives to provide people with a place to talk about their fears and a place in which they can give feedback. Let people know that it's normal to be fearful. Be open; teach them it is acceptable to say they are fearful or uncomfortable. Discuss each source of fear, learn from the discussion, make decisions, and move on. Fear is a common response to change. Forcing people to do something they don't want is detrimental to positive change. Lead by example.

Lisa's Story

Janet and I each joined our first XP teams at a time when many XP practitioners didn't see any place for testers on an XP team. XP had a "Customer Bill of Rights" and a "Programmer Bill of Rights," but the "Tester Bill of Rights" was conspicuously absent. Tip House and I came up with our own "Tester Bill of Rights" in order to give testers the support and courage to succeed on agile teams. Over the years, many testers have told us how much this helped them and their teams learn how testers work together with other team members. I don't like too many rules, but they can be a good thing when they help the team to overcome cultural barriers and to understand how to work in new ways. The following list presents a "Tester Bill of Rights." We encourage you to use it to help testers integrate into agile teams.

- You have the right to bring up issues related to testing, quality, and process at any time.
- You have the right to ask questions of customers, programmers, and other team members and receive timely answers.
- You have the right to ask for and receive help from anyone on the project teams, including programmers, managers, and customers.
- You have the right to estimate testing tasks and have these included in story estimates.
- You have the right to the tools you need to perform testing tasks in a timely manner.
- You have the right to expect your entire team, not just yourself, to be responsible for quality and testing.

—Lisa

Give Team Ownership

A critical success factor is whether the team takes ownership and has the ability to customize its approach. People can change their attitudes and their perceptions if they are given the right help. Lisa was able to observe Mike Cohn work with her team as a coach. As a self-organizing team, the team had to identify and solve its own problems. Mike made sure they had the time and resources to experiment and improve. He made sure that the business understood that quality was more important than quantity or speed. Every team, even a self-organizing team, needs a leader who can effectively interact with the organization's management team.

Celebrate Success

Implementing change takes time and can be frustrating, so be sure to celebrate all successes your team achieves. Pat yourselves on the back when you meet your goal to write high-level test cases for all stories by the fourth day of the iteration. Get the team together for a trivia game or lunch when you've just delivered an iteration's worth of work. Acknowledgment is important if you want a change to stick.

Chapter 18, "Coding and Testing," covers how testers and programmers work together throughout the development process.

Integrating testers into development teams while letting them continue to report to a supportive QA manager is one way to ease the transition to agile development. Testers can find ways to move from an adversarial relationship with programmers to a collaborative one. They can show how they can help

Overcoming Resistance to Agile

Mark Benander, a Quality Assurance Team Lead with Quickoffice, was on his fourth project on an agile team. The first was a major rewrite of their entire application, with a team of eight developers, one tester, and no test automation tool. He told us about his experiences in overcoming his concerns about agile development, especially about reporting to a development manager.

> We were in a matrix management type of system, where a tester reports to a development manager, but the test manager is still officially the supervisor. This comforted me somewhat, but the majority of the issues I expected to occur, such as being overruled whenever I found an issue, never did. My concern wasn't that I'd really end up thinking like a developer and just releasing anything, but that my manager, who was not a tester, wouldn't care as much, and might not back up my concerns with the application.

> Ultimately, I think I ended up thinking slightly more like a developer, being less concerned about some of the small bugs. My better understanding of the application's workings made me understand that the risk and cost of fixing it was potentially much more risky than the benefit. I believe that thinking like this isn't a bad thing as long as we are always mindful of the end customer impact, not just the internal cost.

> The corollary to my thinking more like a developer is that the developers began thinking more like testers. I'm actually a fan of the adversarial role of the tester, but in a relaxed way. I actually give the developers gold stars (the little sticker kind you used to get on your spelling test in second grade) when they implement an area of code that is especially solid and user friendly, and I give out pink stars when they "implement" a bug that is especially heinous. They groan when I come over, wondering what I've found now, and take great joy in "making my job boring" by testing their code themselves and giving me nothing to find. Needless to say, you need the right group to be able to work with this kind of faux-hostile attitude. I've never been in another company where this would have worked, but I've never worked in another company where spontaneous nerf gunfights broke out either.

Mark's experience matches our own and that of many other testers we've met who've moved from traditional to agile development. If you're a tester who just joined an agile team, keep an open mind and consider how your teammates might have different viewpoints.

the team understand the customers' needs and deliver appropriate business value. They can host enjoyable activities to build good team interactions. Having cookies or chocolate available for teammates is a good way to get them to walk over to your desk! Patience and a sense of fun are big advantages.

MANAGEMENT EXPECTATIONS

When we think of challenges involved with adopting agile, we generally think of the actual team and the issues it encounters. However, for successful agile adoption, management buy-in is critical. In a phased project, management gets regular updates and sign-off documents indicating the end of each phase. Upper-level managers might not understand how they'll be able to gauge agile project progress. They might fear a loss of control or lack of "process."

Cultural Changes for Managers

In an agile project, expectations change. In her previous life in waterfall projects, Janet remembers hearing comments like "this feature is 90% done" for weeks. Those types of metrics are meaningless in agile projects. There are no sign-offs to mark the end of a phase, and the "doneness" of a project isn't measured by gates.

Meaningful metrics are determined by each project team. In Scrum, sprint and release burndown charts track story completion and can give managers a measure of progress, but not any hard "dates" to use for billing customers. Test matrices can be used to track functionality test coverage but do not provide sign-off documentation.

The other change that is difficult for some managers to understand is letting the teams make their own technical decisions and manage their own workloads. It's no longer the manager who decides what is good enough. It is the team (which includes the customer) that defines the level of quality necessary to deliver a successful application.

Agile teams estimate and work in smaller chunks of time than traditional teams. Rather than building in contingency, teams need to plan enough time for good design and execution in order to ensure that technical debt does not increase. Rather than managing the team's activities at a low level, managers of agile teams focus on removing obstacles so that team members can do their best work.

Janet's Story

I asked the vice president in charge of a large agile project what he found to be the most difficult part in the new agile environment from a management perspective. He said that in a traditional waterfall type project, the reports all showed that everything was going according to plan until the very end, and then everything was in a panic state and "nothing worked."

In the agile project, there were problems every day that needed to be addressed. Agile projects were more work on a consistent basis, but at least he was getting realistic reports. There were no surprises at the end of the project.

—Janet

Business stakeholders don't like surprises. If they can be convinced to give the team enough time and resources to make the transition, they'll find that agile development lets them plan more accurately and achieve business goals in steady increments.

Sometimes it's actually management that drives the decision to start doing agile development. The business leaders at Lisa's company chose to try agile development in order to solve its software crisis. To be effective, they needed to have a different set of management expectations. They needed to be sensitive to the difficulty of making big changes, especially in an organization that wasn't functioning well.

In all cases, managers need lots of patience during what might be a long transition to a high-functioning agile team. It's their job to make sure they provide the necessary resources and that they enable every individual to learn how to do high-quality work.

A Testing Manager's Transition Tale

Tae Chang manages a team at DoubleClick that conducts end-to-end testing to ensure that all integration points, both up and downstream from the target of change, are covered. When they implemented Scrum, the development teams were reorganized into numerous application teams. Communication problems resulted in missed dependencies, so Tae's team stepped up to help make sure problems were detected early.

Tae told us, "I believe agile development effectively magnified the importance of cross-team communication and a coordinated end-to-end testing effort. It was not easy to work out a noninvasive (in terms of fitting into current sprint structure) integration testing process; in fact, we are still tweaking it, but the overall benefit of such a testing effort is apparent." Their teams began to slide into the "mini-waterfall" trap. "In retrospect," explains Tae, "one of the reasons for this is because we started with the agile process before internalizing agile practices."

Knowing that test automation and continuous integration were key, the teams at DoubleClick came up with new ideas, such as a specialized build and automation team to help the development teams cope. They brought in expert training to help them learn TDD and pair programming. They started taking steps to address their legacy system's technical debt.

Tae's team attends all of the sprint planning and review sessions, using both formal and informal communication to facilitate cross-functional communication and coordinate testing and releases. He has found that it helps to keep meetings small, short, and relevant. He's also a proponent of everyone sitting together in an open work area, as opposed to sectioned-off cubes.

Tae offers the following advice to testers making the transition to agile:

"Agile development in general will initially frustrate testers in that they will not have access to full requirements documentation or defined stages of testing. In my view of agile development, at any given moment, the tester will be engaged in tasks from multiple stages of the traditional development process. A tester can be sitting in a design session with engineering and product management (she should be taking notes here and start thinking of areas of risk where proposed code change will most likely impact) and on the same day work on automating and running test cases for the proposed changes. It's a change in mind-set, and some people are quicker to adapt than others."

Tae's experience mirrors our own and that of many other teams we've talked to.

If you're a QA manager, be prepared to help your testers overcome their frustrations with moving from defined, sequential testing stages to fast-paced iterations where they perform widely varied tasks on any given day. Help them adapt to the idea that testing is no longer a separate activity that occurs after development but that testing and coding are integrated activities.

If you're a tester or other team member who isn't getting the support you need in your transition to agile development, think about the difficulties your managers might be having in understanding agile development. Help them to understand what kinds of support you need.

Speaking the Manager's Language

What do business managers understand best? It's the bottom line—the ROI (return on investment). To get the support you need from your management, frame your needs in a context that they can understand. Your team's velocity translates into new features to make the business more profitable. If you need time and funds to learn and implement an automated test tool, explain to management that over time, automated regression tests will let your team go faster and deliver more functionality in each iteration.

Lisa's Story

My team needs big blocks of time to do risky refactoring, such as trying to split the code base into multiple modules that can be built independently. We also need time to upgrade to the latest versions of our existing tools, or to try out new tools. All of these tasks are difficult to integrate into a two-week sprint when we're also trying to deliver stories for the business.

We explained to our management that if these "engineering" tasks were put off too long, our technical debt would accumulate and our velocity would slow. The number of story points delivered each iteration would decline, and new stories would take longer to code. It would take longer and longer for the business to get the new features it needed in order to attract customers.

It was hard for the business to agree to let us devote a two-week iteration every six months to do the internal work we needed to manage our technical debt, but over time they could see the results in our velocity. Recently, one of the managers actually asked if we might need to have "engineering sprints" more often. Both the product and the team are growing, and the business wants to make sure we grow our infrastructure and tools, too.

—Lisa

Like all members of an agile team, managers need to learn a lot of new concepts and figure out how they fit as team members. Use big visible charts (or their virtual equivalents, as needed) to make sure they can follow the progress of each iteration and release. Look for ways to maximize ROI. Often, the business will ask for a complex and expensive feature when there is a simpler and quicker solution that delivers similar value. Make sure you explain how your team's work affects the bottom line. Collaborate with them to find the best way for stakeholders to express the requirements for each new feature.

Budget limitations are a reality most teams face. When resources are limited, your team needs to be more creative. The whole-team approach helps. Perhaps, like Lisa's team, your team has a limited budget to buy software, and so you tend to look at open-source test automation tools that usually don't have a large up-front purchase cost. A tool that uses the same language as the application won't help the non-programming testers unless the programmers collaborate with them to automate the tests. Leveraging all of the expertise on the team helps you work within the business limitations.

As with all challenges your team encounters, experiment with new ways that the development team and management can help each other to build a valuable product. At the same time, regardless of your development approach, you might have to make sure that some processes, such as conformance to audit requirements, receive the necessary attention.

CHANGE DOESN'T COME EASY

Agile development might seem fast-paced, but change can seem glacial. Teams that are new to agile will be slow to master some practices they've committed to using. We've met many testers who are frustrated that their "agile" development cycles are actually mini-waterfall cycles. These testers are still getting squeezed; it just happens more often. Iterations are over before stories can be tested. Programmers refuse or aren't able to adopt critical practices such as TDD or pairing. The team leaves responsibility for quality in the hands of the testers, who are powerless to make changes to the process.

There's no magic that you can use to get your team to make positive changes, but we have some tips for testers who want to get their teams to change in positive ways.

Be Patient

New skills such as TDD are hard. Find ways to help your team get time to master them. Find changes you can make independently while you wait. For example, while programmers learn to write unit tests, implement a GUI test tool that you can use with minimal help. Help the team make baby steps. Remember that when people panic, they go back to their old habits, even though those habits didn't work. Focus on tiny positive increments.

Let Them Feel Pain

Sometimes you just have to watch the train wreck. If your suggestions for improvement were rebuffed, and the team fails, bring your suggestion up again and ask the team to consider trying it for a few iterations. People are most willing to change in the areas where they feel the most pain.

Build Your Credibility

You might now be working with programmers who haven't worked closely with testers before. Show them how you can help. Go to them with issues you've found rather than opening bug reports. Ask them to review code with you before they check it in. When they realize you're contributing real value, they're more likely to listen to your ideas.

Work On Your Own Professional Development

Read books and articles, go to user group meetings and conferences, and learn a new tool or scripting language. Start learning the language your application is coded in, and ask the programmers on your team if you can pair with them or if they'll tutor you. Your coworkers will respect your desire to improve your skills. If your local user group is willing to listen to your presentation on agile testing, or a software newsletter publishes your automation article, your teammates might notice you have something worth hearing too.

Beware the Quality Police Mentality

Be a collaborator, not an enforcer. It might bug you if programmers don't follow coding standards, but it's not your job to make sure that they do so. Raise your issues with the team and ask for their help. If they ignore a critical problem that is really hurting the team, you might need to go to your coach or manager for help. But do that in a "please help me find a solution" vein rather than a "make these people behave" one. If you're seeing a problem, chances are high that others see it too.

Vote with Your Feet

See the bibliography for some good resources on being an effective change agent for your team.

You've been patient. You've tried every approach you can think of, but your management doesn't understand agile development. The programmers still throw buggy, untestable code "over the wall," and that code is released as is despite your best efforts, including working 14-hour days. Nobody cares about quality, and you feel invisible despite your best efforts. It might be time to look for a better team. Some teams are happy the way they are and simply don't feel enough pain to want to change. Lisa worked on a team that thrived on chaos, because there were frequent opportunities to figure out why the server crashed and be a hero. Despite a successful project using agile practices, they went back to their old habits, and Lisa finally gave up trying to change them.

SUMMARY

In this chapter, we talked about how cultural issues can affect whether testers and their teams can make a successful transition to doing agile development.

- Consider organizational culture before making any kind of change.
- Testers have an easier time integrating into agile teams when their whole organization values quality, but testers with a "quality police" mind-set will struggle.
- Some testers might have trouble adjusting to the "whole team" ownership of quality, but a team approach helps overcome cultural differences.
- Customer teams and developer teams must work closely together, and we showed how testers can be key in facilitating this relationship.
- Large organizations that tend to have more isolated specialist teams face particular cultural challenges in areas such as communication and collaboration.
- Major barriers to success for testers for agile adoption include fear, loss of identity, lack of training, previous negative experiences with new development processes, and cultural differences among roles.
- To help introduce change and promote communication, we suggest encouraging team members to discuss fears and celebrating every success, no matter how small.
- Guidelines such as a "Tester Bill of Rights" give testers confidence to raise issues and help them feel safe as they learn and try new ideas.
- Managers face their own cultural challenges, and they need to provide support and training to help testers succeed on agile teams.
- Testers can help teams accommodate manager expectations by providing the information managers need to track progress and determine ROI.
- Change doesn't come easy, so be patient, and work on improving your own skills so you can help your team.

## Chapter 4

TEAM LOGISTICS

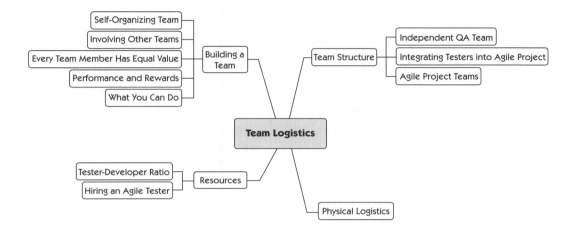

Agile teams stress that face-to-face communication is critical to the success of a project. They also encourage using the "whole-team" approach. What does this mean to the testers? This chapter talks about some of the issues involving team structure and physical logistics. There's more to creating a cohesive team than just moving chairs and desks.

TEAM STRUCTURE

Having separate functional groups can make life difficult for agile teams. Constant communication is critical. Team members need to work closely with one another, whether the work is done virtually or in the same physical location.

We use the terms "QA team" and "test team" interchangeably here. It can be argued whether "QA teams" are really doing quality assurance or not, but the term has become a common one attached to test teams, so we use it too.

Independent QA Teams

Many organizations, both large and small, think it is important to have an independent QA or test team in order to get an honest opinion about the quality of a product. We're often asked the questions, "Is there a place for a test organization in the whole-team approach?" and "If so, what is its role?"

Some of the reasons we're given for wanting to keep the QA team separate from the development team are:

- It is important to have that independent check and audit role.
- The team can provide an unbiased and outside view relating to the quality of the product.
- If testers work too closely with developers, they will start to think like developers and lose their customer viewpoint.
- If the testers and developers report to the same person, there is a danger that the priority becomes delivering *any* code rather than delivering tested code.

Teams often confuse "independent" with "separate." If the reporting structure, budgets, and processes are kept in discrete functional areas, a division between the programmers and testers is inevitable. This can lead to friction, competition, and an "us versus them" attitude. Time is wasted on duplicate meetings, programmers and testers don't share a common goal, and information sharing is nonexistent.

There are reasons for having a QA manager and an independent test team. However, we suggest changing the reasons as well as the structure. Rather than keeping the testers separate as an independent team to test the application after coding, think about the team as a community of testers. Provide a learning organization to help your testers with career development and a place to share ideas and help each other. If the QA manager becomes a practice leader in the organization, that person will be able to teach the skills that testers need to become stronger and better able to cope with the ever-changing environment.

We don't believe that integrating the testers with the project teams prevents testers from doing their jobs well. In fact, testers on agile teams feel very strongly about their role as customer advocate and also feel they can influence the rest of the team in quality thinking.

Integration of Testers into an Agile Project

The whole-team approach in agile development has provoked many organizations that have adopted agile development to disband their independent QA teams and send their testers to work with the project groups. While this sounds great, some organizations have found that it doesn't work as expected. More than one organization has had most, if not all, of their testers quit when they found themselves on an agile development team with no idea what they should be doing.

Developers get training on pair programming, test-driven development, and other agile practices, while testers often seem to get no training at all. Many organizations fail to recognize that testers also need training on pair testing, working with incomplete and changing requirements, automation, and all of the other new skills that are required. It's critical that testers receive training and coaching so that they can acquire the skills and understanding that will help them succeed, such as how to work with customers to write business-facing tests. Programmers also might need coaching to understand the importance of business-facing tests and the whole-team approach to writing and automating tests.

Janet has helped integrate several independent test teams into agile projects. She finds that it can take up to six months for most testers to start feeling confident about working with the new process.

The pairing of programmers and testers can only improve communication about the quality of the product. Developers often need to observe the behavior of the application on the tester's workstation if that behavior can't be reproduced in the development environment. Testers can sometimes sit down with the developer to reproduce a problem more easily and quickly than they can by trying to record the steps in a defect. This interaction reduces the time spent on non-oral communication.

Comments we've heard from testers on this subject include the following:

- "Being closer to the development of the product makes me a better tester."
- "Going to lunch with developers builds a better team, one that wants and likes to work together."

One major advantage of an integrated project team is that there's only one budget and one schedule. There is no "testing" time to cut if all of the functionality is not finished. If there is no time to test a new feature, then there is no time to develop it in the first place. The whole-team approach to taking responsibility for quality is very powerful, as we point out throughout this book.

Lisa's Story

I once joined an XP team that had been depending solely on unit-level testing and had never had anyone in a tester role before. Their customer wasn't all that happy with the results, so they decided to hire a tester. While I attended daily stand-ups, I wasn't allowed to talk about testing tasks. Testing time wasn't included in story estimates, and testing tasks weren't part of iteration planning. Stories were marked "done" as soon as coding tasks were complete.

After the team missed the release date, which was planned for after three two-week iterations, I asked the team's coach to try the whole-team approach to testing. Testing tasks went up on the board along with coding tasks. Stories were no longer considered done until testing tasks were finished. Programmers took on testing tasks, and I was a full participant in daily stand-ups. The team had no more issues meeting the release plans they set.

—Lisa

Testers need to be full-fledged members of the development team, and testing tasks need to be given the same attention as other tasks. Again, the whole-team approach to testing goes a long way toward ensuring that testing tasks are completed by the end of each iteration and release. Be sure to use retrospectives to evaluate what testers need to integrate with their new agile team and what skills they might need to acquire. For example, testers might need more support from programmers, or from someone who's an expert in a particular type of testing.

A smart approach to planning the organizational changes for agile development makes all the difference to a successful transition. Ask the QA and development managers to figure out their own roles in the new agile organization. Let them plan how they will help their testers and developers be productive on the new agile teams. Provide training in agile practices that the team doesn't know. Make sure all of the teams can communicate with each other. Provide a framework that lets each team learn as it goes, and the teams will find a way to succeed.

Transitioning QA and Engineering Teams—Case Study

Christophe Louvion is a CTO and agile coach for high-profile Internet companies. He told us about one experience he had while helping his company implement agile development. As the agile coach, he wanted to truly implement agile development and avoid the common "small waterfall" mistake, where the developers spend a week writing code and the testers spend the next week testing it.

His company at the time was an organization of about 120 engineers, including the internal IT departments. Before transitioning to Scrum, the company was organized functionally. There were directors of QA and Engineering, and the idea of product-based teams was hard for management to accept. The managers of these teams struggled with the following question: "What is my job now?" Christophe turned this around on the managers and said: "You tell me."

He worked with the Engineering and QA managers to help them figure out what their jobs would be in the new agile environment. Only when they were able to speak with one voice did they all go to the teams and explain their findings.

In the new agile organization, managers deal with specific domain knowledge, resources, prioritization, and problems that arise. The Engineering and QA managers work hand-in-hand on a daily basis to resolve these types of issues. Christophe and the two managers looked at what prevented testers from being productive in the first week of the two-week iteration and taught them how to help with design.

For the programmers, the question was "How do I make it so that the code is easy to test?" The engineers weren't trained in continuous integration, because they were used to working in phased cycles. They needed lots of training in test-driven design, continuous integration, and other practices. Their managers ensured that they got this training.

Configuration management (CM) experts were brought in to help with the build process. The CM team is separate from Engineering and QA at the company, and it provides the framework for everything in the build process, including database objects, hardware, and configurations. Once the build process framework was implemented, integrating coding and testing was much easier to talk about.

See the bibliography for a link to some of Christophe's writings on managing agile teams.

Having management figure out their new roles first, and then getting a build process framework in place with everything in source code control, were key to the successful transition to agile. Another success factor was having representatives from all teams—Engineering, QA, the CM, network, and the system administrator groups and product teams—participate in daily stand-ups and planning activities. This way, when testing issues came up, they could be addressed by everyone who could help. As Christophe says, their approach integrates everyone and puts a focus on testing.

Agile Project Teams

Agile project teams are generally considered cross-functional, because each team has members from many different backgrounds. The difference between a traditional cross-functional team and an agile team is the approach to the whole-team effort. Members are not just "representing" their functions in the team but are becoming true members of the team for as long as the project or permanent team exists (see Figure 4-1).

Because projects vary in size, project teams might vary in structure. Organizations with large projects or many projects that happen simultaneously are having success using a matrix-type structure. People from different functional areas combine to form a virtual team while still reporting back to their individual organizational structures. In a large organization, a pool of testers might move from project to project. Some specialists, such as security or performance testers, might be shared among several teams. If you're starting up a project, identify all of the resources the project will need. Determine the number of testers required and the skill set needed before you start. The testers start with the team and keep working until the project is complete, and at that time they go on to the next project.

While testers are part of the team, their day-to-day work is managed the same as the rest of the project team's work. A tester can bounce new ideas off of the larger tester community, which includes testers on different project teams across a large organization. All testers can share knowledge and ideas. In organizations that practice performance reviews, the QA manager (if there is one) might drive the reviews and get input from the project team.

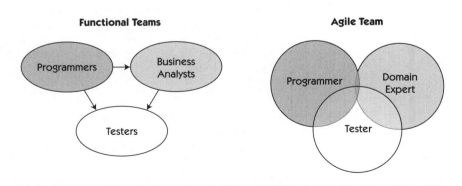

Figure 4-1   Traditional functional teams structure vs. agile team structure

As with any new team, it takes a while for a team to jell. If the length of the project is short and the teams are constantly changing, the organization needs to be aware that the first iteration or two of every project will include the new team members getting used to working with each other. Refactor your organization as needed, and remember to include your customers. The best teams are those that have learned to work together and have developed trust with one another.

PHYSICAL LOGISTICS

Many organizations that are thinking of adopting agile try to create project teams without co-locating the team in an open-plan environment. To support agile values and principles, teams work better when they have ready access to all team members, easy visibility of all project progress charts, and an environment that fosters communication.

Testers and customers sitting close to the programmers enable the necessary communalization. If logistics prohibit co-location, teams can be inventive.

Janet's Story

I worked in a team where space prevented all team members from sitting together. The programmers had an area where they could pair-program with ease, but the testers and the customer were seated in another area. At first, it was the testers that made the trip to the storyboard area where the programmers sat to participate in stand-ups and whenever they had a question for one of the programmers. Few of the programmers made the trip (about 50 feet) to the testers' area. I started keeping a candy dish handy with treats and encouraged the developers to take some as often as they wanted. But there was one rule—they needed to ask a question of one of the testers if they came for candy. Over time, the walk got shorter for all team members. No one side was doing all of the walking, and communication flourished.

—Janet

Team size offers different types of challenges to the organization. Small teams mean small areas, so it is usually easier to co-locate members. Large teams might be spread globally, and virtual communication tools are needed. Co-locating large teams usually means renovating existing space, which some organizations are reluctant to do. Understand your constraints, and try to find solutions to the problems your team encounters rather than just accepting things as "the way it is."

Janet's Story
One team I worked on started in one corner of the floor, but expanded over the course of three years, gradually taking over 70% of the floor. Walls were taken down, offices removed, and large open areas created. The open areas and pods of teams worked well, but all the open space meant wall space was lost. Windows became story boards and whiteboards, and rolling whiteboards were ordered that could be used as teams needed them.

—Janet

Co-located teams don't always live in a perfect world, and distributed teams have a another set of challenges. Distributed teams need technology to help them communicate and collaborate. Teleconferencing, video conferencing, webcams, and instant messaging are some tools that can promote real-time collaboration for teams in multiple locations.

Whether teams are co-located or distributed, the same questions usually come up about what resources are needed on an agile team and how to obtain them. We'll discuss these in the next section.

RESOURCES

New agile team members and their managers have lots of questions about the makeup of the team. Can we use the same testers that we had with our traditional projects, or do we need to hire a different type of tester? How many testers will we need? Do we need people with other specialized skills? In this section, we talk a little about these questions.

Tester-Developer Ratio

There have been many discussions about the "right" ratio of the number of testers to the number of developers. This ratio has been used by organizations to determine how many testers are needed for a project so that they can hire accordingly. As with traditional projects, there is no "right" ratio, and each project needs to be evaluated on its own. The number of testers needed will vary and depends upon the complexity of the application, the skill set of the testers, and the tools used.

We have worked on teams with a tester-developer ratio of anywhere from 1:20 to 1:1. Here are a couple of our experiences.

Janet's Story	I worked on a project with a 1:10 ratio that developed a message-handling system. There was very little GUI, and I manually tested that part of the application, looking at usability and how well it matched the customer's expectations. The programmers did all of the automated regression testing while I worked with them to validate the effectiveness of the test cases written. I pair-tested stories with the developers, including load testing specific stories.

I never felt that I didn't have enough time to do the testing I needed to, because the developers believed that quality was the whole team's responsibility.

—Janet

Lisa's Story	I was once the only professional tester on a team of up to 20 programmers developing a content management system on an Internet shopping website. The team began to get really productive when the programmers took on responsibility for both manual testing and test automation. One or two programmers wore a "tester hat" for each iteration, writing customer-facing tests ahead of coding and performing manual tests. Additional programmers picked up the test automation tasks during the iteration.

Conversely, my current team has had two testers for every three to five programmers. The web-based financial application we produce has highly complex business logic, is high risk, and test intensive. Testing tasks often add up to the same amount of time as programming tasks. Even with a relatively high tester–programmer ratio, programmers do much of the functional test automation and sometimes pick up manual testing tasks. Specialized testing tasks such as writing high-level test cases and detailed customer-facing tests are usually done by the testers.

—Lisa

Rather than focus on a ratio, teams should evaluate the testing skills they need and find the appropriate resources. A team that takes responsibility for testing can continually evaluate whether it has the expertise and bandwidth it needs. Use retrospectives to identify whether there's a problem that hiring more testers would solve.

Hiring an Agile Tester

As we discussed in Chapter 2, "Ten Principles for Agile Testers," there are certain qualities that make a tester suited to working on an agile team. We don't want to go into a lot of detail about what kind of tester to hire, because every team's need is different. However, we do believe that attitude is an important factor. Here's a story of how Lisa's team struggled to hire a new agile tester.

Lisa's Story

Our first attempt at recruiting another tester was not very successful. The first job posting elicited many responses, and we interviewed three candidates without finding a good fit. The programmers wanted someone "techie," but we also needed someone with the skills to collaborate with business people and help them to produce examples and requirements. We struggled to determine the content of the job posting in order to attract candidates with the right attitude and mind-set.

After soliciting opinions and suggestions from Janet and other colleagues in the agile testing community, we decided to look for a tester with the mind-set that is described in Chapter 2. We changed the job posting to include items such as these:

- Experience writing black box and GUI test cases, designing tests to mitigate risks, and helping business experts define requirements
- Experience writing simple SQL queries and insert/update statements and basic grasp of Oracle or another relational database
- At least one year of experience with some scripting or programming language and/or open source test tools
- Ability to use basic Unix commands
- Experience collaborating with programmers and business experts
- Experience in context-based, exploratory, or scenario testing a plus
- Ability to work as part of a self-organizing team in which you determine your tasks on a daily basis in coordination with coworkers rather than waiting for work to be assigned to you

These requirements brought candidates more suited to an agile testing job. I proceeded carefully with screening, ruling out people with a "quality police" mentality. Testers who pursued professional development and showed interest in agile development were more likely to have the right mind-set. The team needed someone who would be strong in the area of test tools and automation, so a passion for learning was paramount.

This more creative approach to recruiting a tester paid off. At that time, it wasn't easy to find good "agile tester" candidates, but subsequent searches went more smoothly. We found that posting the tester position in less obvious places, such as a Ruby mailing list or the local agile user group, helped reach a wider range of suitable candidates.

Hiring an agile tester taught me a lot about the agile testing mind-set. There are testers with very good skill sets who would be valuable to any traditional test team but would not be a good fit on an agile team because of their attitude toward testing.

—Lisa

We need to consider more than just the roles that testers and programmers perform on the team. No matter what role you're trying to fill, the most important consideration is how that person will fit on your team. With the agile whole-team approach, specialists on the team might be asked to step outside their areas of expertise and pitch in on other activities. Each team member needs to have a strong focus on quality and delivering business value. Consider more than just technical skills when you're expanding your team.

BUILDING A TEAM

We've talked a lot about the whole-team approach. But changes like that don't just happen. We get asked questions like, "How do we get the team to jell?" or "How do we promote the whole-team approach?" One of the big ones is: "How do we keep everyone motivated and focused on the goal of delivering business value?"

Self-Organizing Team

In our experience, teams make the best progress when they're empowered to identify and solve their own problems. If you're a manager, resist the temptation to impose all your good ideas on the team. There are problems, such as personnel issues, that are best solved by managers, and there are times a coach needs to provide strong encouragement and lead the team when it needs leadership. It takes time for a new agile team to learn how to prioritize and solve its problems, but it's okay for the team to make mistakes and stumble a few times. We think a high-functioning team has to grow itself. If you're a tester, you're in a good position to help the team figure out ways to get fast feedback, use practices such as retrospectives to prioritize and address issues, and find the techniques that help your team produce better software.

Involving Other Teams

You might need to get other teams on board to help your team succeed. Set up meetings; find ways to communicate as much as possible. Use a Scrum of Scrums to keep multiple teams coordinated, or just get involved with the other teams. If you have to bring in an expert to help with security testing, pair with that expert and learn as much as you can, and help them learn about your project.

If teams are scattered in different locations and time zones, figure out how to get as much direct communication as possible. Maybe representatives from

Chapter 9, "Toolkit for Business-Facing Tests that Support the Team," gives examples of tools that help remote teams collaborate.

each team can adjust their hours once or twice a week so that they can teleconference once a week. Make a phone call instead of sending an email whenever possible. Lisa's team adjusted its planning meeting times to include a remote team member who works late at night. They schedule meetings for a time where his day overlaps with the rest of the team's day.

Every Team Member Has Equal Value

Every team member has equal value to the team. If testers or any other team members feel left out or less valued, the whole-team approach is doomed. Make sure testers are invited to all meetings. If you're a tester and someone forgets to invite you to a meeting, invite yourself. Nontechnical testers might think they'll be out of place or overwhelmed at a design meeting, but sometimes they ask good questions that the techies didn't think of.

Testers have a right to ask for and get help. If you're a tester stuck on an automation problem, have the courage to ask a team member for help. That person might be busy right now, but he or she must commit to helping you in a reasonable amount of time. If you're a manager or leader on your team, make sure this is happening, and raise the issue to the team if it's not.

Performance and Rewards

Measuring and rating performance on an individual basis risks undermining team collaboration. We don't want a programmer to feel she shouldn't take on a testing task because she's rated on delivering production code. We don't want a system administrator to be so busy making sure her individual goals are met that she can't help with a test environment problem.

Conversely, a good performer who was trying to work well with the team shouldn't be knocked because the rest of the team didn't pull together. This is a time when a manager needs to step up and help the team find its way. If major bugs made it to production, nobody should blame the testers. Instead, the whole team should analyze what happened and start taking steps to prevent a recurrence.

The development team needs to keep the business needs in mind. Set goals that serve the business, increase profitability, and make the customers happier. Work closely with the business so that your successes help the whole company succeed.

As we mentioned in Chapter 3, "Cultural Challenges," celebrate every success, however small. A celebration might be a high-five, a company-provided lunch, or maybe just leaving work early to socialize a bit. The ScrumMaster on Lisa's team hands out gold stars at stand-up meetings for special accomplishments. Acknowledge the people who help you and your team.

Read about the "Shout-Out Shoebox" idea in Chapter 19, "Wrap Up the Iteration."

Teams can find novel ways to recognize each other's contributions. Iteration review and demonstration meetings, where both the development team and customer team are present, are a good setting for recognizing both individual and team achievements.

What Can You Do?

If you're a new tester on an agile team, especially a new agile team, what can you do to help the team overcome organizational challenges and succeed? How can you fit in with the team and contribute your particular skills and experience?

Put the ten principles we described in Chapter 2 to work. Courage is especially important. Get up and go talk to people; ask how you can help. Reach out to team members and other teams with direct communication. Notice impediments and ask the team to help remove them.

Agile development works because it gets obstacles out of our path and lets us do our best work. We can feel proud and satisfied, individually and as a team. When we follow agile principles, we collaborate well, use feedback to help improve how we work, and always look for new and better ways to accomplish our goals. All this means we can continually improve the quality of our product.

SUMMARY

In this chapter, we looked at ways to build a team and a structure for successful agile testing and development.

- Consider the importance of team structure; while testers might need an independent mind-set, putting them on a separate team can be counterproductive.
- Testers need access to a larger community of testers for learning and trying out new ideas. QA teams might be able to create this community within their organization.

- It is important for the whole team to be located together, to foster collaboration; if the team is distributed, provide tools to promote communication.
- Hire for attitude.
- There is no right tester–developer ratio. The right answer is, "It depends on your situation."
- Teams need to self-organize, identify and find solutions to their own problems, and look for ways to improve. They can't wait for someone to tell them what to do.
- Management should reward performance in a way that promotes the team's effort to deliver business value but not penalize good individual performance if the team is struggling.
- Testers can use agile principles to improve their own skills and increase their value to the team. They need to be proactive and find ways that they can contribute.

Chapter 5

TRANSITIONING TYPICAL PROCESSES

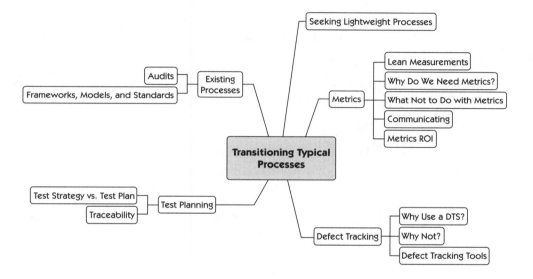

There are many processes in a traditional project that don't transition well to agile because they require heavyweight documentation or are an inherent part of the phased and gated process and require sign-offs at the end of each stage.

Like anything else, there are no hard and fast rules for transitioning your processes to a more agile or lightweight process. In this chapter, we discuss a few of those processes, and give you alternatives and guidance on how to work with them in an agile project. You'll find more examples and details about these alternatives in Parts III, IV, and V.

SEEKING LIGHTWEIGHT PROCESSES

When teams are learning how to use agile processes, some of the more traditional processes can be lost in the shuffle. Most testers who are used to working with traditional phased and gated development methodologies are accustomed to producing and using metrics, recording defects in a formal defect tracking system, and writing detailed test plans. Where do those fit in agile development?

Many software organizations must comply with audit systems or quality process models. Those requirements don't usually disappear just because you start using agile development practices. In fact, some people worry that agile development will be incompatible with such models and standards as CMMI and ISO 9000.

It might be more fun to talk about everything that's new and different when testing on an agile project, but we still need ways to measure progress, track defects, and plan testing. We also need to be prepared to work with our organization's quality models. The key is to keep these processes lightweight enough to help us deliver value in a timely manner. Let's start by looking at metrics.

METRICS

Metrics can be controversial, and we spend a lot of time talking about them. Metrics can be a pit of wasted effort, numbers for the sake of numbers. They are sometimes used in harmful ways, although they don't have to be bad. They can guide your team and help it to measure your team's progress toward its goals. Let's take a look at how to use metrics to help agile testers and their teams.

Lean Measurements

Lean software development practitioners look for ways to reduce the number of measurements and find measurements that will drive the right behaviors. *Implementing Lean Software Development: From Concept to Cash*, by Mary and Tom Poppendieck, is an excellent resource that teaches how to apply lean initiatives to your testing and development efforts.

According to the Poppendiecks [2007], a fundamental lean measurement is the time it takes to go "from concept to cash," from a customer's feature request to delivered software. They call this measurement "cycle time." The focus is on the team's ability to "repeatedly and reliably" deliver new business value. Then the team tries to continuously improve their process and reduce the cycle time.

Measurements such as cycle time that involve the whole team are more likely to drive you toward success than are measures confined to isolated roles or groups. How long does it usually take to fix a defect? What can the team do to reduce that latency, the amount of time it takes? These types of metrics encourage collaboration in order to make improvements.

Another lean measurement the Poppendiecks explain in their book is financial return. If the team is developing a profitable product, it needs to understand how it can work to achieve the most profit. Even if the team is developing internal software or some other product whose main goal isn't profit, it still needs to look at ROI to make sure it is delivering the best value. Identify the business goals and find ways to measure what the team delivers. Is the company trying to attract new customers? Keep track of how many new accounts sign on as new features are released.

Lean development looks for ways to delight customers, which ought to be the goal for all software development. The Poppendiecks give examples of simple ways you can measure whether your customers are delighted.

We like the lean metrics, because they're congruent with our goal to deliver business value. Why are we interested in metrics at all? We'll go into that in the next section.

Why We Need Metrics

There are good reasons to collect and track metrics. There are some really bad ones too. Anyone can use good metrics in terrible ways, such as using them as the basis for an individual team member's performance evaluation. However, without metrics, how do you measure your progress?

When metrics are used as guideposts—telling the team when it's getting off track or providing feedback that it's on the right track—they're worth gathering. Is our number of unit tests going up every day? Why did the code coverage take a dive from 75% to 65%? It might have been a good reason—maybe we got rid of unused code that was covered by tests. Metrics can alert us to problems, but in isolation they don't usually provide value.

Metrics that measure milestones along a journey to achieve team goals are useful. If our goal is to increase unit test code coverage by 3%, we might run the code coverage every time we check in to make sure we didn't slack on unit tests. If we don't achieve the desired improvement, it's more important to figure out why than to lament whatever amount our bonus was reduced as a result. Rather than focus on individual measurements, we should focus on the goal and the trending toward reaching that goal.

Metrics help the team, customers included, to track progress within the iteration and within the release or epic. If we're using a burndown chart, and we're burning up instead of down, that's a red flag to stop, take a look at what's happening, and make sure we understand and address the problems. Maybe the team lacked important information about a story. Metrics, including burndown charts, shouldn't be used as a form of punishment or source of blame. For example, questions like "Why were your estimates too low?" or "Why can't you finish all of the stories?" would be better coming from the team and phrased as "Why were our estimates so low?" and "Why didn't we get our stories finished?"

Metrics, used properly, can be motivating for a team. Lisa's team tracks the number of unit tests run in each build. Big milestones—100 tests, 1000 tests, 3000 tests—are a reason to celebrate. Having that number of unit tests go up every day is a nice bit of feedback for the development and customer teams. However, it is important to recognize that the number itself means nothing. For example, the tests might be poorly written, or to have a well tested product, maybe we need 10,000 tests. Numbers don't work in isolation.

Lisa's Story   Pierre Veragen told me about a team he worked on that was allergic to metrics. The team members decided to stop measuring how much code their tests covered. When they decided to measure again after six months, they were stunned to discover the rate had dropped from 40% to 12%.

How much is it costing you to not use the right metrics?

—Lisa

When you're trying to figure out what to measure, first understand what problem you are trying to solve. When you know the problem statement, you can set a goal. These goals need to be measurable. "Reduce average response time on the XYZ application to 1.5 seconds with 20 concurrent users" works better than "Improve the XYZ application performance." If your goals are measurable, the measurements you need to gather to track the metrics will be obvious.

Remember to use metrics as a motivating force and not for beating down a team's morale. This wisdom bears repeating: Focus on the goal, not the metrics. Maybe you're not using the right metrics to measure whether you're achieving your team's objectives, or perhaps you're not interpreting them in context. An increased number of defect reports might mean the team is doing a better job of testing, not that they are writing more buggy code. If your metrics aren't helping you to understand your progress toward your goal, you might have the wrong metrics.

What Not to Do with Metrics

Mark Twain popularized the saying, which he attributed to Benjamin Disraeli, "There are three kinds of lies: lies, damned lies, and statistics." Measurable goals are a good thing; if you can't gauge them in some way, you can't tell if you achieved them. On the other hand, using metrics to judge individual or team performance is dangerous. Statistics by themselves can be twisted into any interpretation and used in detrimental ways.

Take lines of code, a traditional software measuring stick. Are more lines of code a good thing, meaning the team has been productive, or a bad thing, meaning the team is writing inefficient spaghetti-style code?

What about number of defects found? Does it make any sense to judge testers by the number of defects they found? How does that help them do their jobs better? Is it safe to say that a development team that produces a higher number of defects per lines of code is doing a bad job? Or that a team that finds more defects is doing a good job? Even if that thought holds up, how motivating is it for a team to be whacked over the head with numbers? Will that make the team members start writing defect-free code?

Communicating Metrics

We know that whatever we measure is bound to change. How many tests are running and passing? How many days until we need a "build on the shelf"? Is the full build passing? Metrics we can't see and easily interpret aren't worth having. If you want to track the number of passing tests, make sure that metric is visible in the right way, to the right people. Big visible charts are the most effective way of displaying metrics we know.

Lisa's Story

My previous team had goals concerned with the number of unit tests. However, the number of unit tests passing wasn't communicated to anyone; there were no big visible charts or build emails that referred to that number. Interestingly, the team never got traction on automating unit tests.

At my current company, everyone in the company regularly gets a report of the number of passing tests at the unit, behind-the-GUI, and GUI levels (see Tables 5-1 and 5-2 for examples). Business people do notice when that number goes down instead of up. Over time, the team has grown a huge number of useful tests.

—Lisa

Table 5-1   Starting and Ending Metrics

Metric	At Start	At End
NCSS – Whitney	69943	69887
NCSS – Ghidrah	41044	41978
Number of JUnit tests	3001	3062
Number of Canoo/Watir assertions	3215	3215
Number of FitNesse assertions	57319	61585

Table 5-2   Daily Build Results

Date	Build Result
Friday 1/25/2008	Passed 3026 JUnits
Monday 1/28/2008	Passed 3026 JUnits
Tuesday 1/29/2008	Passed 3027 JUnits
Wednesday 1/30/2008	Passed 3033 JUnits
Thursday 1/31/2008	Passed 3040 JUnits
Friday 2/1/2008	Passed 3058 JUnits
Monday 2/4/2008	Passed 3059 JUnits
Tuesday 2/5/2008	Passed 3060 JUnits
Wednesday 2/6/2008	Passed 3062 JUnits
Thursday 2/7/2008	Passed 3062 JUnits

Are your metrics worth the trouble? Don't measure for the sake of producing numbers. Think about what you'll learn from those numbers. In the next section, we consider the return on investment you can expect from metrics.

Metrics ROI

When you identify the metrics you need, make sure you can obtain them at a reasonable cost. If your continual build delivers useful numbers, it delivers good value. You're running the build anyway, and if it gives us extra information, that's gravy. If you need a lot of extra work to get information, ask yourself if it's worth the trouble.

Lisa's team went to a fair amount of trouble to track actual time spent per story versus estimated time. What did they learn other than the obvious fact that estimates are just that? Not much. Some experienced teams find they can dispense with the sprint burndown chart because the task board gives them enough information to gauge their progress. They can use the time spent estimating tasks and calculating the remaining hours on more productive activities.

This doesn't mean we recommend that you stop tracking these measurements. New teams need to understand their velocity and burndown rate, so that they can steadily improve.

Defect rates are traditional software metrics, and they might not have much value on a team that's aiming for zero defects. There's not much value in knowing the rate of bugs found and fixed during development, because finding and fixing them is an integral part of development. If a tester shows a defect to the programmer who's working on the code, and a unit test is written and the bug is fixed right away, there's often no need to log a defect. On the other hand, if many defects reach production undetected, there can be value in tracking the number to know if the team improves.

When it started to rewrite its buggy legacy application, Lisa's team set a goal of no more than six high-severity bugs in new code reported after the code is in production over a six-month period. Having a target that was straightforward and easy to track helped motivate the team to find ways to head bugs off during development and exceed this objective.

Figure each metric's return on investment and decide whether to track or maintain it. Does the effort spent collecting it justify the value it delivers? Can it be easily communicated and understood? As always, do what works for your situation. Experiment with keeping a particular metric for a few sprints and evaluate whether it's paying off.

One common metric that relates to software quality is the defect rate. In the next section, we look at reasons to track defects, or to not track defects, and what we can learn from them.

DEFECT TRACKING

One of the questions that are asked by every new agile team is, "Do we still track bugs in a defect tracking system?" There's no simple answer, but we'll give you our opinion on the matter and offer some alternatives so that you can determine what fits your team.

Why Should We Use a Defect Tracking System (DTS)?

A lot of us testers have used defect tracking as the only way to communicate the issues we saw, and it's easy to keep using the tools we are familiar with. A DTS is a convenient place to keep track of not only the defect but the priorities, severities, and status, and to see who it is assigned to. Many agile practitioners say that we don't need to do this anymore, that we can track defects on cards or some other simple mechanism. We could write a test to show the failure, fix the code, and keep the test in our regression suite.

However, there are reasons to keep using a tool to record defects and how they were fixed. Let's explore some of them now.

Convenience

One of the concerns about not keeping a defect tracking system is that there is no place to keep all of the details of the bug. Testers are used to recording a bug with lots of information, such as how to reproduce it, what environment it was found in, or what operating system or browser was used. All of this information cannot fit on a card, so how do you capture those details? If you are relying only on cards, you also need conversation. But with conversation, details get lost, and sometimes a tester forgets exactly what was done—especially if the bug was found a few days prior to the programmer tackling the issue.

A DTS is also a convenient place to keep all supplemental documentation, such as screen prints or uploaded files.

Knowledge Base

We have heard reasons to track defects such as, "We need to be able to look at old bug reports." We tried to think of reasons why you would ever need to look at old bug reports, and as we were working on this chapter, Janet found an example.

Janet's Story   When I was testing the pre-seating algorithm at WestJet, I found an anomaly. I asked Sandra, another tester, if she had ever come across the issue before. Sandra vaguely recalled something about it but not exactly what the circumstances were. She quickly did a search in Bugzilla and found the issue right away. It had been closed as invalid because the business had decided that it wasn't worth the time it would take to fix it, and the impact was low.

Being able to look it up saved me from running around trying to ask questions or reentering the bug and getting it closed again. Because the team members sit close to each other, our talking led to another conversation with the business analyst on the team. This conversation sparked the idea of a FAQ page, an outstanding issues list, or something along that line that would provide new testers a place to find all of the issues that had been identified but for which the decision had been made not to address them.

—Janet

This story shows that although the bug database can be used as a knowledge base, there might be other mechanisms for keeping business decisions and their background information. If an issue is old enough to have been lost track of, maybe we should rewrite it and bring it up again. The circumstances may have changed, and the business might decide it is now worthwhile to fix the bug.

The types of bugs that are handy to keep in a DTS are the ones that are intermittent and take a long time to track down. These bugs present themselves infrequently, and there are usually gaps in time during which the investigation stalls for lack of information. A DTS is a place where information can be captured about what was figured out so far. It can also contain logs, traces, and so on. This can be valuable information when someone on the team finally has time to look at the problem or the issue becomes more critical.

The information in bug reports can be used later for several purposes. Here's a story from Lisa's team on how it uses its information.

Lisa's Story

One developer from our team serves on a "production support" rotation for each iteration. Production support requests come in from the business side for manual fixes of past mistakes or production problems that need manual intervention. The "production support person" researches the problem and notes whatever was done to fix it in the bug report. These notes usually include a SQL statement and information about the cause. If anyone encounters the same error or situation later, the solution can be easily found in the DTS. If certain types of problems seem to occur frequently, the team can use the DTS for research and analysis. Even though our team is small, we deal with a lot of legacy code, and we can't rely on people's memory to keep track of every problem and fix.

—Lisa

Remembering the cause of defects or what was done to fulfill a special request is even harder when the team is particularly large or isn't co-located. Customers might also be interested in the solutions to their problems.

Large or Distributed Teams

If projects are so large that defects found by one team might affect other teams, a DTS is probably a good choice. Of course, to be useful it needs to be accessible to all members of the team. Face-to-face communication is always our first choice, but when circumstances make that impractical, we need aids such as a DTS.

Customer Support

When there are defects that have been reported by the customer after the release, the customer usually wants to know when they've been fixed. It's invaluable for the help desk or technical support to know what was fixed in a given release. They can also find defects that are still outstanding at release time and let the customers know. A DTS makes it much simpler to pull this information together.

Metrics

Chapter 18, "Coding and Testing," explores metrics related to defect rates.

There are reasons to track defect rates. There are also reasons why you wouldn't track a defect. For example, we don't think that a bug should be counted as a defect if it never makes it out of the iteration. This, of course, brings up another discussion about what should we track and why, but we won't discuss that here.

Traceability

Another reason we've heard for having a DTS is traceability, linking defects to test cases. We're not sure that this is a valid reason. Not all defects are linked to test cases, nor should they be. For example, errors like spelling mistakes might not need specific test cases. Maybe the product was not intuitive to use; this is a very real bug that often goes unreported. How do you write a test to determine if something is usable? Exploratory testing might find bugs in edge conditions that are not worth the effort of creating automated tests.

If it is an automated test case that caught a bug, then the need to record that defect is further reduced, because it will be caught again if ever reintroduced. The need for traceability is gone. So, maybe we don't need to track defects.

Why Shouldn't We Use a DTS?

Agile and Lean provide us with practices and principles that help reduce the need for a DTS. If the process is solid, and all of the people are committed to delivering a quality product, defects should be rare and very simply tracked.

As a Communication Tool

Defect tracking systems certainly don't promote communication between programmers and testers. They can make it easy to avoid talking directly to each other.

Waste of Time and Inventory

We tend to put lots of information into the DTS in addition to all of the steps to reproduce the defect. Depending on the bug, it can take a long time to write these steps so that the programmer can reproduce it as well. Then there is the triage, and someone has to make comments, interpret the defect, attempt to reproduce it, (ideally) fix it, write more comments, and assign it back to the person who reported it. Finally, the fix can be verified. This whole cycle can double if the programmer misunderstood the problem in the first place. The cost of a single defect report can become exorbitant.

In Chapter 15, "Coding and Testing," we'll explain how tester and programmers work together on bugs.

How much easier would it be if we as testers could just talk to the programmer and show what we found, with the developer then fixing the defect right away? We'll talk more about that later.

Defects in a DTS become a queue or a mini product backlog. According to lean principles, this inventory of defects is a waste. As a team, we should be thinking of ways to reduce this waste.

Janet's Story

Antony will share his ideas about the hidden backlog when we cover iteration planning in Chapter 18, "Coding and Testing."

In 2004, Antony Marcano, author of TestingReflections.com, wrote a blog post about the idea of not using a bug-tracking system. When it was discussed on mailing lists, he was flamed by many testers as introducing something similar to heresy. He finds he has a different reception now, because the idea is making its way into the mainstream of agile thinking.

He suggests that bug-tracking systems in agile teams are just "secret backlogs."

—Janet

Defect Tracking Tools

If you do decide to use a DTS, choose it carefully. Understand your needs and keep it simple. You will want everyone on the team to use it. If it becomes overhead or hard to use, people will find ways to work around it. As with all tools used by your agile development team, you should consider the whole team's opinion. If anyone from the customer team enters bug reports, get his or her opinion too.

One of the simplest tools that Janet has used is Alcea's FIT IssueTrack. It is configurable, does not make you follow a predefined process, and is easy to get metrics out of. Do your homework and find the tool that works for you. There are a variety of open source defect-tracking systems, hosted systems, and integrated enterprise systems available.

Whether or not you use a DTS, you want to make defects as visible as possible.

We use a commercial DTS, but we find value in keeping bugs visible. We color-code bugs and include them as tasks in our story board, shown in Figure 5-1. Yellow cards denote normal bugs, and red cards denote either high production bugs or "test stopper" development bugs—both categories need to be addressed right away. A quick look at the board lets us see how many bugs are in the To Do, WIP, Verify and Done columns. Other cards are color-coded as well: blue for story cards, green for test task cards, and white for development tasks. Striped cards are for tasks added after iteration planning. Yellow and red bug cards stand out easily.

Figure 5-1   Story board with color-coded cards. Used with permission of Mike Thomas. Copyright 2008.

During the time we were writing this book, my team converted to a virtual story board because one of our team members became a remote team member, but we retained this color-coding concept.

—Lisa

We usually recommend experimenting with different tools, using each one for a few iterations, but this is trickier with bug-tracking systems, because you need to port all of the bugs that are in one system to the new one that you're trying on for size. Spend some time thinking about what you need in a DTS, what purposes it will serve, and evaluate alternatives judiciously.

Lisa's Story

My team used a web-based DTS that was basically imposed upon it by management. We found it somewhat cumbersome to use, lacking in basic features such as time-stamping updates to the bug reports, and we chafed at the license restrictions. We testers were especially frustrated by the fact that our license limited us to three concurrent users, so sessions were set to time out quickly.

The team set aside time to evaluate different DTS alternatives. At first, the selection seemed mind-boggling. However, we couldn't find one tool that met all our requirements. Every tool seemed to be missing something important, or we heard negative reports from people who had used the tool. We were concerned about the effort needed to convert the existing bug database into a new system.

The issue was forced when our DTS actually crashed. We had stopped paying for support a couple of years earlier, but the system administrator decided to see what enhancements the vendor had made in the tool. He found that a lot of shortcomings we had experienced had been addressed. For example, all updates were now time stamped. A client application was available that wasn't subject to session timeouts and had enhanced features that were particularly valuable to the testers.

By going with our existing tool and paying for the upgrade and maintenance, plus a license allowing more concurrent users, we got help with converting our existing data to the new version and got a working system easily and at a low cost. A bonus was that our customers weren't faced with having to learn a new system.

Sometimes the best tool is the one you already have if you just look to see how it has improved!

—Lisa

As with all your tool searches, look to others in your community, such as user groups and mailing lists, for recommendations. Define your criteria before you start looking, and experiment as much as you can. If you choose the wrong tool, cut your losses and start researching alternatives.

Keep Your Focus

Decisions about reporting and tracking defects are important, but don't lose track of your main target. You want to deliver the best quality product you can, and you want to deliver value to the business in a timely manner. Projects

Chapter 18, "Coding and Testing," covers alternatives and shows you different ways to attack your bug problems.

succeed when people are allowed to do their best work. Concentrate on improving communication and building collaboration. If you encounter a lot of defects, investigate the source of the problem. If you need a DTS to do that, use it. If your team works better by documenting defects in executable tests and fixing them right away, do that. If some combination enables you continually improve, go with it. The main thing to remember is that it has to work for your whole team.

Defect tracking is one of the typical quality processes that generate the most questions and controversy in agile testing. Another big source of confusion is whether agile projects need documents such as test plans or traceability matrices. Let's consider that next.

TEST PLANNING

Traditional phased software methodologies stress the importance of test plans as part of the overall documentation needs. They're intended to outline the objectives, scope, approach, and focus of the software testing effort for stakeholders. The completed document is intended to help people outside the test group understand the "why" and "how" of product validation. In this section, we look at test plans and other aspects of preparing and tracking the testing effort for an agile project.

Test Strategy vs. Test Planning

In an agile project, teams don't rely on heavy documentation to communicate what the testers need to do. Testers work hand in hand with the rest of the team so that the testing efforts are visible to all in the form of task cards. So the question often put to us is, "Is there still a need for test plans?" To answer that question, let's first take a look at the difference between a test plan and a test strategy or approach.

The more information that is contained in a document, the less likely it is that someone is going to read it all. Consider what information is really necessary for the stakeholders. Think about how often it is used and what it is used for.

We like to think of a test strategy as a static document that seldom changes, while a test plan is created new and is specific to each new project.

Test Strategy

A strategy is a long-term plan of action, the key word being "long-term." If your organization wants documentation about your overall test approach to projects, consider taking this information and putting it in a static document that doesn't change much over time. There is a lot of information that is not project specific and can be extracted into a Test Strategy or Test Approach document.

This document can then be used as a reference and needs to be updated only if processes change. A test strategy document can be used to give new employees a high-level understanding of how your test processes work.

Janet's Story

I have had success with this approach at several organizations. Processes that were common to all projects were captured into one document. Using this format answered most compliance requirements. Some of the topics that were covered were:

- Testing Practices
- Story Testing
- Solution Verification Testing
- User Acceptance Testing
- Exploratory Testing
- Load and Performance Testing
- Test Automation
- Test Results
- Defect Tracking Process
- Test Tools
- Test Environments

—Janet

Test Plan

The power of planning is to identify possible issues and dependencies, to bring risks to the surface to be talked about and to be addressed, and to think about the big picture. Test planning is no different. A team should think about risks and dependencies and the big picture for each project before it starts.

In Chapter 15, "Tester Activities in Release or Theme Planning," we show examples and discuss alternatives you can use when you are planning the release.

Whether your team decides to create a test plan document or not, the planning should be done. Each project is different, so don't expect that the same solution will fit all.

Sometimes our customers insist on a test plan document. If you're contracting to develop an application, a test plan might be part of a set of deliverables that also include items such as a requirements document and a design document.

Talk of test plans often leads to talk of traceability. Did someone execute all planned testing of the desired behavior on the delivered code? How do requirements and test plans relate to the actual testing and final functionality?

Traceability

In traditional projects, we used to need traceability matrices to determine whether we had actually tested all of the requirements. If a requirement changed, we needed to know that we had changed the appropriate test cases. With very large requirements documents, this was the only way that a test team knew it had good coverage.

In an agile project, we don't have those restrictions. We build functionality in tiny, well-defined steps. We work with the team closely and know when something changes. If the programmers work test-first, we know there are unit tests for all of the small chunks of work. We can then collaborate with the customer to define acceptance tests. We test each story as the programmer works on it, so we know that nothing goes untested.

There might be requirements for some kind of traceability for regulated industries. If there is, we suggest that you really look at what problem management is trying to solve. When you understand what is needed, you should try to make the solution as simple as possible. There are multiple ways to provide traceability. Source code check-in comments can refer to the wiki page containing the requirements or test cases, or to a defect number. You can put comments in unit tests tying the test to the location or identifier of the requirement. The tests can be integrated directly with the requirements in a tool such as FitNesse. Your team can easily find the way that works best for your customers' needs.

Documents such as traceability matrices might be needed to fulfill requirements imposed by the organization's audit standards or quality models. Let's consider how these directives get along with agile development.

EXISTING PROCESSES AND MODELS

This question is often asked: "Can traditional quality models and processes coexist with agile development methods?" In theory, there is no reason why they can't. In reality, there is often not a choice. Quality models often fall into the domain of the traditional QA team, and they can follow testers into the new agile structure as well. It might not be easy to fit these into a new agile development model. Let's look at a few typical quality processes and how testers and their teams might accommodate them.

Audits

Different industries have different audit requirements. Quality assurance teams in traditional development organizations are often tasked with providing information for auditors and ensuring compliance with audit requirements. The Sarbanes-Oxley Act of 2002, enacted in response to high-profile corporate financial scandals, sets out requirements for maintaining business records. Ensuring compliance usually falls to the IT departments. SAS 70 is another widely recognized auditing standard for service organizations. These are just a couple of examples of the type of audit controls that affect development teams.

Larger organizations have specialized teams that control compliance and work with auditors, but development teams are often asked to provide information. Examples include what testing has been performed on a given software release, or proving that different accounts reconcile. Testers can be tasked with writing test plans to evaluate the effectiveness of control activities.

Lisa's Story

Our company undergoes regular SAS 70 audits. Whenever one is scheduled, we write a story card for providing support for the audit. Most of this work falls to the system administrators, but I provide support to the business people who work with the auditor. Sometimes we're required to demonstrate system functionality in our demo environment. I can provide data for the demos and help if questions arise. I might also be asked to provide details about how we tested a particular piece of functionality.

Some of our internal processes are required to conform with SAS 70 requirements. For example, every time we release to production, we fill out a form with information about which build was released, how many tests at each level were run on it, who did the release, and who verified it.

—Lisa

Testers who are part of an agile team should be dedicated to that team. If their help is needed in providing information for an audit or helping to ensure compliance, write stories for this and plan them along with the rest of the team's work. Work together with the compliance and internal audit teams to understand your team's responsibilities.

Frameworks, Models, and Standards

There are many quality models, but we'll look at two to show how you can adapt your agile process to fit within their constraints.

1. The Capability Maturity Model Integration (CMMI) aims to help organizations improve their process but doesn't dictate specific development practices to accomplish the improvements.

2. Information Technology Infrastructure Library (ITIL) is a set of best practices for IT service management intended to help organizations develop an effective quality process.

Both of these models can coexist happily with agile development. They're rooted in the same goal, making software development projects succeed.

Let's look at CMMI, a framework for measuring the maturity of your process. It defines each level by measuring whether the process is unknown, defined, documented, permanent, or optimized. Agile projects have a defined process, although not all teams document what they do. For example, managing your requirements with index cards on a release planning wall with a single customer making the final decisions is a defined process as long as you do it all the time.

Retrospectives are aimed at constant process improvement, and teams should be always be looking for ways to optimize processes. If the only thing your team is lacking is documentation, then think about including your process into your test strategy documentation.

See the bibliography for information about CMMI and agile development.

Ask yourself what the minimum amount of documentation you could give to satisfy the CMMI requirements would be. Janet has had success with using diagrams like the one in Figure 5-2.

If ITIL has been introduced into your organization and affects change management, adapt your process to accommodate it. You might even find the new process beneficial.

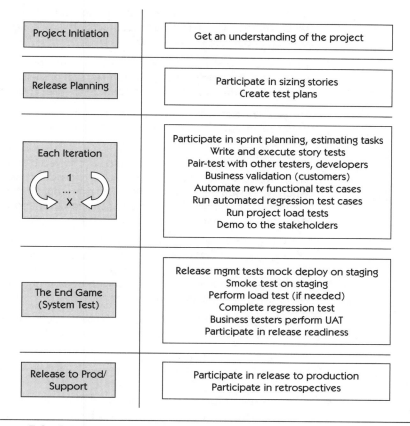

Figure 5-2   Documenting the test strategy

When I worked in one organization that had a central call center to handle all of the customers' support calls, management implemented ITIL for the service part of the organization. We didn't think it would affect the development team until the change management team realized that the number of open problems was steadily increasing. No one understood why the number kept going up, so we held a series of problem-solving sessions. First, we mapped out the process currently in effect.

The call center staff reported an incident in their tracking system. They tried to solve the customer's problem immediately. Often, that meant providing a workaround for a software defect. The call center report was closed, but a problem report in Remedy was then opened, and someone in the development team was sent an email. If the defect was accepted by the development team, a defect was entered into Bugzilla to be fixed.

There was no loop back to the problem issue to close it when the defect was finally fixed. We held several brainstorming sessions with all involved stakeholders to determine the best and easiest solution to that problem.

The problem statement to solve was, "How does the project team report back to the problem and change management folks to tell them when the bug was actually fixed?"

There were a couple of ways we could have solved the problem. One option was to reference the Remedy ticket in Bugzilla and put hooks into Remedy so that when we closed the Bugzilla defect, Remedy would detect it and close the Remedy ticket. Of course, some of the bugs were never addressed, which meant the Remedy tickets stayed open forever.

We actually found a better solution for the whole team, including the problem change folks. We brainstormed a lot of different ideas but decided that when a bug was opened in Bugzilla, we could close the Remedy ticket, because we realistically would never go back to the original complaint and tell the customer who reported it, or when the fix was done.

The change request that covered the release would automatically include all software fixes, so it followed the change management process as well.

—Janet

If your organization is using some kind of process model or quality standards management, educate yourself about it, and work with the appropriate specialists in your organization. Maintain the team's focus on delivering high-quality software that provides real business value, and see how you can work within the model.

Process improvement models and frameworks emphasize discipline and conformance to process. Few software development methodologies require more discipline than agile development. Standards simply enable you to measure your progress toward your goal. Agile's focus is on doing your best work and constantly improving. Agile development is compatible with achieving whatever standards you set for yourself or borrow from a process improvement measurement tool.

Separate your measurement goals and standards from your means to improve those measurements. Set goals, and know what metrics you need to measure success for areas that need improvement. Try using task cards for activities that provide the improvements in order to ensure they get the visibility they need.

Working with existing quality processes and models is one of the biggest cultural issues you may face as you transition to agile development. All of these changes are hard, but when your whole team gets involved, none are insurmountable.

Summary

In this chapter, we looked at traditional quality-oriented processes and how they can be adapted for an agile environment.

- The right metrics can help you to make sure your team is on track to achieve its goals and provide a good return on your investment in them.
- Metrics should be visible, providing necessary milestones upon which to make decisions.
- The reasons to use a defect tracking system include for convenience, for use as a knowledge base, and for traceability.
- Defect tracking systems are too often used as a communication tool, and entering and tracking unnecessary bugs can be considered wasteful.
- All tools, including the DTS, need to be used by the whole team, so consider all perspectives when choosing a tool.
- A test strategy is a long-term overall test approach that can be put in a static document; a test plan should be unique to the project.
- Think about alternatives before blindly accepting the need for specific documents. For example, the agile approach to developing in small, incremental chunks, working closely together, might remove the need for formal traceability documents. Linking the source code control system comments to tests might be another way.
- Traditional quality processes and process improvement models, such as SAS 70 audits and CMMI standards, can coexist with agile development and testing. Teams need to be open to thinking outside the box and work together to solve their problems.

Part III

THE AGILE TESTING QUADRANTS

Software quality has many dimensions, each requiring a different testing approach. How do we know all the different types of tests we need to do? How do we know when we're "done" testing? Who does which tests and how? In this part, we explain how to use the Agile Testing Quadrants to make sure your team covers all needed categories of testing.

Of course, testing requires tools, and we've included examples of tools to use, strategies for using those tools effectively, and guidelines about when to use them. Tools are easier to use when used with code that's designed for testability. These concerns and more are discussed in this part of the book.

Chapter 6

THE PURPOSE OF TESTING

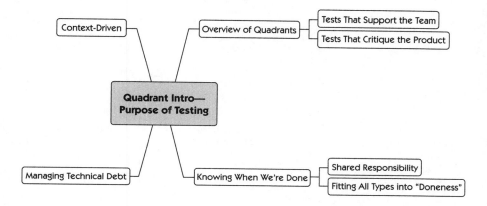

Why do we test? The answer might seem obvious, but in fact, it's pretty complex. We test for a lot of reasons: to find bugs, to make sure the code is reliable, and sometimes just to see if the code's usable. We do different types of testing to accomplish different goals. Software product quality has many components. In this chapter, we introduce the Agile Testing Quadrants. The rest of the chapters in Part III go into detail on each of the quadrants. The Agile Testing Quadrants matrix helps testers ensure that they have considered all of the different types of tests that are needed in order to deliver value.

THE AGILE TESTING QUADRANTS

In Chapter 1, "What Is Agile Testing, Anyway?," we introduced Brian Marick's terms for different categories of tests that accomplish different purposes. Figure 6-1 is a diagram of the agile testing quadrants that shows how each of the four quadrants reflects the different reasons we test. On one axis, we divide the matrix into tests that support the team and tests that critique the product. The other axis divides them into business-facing and technology-facing tests.

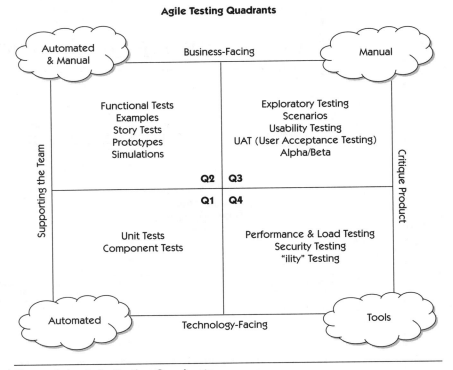

Figure 6-1   Agile Testing Quadrants

The order in which we've numbered these quadrants has no relationship to when the different types of testing are done. For example, agile development starts with customer tests, which tell the team what to code. The timing of the various types of tests depends on the risks of each project, the customers' goals for the product, whether the team is working with legacy code or on a greenfield project, and when resources are available to do the testing.

Tests that Support the Team

The quadrants on the left include tests that support the team as it develops the product. This concept of testing to help the programmers is new to many testers and is the biggest difference between testing on a traditional project and testing on an agile project. The testing done in Quadrants 1 and 2 are more requirements specification and design aids than what we typically think of as testing.

Quadrant 1

The lower left quadrant represents test-driven development, which is a core agile development practice.

Unit tests verify functionality of a small subset of the system, such as an object or method. Component tests verify the behavior of a larger part of the system, such as a group of classes that provide some service [Meszaros, 2007]. Both types of tests are usually automated with a member of the xUnit family of test automation tools. We refer to these tests as programmer tests, developer-facing tests, or technology-facing tests. They enable the programmers to measure what Kent Beck has called the internal quality of their code [Beck, 2000, 2004].

A major purpose of Quadrant 1 tests is test-driven development (TDD) or test-driven design. The process of writing tests first helps programmers design their code well. These tests let the programmers confidently write code to deliver a story's features without worrying about making unintended changes to the system. They can verify that their design and architecture decisions are appropriate. Unit and component tests are automated and written in the same programming language as the application. A business expert probably couldn't understand them by reading them directly, but these tests aren't intended for customer use. In fact, internal quality isn't negotiated with the customer; it's defined by the programmers. Programmer tests are normally part of an automated process that runs with every code check-in, giving the team instant, continual feedback about their internal quality.

Quadrant 2

The tests in Quadrant 2 also support the work of the development team, but at a higher level. These business-facing tests, also called customer-facing tests and customer tests, define external quality and the features that the customers want.

Chapter 8, "Business-Facing Tests that Support the Team," explains business conditions of satisfaction.

Like the Quadrant 1 tests, they also drive development, but at a higher level. With agile development, these tests are derived from examples provided by the customer team. They describe the details of each story. Business-facing tests run at a functional level, each one verifying a business satisfaction condition. They're written in a way business experts can easily understand using the business domain language. In fact, the business experts use these tests to define the external quality of the product and usually help to write them. It's possible this quadrant could duplicate some of the tests that were done at the unit level; however, the Quadrant 2 tests are oriented toward illustrating and confirming desired system behavior at a higher level.

Most of the business-facing tests that support the development team also need to be automated. One of the most important purposes of tests in these two quadrants is to provide information quickly and enable fast troubleshooting. They must be run frequently in order to give the team early feedback in case any behavior changes unexpectedly. When possible, these automated tests run directly on the business logic in the production code without having to go through a presentation layer. Still, some automated tests must verify the user interfaces and any APIs that client applications might use. All of these tests should be run as part of an automated continuous integration, build, and test process.

There is another group of tests that belongs in this quadrant as well. User interaction experts use mock-ups and wireframes to help validate proposed GUI (graphical user interface) designs with customers and to communicate those designs to the developers before they start to code them. The tests in this group are tests that help support the team to get the product built right but are not automated. As we'll see in the following chapters, the quadrants help us identify all of the different types of tests we need to use in order to help drive coding.

Some people use the term "acceptance tests" to describe Quadrant 2 tests, but we believe that acceptance tests encompass a broader range of tests that include Quadrants 3 and 4. Acceptance tests verify that all aspects of the system, including qualities such as usability and performance, meet customer requirements.

Using Tests to Support the Team

The quick feedback provided by Quadrants 1 and 2 automated tests, which run with every code change or addition, form the foundation of an agile team. These tests first guide development of functionality, and when automated, then provide a safety net to prevent refactoring and the introduction of new code from causing unexpected results.

Lisa's Story

We run our automated tests that support the team (the left half of the quadrants) in separate build processes. Unit and component tests run in our "ongoing" build, which takes about eight minutes to finish. Although the programmers run the unit tests before they check in, the build might still fail due to integration problems or environmental differences. As soon as we see the "build failed" email, the person who checked in the offending code fixes the problem. Business-facing functional tests run in our "full build," which also runs continually, kicking off every time a code change is checked in. It finishes in less than two hours. That's still pretty quick feedback, and again, a build failure means immediate action to fix the problem. With these builds as a safety net, our code is stable enough to release every day of the iteration if we so choose.

—Lisa

The tests in Quadrants 1 and 2 are written to help the team deliver the business value requested by the customers. They verify that the business logic and the user interfaces behave according to the examples provided by the customers. There are other aspects to software quality, some of which the customers don't think about without help from the technical team. Is the product competitive? Is the user interface as intuitive as it needs to be? Is the application secure? Are the users happy with how the user interface works? We need different tests to answer these types of questions.

Tests that Critique the Product

If you've been in a customer role and had to express your requirements for a software feature, you know how hard it can be to know exactly what you want until you see it. Even if you're confident about how the feature should work, it can be hard to describe it so that programmers fully understand it.

The word "critique" isn't intended in a negative sense. A critique can include both praise and suggestions for improvement. Appraising a software product involves both art and science. We review the software in a constructive manner, with the goal of learning how we can improve it. As we learn, we can feed new requirements and tests or examples back to the process that supports the team and guide development.

Quadrant 3

Business-facing examples help the team design the desired product, but at least some of our examples will probably be wrong. The business experts might overlook functionality, or not get it quite right if it isn't their field of expertise. The team might simply misunderstand some examples. Even when the programmers write code that makes the business-facing tests pass, they might not be delivering what the customer really wants.

That is where the tests to critique the product in the third and fourth quadrants come into play. Quadrant 3 classifies the business-facing tests that exercise the working software to see if it doesn't quite meet expectations or won't stand up to the competition. When we do business-facing tests to critique the product, we try to emulate the way a real user would work the application. This is manual testing that only a human can do. We might use some automated scripts to help us set up the data we need, but we have to use our senses, our brains, and our intuition to check whether the development team has delivered the business value required by the customers.

Often, the users and customers perform these types of tests. User Acceptance Testing (UAT) gives customers a chance to give new features a good workout and see what changes they may want in the future, and it's a good way to gather new story ideas. If your team is delivering software on a contract basis to a client, UAT might be a required step in approving the finished stories.

Usability testing is an example of a type of testing that has a whole science of its own. Focus groups might be brought in, studied as they use the application, and interviewed in order to gather their reactions. Usability testing can also include navigation from page to page or even something as simple as the tabbing order. Knowledge of how people use systems is an advantage when testing usability.

Exploratory testing is central to this quadrant. During exploratory testing sessions, the tester simultaneously designs and performs tests, using critical thinking to analyze the results. This offers a much better opportunity to learn about the application than scripted tests. We're not talking about ad hoc testing, which is impromptu and improvised. Exploratory testing is a more thoughtful and sophisticated approach than ad hoc testing. It is guided by a strategy and operates within defined constraints. From the start of each project and story, testers start thinking of scenarios they want to try. As small chunks of testable code become available, testers analyze test results, and as they learn, they find new areas to explore. Exploratory testing works the system in the same ways that the end users will. Testers use their creativity and intuition. As a result, it is through this type of testing that many of the most serious bugs are usually found.

Quadrant 4

The types of tests that fall into the fourth quadrant are just as critical to agile development as to any type of software development. These tests are technology-facing, and we discuss them in technical rather than business terms. Technology-facing tests in Quadrant 4 are intended to critique product characteristics such as performance, robustness, and security. As we'll describe in Chapter 11, "Critiquing the Product using Technology-Facing Tests," your team already possesses many of the skills needed to do these tests. For example, programmers might be able to leverage unit tests into performance tests with a multi-threaded engine. However, creating and running these tests might require the use of specialized tools and additional expertise.

In the past, we've heard complaints that agile development seems to ignore the technology-facing tests that critique the product. These complaints might be partly due to agile's emphasis on having customers write and prioritize stories. Nontechnical customer team members often assume that the developers will take care of concerns such as speed and security, and that the programmers are intent on producing only the functionality prioritized by the customers.

If we know the requirements for performance, security, interaction with other systems, and other nonfunctional attributes before we start coding, it's easier to design and code with that in mind. Some of these might be more important than actual functionality. For example, if an Internet retail website has a one-minute response time, the customers won't wait to appreciate the fact that all of the features work properly. Technology-facing tests that critique the product should be considered at every step of the development cycle and not left until the very end. In many cases, such testing should even be done before functional testing.

In recent years we've seen many new lightweight tools appropriate to an agile development project become available to support tests. Automation tools can be used to create test data, set up test scenarios for manual testing, drive security tests, and help make sense of results. Automation is mandatory for some efforts such as load and performance testing.

Checking Nonfunctional Requirements

Alessandro Collino, a computer science and information engineer with Onion S.p.A., who works on agile projects, illustrates why executing tests that critique the product early in the development process is critical to project success.

> Our Scrum/XP team used TDD to develop a Java application that would convert one form of XML to another. The application performed complex calculations on the data. For each simple story, we wrote a unit test to check the conversion of one element into the required format, implemented the code to make the test pass, and refactored as needed.
>
> We also wrote acceptance tests that read subsets of the original XML files from disk, converted them, and wrote them back. The first time we ran the application on a real file to be converted, we got an out-of-memory error. The DOM parser we used for the XML conversion couldn't handle such a large file. All of our tests used small subsets of the actual files; we hadn't thought to write unit tests using large datasets.

> Doing TDD gave us quick feedback on whether the code was working per the functional requirements, but the unit tests didn't test any nonfunctional requirements such as capacity, performance, scalability, and usability. If you use TDD to also check nonfunctional requirements, in this case, capacity, you'll have quick feedback and be able to avoid expensive mistakes.
>
> Alessandro's story is a good example of how the quadrant numbering doesn't imply the order in which tests are done. When application performance is critical, plan to test with production-level loads as soon as testable code is available.

When you and your team plan a new release or project, discuss which types of tests from Quadrants 3 and 4 you need, and when they should be done. Don't leave essential activities such as load or usability testing to the end, when it might be too late to rectify problems.

Using Tests that Critique the Product

The information produced during testing to review the product should be fed back into the left side of our matrix and used to create new tests to drive future development. For example, if the server fails under a normal load, new stories and tests to drive a more scalable architecture will be needed. Using the quadrants will help you plan tests that critique the product as well as tests that drive development. Think about why you are testing to make sure that the tests are performed at the optimum stage of development.

The short iterations of agile development give your team a chance to learn and experiment with the different testing quadrants. If you find out too late that your design doesn't scale, start load testing earlier with the next story or project. If the iteration demo reveals that the team misunderstood the customer's requirements, maybe you're not doing a good enough job of writing customer tests to guide development. If the team puts off needed refactoring, maybe the unit and component tests aren't providing enough coverage. Use the agile testing quadrants to help make sure all necessary testing is done at the right time.

KNOWING WHEN A STORY IS DONE

For most products, we need all four categories of testing to feel confident we're delivering the right value. Not every story requires security testing, but you don't want to omit it because you didn't think of it.

Lisa's Story
My team uses "stock" cards to ensure that we always consider all different types of tests. When unit testing wasn't yet a habit, we wrote a unit test card for each story on the board. Our "end to end" test card reminds the programmers to complete the job of integration testing and to make sure all of the parts of the code work together. A "security" card also gets considered for each story, and if appropriate, put on the board to keep everyone conscious of keeping data safe. A task card to show the user interface to customers makes sure that we don't forget to do this as early as possible, and it helps us start exploratory testing along with the customers early, too. All of these cards help us address all the different aspects of product quality.

Technology-facing tests that extend beyond a single story get their own row on the story board. We use stories to evaluate load test tools and to establish performance baselines to kick off our load and performance-testing efforts.

—Lisa

The technology-facing and business-facing tests that drive development are central to agile development, whether or not you actually write task cards for them. They give your team the best chance of getting each story "done." Identifying the tasks needed to perform the technology-facing and business-facing tests that critique the product ensures that you'll learn what the product is missing. A combination of tests from all four quadrants will let the team know when each feature has met the customer's criteria for functionality and quality.

Shared Responsibility

Our product teams need a wide range of expertise to cover all of the agile testing quadrants. Programmers should write the technology-facing tests that support programming, but they might need help at different times from testers, database designers, system administrators, and configuration specialists. Testers take primary charge of the business-facing tests in tandem with the customers, but programmers participate in designing and automating tests, while usability and other experts might be called in as needed. The fourth quadrant, with technology-facing tests that critique the product, may require more specialists. No matter what resources have to be brought in from outside the development team, the team is still responsible for getting all four quadrants of testing done.

We believe that a successful team is one where everybody participates in the crafting of the product and that everyone shares the team's internal pain when things go wrong. Implementing the practices and tools that enable us to address all four quadrants of testing can be painful at times, but the joy of implementing a successful product is worth the effort.

MANAGING TECHNICAL DEBT

Ward Cunningham coined the term "technical debt" in 1992, but we've certainly experienced it throughout our careers in software development! Technical debt builds up when the development team takes shortcuts, hacks in quick fixes, or skips writing or automating tests because it's under the gun. The code base gets harder and harder to maintain. Like financial debt, "interest" compounds in the form of higher maintenance costs and lower team velocity. Programmers are afraid to make any changes, much less attempt refactoring to improve the code, for fear of breaking it. Sometimes this fear exists because they can't understand the coding to start with, and sometimes it is because there are no tests to catch mistakes.

Each quadrant in the agile testing matrix plays a role in keeping technical debt to a manageable level. Technology-facing tests that support coding and design help keep code maintainable. An automated build and integration process that runs unit tests is a must for minimizing technical debt. Catching unit-level defects during coding will free testers to focus on business-facing tests in order to guide the team and improve the product. Timely load and stress testing lets the teams know whether their architecture is up to the job.

By taking the time and applying resources and practices to keep technical debt to a minimum, a team will have time and resources to cover the testing needed to ensure a quality product. Applying agile principles to do a good job of each type of testing at each level will, in turn, minimize technical debt.

TESTING IN CONTEXT

Categorizations and definitions such as we find in the agile testing matrix help us make sure we plan for and accomplish all of the different types of testing we need. However, we need to bear in mind that each organization, product, and team has its own unique situation, and each needs to do what works for it in its individual situation. As Lisa's coworker Mike Busse likes to say, "It's a tool, not a rule." A single product or project's needs might evolve drastically over time. The quadrants are a helpful way to make sure your team is considering all of the different aspects of testing that go into "doneness."

We can borrow important principles from the context-driven school of testing when planning testing for each story, iteration, and release.

For more on context-driven testing, see www
.context-driven-testing.com.

- The value of any practice depends on its context.
- There are good practices in context, but there are no best practices.
- People, working together, are the most important part of any project's context.
- Projects unfold over time in ways that are often not predictable.
- The product is a solution. If the problem isn't solved, the product doesn't work.
- Good software testing is a challenging intellectual process.
- Only through judgment and skill, exercised cooperatively throughout the entire project, are we able to do the right things at the right times to effectively test our products.

The quadrants help give context to agile testing practices, but you and your team will have to adapt as you go. Testers help provide the feedback the team needs to adjust and work better. Use your skills to engage the customers throughout each iteration and release. Be conscious of when your team needs roles or knowledge beyond what it currently has available.

The Agile Testing Quadrants provide a checklist to make sure you've covered all your testing bases. Examine the answers to questions such as these:

- Are we using unit and component tests to help us find the right design for our application?
- Do we have an automated build process that runs our automated unit tests for quick feedback?
- Do our business-facing tests help us deliver a product that matches customers' expectations?
- Are we capturing the right examples of desired system behavior? Do we need more? Are we basing our tests on these examples?
- Do we show prototypes of UIs and reports to the users before we start coding them? Can the users relate them to how the finished software will work?
- Do we budget enough time for exploratory testing? How do we tackle usability testing? Are we involving our customers enough?
- Do we consider technological requirements such as performance and security early enough in the development cycle? Do we have the right tools to do "ility" testing?

Use the matrix as a map to get started. Experiment, and use retrospectives to keep improving your efforts to guide development with tests and build on what you learn about your product through testing.

SUMMARY

In this chapter we introduced the Agile Testing Quadrants as a convenient way to categorize tests. The four quadrants serve as guidelines to ensure that all facets of product quality are covered in the testing and developing process.

- Tests that support the team can be used to drive requirements.
- Tests that critique the product help us think about all facets of application quality.
- Use the quadrants to know when you're done, and ensure the whole team shares responsibility for covering the four quadrants of the matrix.
- Managing technical debt is an essential foundation for any software development team. Use the quadrants to think about the different dimensions.
- Context should always guide our testing efforts.

Chapter 7

TECHNOLOGY-FACING TESTS THAT SUPPORT THE TEAM

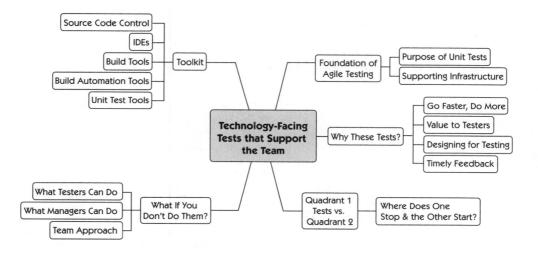

We use the Agile Testing Quadrants as a guide to help us cover all the types of testing we need and to help us make sure we have the right resources to succeed at each type. In this chapter, we look at tests in the first quadrant, technology-facing tests that support the team, and at tools to support this testing. The activities in this quadrant form the core of agile development.

AN AGILE TESTING FOUNDATION

We discuss Quadrant 1 first because the technology-facing tests that support the team form the foundation of agile development and testing. See Figure 7-1 for a reminder of the Agile Testing Quadrants with this quadrant highlighted. Quadrant 1 is about much more than testing. The unit and component tests we talk about in Quadrant 1 aren't the first tests written for each story, but they help guide design and development. Without a foundation of test-driven

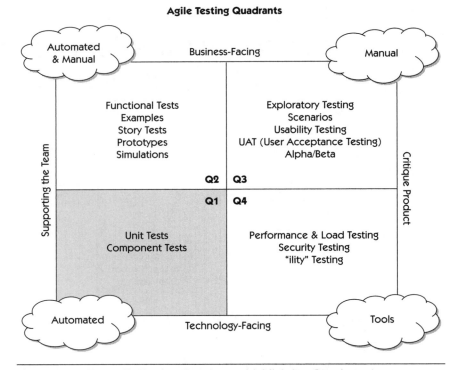

Figure 7-1   The Agile Testing Quadrants, highlighting Quadrant 1

design, automated unit and component tests, and a continuous integration process to run the tests, it's hard to deliver value in a timely manner. All of the testing in the other quadrants can't make up for inadequacies in this one. We'll talk about the other quadrants in the next few chapters and explain how they all fit together.

Teams need the right tools and processes to create and execute technology-facing tests that guide development. We'll give some examples of the types of tools needed in the last section of this chapter.

The Purpose of Quadrant 1 Tests

Unit tests and component tests ensure quality by helping the programmer understand exactly what the code needs to do, and by providing guidance in the right design. They help the team to focus on the story that's being delivered and to take the simplest approach that will work. Unit tests verify the behavior of parts as small as a single object or method [Meszaros, 2007]. Component tests help solidify the overall design of a deployable part of the system by testing the interaction between classes or methods.

Developing unit tests can be an essential design tool when using TDD. When an agile programmer starts a coding task, she writes a test that captures the behavior of a tiny bit of code and then works on the code until the test passes. By building the code in small test-code-test increments, the programmer has a chance to think through the functionality that the customer needs. As questions come up, she can ask the customer. She can pair with a tester to help make sure all aspects of that piece of code, and its communication with other units, are tested.

The term *test-driven development* misleads practitioners who don't understand that it's more about design than testing. Code developed test-first is naturally designed for testability. Quadrant 1 activities are all aimed at producing software with the highest possible internal quality.

When teams practice TDD, they minimize the number of bugs that have to be caught later on. Most unit-level bugs are prevented by writing the test before the code. Thinking through the design by writing the unit test means the system is more likely to meet customer requirements. When post-development testing time is occupied with finding and fixing bugs that could have been detected by programmer tests, there's no time to find the serious issues that might adversely affect the business. The more bugs that leak out of our coding process, the slower our delivery will be, and in the end, it is the quality that will suffer. That's why the programmer tests in Quadrant 1 are so critical. While every team should adopt practices that work for its situation, a team without these core agile practices is unlikely to benefit much from agile values and principles.

Supporting Infrastructure

Solid source code control, configuration management, and continuous integration are essential to getting value from programmer tests that guide development. They enable the team to always know exactly what's being tested. Continuous integration gives us a way to run tests every time new code is checked in. When a test fails, we know who checked in the change that caused the failure, and that person can quickly fix the problem. Continuous integration saves time and motivates each programmer to run the tests before checking in the new code. A continuous integration and build process delivers a deployable package of code for us to test.

Agile projects that lack these core agile practices tend to turn into "mini-waterfalls." The development cycles are shorter, but code is still being thrown "over the wall" to testers who run out of time to test because the code is of poor quality. The term *waterfall* isn't necessarily derogatory. We've worked on successful "waterfall" projects where the programmers stringently automate unit tests, practice continuous integration, and use automated builds to run tests. These successful "waterfall" projects also involve customers and testers throughout the development cycle. When we code without appropriate practices and tools, regardless of what we call the process, we're not going to deliver high-quality code in a timely manner.

WHY WRITE AND EXECUTE THESE TESTS?

We're not going into any details here about how to do TDD, or the best ways to write unit and component tests. There are several excellent books on those subjects. Our goal is to explain why these activities are important to agile testers. Let's explore some reasons to use technology-facing tests that support the team.

Lets Us Go Faster and Do More

Speed should never be the end goal of an agile development team. Trying to do things fast and meet tight deadlines without thinking about the quality causes us to cut corners and revert to old, bad habits. If we cut corners, we'll build up more technical debt, and probably miss the deadline anyway. Happily, though, speed is a long-term side effect of producing code with the highest possible internal quality. Continuous builds running unit tests notify the team of failure within a few minutes of the problem check-in, and the mistake can be found and fixed quickly. A safety net of automated unit and code integration tests enables the programmers to refactor frequently. This keeps the code at a reasonable standard of maintainability and delivers the best value for the time invested. Technical debt is kept as low as possible.

If you've worked as a tester on a project where unit testing was neglected, you know how easy it is to spend all of your time finding unit-level defects. You might find so many bugs while testing the "happy path" that you never have time to test more complex scenarios and edge cases. The release deadline is pushed back as the "find and fix" cycle drags on, or testing is just stopped and a buggy product is foisted off on unsuspecting customers.

Our years on agile teams have been Utopian in contrast to this scenario. Driving coding practices with tests means that the programmers probably understood the story's requirements reasonably well. They've talked extensively with the customers and testers to clarify the desired behaviors. All parties understand the changes being made. By the time the team has completed all of the task cards for coding a story, or a thin, testable slice of one, the feature has been well covered by unit and component tests. Usually the programmers have made sure at least one path through the story works end to end.

This means that we, as testers, waste little time finding low-level bugs. We're likely to try scenarios the programmers hadn't thought of and to spend our time on higher-level business functionality. Well-designed code is usually robust and testable. If we find a defect, we show it to the programmer, who writes a unit test to reproduce the bug and then fixes it quickly. We actually have time to focus on exploratory testing and the other types of in-depth tests to give the code a good workout and learn more about how it should work. Often, the only "bugs" we find are requirements that everyone on our team missed or misunderstood. Even those are found quickly if the customer is involved and has regular demos and test opportunities. After a development team has mastered TDD, the focus for improvement shifts from bug prevention to figuring out better ways to elicit and capture requirements before coding.

Test-First Development vs. Test-Driven Development

Gerard Meszaros [Meszaros 2007, pp. 813–814] offers the following description of how test-first development differs from test-driven development:

> "Unlike test-driven development, test-first development merely says that the tests are written before the production code; it does not imply that the production code is made to work one test at a time (emergent design). Test-first development can be applied at the unit test or customer test level, depending on which tests we have chosen to automate."

Erik Bos [2008] observes that test-first development involves both test-first programming and test-first design, but there's a subtle difference:

> "With test-first design, the design follows the tests, whereas you can do test-first programming of a design that you first write down on a whiteboard. On larger projects, we tend to do more design via whiteboard discussions; the team discusses the architecture around a whiteboard, and codes test-first based on this design. On smaller projects, we do practice test-driven design."

There are several different philosophies about when to write tests and for what purpose. It's up to each team to agree on the approach that helps it achieve its quality objectives, although there is common agreement in the agile community that TDD definitely helps a team achieve better-quality software. This is an important way that programmer tests support the team. Let's look at some more ways.

Making Testers' Jobs Easier

The core practices related to programmer tests make lots of testing activities easier to accomplish. Programmers work in their own sandboxes, where they can test new code without affecting anyone else's work. They don't check in code until it has passed a suite of regression tests in their sandbox.

The team thinks about test environments and what to use for test data. Unit tests usually work with fake or mock objects instead of actual databases for speed, but programmers still need to test against realistic data. Testers can help them identify good test data. If the unit tests represent real-life data, fewer issues will be found later.

Lisa's Story

Here's a small example. When my current team first adopted agile development, we didn't have any automated tests. We had no way to produce a deployable code package, and we had no rudimentary test environments or test databases. I didn't have any means to produce a build myself, either. We decided to start writing code test-first and committed to automating tests at all levels where appropriate, but we needed some infrastructure first.

Our first priority was to implement a continuous build process, which was done in a couple of days. Each build sent an email with a list of checked-in files and comments about the updates. I could now choose which build to deploy and test. The next priority was to provide independent test environments so that tests run by one person would not interfere with other tests. The new database expert created new schemas to meet testing needs and a "seed" database of canonical, production-like data. These schemas could be refreshed on demand quickly with a clean set of data. Each team member, including me, got a unique and independent test environment.

Even before the team mastered TDD, the adopted infrastructure was in place to support executing tests. This infrastructure enabled the team to start testing much more effectively. Another aspect of trying to automate testing was dealing with a legacy application that was difficult to test. The decisions that were made to enable TDD also helped with customer-facing tests. We decided to start rewriting the system in a new architecture that facilitated testing and test automation, not only at the unit level but at all levels.

—Lisa

Writing tests and writing code with those tests in mind means programmers are always consciously making code testable. All of these good infrastructure-related qualities spill over to business-facing tests and tests that critique the product. The whole team is continually thinking of ways to improve design and make testing easier.

Designing with Testing in Mind

One advantage of driving development with tests is that code is written with the express intention of making the tests pass. The team has to think, right from the beginning, about how it will execute and automate tests for every story it codes. Test-driven development means that programmers will write each test before they write the code to make it pass.

Writing "testable code" is a simple concept, but it's not an easy task, especially if you're working on old code that has no automated tests and isn't designed for testability. Legacy systems often have business logic, I/O, database, and user interface layers intertwined. There's no easy way to hook in to automate a test below the GUI or at the unit level.

A common approach in designing a testable architecture is to separate the different layers that perform different functions in the application. Ideally, you would want to access each layer directly with a test fixture and test algorithms with different inputs. To do this, you isolate the business logic into its own layer, using fake objects instead of trying to access other applications or the actual database. If the presentation layer can be separated from underlying business logic and database access, you can quickly test input validation without testing underlying logic.

Layered Architectures and Testability

Lisa's team took the "strangler application" approach to creating a testable system where tests could be use to drive coding. Mike Thomas, the team's senior architect, explains how their new layered architecture enabled a testable design.

A layered architecture divides a code base into horizontal slices that contain similar functionality, often related to a technology. The slices at the highest level are the most specific and depend upon the slices below, which are more general. For example, many layered code bases have slices such as the following: UI, business logic, and data access.

Horizontal layering is just one way to organize a code base: Another is domain-oriented slices (such as payroll or order entry), which are generally thought of as "vertical." These layering approaches can be combined, of course, and all can be used to enhance testability.

Layering has advantages for testing, but only if the mechanism for "connecting" the slices provides flexibility. If a code base has tightly coupled slices via such mechanisms as direct concrete class dependencies and static methods, it is difficult to isolate a unit for testing, despite the layering. This makes most automated tests into integration tests, which can be complicated and can run slowly. In many cases, testing can only be accomplished by running the entire system.

Contrast this with a code base where the layers are separated by interfaces. Each slice depends only upon interfaces defined in the slice beneath it rather than on specific classes. Dependencies on such interfaces are easy to satisfy with test doubles at test time: mocks, stubs, and so on. Unit testing is thus simplified because each unit can truly be isolated. For example, the UI can be tested against mock business layer objects, and the business layer can be tested against mock data access objects, avoiding live database access.

The layered approach has allowed Lisa's team to succeed in automating tests at all levels and drive development with both technology-facing and business-facing tests.

See the bibliography for more information on Alastair Cockburn's Ports and Adapters pattern.

Another example of an approach to testable design is Alistair Cockburn's Ports and Adapters pattern [Cockburn, 2005]. This pattern's intent is to "create your application to work without either a UI or a database so you can run automated regression tests against the application, work when the database becomes unavailable, and link applications together without any user involvement." Ports accept outside events, and a technology-specific adapter converts it into a message that can be understood by the application. In turn, the application sends output via a port to an adapter, which creates the signals needed by the receiving human or automated users. Applications designed using this pattern can be driven by automated test scripts as easily as by actual users.

It's more obvious how to code test-first on a greenfield project. Legacy systems, which aren't covered by automated unit tests, present a huge challenge. It's hard to write unit tests for code that isn't designed for testability, and it's hard to change code that isn't safeguarded with unit tests. Many teams have

The bibliography has links to more articles about "rescue" and "strangler" approaches to legacy code.

followed the "legacy code rescue" techniques explained by Michael Feathers in *Working Effectively with Legacy Code* [Feathers, 2004]. Other teams, such as Lisa's, aim to "strangle" their legacy code. This strategy stems from Martin Fowler's "strangler application" [Fowler, 2004]. New stories were coded test-first in a new architecture while the old system was still maintained. Over time, much of the system has been converted to the new architecture, with the goal of eventually doing away with the old system.

Agile testing in a legacy mainframe type of environment presents particular challenges, not the least of which is the lack of availability of publications and information about how to do it successfully. COBOL, mainframes, and their ilk are still widely used. Let agile principles and values guide your team as you look for ways to enable automated testing in your application. You might have to adapt some techniques; for example, maybe you can't write code test-first, but you can test soon after writing the code. When it's the team's problem to solve, and not just the testers' problem, you'll find a way to write tests.

Testing Legacy Systems

John Voris, a developer with Crown Cork and Seal, works in the RPG language, a cousin of COBOL, which runs on the operating system previously known as AS 400 and now known as System i. John was tasked with merging new code with a vendor code base. He applied tenets of Agile, Lean, and IBM-recommended coding practices to come up with an approach he calls "ADEPT" for "AS400 Displays for External Prototyping and Testing." While he isn't coding test-first, he's testing "Minutes Afterward." Here's how he summed up his approach:

For more information about Presenter First development, see the bibliography.

- Write small, single-purpose modules (not monolithic programs), and refactor existing programs into modules. Use a Presenter First development approach (similar to the Model View Presenter or Model View Controller pattern).
- Define parameter interfaces for the testing harness based on screen formats and screen fields. The only drawback here is numbers are defined as zoned decimals rather than packed hexadecimal, but this is offset by the gain in productivity.
- "Minutes after" coding each production module, create a testing program using the screen format to test via the UI. The UI interface for the test is created prior to the production program, because the UI testing interface is the referenced interface for the production module. The impetus for running a test looms large for the programmer, because most of the coding for the test is already done.

For more about
RPGUnit, see www
.RPGUnit.org.

> - Use standard test data sets, which are unchanging, canonical test data, to drive the tests.
> - This approach, in which the test programs are almost auto-generated, lends itself to automation with a record/playback tool that would capture data inputs and outputs, with tests run in a continuous build, using RPGUnit.

Your team can find an approach to designing for testability that works for you. The secret is the whole-team commitment to testing and quality. When a team is constantly working to write tests and make them pass, it finds a way to get it done. Teams should take time to consider how they can create an architecture that will make automated tests easy to create, inexpensive to maintain, and long-lived. Don't be afraid to revisit the architecture if automated tests don't return enough value for the investment in them.

Timely Feedback

The biggest value of unit tests is in the speed of their feedback. In our opinion, a continuous integration and build process that runs the unit tests should finish within ten minutes. If each programmer checks code in several times a day, a longer build and test process will cause changes to start stacking up. As a tester, it can be frustrating to have to wait a long time for new functionality or a bug fix. If there's a compile error or unit test failure, the delay gets even worse, especially if it's almost time to go home!

A build and test process that runs tests above the unit level, such as functional API tests or GUI tests, is going to take longer. Have at least one build process that runs quickly, and a second that runs the slower tests. There should be at least one daily "build" that runs all of the slower functional tests. However, even that can be unwieldy. When a test fails and the problem is fixed, how long will it take to know for sure that the build passes again?

If your build and test process takes too long, ask your team to analyze the cause of the slowdown and take steps to speed up the build. Here are a few examples.

- Database access usually consumes lots of time, so consider using fake objects, where possible, to replace the database, especially at the unit level.
- Move longer-running integration and database-access tests to the secondary build and test process.
- See if tests can run in parallel so that they finish faster.

- Run the minimum tests needed for regression testing your system.
- Distribute tasks across multiple build machines.
- Upgrade the hardware and software that run the build.
- Find the area that takes the most time and take incremental steps to speed it up.

Lisa's Story

Early in my current team's agile evolution, we had few unit tests, so we included a few GUI smoke tests in our continual build, which kicked off on every check-in to the source code control system. When we had enough unit tests to feel good about knowing when code was broken, we moved the GUI tests and the FitNesse functional tests into a separate build and test process that ran at night, on the same machine as our continual build.

Our continual ongoing build started out taking less than 10 minutes, but soon was taking more than 15 minutes to complete. We wrote task cards to diagnose and fix the problem. The unit tests that the programmers had written early on weren't well designed, because nobody was sure of the best way to write unit tests. Time was budgeted to refactor the unit tests, use mock data access objects instead of the real database, and redesign tests for speed. This got the build to around eight minutes. Every time it has started to creep up, we've addressed the problem with refactoring, removing unnecessary tests, upgrading the hardware, and choosing different software that helped the build run faster.

As our functional tests covered more code, the nightly build broke more often. Because the nightly build ran on the same machine as the continual ongoing one, the only way to verify that the build was "green" again was to stop the ongoing build, which removed our fast feedback. This started to waste everyone's time. We bought and set up another build machine for the longer build, which now also runs continuously. This was much less expensive than spending so much time keeping two builds running on the same machine, and now we get quick feedback from our functional tests as well.

—Lisa

Wow, multiple continuous build and test processes providing constant feedback—it sounds like a dream to a lot of testers. Regression bugs will be caught early, when they're cheapest to fix. This is a great reason for writing technology-facing tests. Can we get too carried away with them, though? Let's look at the line between technology-facing tests and business-facing tests.

WHERE DO TECHNOLOGY-FACING TESTS STOP?

We often hear people worry that the customer-facing tests will overlap so much with the technology-facing tests that the team will waste time. We know that business-facing tests might cover a bit of the same ground as unit or code integration tests, but they have such different purposes that waste isn't a worry.

For example, we have a story to calculate a loan amortization schedule and display it to a user who's in the process of requesting a loan. A unit test for this story would likely test for illegal arguments, such as an annual payment frequency if the business doesn't allow it. There might be a unit test to figure the anticipated loan payment start date given some definition of amount, interest rate, start date, and frequency. Unit-level tests could cover different combinations of payment frequency, amount, interest date, term, and start date in order to prove that the amortization calculation is correct. They could cover scenarios such as leap years. When these tests pass, the programmer feels confident about the code.

Each unit test is independent and tests one dimension at a time. This means that when a unit test fails, the programmer can identify the problem quickly and solve the issue just as quickly. The business-facing tests very seldom cover only one dimension, because they are tackled from a business point of view.

The business-facing tests for this story would define more details for the business rules, the presentation in the user interface, and error handling. They would verify that payment details, such as the principal and interest applied, display correctly in the user interface. They would test validations for each field on the user interface, and specify error handling for situations such as insufficient balance or ineligibility. They could test a scenario where an administrator processes two loan payments on the same day, which might be harder to simulate at the unit level.

Chapter 13, "Why We Want to Automate Tests and What Holds Us Back," talks more about the ROI of the different types of tests.

The business-facing tests cover more complex user scenarios and verify that the end user will have a good experience. Push tests to lower levels whenever possible; if you identify a test case that can be automated at the unit level, that's almost always a better return on investment.

If multiple areas or layers of the application are involved, it might not be possible to automate at the unit level. Both technology-facing and business-facing levels might have tests around the date of the first loan payment, but they check for different reasons. The unit test would check the calculation of the date, and the business-facing test would verify that it displays correctly in the borrower's loan report.

Learning to write Quadrant 1 tests is hard. Many teams making the transition to agile development start out with no automated unit tests, not even a continuous integration and build process. In the next section, we suggest actions agile testers can take if their teams don't tackle Quadrant 1 tests.

WHAT IF THE TEAM DOESN'T DO THESE TESTS?

Many an organization has decided to try agile development, or at least stated that intention, without understanding how to make a successful transition. When we're in a tester role, what can we do to help the development team implement TDD, continuous integration, and other practices that are key to successful development?

Our experience over the years has been that if we aren't programmers ourselves, we don't necessarily have much credibility when we urge the programmers to adopt practices such as TDD. If we could sit down and show them how to code test-first, that would be persuasive, but many of us testers don't have that kind of experience. We've also found that evangelizing doesn't work. It's not that hard to convince someone conceptually that TDD is a good idea. It's much trickier to help them get traction actually coding test-first.

What Can Testers Do?

If you're a tester on a so-called "agile" team that isn't even automating unit tests or producing continuous builds—or at a minimum, doing builds on a daily basis—you're going to get frustrated pretty quickly. Don't give up; keep brainstorming for a way to get traction on a positive transition. Try using social time or other relaxing activity to take some quality time to see what new ideas you can generate to get all team members on board.

One trap to avoid is having testers write the unit tests. Because TDD is really-more of a design activity, it's essential that the person writing the code also write the tests, before writing the code. Programmers also need the immediate feedback that automated unit tests give. Unit tests written by someone else after the code is written might still guard against regression defects, but they won't have the most valuable benefits of tests written by the programmer.

Lisa's Story

Whenever I've wanted to effect change, I've turned to the patterns in *Fearless Change* by Mary Lynn Manns and Linda Rising [2004]. After working on two XP teams, I joined a team that professed a desire to become agile but wasn't making strides toward solid development practices. I found several patterns in *Fearless Change* to try to move the team toward agile practices.

"Ask for Help" was one pattern that helped me. This pattern says, in part: "Since the task of introducing a new idea into an organization is a big job, look for people and resources to help your efforts" [Manns and Rising, 2004]. When I wanted my team to start using FitNesse, I identified the programmer who was most sympathetic to my cause and asked him to pair with me to write FitNesse tests for the story he was working on. He told the other programmers about the benefits he derived from the FitNesse tests, which encouraged them to try it too. Most people want to help, and agile is all about the team working together, so there's no reason to go it alone.

"Brown Bag" is another change pattern that my teams have put to good use. For example, my current team held several brown bag sessions where they wrote unit tests together. "Guru on Your Side" is a productive pattern in which you enlist the help of a well-respected team member who might understand what you're trying to achieve. A previous team I was on was not motivated to write unit tests. The most experienced programmer on the team agreed with me that test-driven development was a good idea, and he set an example for the rest of the team.

We think you'll find that there's always someone on an agile team who's sympathetic to your cause. Enlist that person's support, especially if the team perceives him or her as a senior-level guru.

—Lisa

As a tester on an agile team, there's a lot you can do to act as a change agent, but your potential impact is limited. In some cases, strong management support is the key to driving the team to engage in Quadrant 1 activities.

What Can Managers Do?

If you're managing a development team, you can do a lot to encourage test-driven development and unit test automation. Work with the product owner to make quality your goal, and communicate the quality criteria to the team. Encourage the programmers to take time to do their best work instead of worrying about meeting a deadline. If a delivery date is in jeopardy, push to reduce the scope, not the quality. Your job is to explain to the business managers how making quality a priority will ensure that they get optimum business value.

Give the team time to learn, and provide expert, hands-on training. Bring in an experienced agile development coach or hire someone with experience in using these practices who can transfer those skills to the rest of the team. Budget time for major refactoring, for brainstorming about the best approach to writing unit and code integration tests, and for evaluating, installing, and upgrading tools. Test managers should work with development managers to encourage practices that enhance testability and allow testers to write executable tests. Test managers can also make sure testers have time to learn how to use the automation tools and frameworks that the team decides to implement.

It's a Team Problem

More about retrospectives and process improvement in Chapter 19, "Wrap Up the Iteration."

While you can find ways to be an effective change agent, the best thing to do is involve the whole team in solving the problems. If you aren't already doing retrospectives after every iteration, propose trying this practice or some other type of process improvement. At the retrospective, raise issues that are hampering successful delivery. For example, "We aren't finishing testing tasks before the end of the iteration" is a problem for the whole team to address. If one reason for not finishing is the high number of unit-level bugs, suggest experimenting with TDD, but allow programmers to propose their own ways to address the problem. Encourage the team to try a new approach for a few iterations and see how it works.

Technology-facing tests that support the team's development process are an important foundation for all of the testing that needs to happen. If the team isn't doing an adequate job with the tests in this quadrant, the other types of testing will be much more difficult. This doesn't mean you can't get value from the other quadrants on their own—it just means it will be harder to do so because the team's code will lack internal quality and everything will take longer.

Technology-facing tests can't be done without the right tools and infrastructure. In the next section, we look at examples of the types of tools a team needs to be effective with Quadrant 1 tests.

TOOLKIT

There's no magical tool that will ensure success. However, tools can help good people do their best work. Building up the right infrastructure to support technology-facing tests is critical. There's a huge selection of excellent tools available, and they improve all the time. Your team must find the tools that work best for your situation.

Source Code Control

Source code control is known by other names too, such as version control or revision control. It's certainly not new, or unique to agile development, but no software development team can succeed without it. That's why we're discussing it here. Without source code control, you'll never be sure what you're testing. Did the programmer change only the module he said he changed, or did he forget changes he made to other modules? You can't back out unwanted or erroneous changes without some kind of versioning system. Source code control keeps different programmers from walking on each other's changes to the same modules. Without versioning, you can't be sure what code to release to production.

Software Configuration Management Patterns: Effective Teamwork, Practical Integrations [2003], by Stephen Berczuk and Brad Appleton, is a good resource to use to learn how and why to use source code control. Source code control is essential to any style of software development.

Use source code control for automated test scripts, too. It's important to tie the automated tests with the corresponding code version that they tested in case you need to rerun tests against that version in the future. When you label or tag a build, make sure you label or tag the test code too, even if it doesn't get released to production.

Teams can organize their code hierarchy to provide a repository for production code, corresponding unit tests, and higher-level test scripts. Doing this might require some brainstorming and experimenting in order to get the right structure.

There are many terrific options to choose from. Open source systems such as CVS and Subversion (SVN) are easy to implement, integrate with a continuous build process and IDEs, and are robust. Vendor tools such as IBM Rational ClearCase and Perforce might add features that compensate for the increased overhead they often bring.

Source code control is tightly integrated with development environments. Let's look at some IDEs used by agile teams.

IDEs

A good IDE (integrated development environment) can be helpful for programmers and testers on an agile team. The IDE integrates with the source code control system to help prevent problems with versioning and changes walking on each other. The editors inside an IDE are specific to the programming language and flag errors even as you write the code. Most importantly, IDEs provide support for refactoring.

Programmers who use an IDE tend to have strong personal preferences. However, sometimes an organization decrees that all programmers must use a specific IDE. This might be because of licensing, or it might be intended to encourage open pair programming. It is easier to pair with another programmer if the other person uses the same IDE, but it's generally not essential for the same one to be used. Most tools work similarly, so it's not hard to change from one IDE to another in order to meet new needs or take advantage of new features. Some diehards still prefer to use tried-and-true technology such as vi, vim, or emacs with make files rather than an IDE.

Open source IDEs such as Eclipse and NetBeans are widely used by agile teams, along with proprietary systems such as Visual Studio and IntelliJ IDEA. IDEs have plug-ins to support different languages and tools. They work as well with test scripts as they do with production code.

Lisa's Story

On my current team, some programmers were using IntelliJ IDEA, while others used Eclipse. Environmental differences in rare cases caused issues, such as tests passing in the IDE but not the full build, or check-ins via the IDE causing havoc in the source code control system. Generally, though, use of different IDEs caused no problems. Interestingly, over time most of the Eclipse users switched. Pairing with the IntelliJ users led them to prefer it.

I use Eclipse to work with the automated test scripts as well as to research issues with the production code. The Ruby plug-in helps us with our Ruby and Watir scripts, and the XML editor helps with our Canoo WebTest scripts. We can run unit tests and do builds through the IDE. Programmers on the team helped me set up and start using Eclipse, and it has saved huge amounts of time. Maintaining the automated tests is much easier, and the IDE's "synchronize" view helps me remember to check in all of the modules I've changed.

Test tools are starting to come out with their own IDEs or plug-ins to work with existing IDEs such as Eclipse. Take advantage of these powerful, time-saving, quality-promoting tools.

—Lisa

Testers who aren't automating tests through an IDE, but who want to be able to look at changed snippets of code, can use tools such as FishEye that enable the testers to get access to the code through the automated build.

As of this writing, IDEs have added support for dynamic languages such as Ruby, Groovy, and Python. Programmers who use dynamic languages may prefer lighter-weight tools, but they still need good tools that support good coding practices, such as TDD and refactoring.

Regardless of the development environment and tools being used, agile teams need a framework that will integrate code changes from different programmers, run the unit tests to verify no regression bugs have occurred, and provide the code in a deployable format.

Build Tools

Your team needs some way to build the software and create a deployable jar, war, or other type of file. This can be done with shell-based tools such as make, but those tools have limitations, such as the platforms where they work. Agile teams that we know use tools such as ant, Nant, and Maven to build their projects. These tools not only manage the build but also provide easy ways to report and document build results, and they integrate easily with build automation and test tools. They also integrate with IDEs.

Build Automation Tools

Continuous integration is a core practice for agile teams. You need a way to not only build the project but also run automated tests on each build to make sure nothing broke. A fully automated and reproducible build that runs many times a day is a key success factor for agile teams. Automated build tools provide features such as email notification of build results, and they integrate with build and source code control tools.

Commonly used tools as of the writing of this book include the open source tools CruiseControl, CruiseControl.net, CruiseControl.rb, and Hudson. Other open source and proprietary tools available at publication time are AnthillPro, Bamboo, BuildBeat, CI Factory, Team City, and Pulse, just to name a few.

Without an automated build process you'll have a hard time deploying code for testing as well as releasing. Build management and build automation tools are easy to implement and absolutely necessary for successful agile projects. Make sure you get your build process going early, even before you start coding. Experiment with different tools when you find you need more features than your current process provides.

Unit Test Tools

Unit test tools are specific to the language in which you're coding. "xUnit" tools are commonly used by agile teams, and there's a flavor for many different languages, including JUnit for Java, NUnit for .NET, Test::Unit for Perl and Ruby, and PyUnit for Python.

See Chapter 9, "Toolkit for Business-Facing Tests that Support the Team," for more information on behavior-driven development tools.

See the bibliography for links and books to help your team search for the right unit test tools.

Behavior-driven development is another flavor of test-driven development, spelling out expected behavior to drive tests with tools such as RSpec and easyb.

GUI code can and should be developed test-first as well. Some tools for rich-client unit testing are TestNG, Abbot, and SWTBot.

Tools such as EasyMock and Ruby/Mock help with implementing mock objects and test stubs, an integral part of well-designed unit tests.

The tools programmers use to write technology-facing tests can also be used for business-facing tests. Whether they are suited for that purpose in your project depends on the needs of your team and your customers.

SUMMARY

In this chapter, we explained the purpose of technology-facing tests that support the team, and we talked about what teams need to use them effectively.

- Technology-facing tests that support programming let the team produce the highest quality code possible; they form the foundation for all other types of testing.
- The benefits of this quadrant's tests include going faster and doing more, but speed and quantity should never be the ultimate goal.
- Programmers write technology-facing tests that support the team and provide great value to testers by enhancing the internal quality and testability of the system.
- Teams that fail to implement the core practices related to agile development are likely to struggle.
- Legacy systems usually present the biggest obstacles to test-driven development, but these problems can be overcome with incremental approaches.
- If your team doesn't now do these tests, you can help them get started by engaging other team members and getting support from management.
- There can be some overlap between technology-facing tests and business-facing tests that support the team. However, when faced with a choice, push tests to the lowest level in order to maximize ROI.
- Teams should set up continuous integration, build, and test processes in order to provide feedback as quickly as possible.
- Agile teams require tools for tasks such as source code control, test automation, IDEs, and build management in order to facilitate technology-facing tests that support the team.

Chapter 8

BUSINESS-FACING TESTS THAT SUPPORT THE TEAM

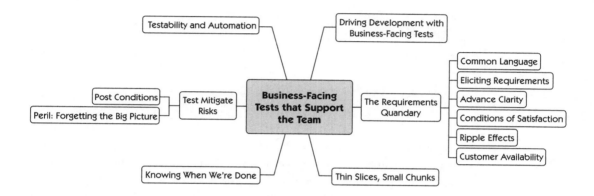

In the last chapter, we talked about programmer tests, those low-level tests that help programmers make sure they have written the code right. How do they know the right thing to build? In phased and gated methodologies, we try to solve that by gathering requirements up front and putting as much detail in them as possible. In projects using agile practices, we put all our faith in story cards and tests that customers understand in order to help code the right thing. These "understandable" tests are the subject of this chapter.

DRIVING DEVELOPMENT WITH BUSINESS-FACING TESTS

Yikes, we're starting an iteration with no more information than what fits on an index card, something like what's shown in Figure 8-1.

That's not much information, and it's not meant to be. Stories are a brief description of desired functionality and an aid to planning and prioritizing work. On a traditional waterfall project, the development team might be

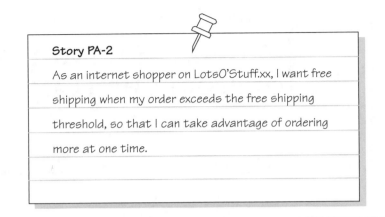

Figure 8-1   Story to set up conversation

given a wordy requirements document that includes every detail of the feature set. On an agile project, the customer team and development team strike up a conversation based on the story. The team needs requirements of some kind, and they need them at a level that will let them start writing working code almost immediately. To do this, we need examples to turn into tests that will confirm what the customer really wants.

These business-facing tests address business requirements. These tests help provide the big picture and enough details to guide coding. Business-facing tests express requirements based on examples and use a language and format that both the customer and development teams can understand. Examples form the basis of learning the desired behavior of each feature, and we use those examples as the basis for our story tests in Quadrants 2 (see Figure 8-2).

Business-facing tests are also called "customer-facing," "story," "customer," and "acceptance" tests. The term "acceptance test" is particularly confusing, because it makes some people think only of "user acceptance tests." In the context of agile development, acceptance tests generally refer to the business-facing tests, but the term could also include the technology-facing tests from Quadrant 4, such as the customer's criteria for system performance or security. In this chapter, we're discussing only the business-facing tests that support the team by guiding development and providing quick feedback.

As we explained in the previous two chapters, the order in which we present these four quadrants isn't related to the order in which we might perform

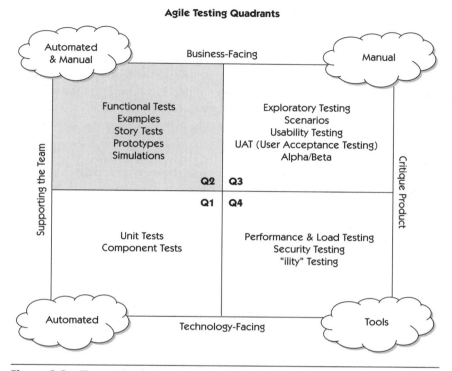

Figure 8-2 The Agile Testing Quadrants, highlighting Quadrant 2

Part V, "An Iteration in the Life," examines the order in which we perform tests from the different quadrants.

activities from each quadrant. The business-facing tests in Quadrant 2 are written for each story before coding is started, because they help the team understand what code to write. Like the tests in Quadrant 1, these tests drive development, but at a higher level. Quadrant 1 activities ensure internal quality, maximize team productivity, and minimize technical debt. Quadrant 2 tests define and verify external quality, and help us know when we're done.

The customer tests to drive coding are generally written in an executable format, and automated, so that team members can run the tests as often as they like in order to see if the functionality works as desired. These tests, or some subset of them, will become part of an automated regression suite so that future development doesn't unintentionally change system behavior.

As we discuss the stories and examples of desired behavior, we must also define nonfunctional requirements such as performance, security, and usability. We'll also make note of scenarios for manual exploratory testing. We'll talk about these other types of testing activities in the chapters on Quadrants 3 and 4.

We hear lots of questions relating to how agile teams get requirements. How do we know what the code we write should do? How do we obtain enough information to start coding? How do we get the customers to speak with one voice and present their needs clearly? Where do we start on each story? How do we get customers to give us examples? How do we use those to write story tests?

This chapter explains our strategy for creating business-facing tests that support the team as it develops each story. Let's start by talking more about requirements.

THE REQUIREMENTS QUANDARY

Just about every development team we've known, agile or not, struggles with requirements. Teams on traditional waterfall projects might invest months in requirements gathering only to have them be wrong or quickly get out of date. Teams in chaos mode might have no requirements at all, with the programmers making their best guess as to how a feature should work.

Agile development embraces change, but what happens when requirements change during an iteration? We don't want a long requirements-gathering period before we start coding, but how can we be sure we (and our customers) really understand the details of each story?

In agile development, new features usually start out life as stories, or groups of stories, written by the customer team. Story writing is not about figuring out implementation details, although high-level discussions can have an impact on dependencies and how many stories are created. It's helpful if some members of the technical team can participate in story-writing sessions so that they can have input into the functionality stories and help ensure that technical stories are included as part of the backlog. Programmers and testers can also help customers break stories down to appropriate sizes, suggest alternatives that might be more practical to implement, and discuss dependencies between stories.

Stories by themselves don't give much detail about the desired functionality. They're usually just a sentence that expresses who wants the feature, what the feature is, and why they want it. "As an Internet shopper, I need a way to delete items from my shopping cart so I don't have to buy unwanted items" leaves a lot to the imagination. Stories are only intended as a starting point for an on-going dialogue between business experts and the development team. If team members understand what problem the customer is trying to solve, they can suggest alternatives that might be simpler to use and implement.

In this dialogue between customers and developers, agile teams expand on stories until they have enough information to write appropriate code. Testers help elicit examples and context for each story, and help customers write story tests. These tests guide programmers as they write the code and help the team know when it has met the customers' conditions of satisfaction. If your team has use cases, they can help to supplement the example or coaching test to clarify the needed functionality (see Figure 8-3).

In agile development, we accept that we'll never understand all of the requirements for a story ahead of time. After the code that makes the story tests pass is completed, we still need to do more testing to better understand the requirements and how the features should work.

After customers have a chance to see what the team is delivering, they might have different ideas about how they want it to work. Often customers have a vague idea of what they want and a hard time defining exactly what that is. The team works with the customer or customer proxy for an iteration and might deliver just a kernel of a solution. The team keeps refining the functionality over multiple iterations until it has defined and delivered the feature.

Being able to iterate is one reason agile development advocates small releases and developing one small chunk at a time. If our customer is unhappy with the behavior of the code we deliver in this iteration, we can quickly rectify that in the next, if they deem it important. Requirements changes are pretty much inevitable.

We must learn as much as we can about our customers' wants and needs. If our end users work in our location, or it's feasible to travel to theirs, we should sit with them, work alongside them, and be able to do their jobs if we can. Not only will we understand their requirements better but we might even identify requirements they didn't think to state.

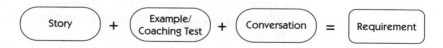

Figure 8-3   The makeup of a requirement

Tests need to include more than the customers' stated requirements. We need to test for post conditions, impact on the system as a whole, and integration with other systems. We identify risks and mitigate those with tests as needed. All of these factors guide our coding.

Common Language

We can also use our tests to provide a common language that's understood by both the development team and the business experts. As Brian Marick [2008] points out, a shared language helps the business people envision the features they want. It helps the programmers craft well-designed code that's easy to extend. Real-life examples of desired and undesired behavior can be expressed so that they're understood by both the business and technical sides. Pictures, flow diagrams, spreadsheets, and prototypes are accessible to people with different backgrounds and viewpoints. We can use these tools to find examples and then easily turn those examples into tests. The tests need to be written in a way that's comprehensible to a business user reading them yet still executable by the technical team.

More on Fit in Chapter 9, "Toolkit for Business-Facing Tests that Support the Team."

Business-facing tests also help define scope, so that everyone knows what is part of the story and what isn't. Many of the test frameworks now allow teams to create a domain language and define tests using that language. Fit (Functional for Integrated Framework) is one of those.

The Perfect Customer

Andy Pols allowed us to reprint this story from his blog [Pols, 2008]. In it, he shows how his customer demanded a test, wrote it, and realized the story was out of scope.

On a recent project, our customer got so enthusiastic about our Fit tests that he got extremely upset when I implemented a story without a Fit test. He refused to let the system go live until we had the Fit test in place.

The story in question was very technical and involved sending a particular XML message to an external system. We just could not work out what a Fit test would look like for this type of requirement. Placing the expected XML message, with all its gory detail, in the Fit test would not have been helpful because this is a technical artifact and of no interest to the business. We could not work out what to do. The customer was not around to discuss this, so I just went ahead and implemented the story (very naughty!).

What the customer wanted was to be sure that we were sending the correct product information in the XML message. To resolve the issue, I suggested that we have a Fit test that shows how the product attributes get mapped onto the XML message using Xpath, although I still thought this was too technical for a business user.

We gave the customer a couple of links to explain what XPath was so that he could explore whether this was a good solution for him. To my amazement, he was delighted with XPath (I now know who to turn to when I have a problem with XPath) and filled in the Fit test.

The interesting bit for me is that as soon as he knew what the message looked like and how it was structured, he realized that it did not really support the business—we were sending information that was outside our scope of our work and that should have been supplied by another system. He was also skeptical about the speed at which the external team could add new products due to the complex nature of the XML.

Most agile people we tell this story to think we have the "perfect customer!"

Even if your customers aren't perfect, involving them in writing customer tests gives them a chance to identify functionality that's outside the scope of the story. We try to write customer tests that customers can read and comprehend. Sometimes we set the bar too low. Collaborate with your customers to find a tool and format for writing tests that works for both the customer and development teams.

It's fine to say that our customers will provide to us the examples that we need to have in order for us to understand the value that each story should deliver. But what if they don't know how to explain what they want? In the next section, we'll suggest ways to help customers define their conditions of satisfaction.

Eliciting Requirements

If you've ever been a customer requesting a particular software feature, you know how hard it is to articulate exactly what you want. Often, you don't really know exactly what you want until you can see, feel, touch and use it. We have lots of ways to help our customers get clarity about what they want.

Ask Questions

Start by asking questions. Testers can be especially good at asking a variety of questions because they are conscious of the big picture, the business-facing and technical aspects of the story, and are always thinking of the end user experience. Types of general questions to ask are:

- Is this story solving a problem?
- If so, what's the problem we're trying to solve?
- Could we implement a solution that doesn't solve the problem?
- How will the story bring value to the business?
- Who are the end users of the feature?
- What value will they get out of it?
- What will users do right before and right after they use that feature?
- How do we know we're done with this story?

One question Lisa likes to ask is, "What's the worst thing that could happen?" Worst-case scenarios tend to generate ideas. They also help us consider risk and focus our tests on critical areas. Another good question is, "What's the best thing that could happen?" This question usually generates our happy path test, but it might also uncover some hidden assumptions.

Use Examples

Most importantly, ask the customer to give you examples of how the feature should work. Let's say the story is about deleting items out of an online shopping cart. Ask the customer to draw a picture on a whiteboard of how that delete function might look. Do they want any extra features, such as a confirmation step, or a chance to save the item in case they want to retrieve it later? What would they expect to see if the deletion couldn't be done?

Examples can form the basis for our tests. Our challenge is to capture examples, which might be expressed in the business domain language, as tests that can actually be executed. Some customers are comfortable expressing examples using a test tool such as Fit or FitNesse as long as they can write them in their domain language.

Let's explore the difference between an example and a test with a simple story (see Figure 8-4). People often get confused between these two terms.

An example would look something like this:

> There are 5 items on a page. I want to select item 1 for $20.25 and put it in the shopping cart. I click to the next page, which has 5 more items. I select a second item on that page for $5.38 and put it in my shopping cart. When I say I'm done shopping, it will show both the item from the

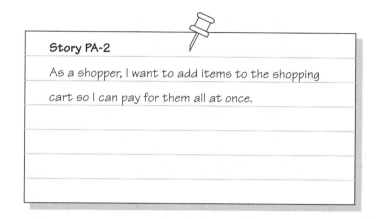

Figure 8-4 Story to use as a base for examples and tests

first page and the item from the second page in my shopping cart, with the total of $25.63

The test could be quite a bit different. We'll use a Fit type format in Table 8-1 to show you how the test could be represented.

The test captures the example in an executable format. It might not use exactly the same inputs, but it encapsulates the sample user scenario. More test cases can be written to test boundary conditions, edge cases, and other scenarios.

Multiple Viewpoints

Each example or test has one point of view. Different people will write different tests or examples from their unique perspectives. We'd like to capture as many different viewpoints as we can, so think about your users.

Table 8-1 Test for Story PA-2

	Inputs		Expected Results	
ID	Item	Price	Total Cost	# of Items
001	Item A	20.25	20.25	1
002	Item D	0.01	20.26	2
003	Item F	100.99	121.25	3

Getting the requirements right is an area where team members in many different roles can jump in to help. Business analysts, subject matter experts, programmers, and various members of the customer team all have something to contribute. Think about other stakeholders, such as your production support team. They have a very unique perspective.

We often forget about nonfunctional requirements such as "How long does the system need to be up? What happens if it fails? If we have middleware that passes messages, do we expect messages to be large enough that we might need to consider loss during transmission? Or will they be a constant size? What happens if there is no traffic for hours? Does the system need to warn someone?" Testing for these types of requirements usually falls into quadrants 3 and 4, but we still need to write tests to make sure they get done.

All of the examples that customers give to the team add up quickly. Do we really have to turn all of these into executable tests? Not as long as we have the customers there to tell us if the code is working the way they want. With techniques such as paper prototyping, designs can be tested before a line of code is written.

Wizard of Oz Testing

Gerard Meszaros, a Certified ScrumMaster (Practicing) and Agile Coach, shared his story about Wizard of Oz Testing on Agile Projects. He describes a good example of how artifacts we generate to elicit requirements can help communicate meaning in an unambiguous form.

> We thought we were ready to release our software. We had been building it one iteration at a time under the guidance of an on-site customer who had prioritized the functionality based on what he needed to enter into integration testing with his business partners. We consciously deferred the master data maintenance and reporting functionality to later iterations to ensure we had the functionality needed for integration testing ready. The integration testing went fine, with just a few defects logged (all related to missing or misunderstood functionality). In the meantime, we implemented the master data maintenance in parallel with integration testing in the last few iterations. When we went into acceptance testing with the business users, we got a rude shock: They hated the maintenance and reporting functionality! They logged so many defects and "must-have improvements" that we had to delay the release by a month. So much for coming up with a plan that would allow us to deliver early!

While we were reimplementing the master data maintenance, I attended the Agile 2005 conference and took a tutorial by Jeff Patton. One of the exercises was building paper prototypes of the UI for a sample application. Then we "tested" the paper prototypes with members of the other groups as our users and found out how badly flawed our UI designs were. Déjà vu! The tutorial resembled my reality.

On my return to the project back home, I took the project manager I was mentoring in agile development aside and suggested that paper prototyping and "Wizard of Oz" testing (the Wizard of Oz reference is to a human being acting as a computer—sort of the "man behind the curtain") might have avoided our one-month setback. After a very short discussion, we decided to give it a try on our release 2 functionality. We stayed late a couple of evenings and designed the UI using screenshots from the R1 functionality overlaid with hand-drawn R2 functionality. It was a long time since either of us had used scissors and glue sticks, and it was fun!

For the Wizard of Oz testing with users, we asked our on-site customers to find some real users with whom to do the testing. They also came up with some realistic sample tasks for the users to try to execute. We put the sample data into Excel spreadsheets and printed out various combinations of data grids to use the in the testing. Some future users came to town for a conference. We hijacked pairs of them for an hour each and did our testing.

I acted as the "wizard," playing the part of the computer ("it's a 286 processor so don't expect the response times to be very good"). The on-site customer introduced the problem and programmers acted as observers, recording the missteps the users made as "possible defects." After just a few hours, we had huge amounts of valuable data about which parts of our UI design worked well and which parts needed rethinking. And there was little argument about which was which! We repeated the usability testing with other users when we had alpha versions of the application available and gained further valuable insights. Our business customer found the exercise so valuable that on a subsequent project the business team set about doing the paper prototyping and Wizard of Oz testing with no prompting from the development team. This might have been influenced somewhat by the first e-mail we got from a real user 30 minutes after going live: "I love this application!!!"

Developing user interfaces test-first can seem like an intimidating effort. The Wizard of Oz technique can be done before writing a single line of code. The team can test user interaction with the system and gather plenty of information to understand the desired system behavior. It's a great way to facilitate communication between the customer and development teams.

Close, constant collaboration between the customer team and the developer team is key to obtaining examples on which to base customer tests that drive coding. Communication is a core agile value, and we talk about it more in the next section.

Communicate with Customers

In an ideal world, our customers are available to us all day, every day. In reality, many teams have limited access to their business experts, and in many cases, the customers are in a different location or time zone. Do whatever you can to have face-to face conversations. When you can't, conference calls, phone conversations, emails, instant messages, cameras, and other communication tools will have to substitute. Fortunately, more tools to facilitate remote communication are available all the time. We've heard of teams, such as Erika Boyer's team at iLevel by Weyerhaeuser, that use webcams that can be controlled by the folks in the remote locations. Get as close to you can to direct conversation.

Lisa's Story

I worked on a team where the programmers were spread through three time zones and the customers were in a different one. We sent different programmers, testers, and analysts to the customer site for every iteration, so that each team member had "face time" with the customers at least every third iteration. This built trust and confidence between the developer and customer teams. The rest of the time we used phone calls, open conference calls, and instant messages to ask questions. With continual fine-tuning based on retrospective discussions, we succeeded in satisfying and even delighting the customers.

—Lisa

Even when customers are available and lines of communication are wide open, communication needs to be managed. We want to talk to each member of the customer team, but they all have different viewpoints. If we get several different versions of how a piece of functionality should work, we won't know what to code. Let's consider ways to get customers to agree on the conditions of satisfaction for each story.

Advance Clarity

If your customer team consists of people from different parts of the organization, there may be conflicting opinions among them about exactly what's intended by a particular story. In Lisa's company, business development wants features that generate revenue, operations wants features that cut down on phone support calls, and finance wants features that streamline accounting, cash management, and reporting. It's amazing how many unique interpretations of the same story can emerge from people who have differing viewpoints.

Lisa's Story

Although we had a product owner when we first implemented Scrum, we still got different directives from different customers. Management decided to appoint a vice president with extensive domain and operations knowledge as the new product owner. He is charged with getting all of the stakeholders to agree on each story's implications up front. He and the rest of the customer team meet regularly to discuss upcoming themes and stories, and to agree on priorities and conditions of satisfaction. He calls this "advance clarity."

—Lisa

A Product Owner is a role in Scrum. He's responsible not only for achieving advance clarity but also for acting as the "customer representative" in prioritizing stories. There's a downside, though. When you funnel the needs of many different viewpoints through one person, something can be lost. Ideally, the development team should sit together with the customer team and learn how to do the customer's work. If we understand the customer's needs well enough to perform its daily tasks, we have a much better chance of producing software that properly supports those tasks.

Janet's Story

Our team didn't implement the product owner role at first and used the domain experts on the team to determine prioritization and clarity. It worked well, but the achieving consensus took many meetings because each person had different experiences. The product was better for it, but there were trade-offs. The many meetings meant the domain experts were not always available for answering questions from the programmers, so coding was slower than anticipated.

There were four separate project teams working on the same product, but each one was focused on different features. After several retrospectives, and a lot of problem-solving sessions, each project team appointed a Product Owner. The number of meetings was cut down significantly because most business decisions were made by the domain experts on their particular project. Meetings were held for all of the domain experts if there were any differences of opinion, and the Product Owner facilitated bringing consensus on an issue. Decisions were made much faster, the domain experts were more available for answering questions by the team, and were able to keep up with the acceptance tests.

—Janet

However your team chooses to bring together varying viewpoints, it is important that there is only "one voice of the customer" presented to the team.

We said that product owners provide conditions of satisfaction. Let's look more closely at what we mean.

Conditions of Satisfaction

There are conditions of satisfaction for the whole release as well as for each feature or story. Acceptance tests help define the story acceptance. Your development team can't successfully deliver what the business wants unless conditions of satisfaction for a story are agreed to up front. The customer team needs to "speak with one voice." If you're getting different requirements from different stakeholders, you might need to push back and put off the story until you have a firm list of business satisfaction conditions. Ask the customer representative to provide a minimum amount of information on each story so that you can start every iteration with a productive conversation.

The best way to understand the customer team's requirements is to talk with the customers face to face. Because everyone struggles with "requirements," there are tools to help the customer team work through each story. Conditions of satisfaction should include not only the features that the story delivers but also the impacts on the larger system.

Lisa's product owner uses a checklist format to sort out issues such as:

- Business satisfaction conditions
- Impact on existing functions such as the website, documents, invoices, forms, or reports
- Legal considerations
- The impact on regularly scheduled processes
- References to mock-ups for UI stories
- Help text, or who will provide it
- Test cases
- Data migration (as appropriate)
- Internal communication that needs to happen
- External communication to business partners and vendors

Chapter 9, "Toolkit for Business-Facing Tests that Support the Team," includes example checklists as well as other tools for expressing requirements.

The product owner uses a template to put this information on the team's wiki so that it can be used as team members learn about the stories and start writing tests.

These conditions are based on key assumptions and decisions made by the customer team for a story. They generally come out of conversations with the customer about high-level acceptance criteria for each story. Discussing conditions of satisfaction helps identify risky assumptions and increases the team's confidence in writing and correctly estimating all of the tasks that are needed to complete the story.

Ripple Effects

In agile development, we focus on one story at a time. Each story is usually a small component of the overall application, but it might have a big ripple effect. A new story drops like a little stone into the application water, and we might not think about what the resulting waves might run into. It's easy to lose track of the big picture when we're focusing on a small number of stories in each iteration.

Lisa's team finds it helpful to make a list of all of the parts of the system that might be affected by a story. The team can check each "test point" to see what requirements and test cases it might generate. A small and innocent story might have a wide-ranging impact, and each part of the application that it touches might present another level of complexity. You need to be aware of all the potential impacts of any code change. Making a list is a good place to start. In the first few days of the iteration, the team can research and analyze affected areas further and see whether any more task cards are needed to cover them all.

Janet's Story

In one project I was on, we used a simple spreadsheet that listed all of the high-level functionality of the application under test. During release planning, and at the start of each new iteration, we reviewed the list and thought about how the new or changing functionality would affect those areas. That became the starting point for determining what level of testing needed to be done in each functional area. This impact analysis was in addition to the actual story testing and enabled our team to see the big picture and the impact of the changes to the rest of the system.

—Janet

Chapter 16, "Hit the Ground Running," and Chapter 17, "Iteration Kickoff," give examples of when and how teams can plan customer tests and explore the wider impact of each story.

Stories that look small but that impact unexpected areas of the system can come back to bite you. If your team forgets to consider all dependencies, and if the new code intersects with existing functionality, your story might take much longer than planned to finish. Make sure your story tests include the less obvious fallout from implementing the new functionality.

Take time to identify the central value each story provides and figure out an incremental approach to developing it. Plan small increments of writing tests, writing code, and testing the code some more. This way, your Quadrant 2 tests ensure you'll deliver the minimum value as planned.

THIN SLICES, SMALL CHUNKS

Writing stories is a tricky business. When the development team estimates new stories, it might find some stories too big, so it will ask the customer team to go back and break them into smaller stories. Stories can be too small as well, and might need to be combined with others or simply treated as tasks. Agile development, including testing, takes on one small chunk of functionality at a time.

When your team embarks on a new project or theme, ask the product owner to bring all of the related stories to a brainstorming session prior to the first iteration for that theme. Have the product owner and other interested stake-holders explain the stories. You might find that some stories need to be sub-divided or that additional stories need to be written to fill in gaps.

After you understand what value each story should deliver and how it fits in the context of the system, you can break the stories down into small, manageable pieces. You can write customer tests to define those small increments, while keeping in mind the impact on the larger application.

A smart incremental approach to writing customer tests that guide development is to start with the "thin slice" that follows a happy path from one end to the other. Identifying a thin slice, also called a "steel thread" or "tracer bullet," can be done on a theme level, where it's used to verify the overall architecture. This steel thread connects all of the components together, and after it's solid, more functionality can be added.

See Chapter 10, "Business-Facing Tests that Critique the Product," for more about exploratory testing.

We find this strategy works at the story level, too. The sooner you can build the end-to-end path, the sooner you can do meaningful testing, get feedback, start automating tests, and start exploratory testing. Begin with a thin slice of the most stripped-down functionality that can be tested. This can be thought of as the critical path. For a user interface, this might start with simply navigating from one page to the next. We can show this to the customer and see whether the flow makes sense. We could write a simple automated GUI test. For the free-shipping threshold story at the beginning of this chapter, we might start by verifying the logic used to sum up the order total and determine whether it

See Part IV, "Automation," for more about regression test automation.

qualifies for free shipping, without worrying about how it will look on the UI. We could automate tests for it with a functional test tool such as FitNesse.

After the thin slice is working, we can write customer tests for the next chunk or layer of functionality, and write the code that makes those tests pass. Now we'll have feedback for this small increment, too. Maybe we add the UI to display the checkout page showing that the order qualified for free shipping, or add the layer to persist updates to the database. We can add on to the automated tests we wrote for the first pass. It's a process of "write tests—write code—run tests—learn." If you do this, you know that all of the code your team produces satisfies the customer and works properly at each stage.

Lisa's Story

My team has found that we have to focus on accomplishing a simple thin slice and add to it in tiny increments. Before we did this, we tended to get stuck on one part of the story. For example, if we had a UI flow that included four screens, we'd get so involved in the first one that we might not get to the last one, and there was no working end-to-end path. By starting with an end-to-end happy path and adding functionality a step at a time, we can be sure of delivering the minimum value needed.

Here's an example of our process. The story was to add a new conditional step to the process of establishing a company's retirement plan. This step allows users to select mutual fund portfolios, but not every user has access to this feature. The retirement plan establishment functionality is written in old, poorly designed legacy code. We planned to write the new page in the new architecture, but linking the new and old code together is tricky and error prone. We broke the story down into slices that might look tiny but that allowed us to manage risk and minimize the time needed to code and test the story. Figure 8-5 shows a diagram of incremental steps planned for this story.

The #1 thin slice is to insert a new, empty page based on a property. While it's not much for our customers to look at, it lets us test the bridge between old and new code, and then verify that the plan establishment navigation still works properly. Slice #2 introduces some business logic: If no mutual fund portfolios are available for the company, skip to the fund selection step, which we're not changing yet. If there are fund portfolios available, display them on the new step 3. In slice #3, we change the fund selection step, adding logic to display the funds that make up the portfolios. Slice #4 adds navigational elements between various steps in the establishment process.

We wrote customer tests to define each slice. As the programmers completed each one, we manually tested it and showed it to our customers. Any problems found were fixed immediately. We wrote an automated GUI test for slice #1, and added to it as the remaining steps were finished. The story was difficult because of the old legacy code interacting with the new architecture, but the stepwise approach made implementation smooth, and saved time.

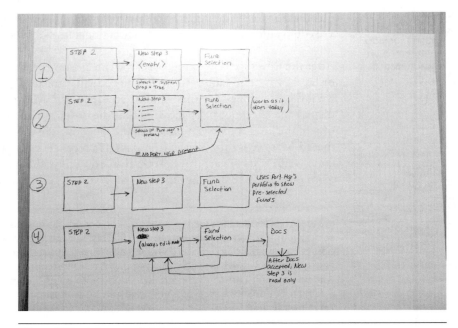

Figure 8-5   Incremental steps

Check the bibliography for Gerard Meszaros's article "Using Storyotypes to Split Bloated XP Stories."

When we draw diagrams such as this to break stories into slices, we upload photos of them to our team wiki so our remote team member can see them too. As each step is finished, we check it off in order to provide instant visual feedback.

—Lisa

If the task of writing customer tests for a story seems confusing or overwhelming, your team might need to break the story into smaller steps or chunks. Finishing stories a small step at a time helps spread out the testing effort so that it doesn't get pushed to the end of the iteration. It also gives you a better picture of your progress and helps you know when you're done—a subject we'll explore in the next section.

HOW DO WE KNOW WE'RE DONE?

We have our business-facing tests that support the team—those tests that have been written to ensure the conditions of satisfaction have been met. They start with the happy path and show that the story meets the intended need. They cover various user scenarios and ensure that other parts of the system aren't adversely affected. These tests have been run, and they pass (or at least they've identified issues to be fixed).

Are we done now? We could be, but we're not sure yet. The true test is whether the software's user can perform the action the story was supposed to provide. Activities from Quadrants 3 and 4, such as exploratory testing, usability testing, and performance testing will help us find out. For now, we just need to do some customer tests to ensure that we have captured all of the requirements. The business users or product owners are the right people to determine whether every requirement has been delivered, so they're the right people to do the exploring at this stage.

When the tests all pass and any missed requirements have been identified, we are done for the purpose of supporting the programmers in their quest for code that does the "right thing." It does not mean we are done testing. We'll talk much more about that in the chapters that follow.

Another goal of customer tests is to identify high-risk areas and make sure the code is written to solidify those. Risk management is an essential practice in any software development methodology, and testers play a role in identifying and mitigating risks.

TESTS MITIGATE RISK

Customer tests are written not only to define expected behavior of the code but to manage risk. Driving development with tests doesn't mean we'll identify every single requirement up front or be able to predict perfectly when we're done. It does give us a chance to identify risks and mitigate them with executable test cases. Risk analysis isn't a new technique. Agile development inherently mitigates some risks by prioritizing business value into small, tested deliverable pieces and by having customer involvement in incremental acceptance. However, we should still brainstorm potential events, the probability they might occur, and the impact on the organization if they do happen so that the right mitigation strategy can be employed.

Coding to predefined tests doesn't work well if the tests are for improbable edge cases. While we don't want to test only the happy path, it's a good place to start. After the happy path is known, we can define the highest risk scenarios—cases that not only have a bad outcome but also have a good possibility of happening.

In addition to asking the customer team questions such as "What's the worst thing that could happen?," ask the programmers questions like these: "What are the post conditions of this section of code? What should be persisted in the database? What behavior should we look for down the line?" Specify tests to cover potentially risky outcomes of an action.

Lisa's Story

My team considers worst-case scenarios in order to help us identify customer tests. For example, we planned a story to rewrite the first step of a multistep account creation wizard with a couple of new options. We asked ourselves questions such as the following: "When the user submits that first page, what data is inserted in the database? Are any other updates triggered? Do we need to regression test the entire account setup process? What about activities the user account might do after setup?" We might need to test the entire life cycle of the account. We don't have time to test more than necessary, so decisions about what to test are critical. The right tests help us mitigate the risk brought by the change.

—Lisa

Programmers can identify fragile parts of the code. Does the story involve stitching together legacy code with a new architecture? Does the code being changed interact with another system or depend on third-party software? By discussing potential impacts and risky areas with programmers and other team members, we can plan appropriate testing activities.

There's another risk. We might get so involved writing detailed test cases up front that the team loses the forest in the trees; that is, we can forget the big picture while we concentrate on details that might prove irrelevant.

> **Peril: Forgetting the Big Picture**
>
> It's easy to slip into the habit of testing only individual stories or basing your testing on what the programmer tells you about the code. If you find yourself finding integration problems between stories late in the release or that a lot of requirements are missing after the story is "done," take steps to mitigate this peril.
>
> Always consider how each individual story impacts other parts of the system. Use realistic test data, use concrete examples as the basis of your tests, and have a lot of whiteboard discussions (or their virtual equivalent) in order to make sure everyone understands the story. Make sure the programmers don't start coding before any tests are written, and use exploratory testing to find gaps between stories.
>
> Remember the end goal and the big picture.

As an agile team, we work in short iterations, so it's important to time-box the time spent writing tests before we start. After each iteration is completed, take the time to evaluate whether more detail up front would have helped. Were there enough tests to keep the team on track? Was there a lot of wasted time because the story was misunderstood? Lisa's team has found it best to write high-level story tests before coding, to write detailed test cases once coding starts, and then to do exploratory testing on the code as it's delivered in order to give the team more information and help make needed adjustments.

Janet worked on a project that had some very intensive calculations. The time spent creating detailed examples and tests before coding started, in order to ensure that the calculations were done correctly, was time well spent. Understanding the domain, and the impact of each story, is critical to assessing the risk and choosing the correct mitigation strategy.

While business-facing tests can help mitigate risks, other types of tests are also critical. For example, many of the most serious issues are usually uncovered during manual exploratory testing. Performance, security, stability, and usability are also sources of risk. Tests to mitigate these other risks are discussed in the chapters on Quadrants 3 and 4.

Experiment and find ways that your team can balance using up-front detail and keeping focused on the big picture. The beauty of short agile iterations is that you have frequent opportunities to evaluate how your process is working so that you can make continual improvements.

TESTABILITY AND AUTOMATION

When programmers on an agile team get ready to do test-driven development, they use the business-facing tests for the story in order to know what to code. Working from tests means that everyone thinks about the best way to design the code to make testing easier. The business-facing tests in Quadrant 2 are expressed as automated tests. They need to be clearly understood, easy to run, and provide quick feedback; otherwise, they won't get used.

It's possible to write manual test scripts for the programmers to execute before they check in code so that they can make sure they satisfied the customer's conditions, but it's not realistic to expect they'll go to that much trouble for long. When meaningful business value has to be delivered every two weeks or every 30 days, information has to be direct and automatic. Inexperienced agile teams might accept the need to drive coding with automated tests at the developer test level more easily than at the customer test level. However, without the customer tests, the programmers have a much harder time knowing what unit tests to write.

Part IV, "Test Automation," will guide you as you develop an automation strategy.

Each agile team must find a process of writing and automating business-facing tests that drive development. Teams that automate only technology-facing tests find that they can have bug-free code that doesn't do what the customer wants. Teams that don't automate any tests will anchor themselves with technical debt.

Quadrant 2 contains a lot of different types of tests and activities. We need the right tools to facilitate gathering, discussing, and communicating examples and tests. Simple tools such as paper or a whiteboard work well for gathering examples if the team is co-located. More sophisticated tools help teams write business-facing tests that guide development in an executable, automatable format. In the next chapter, we'll look at the kinds of tools needed to elicit examples, and to write, communicate, and execute business-facing tests that support the team.

SUMMARY

In this chapter, we looked at ways to support the team during the coding process with business-facing tests.

- In agile development, examples and business-facing tests, rather than traditional requirements documents, tell the team what code to write.
- Working on thin slices of functionality, in short iterations, gives customers the opportunity to see and use the application and adjust their requirements as needed.
- An important area where testers contribute is helping customers express satisfaction conditions and create examples of desired, and undesired, behavior for each story.
- Ask open-ended questions to help the customer think of all of the desired functionality and to prevent hiding important assumptions.
- Help the customers achieve consensus on desired behavior for stories that accommodate the various viewpoints of different parts of the business.
- Help customers develop tools (e.g., a story checklist) to express information such as business satisfaction conditions.
- The development and customer teams should think through all of the parts of the application that a given story affects, keeping the overall system functionality in mind.

- Work with your team to break feature sets into small, manageable stories and paths within stories.
- Follow a pattern of "write test—write code—run tests—learn" in a step-by-step manner, building on each pass through the functionality.
- Use tests and examples to mitigate risks of missing functionality or losing sight of the big picture.
- Driving coding with business-facing tests makes the development team constantly aware of the need to implement a testable application.
- Business-facing tests that support the team must be automated for quick and easy feedback so that teams can deliver value in short iterations.

Chapter 9

TOOLKIT FOR BUSINESS-FACING TESTS THAT SUPPORT THE TEAM

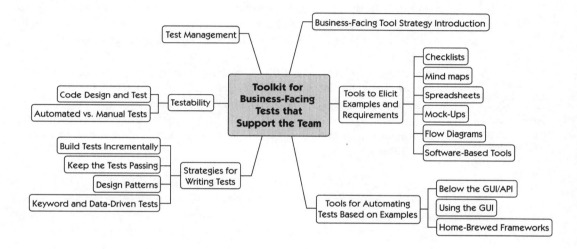

In the previous chapter, we talked about how to approach business or functional testing to support the team in its effort to build the right software. In this chapter, we'll examine some of the tools you can use to help your team succeed with Quadrant 2 tests.

BUSINESS-FACING TEST TOOL STRATEGY

How do we capture the business-facing tests that help the programmers know what to code? Face-to-face conversations between programmers and customers are usually the best way, but even when customers are part of your team, they don't have all day to hang out with programmers and explain features. If any customer or developer team members are in different locations, impromptu hallway conversations might not be feasible. Besides, six months from now, we might want a way to remember why we coded a piece of functionality a certain way. If some of our team members are in different locations, we're definitely going to need some way to share information electronically.

As agile development has gained in popularity, we have more and more tools to help us capture examples and use them to write executable tests. The tools available are changing too fast for us to include an inventory of them in this book, but we can offer some examples of tools and some strategies for using them to help provide business-facing tests that support the team's development of new stories. Some of the tools we discuss here aren't new, or specific to agile development, but they work well in an agile project.

For more information about a general approach to test automation, see Chapter 14, "An Agile Test Automation Strategy."

Your strategy for selecting the tools you need should be based on your team's skill set, the technology your application uses, your team's automation priorities, time and budget constraints, and other concerns unique to your situation. Your selection of a tool or tools should not be based on the latest and coolest tool offered by a salesman. You might need many different tools to solve different problems.

We encourage customers to do some advance preparation and to be ready to explain examples for each story during iteration planning. Testers are in a good position to help customers figure out how to provide the right amount of detail at the beginning of the iteration. It's hard to strike just the right balance.

Lisa's Story

Soon after our team chose to use FitNesse for specifying and automating business-facing tests, our product owner and I tried to make good use of the new tool. We had an extremely complex epic coming up. We spent many hours writing detailed test cases for highly complex business rules weeks in advance of the iteration where the first story of the epic was started. We felt good about getting a running start on developing the new functionality.

When they started working on these stories, the programmers complained that they couldn't get the big picture from these detailed tests. The tests were also designed in a way that was incompatible with the actual code design. I ended up spending hours refactoring them. It wasn't a complete waste of time, because at least I understood the stories well and we had a number of test cases we could use eventually, but it wasn't the right approach for our team. Trial and error has shown us that high-level tests combined with a few examples of desired and undesired behavior are the best way for the programmers to know what to start coding.

—Lisa

Experiment with different levels of up-front detail in test cases to figure out what works best for your team. Whatever level of detail you're after, you need some way to help customers find and express examples of desired system behavior. In the next section, we look at the types of tools that can do that.

Tools to Elicit Examples and Requirements

As we pointed out in Chapter 8, stories are only a starting place for a prolonged conversation about the desired behavior. Having correctly sized stories where the feature, user, and purpose are clearly stated gives us a head start. They aren't very detailed, because as Mike Cohn [2004] points out, it's best to defer collecting details until the story is included in an iteration. Collecting details for a story that might never be included is a waste of resources. We like the "role, function, business value" pattern for user stories that Mike Cohn describes in *User Stories Applied*, as in:

As a (role), I want (function) so that (business value).

This format doesn't work for everyone, so we encourage you to experiment and see what works best in your situation. Regardless of how your user stories read, you need some way to flesh those stories out with examples and business-facing tests that guide development.

One simple story can have a wide-ranging impact, not only on the application, but across the organization, its clients, its associates, vendors, or partners. If we change an API, we have to notify any customers or vendors who might be using it. If we plan a UI change, we want, or might even be contractually obligated, to give a certain amount of advance notice to users. Stories may affect legal concerns or impact external reporting. New features often mean new or updated documentation. Of course, changed functionality is likely to affect other parts of the system.

The software development team, including the testers, should help the customer capture and communicate all of the requirements related to each story or theme. Developing new features, only to be prevented from releasing them for legal reasons or because a business partner wasn't informed in time, is a frustrating waste of time (just ask Lisa!). Lean development teaches us to avoid waste while we develop software.

What tools can help us illustrate desired behavior with examples, brainstorm potential implementations and ripple effects, and create requirements we can turn into tests? Some examples are:

- Checklists
- Mind maps
- Spreadsheets
- Mock-ups
- Flow diagrams
- Software-based tools

The list includes a number of simple tools that aren't unique to agile testing but that shouldn't be neglected. In agile development, simple solutions are usually best. Let's look at these in more detail.

Checklists

Checklists are one way for product owners to make sure they correctly assess and communicate all of the aspects of a story. The product owner for Lisa's team, Steve Perkins, came up with his own "story checklist" to make sure he and the stakeholders think through everything affected by the story. He created a template on the team wiki for this purpose. The checklist specifies the conditions of satisfaction—what the business needs from the story. It also includes impacts on existing functions such as the website, documents, administrative forms, account statements, and other components of the system and the daily operation of the business. The checklist makes sure the team doesn't miss requirements such as data migration, notifications, legal considerations, and communications to vendors and business partners because they forgot to consider them. Figure 9-1 shows a sample story checklist.

Mind Maps

Mind maps are a simple but effective way to search out ideas that that might not occur to you in a simple brainstorming session. Mind maps are diagrams created to represent concepts, words, or ideas linked to a central key concept. We used mind maps to organize this book.

It really doesn't matter whether you purchase a tool such as the one we used or draw on a whiteboard or a big piece of paper. The effect is the same. Mind maps enable you to generate ideas and work in a way that is consistent with the way you think about problems.

As a plan sponsor I can have an updated summary statement so that I can:

SATISFACTION CONDITIONS

1. separate (smart) dividends/interest detail on summary and activity;
2. separate (smart) concessions detail on summary and activity;
3. add balance by fund to investment performance page;
4. update font, point size, style and coloring (see attached prototype)

IMPACT

New Product Website	
Legal contracts	
Documents - Invoices	
Documents - Plan	
Administrative Forms	
Reports - Existing or new	
Account Statements	Revised, smart to not show new details prior to 01/01/2008;

U/I MOCKUPS PREPARED, REVIEW AND FINALIZED

Screens	see attached docs
Help Text Written	

ADDITIONAL ISSUES

Data migration	
Impact on Processing	
Vendor APIs	
Impact if incomplete	
Audit tracking	

TEST CASE OUTLINES

1. test smartness of divs/int and concessions;
2. further systematic testing;
3. test statements with period dates prior to 01/01/2008

COMMUNICATION (INTERNAL/EXTERNAL)

Pieces Written	Notify partners, plan sponsors
Delivery method	

Figure 9-1   Sample story checklist

How about an example? We're discussing the story shown in Figure 9-2.

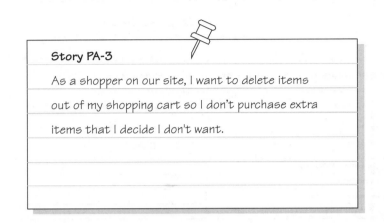

Figure 9-2   Shopping cart delete story

We gather around the whiteboard and start asking questions. Where should the deleted items go? Should they be saved for later approval, or should they just disappear? What should the screen look like after we delete an item? Figure 9-3 shows an example of the sort of mind map we might draw on a whiteboard.

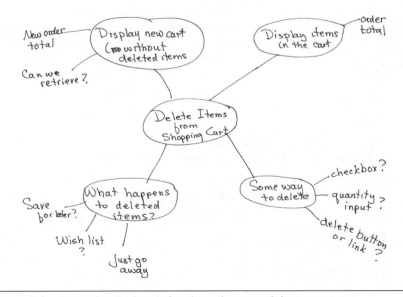

Figure 9-3   Example mind map for shopping cart delete story

Spreadsheets

When possible, tools for specifying business-facing tests should fit well with your business domain. For example, spreadsheets are widely used by financial services companies, so for a project in the financial services area it makes sense to use spreadsheets to define examples of the functionality that a story should deliver.

Customers can write a few high-level test cases to help round out a story prior to the start of the iteration, possibly using some type of checklist. Some customer teams simply write a couple of tests, maybe a happy path and a negative test, on the back of each story card. Some write more detailed examples in spreadsheets or whatever format they're comfortable working with.

Steve Perkins, the product owner for Lisa's team, often illustrates complex calculations and algorithms in spreadsheets, which the team can turn into tests later. Figure 9-4 shows one of his worksheets, which performs calculations on the input values to produce the values in the ADR and ACR columns. This format is easy to get into an automated test framework (refer to Figure 9-8 for the corresponding FitNesse example).

Look at tools already used by your business experts and see whether they can be adapted to document examples of desired feature behavior to help the development team better understand the story.

Janet has worked with several teams that have used spreadsheets as input into their Fit tests. This allows customers to work in a tool that is familiar to them but not waste any effort in translating them to an automation tool.

EE	HCE	Testing Year Eligible Compensation	Testing Year Deferral	Testing Year Match	Catch-up Deferral	ADR	ACR
E-1001	Y	102,500.00	16,000.00	16,000.00	3,000.00	12.68	15.61
E-1002	Y	102,500.00	13,000.00	13,000.00	-	12.68	12.68
E-1003	Y	30,000.00	7,500.00	7,500.00	-	25.00	25.00
E-1004	Y	30,000.00	3,000.00	3,000.00	-	10.00	10.00
E-1005	Y	40,000.00	8,000.00	8,000.00	-	20.00	20.00
E-1006	Y	150,000.00	13,000.00	13,000.00	-	8.67	8.67
E-1007	Y	100,000.00	-	-	-	-	-
						12.72	13.14

Figure 9-4 Spreadsheet example from product owner

Mock-Ups

See Chapter 8 for Gerard Meszaros' description of using paper prototypes and Wizard of Oz testing.

Mock-ups can take many forms. Paper prototypes are a simple but effective way to test how screens will work together. Drawing on a whiteboard can accomplish the same goal, but it can't be passed around. Screenshots from existing applications can form the basis of a discussion about how to add a new feature and where it will fit into the UI. You may have used tools like these in other development methodologies. The big difference in agile development is that we create and discuss the mock-ups just as we're about to start writing the code, rather than weeks or months beforehand. We can be confident that the mock-up represents what the customers want right now.

Lisa's Story

We use simple approaches to creating mock-ups so that we aren't tempted to invest time coding before we're finished working through the mock-up. Often, we draw a UI or workflow on the whiteboard and then take photos of it to upload to our team wiki so our remote team member can also see it. At other times, a customer or our product owner draws the mock-up on paper or modifies an existing UI page or report to show what should be added and changed. The paper mock-ups are scanned in and posted on the wiki.

A picture's worth a thousand words, even in agile software development. Mock-ups show the customer's desires more clearly than a narrative possibly could. They provide a good focal point for discussing desired code behavior.

—Lisa

Figure 9-5 shows an example of a mock-up that Lisa's team used to mock up a new report—simply by marking up an existing report that's similar.

Mock-ups don't need to be fancy or pretty, or to take a lot of time to create. They do need to be understandable to both the customer and developer teams.

Flow Diagrams

Simple diagramming tools are helpful, whether the team is co-located or not. It's often a good idea to capture in a more permanent form a workflow or decision tree worked out during a discussion. Flow diagrams can become the basis of a user scenario that might help you tie two or three user stories together. Let's look at the shipping order story again that we introduced in Chapter 8 (see Figure 9-6).

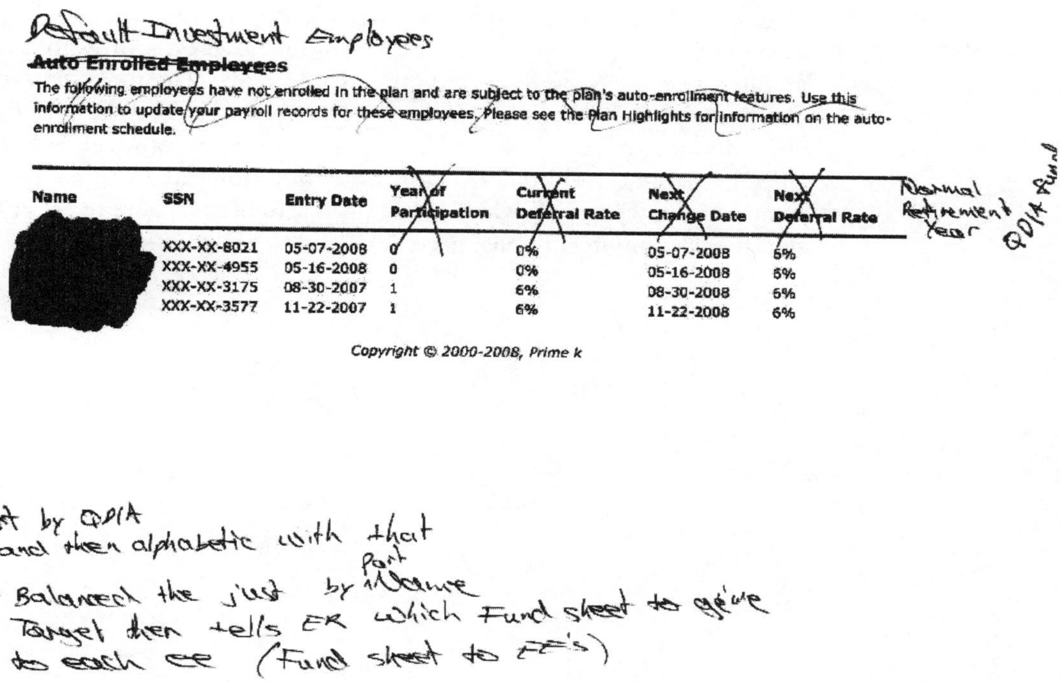

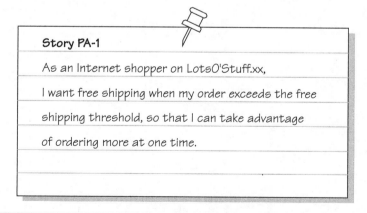

Figure 9-5 Sample report mock-up

Figure 9-6 Story for shipping charges

Figure 9-7 shows a very simple flowchart of a decision process for whether a customer's order is eligible for free shipping based on a threshold order amount. Because we've discussed this story with our customer, we've found out that the customer's order must not only exceed a threshold dollar amount but also must be to one address only, and it must weigh less than a shipping weight threshold. If all of these conditions are satisfied, the customer's order will ship free; otherwise, the customer will have to select from the "choose shipping options" page.

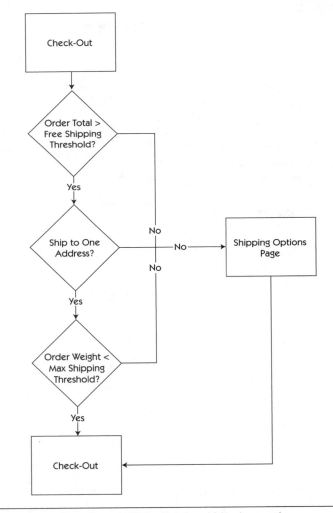

Figure 9-7   Flow chart for qualifying for free shipping option

Visuals such as flow diagrams and mind maps are good ways to describe an overview of a story's functionality, especially if they're drawn by a group of customers, programmers, and testers. In agile development, we create these diagrams as we're about to start writing tests and code. From these, the team can immediately start digging down to the detailed requirements.

Software-Based Tools

If we're in a different location than our customers, we need tools to help us converse with them. Distributed teams tell us that desktop sharing is the number one tool that helps them deal with working in separate locations. Windows NetMeeting and VNC are examples of tools that let two team members in different locations pair-test. Video conferencing tools such as WebEx and Skype enable collaboration and demos between remote teams and customers. Online whiteboards such as Scriblink and interactive whiteboard tools such as Mimeo facilitate distributed whiteboard discussions.

More tools that are geared for direct use by product owners and business experts are becoming available, and many teams develop their own. Tools such as Fit (Framework for Integrated Tests) and FitNesse were designed to facilitate collaboration and communication between the customer and development teams. We're hearing about more teams where the customers actually write the tests in a tool such as those.

Notes from a Distributed Team

Pierre Veragen and Erika Boyer of iLevel by Weyerhaeuser told us that every iteration begins with everyone on the team writing acceptance tests. That's how they start their iteration planning. Most interesting is the fact that their product owners, who are mechanical engineers, write FitNesse tests themselves. Pierre explains that an advantage of a tool such as FitNesse is the ability to use their own domain language in the FitNesse tests. It doesn't matter what they end up choosing as a UI. They can test all of their complex calculations in the tests.

With this process, tests can be written before writing the testing code or the system under test. It's true test-driven development. Behavior changes and bug fixes can follow.

Some teams build their own frameworks that allow customers, business analysts, and testers to document examples that can be directly turned into executable tests. These are often based on open source tools such as xUnit, Fit, Selenium, and Watir. We like this approach, because it saves time and resources. When you're delivering production-ready code in short iterations, you need a streamlined process.

Online forum tools are a good alternative to email conversations for ongoing discussions about features or technical concerns, especially for teams that don't all sit together. Emails often get missed or lost, people have to remember to choose "Reply all," and it can be hard to put together the details of the discussion later. Lisa's team uses an online forum to elicit opinions about different tools, propose different behavior for features, and conduct philosophical discussions such as whether to track defects.

Finding the right electronic tools is particularly vital for distributed teams. Instant messaging, the telephone, VoIP, and Skype help us communicate, but they lack the visual component. Some global teams ask their members to meet at nonstandard hours so that they can have real-time conversations, but frameworks for written and visual communication are still critical.

Wikis are a common tool used to enhance communication and record discussions and decisions. Wikis enable users to edit web page content in a web browser. Users can add hyperlinks and easily create new pages. You can upload mock-ups, samples, and pictures of whiteboard drawings and make them easily visible on Wiki pages. The hierarchical organization can get tricky to maintain, but there are lots of open source and vendor wiki software packages available that make managing your knowledgebase and sharing information easier to administer. If your wiki knowledgebase has grown to the point where it's hard to find anything, hire a technical writer to transform it into organized, usable documentation.

Open source and commercial tools provide ways to let teams collaborate on requirements and test cases online. We can't emphasize enough the need for you to identify tools that might be helpful, to experiment with them for a few iterations, and to decide how well they work for you. Your team's needs will change with time, so always be open to trying new techniques and frameworks.

These tools help create the conversation about the story. With these techniques, and as much real-time conversation and visual sharing as we can manage, we can define the right product from the get-go.

TOOLS FOR AUTOMATING TESTS BASED ON EXAMPLES

What about test tools? We like the collaboration inherent with tools such as Fit and FitNesse. However, in our opinion, any tool that gets testers and programmers, programmers and customers, and testers and customers talking is a great one. We know teams where customers actually write tests in Fit, Fit-Nesse, Expect, or other tools. This works when the tool has been set up in a manner that's clear to everyone writing tests, with the domain language easy to understand and the appropriate fixtures provided.

Tools to Test below the GUI and API Level

There are a multitude of open source tools that enable you to test below the GUI or at the API layer. We are listing just a few, but your team will need to determine the right tool for you.

Unit-Level Test Tools

Some teams use the xUnit tools such as JUnit or NUnit for business-facing tests as well as technology-facing tests. If the testers and customers are comfortable with these tools, and they provide for all of the functional testing behind the GUI needed, they're fine. To make these tools more customer-friendly, teams might build a framework on top of the unit-level tools that testers and customers can use to specify tests.

Janet has worked on a couple of applications like that. One was a message handling system that was being deployed in an organization. The programmers used JUnit for all of the component and integration testing. They built a load test framework that could make use of the JUnit tests, so no other testing tools were needed. The GUI front end was so small that Janet was able to test it manually. It made no sense to automate the GUI testing in this case.

Behavior-driven development (BDD) tools are also suited to this purpose, because they use a more natural language for specifying the tests. Behavior-driven development is a variation of test-driven development, pioneered by Dan North [2006], and evolved by many others. It's related to domain-driven design, with a focus on the domain rather than on the technology, and driving design with a model. Instead of the word "test" or "assert," BDD uses the word "should." By thinking in terms of behavior, it's natural to write specifications ahead of code. Test specifications use a domain-specific language to provide tests that customers can read but that can also be easily automated.

Some of the many BDD tools available as of this writing include easyb and JBehave for the Java platform, NBehave and NSpec for .NET, and RSpec for Ruby. These tools, like the XUnit tools, are intended for use by programmers to guide coding, but they can also be used to express business-facing tests that drive development, involving customers more closely in the development process.

Behavior-Driven Development

Andrew Glover, president of Stelligent Incorporated and author of books including *Continuous Integration* and *Java Testing Patterns*, explains the thinking behind one of the BDD tools, easyb.

> `assertEquals(42.50, order.price(), 0.0)`. Without examining the context in which this statement appears, this code is somewhat incomprehensible. Now imagine you don't even read code—that is, you are a stakeholder asking (actually *paying*) for new features. The previous code statement might as well be Farsi (assuming you can't actually read Farsi!).
>
> `order.price().shouldBe 42.50`. While the context in which this statement appears is still absent, this line of code is a bit more coherent. In fact, it reads like a normal sentence (and this time knowledge of Farsi isn't required!). Stakeholders, in this case, could understand this code if they chose to read it; on top of that, it turns out that this line of code essentially matches what they asked for in the first place. This line of code describes behavior in a more literal manner too—the code uses a normal everyday phrase like `shouldBe`, which is distinctly different than the previously written `assertEquals`.
>
> Both lines of code from the previous paragraphs convey the same meaning and indeed validate the same requirement, yet the latter one comes awfully close to leveraging the customer's language. This is a fundamental point of the notion of behavior-driven development, which strives to more appropriately validate a software system by thinking in terms of the term "should" rather than test. In fact, by focusing on behavior and closely modeling behavior after what stakeholders ask for, behavior-driven development converges on the idea of executable documentation. Indeed, through leveraging a stakeholder's language, there is a decreased impedance mismatch between what he wants and what he ultimately receives; moreover, employing a stakeholder's language facilitates a deeper level of collaboration between all parties. Listen to how a conversation might go:
>
> > **Stakeholder:** For the next release of our online store, our Gold-level customers should receive a discount when they make a purchase.
> >
> > **Developer:** What kind of discount—what criteria do they have to meet in order to receive it?
> >
> > **Stakeholder:** When they have at least $50 dollars in their shopping cart.
> >
> > **Developer:** Does the discount increase based upon the amount, or is it fixed regardless of the value of the shopping cart?
> >
> > **Stakeholder:** Good question—the discount is fixed at 15% regardless of price. So, given a Gold-level customer, when the shopping cart totals $50 or more, it should receive a 15% discount off the total price.

The last statement of the stakeholder is key—note how the requirement has been specified and the means for validating it. In fact, the stakeholder has essentially narrated a specific scenario in a larger story related to discounts.

Given this scenario, a developer can take the stakeholder's comments— word for word—and execute them. For example, one behavior-driven development framework, dubbed easyb, facilitates system validation through a domain-specific language that supports stories and scenarios. For example:

```
scenario "Gold-level customer with $50 in shopping cart", {
  given " a Gold-level customer"
  when "their shopping cart totals $50 or more"
  then " they should receive a 15% discount off the total price"
}
```

Of course, this particular scenario doesn't actually do anything (other than capturing the stakeholder's requirements, which is still quite important!); consequently, it is considered pending. This status alone conveys valuable information—stakeholders can, first and foremost, see their words as a means to validate their requests, and secondly, gauge if their requirement has been fulfilled. After this scenario has been implemented, it can, of course, take on two other states—success or failure, both of which serve to convey further status information to interested parties.

Now, with a collaborative scenario defined, development can proceed to the implementation—the beauty in this case is that they can directly implement the desired behavior inline with the requirements, like this:

```
scenario "Gold-level customer with $50 in shopping cart", {
  given "a Gold-level customer", {
        customer = new GoldCustomer()
        }
  when "their shopping cart totals $50 or more", {
        customer.shoppingCart << new Item("widget", 50.00)
  }
  then "they should receive a 15% discount off the total price" , {
        customer.orderPrice.shouldBe 42.50
        }
}
```

This scenario is now executable within the context of the application it serves to validate! The scenario leverages the customer's exact words, too; what's more, regardless of the customer's ability to read code, the code itself leverages natural language: `customer.orderPrice.shouldBe 42.50`.

By leveraging the customer's language, the customer has the ability to collaboratively facilitate in validating the system he or she wants built. Also, with development leveraging the stakeholders' language, there is a direct link between what stakeholders ask for and what they receive. And you don't even need to understand Farsi to see the benefit in that.

Two of the most common questions we're asked by new agile teams are, "What about documentation?" and "How can test automation keep up with development in two-week iterations?" Tools such as easyb answer that question with executable documentation using a domain-specific language that everyone on both the customer and developer teams understands.

The goal of business-facing tests that support the team is to promote communication and collaboration between customers and developers, and to enable teams to deliver real value in each iteration. Some teams do this best with unit-level tools, and others adapt better to functional-level test tools.

API-Layer Functional Test Tools

Before Lisa joined her first agile team, testing "behind the GUI" was a concept that sounded good, but she'd never had the opportunity to try it. Fit, and FitNesse, which is built on top of Fit, are functional test tools that grew from the need for the customer team to be able to write and understand the business-facing tests that drive development. With these tools, teams can test business logic without involving the presentation layer.

Fit and FitNesse. Fit (Framework for Integrated Tests) is an open source testing framework that promotes collaboration, which makes it a good tool to help refine requirements. The invention of Ward Cunningham, Fit has enjoyed an illustrious roster of contributing developers. Fit enables customers, testers, and programmers to use examples to specify what they expect the system to do. When the tests run, Fit automatically compares customers' expectations to actual results.

With Fit, customers can provide guidance using their subject matter expertise to define the examples that the programmers can code against. The programmers participate by writing the fixtures that do the actual checks against the examples. These fixtures use the data specified in the examples to run with the actual program.

Fit tests are automated by fixtures that pass the test inputs to the production code and then accept the outputs, which it then compares with expected results. The test results are color-coded, so it's easy to spot a failure or exception.

Learn more about
Fit at fit.c2.com.

Fit tests are written as HTML tables, but teams can customize Fit so that tests can be written in spreadsheets or whatever form the customers, testers, and analysts find usable.

Learn more about
FitNesse at
www.fitnesse.org.

FitNesse is a web server, a wiki, and a software testing tool that is based on Fit. Originally developed by Robert C. "Uncle Bob" Martin and Micah Martin, it's an open source tool with an active developer community. The main difference between FitNesse and Fit is that FitNesse tests are written in wiki markup instead of HTML tables, which some users find easier. It also supports creating tests in spreadsheets and importing those into the tests.

Figure 9-8 shows part of the FitNesse test that was built from the example in Figure 9-4. More inputs were added to make the production code run, but the essential test data is from the spreadsheet. The test results are color-coded green when they pass, red when they fail.

Another benefit of a Fit or FitNesse type of tool is that it promotes collaboration among different team members in order to come up with the right tests

Add Employees

Build Employees Fixture												
userId	dob	doh	doe	dot	directOwnerPct	lookbackTotalOwnerPct	lookbackAnnualComp	annualComp	deferral	eligibleComp	match	add!
1001	01-01-1950	01-01-1993	01-01-1994	null	0	0	101500.00	102500.00	16000.00	102500.00	16000.00	true
1002	01-01-1960	01-01-1993	01-01-1994	null	4	3	102500.00	102500.00	13000.00	102500.00	13000.00	true
1003	01-01-1960	01-01-1993	01-01-1994	null	5.01	5.01	30000.00	30000.00	7500.00	30000.00	7500.00	true
1004	01-01-1960	01-01-1993	01-01-1994	null	10	10	20000.00	30000.00	3000.00	30000.00	3000.00	true
1005	01-01-1960	01-01-1993	01-01-1994	null	8	0	40000.00	40000.00	8000.00	40000.00	8000.00	true
1006	01-01-1960	01-01-1993	01-01-1994	null	5.01	0	150000.00	150000.00	13000.00	150000.00	13000.00	true
1007	01-01-1960	01-01-1993	01-01-1994	null	0	0	100000.00	100000	0	100000	0	true
1008	01-01-1960	01-01-1993	01-01-1994	null	0	0	40000.00	50000.00	3000.00	50000.00	3000.00	true

OPERATE ON INPUT BY RUNNING ADP TEST

Operate Adp Test Fixture
operate!
true

MAKE ASSERTIONS ABOUT ADP TEST RESULTS

Check Employee Fixture				
userId	isHce?	isEligible?	adr?	acr?
1001	true	true	12.682927	15.61
1002	true	true	12.682927	12.68
1003	true	true	25.00	25
1004	true	true	10.00	10
1005	true	true	20.00	20
1006	true	true	8.666667	8.67
1007	true	true	0	0
1008	false	true	6	6

Figure 9-8 Automated FitNesse test from customer example

to guide development. Customers, programmers, testers, and others work together to specify and automate the tests.

Testing Web Services.   Web services is just another form of an API that enables other applications to access your application. Let's talk about some of the tools you can use to test various inputs into your system.

CrossCheck. CrossCheck is one example of a tool for testing web services. You supply the WSDL (Web Services Description Language); CrossCheck compiles the page and then presents you with a tabbed menu that contains textboxes for you to fill in. It has a Run mode where you can add your tests to a suite and then run the suite. Neither Lisa or Janet have tried this tool, but it was noted on the Yahoo agile-testing group as a tool to use for testing web services if you were running the same data through each time.

Ruby Test::Unit. One project Janet was on used Ruby's unit testing framework, Test::Unit, to test web services, with great success. In fact, the team was able to test early to give the programmers immediate feedback, which helped with the final design.

soapUI. Another tool suggested for testing web services is soapUI. It has a steep learning curve but can be used for performance and load testing. Because it can loop though rows in an Excel spreadsheet or text file, it can be used for data-driven testing.

See the "System Test" example in Chapter 12, "Summary of Testing Quadrants," to see how Janet's team used Ruby Test::Unit to test web services.

Tests that work at the layers below the presentation layer are well suited for writing and automating customer tests that guide coding. Some practitioners haven't gotten the value they expected from story test-driven development. Brian Marick [2008] hypothesized that an application built with programmer test-driven development, example-heavy business-facing design that relies heavily on whiteboard discussions, a small set of automated sanity tests, and lots of exploratory testing could be a less expensive and equally effective approach. Whichever approach you take, if you're testing an application with a user interface, you'll need some automation at the GUI level.

Tools for Testing through the GUI

Wait a minute. How can we use GUI tests to drive development, because the GUI won't be ready until the story is complete? It sound counterintuitive, but automated GUI tests are important to help us while we're developing new functionality. Test frameworks can be used to specify test cases for a GUI tool before the code is written. In addition, you can automate GUI tests be-

A Tool Selection Rationale

David Reed, a test automation engineer, and his team went with soapUI Pro to automate testing for their web services. Here are some reasons he gave for choosing this particular tool.

- It has an open source version, so you can try it out it for free. You can learn it, kick the tires, expand stuff, and learn its strengths and weaknesses.
- It was easy to figure out what requests to make for what service.
- The assertions provided for verifying the results from requests are great and expandable. One really helpful one is verifying that the response comes back in an acceptable amount of time, raising an error if it doesn't.
- The Pro version takes a lot of the hassle out of designing XPath queries to verify results. It also adds some nice touches for retrieving database data.
- It's expandable with Groovy, a Java-based scripting language. (They're working on a Java application, so it pays to have Java-friendly tools.)
- Developers can use it without sneering at it as a "test tool."
- It's easily integrated with our continuous integration environment.
- It has a feature to check code coverage.
- The price is right.

fore coding is finished, either by using HTML mock-ups or by developing an end-to-end bare-bones slice through all of the screens that simply navigates but doesn't provide all of the functionality yet. Even if you're not using a lot of automated story tests to drive development, manual exploratory testing that helps us learn about the functionality and provides immediate feedback gets pretty tedious and slow without any assistance from automation. Let's look at the types of GUI test tools that help drive development using business-facing tests.

Record/Playback Tools

Record/playback tools are appealing because you can usually learn how to record a script and play it back quickly, and you can create lots of scripts in a short time. However, they have drawbacks. Early GUI test tools recorded mouse movements using X-Y screen coordinates. Scripts using those tools might also be sensitive to changes in screen resolution, color depth, and even where the window is placed on the screen.

Most modern GUI test tools use objects to recognize the controls in a graphical application, like buttons, menus, and text input widgets, so they can refer to them symbolically rather than with raw screen coordinates. This makes the application much more testable, because it's more robust standing up to changes. A button might move to a different part of the screen, but the test can still find it based on its object name.

Even with improved object recognition, scripts created with record/playback are usually brittle and expensive to maintain. Recording can be a good way to start creating a script. Testers or programmers who know the tool's scripting language can refactor the recorded script into an object-oriented model that's easier to use and maintain. Historically, record/playback tools used proprietary scripting languages, which programmers aren't interested in learning. It's also more difficult to change the design patterns used in the tests.

Some script-based tools such as the ones we'll talk about in the next few sections offer a record feature to help people get a quick start on writing the test script. However, with those tools, the recorded scripts aren't intended for straight playback; they're just a starting point to creating a well-designed and easily maintained suite of tests.

Many agile teams prefer tools and scripting languages that let them create their own domain-specific language (DSL). This makes tests much easier for business experts to understand and even write. Let's look at some of these next.

Agile Open Source Test Tools

Each of the tools in this section was originally written by an agile development team that needed a GUI test tool and couldn't find any third-party tools that worked for its situation. With these tools, you can write scripts that use web applications just like a human user. They fill in text fields, select from lists, and click checkboxes and buttons. They provide a variety of ways to verify correct navigation and contents of pages, such as tool-specific verify steps or XPath. Some of these tools have a higher learning curve than simple record/playback tools, but the extra investment of time usually pays off in scripts with a low total cost of ownership.

Ruby with Watir. Watir (Web Application Testing in Ruby) is a simple open source Ruby library for automating web browsers that works with Internet Explorer on Windows. There are different flavors for other browsers, including FireWatir for Firefox and SafariWatir for Safari.

Janet's Story

I worked on a project that developed a three-layer test framework using Ruby and Watir. The first layer was a common set of libraries, and the second layer was to access the pages and provide navigation. The third and top layer created a domain language using fixture-type methods that mapped to the business needs. This allowed the manual testers to write high-level automated tests for workflows before coding was completed. If a fixture didn't exist because of new functionality, the test could be created and the action word for the missing fixture could be "dummied" in. As soon as the fixture was coded, the test could be run as an acceptance test.

A very simple example of using Ruby with Watir incorporates the idea of DSL. Methods were created to simplify the tests so that any of the testers could actually create an automated script without knowing any Ruby or Watir.

This next example shows a test, and then two of the methods used in the test.

```
def test_create_new_user

    login 'administrator','admin'
    navigate_to_tab 'Manage Users'
    click_button "Create New User"
    set_text_field "userFirstNameInput", "Ruby"
    set_text_field "userLastNameInput", "RubyTester"
    click_button "Save Changes"
    verify_text "Saved changes"
end


# methods created to support easier test writing
def navigate_to_tab(menuItemName)
    @browser.link(:text,menuItemName).click
  end

def set_text_field(id, value)
    @browser.text_field(:id,id).set value
  end
```

A third level could easily be added if `create_new_user` was called more than once. Just extract the common code that the test could call:

```
create_new_user (Ruby, RubyTester)
```

These tests were well suited to guiding development and providing quick feedback. Making tests easy for testers and customers to write, while keeping the automation framework designed for optimum maintainability, reduced the total cost of ownership of the tests.

—Janet

There are always drawbacks to any tool you use. For example, there are limitations to using objects. Sometimes programmers use custom controls or a new toolkit that your tool might not understand.

Janet's Story

I started a new job as QA manager, and after much deliberation we decided to drop the vendor tool that the team had been using for a couple of years. We could not figure out what tests were actually being run, or what the real coverage was. We decided to start automating the tests using Ruby and Watir. The automation went fairly quickly at first, but then the tests started failing. We spent a lot of time changing the tests to reflect new object names. The developers were just using the default WebLogic object names, which would change every time a new object was added to the page. The testers went to the developers to ask if they could change the way they were coding. It took a little convincing, but when the developers realized the problems their practice was causing, they changed their habits. Over time, all of the defaults were changed, and each object had an assigned name. The tests became much more robust, and we spent much less time in maintenance mode.

—Janet

Implementing a new test automation tool usually requires some experimentation to get a good balance of testable code and well-designed test scripts. Involving the whole team makes this much easier. Watir is one example of a GUI test tool that we've found is well suited to agile projects. Let's look at a couple more, Selenium and Canoo WebTest.

Selenium.   Selenium is another open source tool, actually a suite of tools, for testing web applications. The tests can be written as HTML tables or coded in a number of popular programming languages, and can be run directly in most modern web browsers. A Firefox plug-in called "Selenium IDE" provides a way to learn the tool quickly. A recorder is provided to help create the tests, including writing assertions. Tests can be written in several different common programming and scripting languages, including Java, C#, and Ruby.

See Chapter 14, "An Agile Test Automation Strategy," for an example of using Selenium RC to create a domain-specific test automation framework.

Canoo WebTest.   In WebTest scripts, tests are specified as "steps" in XML files, simulating a user's actions through a web UI. Here's an example of how a WebTest script might invoke a page and verify the results:

```
<setInputField description="set query" name="q" value="Agile Tester"/>
<clickButton description="submit query" label="Google Search"/>
<verifyText description="check for result" text="Lisa Crispin" />
<verifyText description="check for result" text="Janet Gregory" />
```

Rather than driving an actual browser, as Selenium and Watir do, WebTest simulates the desired browser using HtmlUnit. The advantage of specifying tests as opposed to coding test scripts, is because there's no logic in them, you don't have to test the test.

My team chose WebTest to automate smoke tests for our legacy application for several reasons. Because the scripts are written in XML, the programmers on the team were comfortable using the tool. It uses Ant to run the tests, so integrating it into the continuous build process was simple. It's easy to learn, and the tests can be designed in a modular fashion, so they're fairly easy to maintain. WebTest supports testing PDF files, emails, and Excel files, all of which are widely used in our application.

Being accustomed to powerful commercial test tools, I was skeptical of the concept of specifying tests, as opposed to programming them. I was amazed at how effective the simple tests were at catching regression bugs. It's possible to put logic into the tests using Groovy or other scripting languages, but we've only found the need in a few cases.

Writing a few tests per iteration, I automated smoke tests for all of the critical areas of our application in eight months. These simple tests find regression bugs regularly. We refactor the tests frequently, so they are relatively easy to maintain. Our ROI on these tests has been tremendous.

—Lisa

Selenium, WebTest, and Watir are just three examples of the many open source tools available for GUI testing as of the time we wrote this book. Many teams write their own test automation frameworks. Let's look at an example in the next section.

"Home-Brewed" Test Automation Tools

Bret Pettichord [2004] coined the term "home-brewed" for the tools agile teams create to meet their own unique testing needs. This allows even more customization than an open source tool. The goal of these tools is usually to provide a way for nontechnical customer team members and testers to write tests that are actually executable by the automated tool. Home-brewed tools are tailored to the exact needs of the project. They can be designed to minimize the total cost of ownership. They're often built on top of existing open source tools.

Janet has been involved in a few projects that have used Ruby and Watir to create a full framework for functional testing. These frameworks allowed customers to specify tests that were then turned into a functional regression suite.

No test tool guarantees success. In fact, the history of test automation is littered with failed attempts. Having the whole team think about the best tools to use is a big help, but no matter what tool you use, you need a smart approach to writing tests. We'll discuss that in the next section.

PAS Functional Testing

This next story is about one project Janet worked on that enjoyed success with home-brewed test automation.

PAS is a production accounting application for the oil and gas industry. Using gross meter readings and contract agreements, it must calculate ownership of the various products down to a very precise level (i.e., the components in gas). There are literally thousands of interactions between the combinations available in configuring the system and the actual outputs visible to a user. Given the large number of interactions, PAS has employed many complementary strategies for testing.

Joseph King, one of the initial programmers and agile coach for the team, tells us the story of how they accomplished their functional testing.

> At the lowest level, there are developer functional tests that exercise specific functions via an API and verify the results using another read-only user API. There are currently over 24,000 tests implemented in JUnit that every developer must run before they can "check in" their changes to the source code.
>
> The next level is a set of GUI tests that test the marshalling of user data back and forth to the API, particularly around "master-data" creation and updates. There are currently over 500 of these tests implemented using Watij (an open source library similar to Watir but using Java) and JUnit that run multiple times a day.
>
> The final level of testing is a set of integration tests created by the users that run in a Fit-like harness. Users identify dense test cases that reflect real-world cases covering many of the functions that work together to produce financial and regulatory outputs. These test cases are then transcribed into import templates and then processed using a domain language that mirrors the way end customers think about their processes.
>
> For example, after an end customer has created the configuration of facilities and contracts they wish to exercise in their test, they work with a developer to use the domain language to process their facilities in the correct order. The end users also supply a set of expected outputs that are then verified using a read-only API. These outputs can contain thousands of numbers, any of which can change for seemingly minor reasons in an evolving product. It is a constant challenge to sort through what is a legitimate business change from what is a defect. There are currently over 400 integration tests, and they run twice per day, providing feedback to the end customers and developers.
>
> Exploratory testing is done continuously throughout the development cycle and is augmented at the end of releases.
>
> Our first attempt at PASFIT (which is what we called the functional test framework) was a spreadsheet of color-coded inputs and outputs. We

then generated Java code based on the color of the cells to create the data in PAS. That proved difficult to maintain, partly because the application was in major flux both at the GUI and database level.

Our next iteration of PASFIT didn't evolve for nearly a year after the previous attempt. After we had a more stable set of database views and GUI, we were able to create an engine that used simple imperative language (i.e., a script) to do actions with arguments against a GUI (e.g., Go to Balancing Page, Balance Battery: Oil, Water). The script evolved into following the thought process of a production accountant and became a domain-specific language. The engine was written using Ruby and Watir, and an instruction from the script was basically a Ruby method that was invoked dynamically so that it was easy to update. After the script ran, the framework then loaded a snapshot of the views that the test wished to compare and did a simple row-by-row, cell-by-cell comparison of what was to be asserted and what actually happened. Eventually this was enhanced in the spreadsheet to use Pivot tables to enable the users to focus in on only the results they wished to assert for their test. All in all it has been quite successful, although the requirements for our application mean that 300 tests take about 12 hours to run, which is a long time.

Getting the business more involved in maintaining the regression tests has also been difficult, but when it happens it is very good. Currently, we have a stand-up where the business users and the developers meet for 15 minutes to pick up any of the scenario tests that are breaking that day. It is quite effective in that people often know when they come to the stand-up what they might have broken the day before. Future enhancements are likely to include asserting against actual user reports instead of the views and running a migration each night against the scenario script.

PASFIT achieved a balance between letting business experts write tests in a DSL and automating those tests with a highly complex application. Success came with some trial and error. Teams that write their own test frameworks need time to experiment to find the right solution for both the business and the development team.

STRATEGIES FOR WRITING TESTS

The best tools in the world won't help if you don't use them wisely. Test tools might make it very easy to specify tests, but whether you're specifying the right tests at the right time is up to you. Lisa's team found that too much detail up front clouded the big picture to such a degree that the programmers didn't know what to code. This won't be true for every team, and at some point we do need details. The latest time to provide them is when a programmer picks up a coding task card and starts working on a story.

Writing detailed test cases that communicate desired behavior effectively requires both art and science. Poorly expressed scenarios and poorly designed test cases can create more confusion than they resolve. Experiment so that you can find the right level of detail and the right test design for each story. Let's look at some strategies to help you use tools successfully to write useful business-facing tests.

Build Tests Incrementally

After we have defined our high-level acceptance tests so that the programmer knows what to start coding, we can start elaborating on the rest of the story tests. We can work closely with the programmer to ensure we automate the best possible way.

When a programmer starts working on the programming tasks for a story, start writing detailed tests. For those of us who enjoy testing, it's tempting to go for the biggest "smells" right away, the areas where we think the code might be fragile. Resist the temptation. Make sure the most obvious use case is working first. Write a simple, happy path automated test to show the code accomplishes the most basic task that it should. After that test passes, you can start getting more creative. Writing the business-facing tests is an iterative process.

Lisa's Story

I start writing executable business-facing tests that support the team by writing a simple FitNesse test based on examples that the product owner provides. I show this to the programmer working on the code. He can make suggestions for changes right then, or he might modify the test himself as appropriate when he's ready to automate it. Discussing the test often leads the programmer to realize he missed or misunderstood a requirement. We might need another three-way conversation with the customer. The programmer updates the code accordingly. We can also show the test to the product owner to make sure we captured the behavior correctly.

Chapter 18, "Coding and Testing," goes into more detail about how testers and programmers work together to test and code.

After the simple test passes, I write more tests, covering more business rules. I write some more complex tests, run them, and the programmer updates the code or tests as needed. The story is filling out to deliver all of the desired value.

—Lisa

Confine each test to one business rule or condition. At some point you can automate or manually perform more complex scenarios, but start by covering each condition with a simple test. If you've followed our recommended thin slice or steel thread pattern, the first set of tests should prove the first thin slice end-to-end. As your automated tests pass, add them to the regression suite that runs in a frequent build process.

Keep the Tests Passing

After a test passes, it shouldn't fail unless the requirements were changed. If that happens, the test should be updated before the code is altered. Of course, if a test was forgotten as part of a requirement change, we expect it to fail. It did its job as change detector. At this time, the test will likely need to change to get it passing.

Whenever a test fails in a continuous integration and build process, the team's highest priority (other than a critical production problem) should be to get the build passing again. Don't comment out the failing test and fix it later; that's the road to perdition. Soon you'll have dozens of commented-out tests and a lot of technical debt. Everyone on the team should stop what they're doing and make sure the build goes "green" again. Determine if a bug has been introduced, or if the test simply needs to be updated to accommodate intentionally changed behavior. Fix the problem, check it in, and make sure all of the tests pass.

Lisa's Story   Early on in our agile efforts, my team wasn't fixing broken tests fast enough. I wrote "Tests are not temporary!" on the whiteboard to remind everyone that once a test passes, it needs to keep passing. A few days later, the words "but testers are!" had been added to get back at me. We did get much better at keeping our builds "green" after that.

—Lisa

One passing test leads to another. Keep your tests current and maintainable with refactoring. Extend them to cover other test cases. The various combinations and scenarios might or might not become part of the regression suite after they pass. We want our regression suite to run in a timely manner, and having too many tests for edge cases would slow it down.

Use Appropriate Test Design Patterns

When designing tests, look at different patterns and choose the ones that work for you. Keep them as simple as you can. Before you can design tests, you have to identify the ones you need. Pierre Veragen coined the term *test genesis patterns* to note the patterns that help you think of tests. Examples and use cases feed into our test genesis patterns.

Build/Operate/Check

Lisa's team often goes with a build/operate/check pattern: Build the input data, in memory or actually in the database, depending on the purpose of the test; invoke the production code to operate on those inputs; and check the results of that operation. Some teams call this setup/execute/validate. For example, to test the invoice presented to a new account holder, set up the fees to be charged, input the properties of the account that relate to fee amounts, run the code that calculates the fees, and then check to see what fees were actually charged. See Figure 9-9 for an example of a test that sets up a loan with a specified amount, interest rate, term, payment frequency, and service start date and then checks the resulting amortization schedule. The test data is built in memory, which makes for a speedy test. A "teardown" fixture (not shown) removes the test data from memory so it won't interfere with subsequent tests.

If there's a need to test the application's data access layer, tests can run using an actual database. Each test can insert the test data it needs, operate on it, check results, and delete the data. Testing with data in a real database can be a means of automating a test against legacy code whose data access and business logic layers aren't easily separated.

BUILD THE DATA

Loan Fixture					
loanAmount	interestRate	term	frequency	serviceStartDate	amortize!
1000	6	1	Monthly	10-01-2005	true

CHECK THE RESULTS

Check Loan Amortization Fixture				
paymentNumber	paymentAmount	principalAmount	interestAmount	endingBalance
1	86.07	81.07	5.00	918.93
2	86.07	81.48	4.59	837.45
3	86.07	81.88	4.19	755.57
4	86.07	82.29	3.78	673.28
5	86.07	82.70	3.37	590.58
6	86.07	83.12	2.95	507.46
7	86.07	83.53	2.54	423.93
8	86.07	83.95	2.12	339.98
9	86.07	84.37	1.70	255.61
10	86.07	84.79	1.28	170.82
11	86.07	85.22	0.85	85.60
12	86.03	85.60	0.43	0.00

Figure 9-9   Example test with build/operate/check pattern

Notice that the "check" table in the example uses a declarative style, with each row forming an independent test case, without changing the state of the system. Each row in our example tests a line in the loan amortization schedule. In the next section, we'll look at patterns that are in a procedural style, with steps that change or test the state of the system.

Time-Based, Activity, and Event Patterns

Sometimes a timeline-based procedural pattern reflects the business better. For example, when testing a loan, we want to make sure interest and principal are applied correctly for each payment. The amount of interest depends on the date the payment was received and the date of the last payment processed. We want a test that simulates taking out a loan for a certain dollar amount, interest rate, and time period, and then over time simulates the borrower sending in payments, which are received and processed. Figure 9-10 shows a simple example of a FitLibrary "DoFixture" test that takes out a loan, checks the payment amount, posts the borrower's payments, receives the payments and processes them, and then checks the interest, principal, and loan balance amount. It also checks the loan default state.

Depending on the domain, a time- or event-based approach might simulate the actual business processes better and be more understandable to business experts than a declarative type test. Other customers might find the declarative table style simpler to understand, because it hides the procedural details. Different patterns work best for different situations, so experiment with them.

1. Take out a loan
2. Check the calculated loan payment
3. Post the payment, then receive it
4. Settle and confirm the payment
5. Check the interest, principal, loan balance and default state

Loan Processing Fixture										
take loan in the amount of	1000		with interest rate	6.0		frequency	Monthly	and term	1	year with loan origination date	12-31-2005
check		periodic payment is	86.07							
post payment	1		of	86.07	on	01-30-2006				
receive payment	1		of	86.07	on	01-31-2006				
settle and confirm payment	1									
check		interest applied for	1		is	5.10				
check		principal applied for	1		is	80.97				
check		loan balance is	919.03							
as of		02-01-2006								
check		default state is	Not in Default							

Figure 9-10 Sample time-based test

Learning More

Your team should educate itself on test patterns that help drive programming. Finding the right pattern for each type of test ensures the test communicates clearly, is easy to maintain, and runs in an optimal amount of time. See the bibliography for more invaluable resources on test design, such as Gerard Meszaros's *xUnit Test Patterns: Refactoring Test Code.*

Bring programmers and testers together to brainstorm test approaches and to help decide what tests can be automated and how the code should be designed to support testing. Business logic and algorithms should be accessible by test fixtures, without having to go through a user interface or batch scheduling process. This enables test-driven development, which in turn produces testable architecture.

A common approach to automating tests is by driving tests with keywords or action words. This can be used with tools such as Fit and FitNesse, or Ruby with Watir. We'll explain this next.

Keyword and Data-Driven Tests

Data-driven testing is a tool that can help reduce test maintenance and enable you to share your test automation with manual testers. There are many times when you want to run the same test code over and over, repeating only the inputs and expected results. Spreadsheets or tables, such as those supported by Fit, are excellent ways to specify inputs. The test fixture, method, or script can loop through each data value one at a time, matching expected results to actual results. By using data-driven tests, you are actually using examples to show what the application is supposed to do.

Keyword-driven testing is another tool used in automated testing, where predefined keywords are used to define actions. These actions correspond to a process related to the application. It is the first step in creating a domain testing language. These keywords (or action words) represent a very simple specification language that non-programmers can use to develop automated tests. You still need programmers or technical automation specialists to implement the fixtures that the action words act on. If these keywords are extended to emulate the domain language, customers and nontechnical testers can specify tests that map to the workflow more easily.

The sample spreadsheet in Figure 9-11 shows how one company used action words to automate their test setup. The same action words can be used to test. The words Signup, Signoff, and CCDeposit are words that are domain-

ScriptID	Logging	Environment	Site	Lang	Email			
8	ON	STAGING	Global	English	ON			

Test ID	Description	ClassName	Action	Input 1	Input 2	Input 3	Input 4	Input 5
# Signup Customer								
123	Cdn customer	Member	**Signup**	Janet	Gregory	Calgary	123 St	T1T 2A2
123	Reg complete	Member	**signoff**	TRUE				
123	Log out	Member	**Log_out**	TRUE				

# Perform CC Deposit								
Setup	Description	ClassName	Action	Input 1	Input 2	Input 3	Input 4	Input 5
234	Log in mbr	Member	**Login**	get.AcctId	get.ID_greg	get.pwd_		
234	Submit CC Txn	Member	**CCDeposit**	VISA	4444333322	02	2008	25.86
234	Member Logout	Member	**log_out**					
END								

Figure 9-11 Sample test spreadsheet with action words

specific. Their users could easily write tests without understanding the underlying code.

Combining data-driven and keyword-driven testing techniques can be very powerful. Fit and FitNesse use both keywords and data to drive tests. The other tools we've described in this chapter can also accommodate this approach.

Any test strategy can run into trouble if the code isn't designed to be easily tested. Let's take a look at testability concerns.

TESTABILITY

Business-facing tests built with appropriate design patterns and written ahead of any coding help the team achieve a testable code design. The programmers start by looking at the business-facing tests, perhaps together with a tester, analyst, or customer, so that the need to execute those tests are always in their minds as they proceed with their test-driven design. They can build so that the tests provide inputs and control run-time conditions.

Janet's Story

I ran into a snag when I was trying to automate some GUI workflow with Ruby and Watir. The calendar pop-up feature was not recognized, and the data field was read-only. I took my problem to one of the programmers. We paired together so that he could see the issue I was having. The first thing he did was to understand the calendar feature. He thought it would be too difficult to automate the test, so he suggested another alternative. He created a new method that would "fool" the input field so it would accept a date into the text field. We knew the risk was no automation on the calendar, but for simplicity's sake we went with his option.

Not all code is testable using automation, but work with the programmers to find alternative solutions to your problems.

—Janet

Let's look at techniques that promote design of testable code.

Code Design and Test Design

In Chapter 7, "Technology-Facing Tests that Support the Team," we explained how test-driven development at the unit level ensures a testable architecture. This is true for business-facing tests as well. The layered architecture Lisa's team designed works just as well for functional testing. Testing can be done directly against the business logic without involving the user interface, and if appropriate, without involving the database layer. This doesn't mean that the database layer doesn't need to be tested. It still needs to be tested, just maybe somewhere else.

Testability has to be considered when coding the presentation layer as well. GUI test tools work better on well-designed code developed with good practices.

Lisa's Story

When I first started trying to automate GUI tests using Canoo WebTest, I discovered that the HTML and JavaScript used in the system didn't comply with standards and contained many errors. WebTest and the tool it's built on, HtmlUnit, required correct, standard HTML and Javascript. Specifying tests depended on good HTML practices such as giving each element a unique ID. The programmers started writing HTML and JavaScript (and later, Ajax) with the test tool in mind, making test automation much easier. They also started validating their HTML and making sure it was up to industry standards. This also reduced the possibility of the application having problems in different browsers and browser versions.

—Lisa

Coding and testing are part of one process in agile development. Code design and test design are complementary and interdependent. It's a chicken-and-egg scenario: You can't write tests without a testable code design, and you can't write code without well-designed tests that clearly communicate requirements and are compatible with the system architecture. This is why we always consider coding and testing together. When we estimate stories, we include time for both coding and testing, and when we plan each iteration and story, we budget time to design both tests and code. If automating a test proves difficult, evaluate the code design. If programmers are writing code that doesn't match customer expectations, the problem might be poorly designed tests.

Automated vs. Manual Quadrant 2 Tests

In Part IV, "Test Automation," we'll dive into developing a successful test automation strategy and look at considerations such as building your own tools versus using third-party or open source tools.

We've assumed that at least a good-sized portion of the tests that guide programming will be automated. Manual test scenarios can also drive programming if you share them with the programmers early. The earlier you turn them into automated tests, the faster you will realize the benefit. Most manual tests fall more into the "critique product" quadrant where we might learn things about the story we hadn't anticipated with the initial set of tests.

That doesn't stop us from writing tests that might not be appropriate for automation. Don't sweat the details when you're writing tests. You might come up with one-off tests that are important to do but not important to repeat over and over in a regression suite. You might start thinking about end-to-end scenarios or springboards to exploratory test sessions that might be facilitated with some automation but need an intelligent human to conduct them in full. You'll figure that out later. Right now, we want to make sure we capture the customer's critical requirements.

Start with a simple approach, see how it works, and build on it. The important thing is to get going writing business-facing tests to support the team as you develop your product.

TEST MANAGEMENT

Chapter 14, "An Agile Test Automation Strategy," goes into more detail on how to manage automated tests.

If we're automating tests, it makes sense to present them in the automation tool framework, even if they're not yet executable. We want some way for all tests, even those that won't be automated, to be accessible to everyone on the development team and understandable to our customers. There are lots of options available that let everyone on the team see tests. Wikis are a common way to share test cases, and some tools such as FitNesse use a wiki or similar tool, enabling narrative requirements, examples, and executable tests to co-exist in one place.

Tests should be included in your source code control, so that you can track which versions of the tests go with which versions of the code. At the very least, have some kind of version control for your tests. Some teams use test management tools or comprehensive test frameworks that might integrate with requirements management, defect tracking, or other components.

SUMMARY

In this chapter, we've looked at tools you might want in your toolkit to help create business-facing tests that help drive development and guidelines to make sure the tools help rather than get in the way. The tools and guidelines included the following:

- Teams need the right tools to elicit requirements and examples, from the big picture down to details, including checklists, mind maps, spreadsheets, mock-ups, flow diagrams, and various software-based tools.
- Tools to express examples and automate tests, below and through the GUI, are also essential to agile test automation. Some of these tools include unit test tools, behavior-driven development tools, FitNesse, Ruby with Watir, Selenium, and Canoo WebTest.
- "Home brewed" test automation helps teams keep the total cost of ownership of their automated tests low.
- Driving development with business-facing tests is one way agile teams are motivated to design testable code.
- Test strategies for building your automation should include building your tests incrementally and making sure they always pass. Design patterns can be used to help you create effective tests.

- Keyword and data-driven testing is a common approach that works with the tools we've discussed in this chapter.
- Consider testability in your code design, and choose your test tools wisely, because they need to work with your code.
- We need some way to organize tests so that they can be used effectively and put into version control.

Chapter 10

BUSINESS-FACING TESTS
THAT CRITIQUE THE PRODUCT

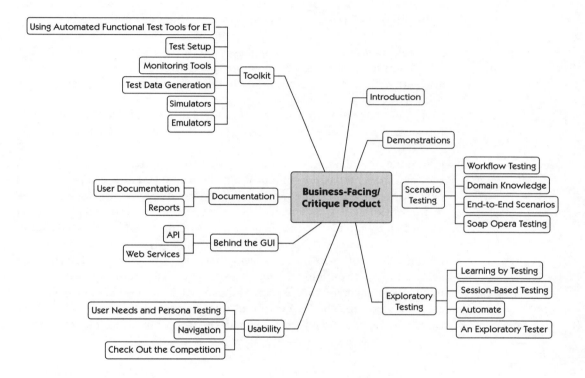

This chapter covers the third quadrant of the testing matrix. In Chapter 8, "Business-Facing Tests that Support the Team," we talked about the second quadrant and how to use business-facing tests to support programming. In this chapter, we show you how to critique the product with different types of business-facing tests. We'll also talk about tools that might help with these activities.

INTRODUCTION TO QUADRANT 3

Remember that business-facing tests are those you could describe in terms that would (or should) be of interest to a business expert. When we mention testing in traditional phased approaches, it pretty much always means critiquing the product after it is built. By now, you might think that in agile development this part of testing should be easy. After all, we just spent all that time making sure it works as expected. The requirements have all been tested as they were built, including security and other nonfunctional requirements, right? All that's left is to possibly find some obscure or interesting bugs.

As testers, we know that people make mistakes. No matter how hard we try to get it right the first time, we sometimes get it wrong. Maybe we used an example that didn't test what we thought it did. Or maybe we recorded a wrong expected result so the test passed, but it was a false positive. The business expert might have forgotten some things that real users needed. The best customer may not know what she wants (or doesn't want) until she sees it.

Critiquing or evaluating the product is what testers or business users do when they assess and make judgments about the product. These evaluators form perceptions based on whether they like the way it behaves, the look and feel, or the workflow of new screens. It is easier to see, feel, and touch a product and respond than to imagine what it will look like when it is described to you.

It's difficult to automate business-facing tests that critique the product, because such testing relies on human intellect, experience, and instinct. However, automated tools can assist with aspects of Quadrant 3 tests (see Figure 10-1), such as test data setup. The last section of this chapter contains examples of the types of tools that help teams focus on the important aspects of evaluating the product's value.

While much of the testing we discuss in this chapter is manual, don't make the mistake of thinking that this manual testing will be enough to produce high-quality software and that you can get away with not automating your regression tests. You won't have time to do any Quadrant 3 tests if you haven't automated the tests in Quadrants 1 and 2.

Evaluating or critiquing the product is about manipulating the system under test and trying to recreate actual experiences of the end users. Understanding different business scenarios and workflows helps to make the experience more realistic.

Agile Testing Quadrants

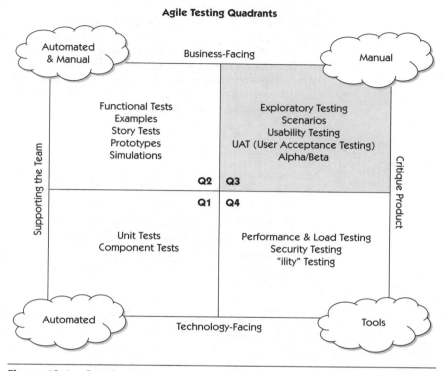

Figure 10-1   Quadrant 3 tests

DEMONSTRATIONS

We recommend showing customers what you're developing early and often. As soon as a rudimentary UI or report is available during story development, show it to the product owner or other domain expert on the team. However, not everyone on the business side will get a chance to see the iteration's deliverables until the iteration demo. End-of-iteration demonstrations are an opportunity for the business users and domain experts to see what has been delivered in the iteration and revise their priorities. It gives them a chance to say, "That's what I said, but it's not what I meant." This is a form of critiquing the product.

Janet's Story

I worked on a project that had five separate teams of eight to ten members, all developing the same system. Even though they were on the same floor, communication was an issue. There were many dependencies and overlaps, so the programmers depended on team-lead meetings to share information. However, the business users and testers needed to see what was being developed by other teams. They relied on end-of-iteration demonstrations given by each team to learn what the other teams were doing.

—Janet

Demonstrations to the executives or upper management can instill confidence in your project as well. One of the downfalls of a phased project is there is nothing to see until the very end, and management has to place all of its trust in the development team's reports. The incremental and iterative nature of agile development gives you a chance to demonstrate business value as you produce it, even before you release it. A live demonstration can be a very powerful tool if the participants are actively asking questions about the new features.

Rather than waiting until the end of the iteration, you can use any opportunity to demonstrate your changes. A recent project Janet worked on used regularly scheduled meetings with the business users to demonstrate new features in order to get immediate feedback. Any desired changes were fed into the next iteration.

Chapter 19, "Wrap Up the Iteration," talks about end-of-iteration demonstrations and reviews.

Choose a frequency for your demonstrations that works for your team so that the feedback loop is quick enough for you to incorporate changes into the release.

Informal demos can be even more productive. Sit down with a business expert and show her the story your team is currently coding. Do some exploratory testing together. We've heard of teams that get their stakeholders to do some exploratory testing after each iteration demo in order to help them think of refinements and future stories to change or build on the functionality just delivered.

SCENARIO TESTING

Business users can help define plausible scenarios and workflows that can mimic end user behavior. Real-life domain knowledge is critical to creating accurate scenarios. We want to test the system from end to end but not necessarily as a black box.

One good technique for helping the team understand the business and user needs is "soap opera testing," a term coined by Hans Buwalda [2004]. The idea here is to take a scenario that is based on real life, exaggerate it in a manner similar to the way TV soap operas exaggerate behavior and emotions, and compress it into a quick sequence of events. Think about questions like, "What's the worst thing that can happen, and how did it happen?"

Soap Opera Test Example

Lisa worked on an Internet retail site, where she found soap opera tests to be effective. Here's an example of a soap opera scenario to test inventory, preorder, and backorder processes of an Internet retailer's warehouse.

> The most popular toy at our online toy store this holiday season is the Super Tester Action Figure. We have 20 preorders awaiting receipt of the items in our warehouse. Finally, Jane, a warehouse supervisor, receives 100 Super Tester Action figures. She updates the inventory system to show it is available inventory against the purchase order and no longer a preorder. Our website now shows Super Tester Action Figures available for delivery in time for the holidays. The system releases the preorders, which are sent to the warehouse. Meanwhile, Joe, the forklift driver, is distracted by his cell phone, and accidentally crashes into the shelf containing the Super Tester Action Figures. All appear to be smashed up beyond recognition. Jane, horrified, removes the 100 items from available inventory. Meanwhile, more orders for this popular toy have piled up in the system item. Sorting through the debris, Jane and Joe find that 14 of the action figures have actually survived intact. Jane adds them back into the available inventory.

This scenario tests several processes in the system, including preorder, purchase order receipt, backorder, warehouse cancels, and preorder release. How many Super Tester toys will show as available on the shopping website at the end of all that? While executing the scenario, we'll probably find other areas we want to investigate; maybe the purchase order application is difficult to use or the warehouse inventory updates aren't reflected properly in the website. Thinking up and executing these types of tests will teach us more about what our users and other external customers need than running predefined functional tests on narrower areas of the application. As a bonus, it's fun!

Chapter 14, "An Agile Test Automation Strategy," examines different approaches to obtaining test data.

As a tester, we often "make up" test data, but it is usually simple so we can easily check our results. When testing different scenarios, both the data and the flow need to be realistic. Find out if the data comes from another system or if it's input manually. Get a sample if you can by asking the customers to provide data for testing. Real data will flow through the system and can be checked along the way. In large systems, it will behave differently depending on what decisions are made.

Tools to help define the scenarios and workflows can be simple. Data flow or process flow diagrams will help identify some of the common scenarios. These scenarios can help you think through a complex problem if you take the time. Consider the users and their motivation.

Lisa's Story

Our team planned to rewrite the core functionality of the application that processes the daily buys and sells of mutual funds. These trades are the result of retirement plan participants making contributions, exchanging balances from one fund to another, or withdrawing money from their accounts. Lisa's coworker, Mike Thomas, studied the existing trade processing flow and diagrammed it so that the team could understand it well before trying to rewrite the code. Figure 10-2 shows a portion of the flow diagram. WT stands for the custodian who does the actual trading. Three different file types are downloaded and translated into readable format: CFM, PRI, and POS. Each of these files feeds into a different part of the application to perform processing and produce various outputs: settled trades, a ticker exception report, and a fund position report.

—Lisa

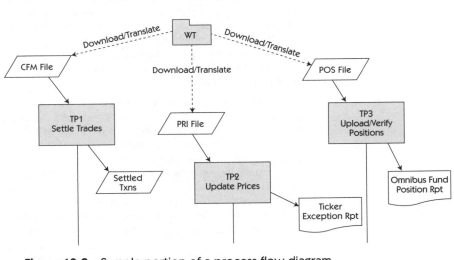

Figure 10-2   Sample portion of a process flow diagram

When testing end-to-end, make spot checks to make sure the data, status flags, calculations, and so on are behaving as expected. Use flow diagrams and other visual aids to help you understand the functionality. Many organizations depend on reports to make decisions, and those reports seem to be the last thing we verify. If your scenarios have been identified correctly, you might be able to use your application reports to provide a final check.

EXPLORATORY TESTING

Exploratory testing (ET) is an important approach to testing in the agile world. As an investigative tool, it's a critical supplement to the story tests and our automated regression suite. It is a sophisticated, thoughtful approach to testing without a script, and it enables you to go beyond the obvious variations that have already been tested. Exploratory testing combines learning, test design, and test execution into one test approach. We apply heuristics and techniques in a disciplined way so that the "doing" reveals more implications that just thinking about a problem. As you test, you learn more about the system under test and can use that information to help design new tests.

The bibliography lists more resources you should investigate to learn more about exploratory testing.

Exploratory testing is not a means of evaluating the software through exhaustive testing. It is meant to add another dimension to your testing. You do just enough to see if the "done" stories are really done to your satisfaction.

A valuable side effect of exploratory testing is the learning that comes out of it. It reveals areas of the product that could use more automated tests and brings up ideas for new or modified features that lead to new stories.

See the bibliography for some links to more about Rapid Software Testing.

Exploratory Testing Explained

Michael Bolton is a trainer and consultant in rapid and exploratory testing approaches. He teaches a course called Rapid Software Testing, which he co-writes with senior author James Bach. Here's Michael's definition of exploratory testing.

> Cem Kaner didn't invent exploratory testing, but he identified and named it in 1983, in the first edition of *Testing Computer Software*, as an approach all testers use when their brains are engaged in their work. He and James Bach, the other leading advocate of the approach, have long defined exploratory testing as "simultaneous test design, test execution, and learning." Kaner also defines exploratory testing more explicitly as "a style of testing that emphasizes the freedom and responsibility of the individual tester to continually optimize the value of her work by treating learning, test design, test execution, and test result interpretation as activities that continue in parallel throughout the project." That's quite a mouthful. What does it mean?

The most important thing to remember about exploratory testing is that it's not a test technique on its own. Instead, it's an approach or a mindset that can be applied to any test technique. The second thing to remember is that exploratory testing is not merely about test execution; testers can also take an exploratory approach when they're designing new tests at the beginning of the iteration or analyzing the results of tests that have already been performed. A third important note is that exploratory testing isn't sloppy or slapdash or unprepared testing. An exploratory approach might require very extensive and elaborate preparation for certain tests—and an exploratory tester's knowledge and skill set, developed over years, is an often invisible yet important form of preparation. An exploratory test might be performed manually, or might employ extensive use of test automation—that is, any use of tools to support testing. So if exploratory testing isn't a technique, nor test execution, nor spontaneous, nor manual, what is it that makes a test activity exploratory? The answer lies in the cognitive engagement of the tester— how the tester responds to a situation that is continuously changing.

Suppose that a tester is given the mission to test a configuration dialog for a text editor. A tester using an exploratory approach would use specifications and conversations about the desired behavior to inform test ideas, but would tend to record these ideas in less detail than a tester using a scripted approach. A skilled tester doesn't generally need much explicit instruction unless the test ideas require some specific actions or data. If so, they might be written down or supplied to a program that could exercise them quickly. Upon seeing the dialog, the exploratory tester would interact with it, usually performing tests in accordance with the original test ideas—but she might also turn her attention to other ideas based on new problems or risks in the dialog as it appeared in front of her. Can two settings conflict in a way not covered by existing tests? The exploratory tester immediately investigates by performing a test on the spot. Does the dialog have a usability issue that could interfere with a user's work flow? The exploratory tester quickly considers a variety of users and scenarios and evaluates the significance of the problem. Is there a delay upon pressing the OK button? The exploratory tester performs a few more tests to seek a general pattern. Is there a possibility that some configuration options might not be possible on another platform? The exploratory tester notes the need for additional testing and moves on. Upon receiving new builds, the exploratory tester would tend to deemphasize repetition and emphasize variation in order to discover problems missed by older tests that are no longer revealing interesting information. This approach, which has always been fruitful, is even more powerful in environments where the need for repeated testing is handled by the developers' low-level, automated regression tests.

Exploratory testing is characterized by the degree to which the tester is under her own control, making informed choices about what he or she is going to do next, and where the last outcome of the last activity consciously informs the next choice. Exploratory and scripted approaches are at the opposite poles of a continuum. At the extreme end of the scripted mind-set, the decision as to what to do next comes exclusively from someone else, at some point in the past. In the exploratory mind-set, the decision to continue on the same line of inquiry or to choose a new path comes entirely from the individual tester, in the moment in which the activity occurs, The result of the last test strongly informs the tester's choices for the next test. Other influences include the stakeholders for whom test information might be important, the quality criteria that are important to stakeholders, the test coverage that stakeholders seek, specific risks associated with the item being tested, the needs of the end user of the product, the skills of the tester, the skills of the developers, the state of the item under test, the schedule for the project, the equipment and tools that are available to the tester, and the extent to which she can use them effectively—and that's only a partial list.

No test activity performed by a thinking human is entirely scripted. Humans have an extraordinary capacity to recognize things even when people are telling them not to, and as a result we can be distracted and diverted—but we can learn and adapt astonishingly quickly to new information and investigate its causes and effects. Machines only recognize what they've been programmed to recognize. When they're confronted with a surprising test result, at best they ignore it; at worst, they crash or destroy data.

Yet no test activity performed on behalf of a client is entirely exploratory, either. The exploratory tester is initially driven by the testing mission, which is typically set out by the client early in the project. Exploratory work can also be guided by checklists, strategy models, coverage outlines, risk lists—ideas that might come from other people at other times. The more that the tester is controlled by these ideas rather than guided by them, the more testing takes on a scripted approach.

Good exploration requires continuous investigation of the product by engaged human testers, in collaboration with the rest of the project community, rather than following a procedurally structured approach, performed exclusively by automation. *Exploration emphasizes individuals and interactions over processes and tools.* In an agile environment, where code is produced test-first and is covered with automated regression tests, testers can have not only the confidence but also the mandate to develop new tests and seek out new problems in the moment. *Exploration emphasizes responding to change versus following a plan.* Exploratory approaches use variation to drive an active search for problems instead of scripted manual or automated test cases that merely confirm what we already knew. *Exploration emphasizes working software over comprehensive documentation.* And to be effective, good exploration requires frequent feedback between testers, developers, customers, and the rest of the project community, not merely repetition of tests that were prepared at the beginning of the iteration, before we had learned important things about the project. *Exploration emphasizes customer collaboration over negotiated contracts.* Exploratory approaches are fundamentally agile.

Exploratory testing embraces the same values as agile development. It's an important part of the "agile testing mind-set" and critical to any team's success.

People unfamiliar with exploratory testing often confuse it with ad hoc testing. Exploratory testing isn't sitting down at a keyboard and typing away. Unskilled "black box" testers may not know how to do exploratory testing.

Exploratory testing starts with a charter of what aspects of the functionality will be explored. It requires critical thinking, interpreting the results, and comparing them to expectations or similar systems. Following "smells" when testing is an important component. Testers take notes during their exploratory testing sessions so that they can reproduce any issues they see and do more investigation as needed.

Technique: Exploratory Testing and Information Evaluation

Jon Hagar, an experienced exploratory tester, learner, and trainer, shares some activities, characteristics, and skills that are vital to effective exploratory testing.

Exploratory testing uses the tester's understanding of the system, along with critical thinking, to define focused, experimental "tests" which can be run in short time frames and then fed back into the test planning process.

An agile team has many opportunities to do exploratory testing, since each development cycle creates production-ready, working software. Starting early in each development cycle, consider exploratory tests based on:

- Risk (analysis): The critical things you and the customer/user think can go wrong or be potential problems that will make people unhappy.
- Models (mental or otherwise) of how software should behave: You and/or the customer have a great expectation about what the newly produced function should do or look like, so you test that.
- Past experience: Think about how similar systems have failed (or succeeded) in predictable patterns that can be refined into a test, and explore it.

- What your development team is telling you: Talk to your developers and find out what "is important to us."
- Most importantly: What you learn (see and observe) as you test. As a tester on an agile team, a big part of your job is to constantly learn about your product, your team, and your customer. As you learn, you should quickly see tests based on such things as customer needs, common mistakes the team seems to be making, or good/bad characteristics of the product.

Some tests might be good candidates for automated regression suites. Some might just answer your exploratory charter and be "done." The agile team must critically think about what they are learning and "evolve" tests accordingly. The most important aspect here is to be "brain on" while testing, where you are looking for the "funny," unexpected, or new, which automated tests would miss. Use automation for what it is good at (repetitive tasks) and use agile humans for what we are good at (seeing, thinking, and dealing with the unexpected).

Several components are typically needed for useful exploratory testing:

- Test Design: An exploratory tester as a good test designer understands the many test methods. You should be able to call different methods into play on the fly during the exploration. This agility is a big advantage of exploratory testing over automated (scripted) procedures, where things must be thought out in advance.
- Careful Observation: Exploratory testers are good observers. They watch for the unusual and unexpected and are careful about assumptions of correctness. They might observe subtle software characteristics or patterns that drive them to change the test in real time.
- Critical Thinking: The ability to think openly and with agility is a key reason to have thinking humans doing nonautomated exploratory testing. Exploratory testers are able to review and redirect a test into unexpected directions on the fly. They should also be able to explain their logic of looking for defects and to provide clear status on testing. Critical thinking is a learned human skill.
- Diverse Ideas: Experienced testers and subject matter experts can produce more and better ideas. Exploratory testers can build on this diversity during testing. One of the key reasons for exploratory tests is to use critical thinking to drive the tests in unexpected directions and find errors.
- Rich Resources: Exploratory testers should develop a large set of tools, techniques, test data, friends, and information sources upon which they can draw. The agile test team members should grow their exploratory resources throughout a project and throughout their careers.

To help you understand a day in the life of an agile exploratory tester, here is a short tester's story:

> I arrived at 8:00 a.m. and reviewed what had happened the night before during automated testing. The previous night's automated tests found some minor but interesting errors. A password field on a login form had accepted a special character, which should have been rejected by the validation. I created an outline as a starting point for my "attack" (a top-level plan and/or risk list).
>
> As I thought about my "plan of attack," I sketched a small state model of the problem on a flip chart and showed this to a developer and my team's customer rep. I designed a test incorporating their suggestions, using some data stress inputs that I expected the validation to reject (a 1 MG file of special characters). I executed my test with my stress input, and, sure enough, the system rejected them as expected. I tried a different data set and the system failed with a buffer overflow in the database. I was learning, and we were on the trail of a potentially serious security bug. As the day went on, I explored different inputs to the password field and worked with the team to get the bug fixed.

You can learn from automated test results as well as from exploratory testing. Each type of testing feeds into the other. Develop a broad range of skills so you'll be able to identify important issues and write tests to prevent them from reoccurring.

The term *exploratory testing* was popularized by the "context-driven school" of testing. It's a highly disciplined activity, and it can be learned. Session-based test management is one method of testing that's designed to make exploratory testing auditable and measurable [Bach, 2003].

Session-Based Testing

Session-based testing combines accountability and exploratory testing. It gives a framework to a tester's exploratory testing experience so that they can report results in a consistent way.

Janet's Story

James Bach [2003] compares exploratory testing to putting together a jigsaw puzzle. When I first read his article with the jigsaw puzzle analogy, exploratory testing made perfect sense to me.

I start a jigsaw puzzle by dumping out all of the pieces of the puzzle and then sorting them into the different colors and edge pieces. Next, I put the edge pieces together, which gives me a framework in which to start. The edge of the jigsaw is analogous both to the mission statement, which helps me focus, and to the timeboxing of a session, which keeps me within certain limits.

> Session-based testing is a form of exploratory testing, but it is time-boxed and a bit more structured. I learned about session-based testing from Jonathan Bach and found it gave me the structure I needed to do exploratory testing well. I use the same skills as I do for a jigsaw puzzle: I look for patterns in color or shapes or perhaps something that just doesn't look right, an anomaly. My thought process can take those patterns and make sense of them, using heuristics I have developed to help me solve a puzzle.
>
> —Janet

Like solving the jigsaw puzzle by putting together the outside pieces first, we can use session-based testing to give us the framework in which we work. In session-based testing, we create a mission or a charter and then time-box our session so we can focus on what's important. Too often as testers, we can go off track and end up chasing a bug that might or might not be important to what we are currently testing.

For more information on session-based testing, check the bibliography for work by Jonathan Bach.

Sessions are divided into three kinds of tasks: test design and execution, bug investigation and reporting, and session setup. We measure the time we spend on setup versus actual test execution so that we know where we spend the most time. We can capture results in a consistent manner so that we can report back to the team.

Automation and Exploratory Testing

We can combine exploratory testing with test automation as well. Jonathan Kohl, in his article "Man and Machine" [2007], talks about interactive test automation to assist exploratory testing. Use automation to do test set up, data generation, repetitive tasks, or to progress along a workflow to the place you want to start. Then you start using your testing skills and experience to find the really "good" bugs, the insidious ones that otherwise escape attention. You can also use an automated test suite to explore. Just modify it a bit, watch the results as it runs, modify it again, and watch what happens.

An Exploratory Tester

With exploratory testing, each tester has a different approach to a problem, and has a unique style of working. However, there are certain attributes that make for a good exploratory tester. A good tester:

- Is systematic, but pursues "smells" (anomalies, pieces that aren't consistent)
- Learns to recognize problems through the use of Oracles (principle or mechanism by which we recognize a problem)

- Chooses a theme or role or mission statement to focus testing
- Time-boxes sessions and side trips
- Thinks about what the expert or novice user would do
- Explores together with domain experts
- Checks out similar or competitive applications

Exploratory testing helps us learn about the behavior of an application. Testers generally know a lot about the application they're testing. How do they judge whether the application is usable by users who are less technical or not familiar with it? Usability testing is vital for many software systems. We'll talk about that in the next section.

USABILITY TESTING

There are two types of usability testing. The first type is the kind that is done up front by the user experience folks, using tools such as wire frames to help drive programming. Those types of tests belong in Quadrant 2. In this section, we're talking about the kind of usability testing that critiques the product. We use tools such as personas and our intuition to help us look at the product with the end user in mind.

User Needs and Persona Testing

Let's look at an online shopping example. We think about who will use the site. Will it be people who have shopped online before, or will it be brand new users who have no idea how to proceed? We're guessing it will be a mixture of both, as well as others. Take the time to ask your marketing group to get the demographics of the end users. The numbers might help you plan your testing.

One approach to using personas is for your team to invent several different users of your application representing different experience levels and needs. For our Internet retail application, we might have the following personas:

- Nancy Newbie, a senior citizen who is new to Internet shopping and nervous about identity theft
- Hudson Hacker, who looks for ways to cheat the checkout page
- Enrico Executive, who does all his shopping online and ships gifts to all his clients worldwide
- Betty Bargain, who's looking for great deals
- Debbie Ditherer, who has a hard time deciding what items she really wants to order

We might hang photos representing these different personas and their biographies in our work area so that we always keep them in mind. We can test the same scenario as each persona in turn and see what different experiences they might encounter.

Another way to approach persona testing, which we learned from Brian Marick and Elisabeth Hendrickson, is to pick a fictional character or famous celebrity and imagine how they would use our application. Would the Queen of England be able to navigate our checkout process? How might Homer Simpson search for the item he wants?

Real World Projects: Personas

The OneNote team at Microsoft uses personas as part of their testing process. Mike Tholfsen [2008], the Test Manager for OneNote, says they use seven personas that might use OneNote, specific customer types such as Attorneys, Students, Real Estate Agents, and Salespersons. The personas they create contain information such as:

- General job description
- "A Day in the Life"
- Primary uses for OneNote
- List of features the persona might use
- Potential notebook structures
- Other applications used
- Configuration and hardware environment

You can also just assume the roles of novice, intermediate, and expert users as you explore the application. Can users figure out what they are supposed to do without instructions? If you have a lot of first-time users, you might need to make the interface very simple.

Janet's Story

When I first started testing a new production accounting system, I found it very difficult to understand the flow, but the production accountants on the team loved it. After I worked with it for a while, I understood the complexity behind the application and knew why it didn't have to be intuitive for a first-time user. This was a good lesson for me, because I always assumed applications had to be user-friendly.

—Janet

If your application is custom-built for specific types of users, it might need to be "smart" rather than intuitive. Training sessions might be sufficient to get over the initial lack of usability so that the interface can be designed for maximum efficiency and utility.

Navigation

Navigation is another aspect of usability testing. It's incredibly important to test links and make sure the tabbing order makes sense. If a user has a choice of applications or websites, and has a bad first experience, they likely won't use your application again. Some of this testing is automatable, but it's important to test the actual user experience.

If you have access to the end users, get them involved in testing the navigation. Pair with a real user, or watch one actually use the application and take notes. When you're designing a new user interface, consider using focus groups to evaluate different interfaces. You can start with mock-ups and flows drawn on paper, get opinions, and try HTML mock-ups next, to get early feedback.

Check Out the Competition

When evaluating your application for usability, think about other applications that are similar. How do they accomplish tasks? Do you consider them user-friendly or intuitive? If you can get access to competing software, take some time to research how those applications work and compare them with your product. For example, you're testing a user interface that takes a date range, and it has a pop-up calendar feature to select the date. Take a look at how a similar calendar function works on an airline reservation website.

Usability testing is a fairly specialized field. If you're producing an internal application to be used by a few users who will be trained in its use, you probably don't need to invest much in usability testing. If you're writing the online directory assistance for a phone company, usability might be your main focus, so you need to learn as much as you can about it, or bring in a usability expert.

BEHIND THE GUI

In a presentation titled "Man and Machine" [2007], Jonathan Kohl talked about alternatives for testing interfaces. Instead of always thinking about testing through the user interface, consider attacking the problem in other ways. Think about testing the whole system from every angle that you can approach. Consider using tools like simulators or emulators.

See Chapter 8, "Business-Facing Tests that Support the Team," for an example of Wizard of Oz testing, which is one approach to designing for usability.

See the bibliography for links to articles by Jeff Patton, Gerard Meszaros, and others on usability testing.

Chapter 9, "Toolkit for Business-Facing Tests that Support the Team," provides more detail about tools that facilitate these tests.

API Testing

In Chapter 8 and Chapter 9, we talked about testing behind the GUI to drive development. In this section, we show that you can extend your tests for the API in order to try different permutations and combinations.

An API (application programming interface) is a collection of functions that can be executed by other software applications or components. The end user is usually never aware that an API exists; she simply interacts with the interface on top.

Each API call has a specific function with a number of parameters that accept different inputs. Each variation will return a different result. The easy tests are simple inputs. The more complicated testing patterns occur when the parameters work together to give many possible variations. Sometimes parameters are optional, so it's important that you understand the possibilities. Boundary conditions should be considered as well, for both the inputs and expected results. For example, use both valid and invalid strings for parameters, vary the content, and vary the length of the strings' input.

Another way to test is to vary the order of the API calls. Changing the sequence might produce unexpected results and reveal bugs that would never be found through UI testing. You can control the tests much more easily than when using the UI.

Lisa's Story

My team was working on a set of stories to enable retirement plan sponsors to upload payroll contribution files. We wrote FitNesse test cases to illustrate the file parsing rules, and the programmer wrote unit tests for those as well. When the coding for the parser was complete, we wanted to throw a lot more combinations of data at the parser, including some really bizarre ones, and see what happened. We could use the same fixture as we used for our tests to drive development, enter all of the crazy combinations we could think of, and see the results. We tested about 100 variations of both valid and invalid data. Figure 10-3 shows an example of just a few of the tests we tried. We found several errors in the code this way.

We didn't keep all of these tests in the regression suite because they were just a means of quickly trying every combination we could think of. We could have done these tests in a semi-automated, ad hoc manner too, not bothering to type the expected results into the result checking table, and just eyeballing the outputs to make sure they looked correct.

—Lisa

Build the data

ContributionsFileFormatFixture		
line	parse()	
1 pAyRoLl, 701-00-0003, 40,"$2,309.01","$145.09", "125.00", "$32.88"	valid	valid (mixed case, decimals, spaces)
2 payroll, 701-00-0008,167,"$999,999,999.99","$1,500,000",200000,"$75,000"	valid	valid (outrageous amounts)
3 payroll, 701-00-0011,",3509,175,"$0.01",25	invalid	invalid (invalid hours)
4 payroll, 701-00-0013,40,1,200,,100,50	invalid	invalid (unquoted comma)
5 payroll, 701-00-0016,40,1347.22,160,56.0,{},0	invalid	invalid (invalid characters)
6 payroll, 701-00-0021, 80, 2300.98, 174.01, 34.90, 84	valid	valid (variable whitespace)
7 loan, 700000041, 4100220,110	valid	valid (no dashes in SSN)
8 loan, 702-00-0054,"$466"	invalid	invalid (missing field)

Operate and Check

ContributionsFileResultsFixture										
line	ssn	hours	comp	deferral	match	roth	loanId	loan	lineProblem	firstFieldProblem
1	701-00-0003	40	2309.01	145.09	125.00	32.88	null	null	null	null
2	701-00-0008	167	999999999.99	1500000.00	200000.00	75000.00	null	null	null	null
3	701-00-0011	0	3509.00	175.00	0.01	25.00	null	null	null	invalid hours
4	701-00-0013	40	1.00	200.00	0.00	100.00	null	null	null	extra field
5	701-00-0016	40	1347.22	160.00	56.00	0.00	null	null	null	invalid Roth deferral
6	701-00-0021	80	2300.98	174.01	34.90	84.00	null	null	null	null
7	700-00-0041	null	null	null	null	null	4100220	110.00	null	null
8	702-00-0054	null	null	null	null	null	null	null	null	invalid loan identifier

Figure 10-3   Sample of parsing rules test

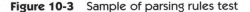

I recently worked with a web application that interfaces to a legacy system through a well-defined API. Due to the design of the legacy system and the fact that the data is hard to replicate, the team hasn't yet found a way to automate this testing. However, we could look in the log files to verify the correct inputs were passed and the expected result was returned. Valuable exploratory testing of APIs is possible with or without benefit of automation.

—Janet

API calls can be developed early in an application life cycle, which means testing can occur early as well. Testing through an API can give confidence in the system before a UI is ever developed. Because this type of testing can be automated, you will need to work with your programmers to understand all of the parameters and the purpose of each function. If your programmers or automation team develop a test harness that is easy to use, you should be able to methodically create a suite of test cases that exercises the functionality.

Web Services

Web services generally require plenty of security, stress, and reliability testing. See Chapter 12, "Critiquing the Product using Technology-Facing Tests," for more on these types of tests.

Web services are a services-based architecture that provides an external interface so that others can access the system. There might be multiple stakeholders, and you may not even know who will be using your product. Your testing will need to confirm the quality of service that the external customers expect.

Consider levels of service that have been promised to clients when you are creating your test plans. Make time for exploratory testing to simulate the different ways users might access the web services.

The use of web services standards also offers other implications for current testing tools. As with API calls, web services-based integration highlights the importance of validating interface points. However, we also need to consider message formats and processing, queuing times, and message response times.

Chapter 12, "Summary of Testing Quadrants," has an example of testing web services.

Using testing tools that utilize GUI-driven automation is simply inadequate for a web services project. A domain-specific language that encapsulates implementation details "behind the scenes" works well for testing web services.

TESTING DOCUMENTS AND DOCUMENTATION

One of the components of the system that is often overlooked during testing is documentation. As agile developers, we may value working software over documentation, but we still value documentation! User manuals and online help need validation just as much as software. Your team may employ specialists such as technical writers who create and verify documentation. As with all other components of the product, your whole team is responsible for the quality of the documentation, and that includes both hard copy and electronic.

User Documentation

Your team might do Quadrant 2 tests to support the team as they produce documentation; in fact we encourage it. Lisa's team writes code that produces documents whose contents are specified by government regulations, and programmers can write much of the code test-first. However, it's difficult for automated tests to judge whether a document is formatted correctly or uses a readable font. They also can't evaluate whether the contents of documents such as user manuals are accurate or useful. Because documentation has many subjective components, validating it is more of a critiquing activity.

Technical writers and testers can work very closely together. Stephanie, a technical writer I worked with on one project, talked with the programmers to understand how the application worked. She would also work through the application to make sure she wrote it down correctly. This seemed to be a duplication of the testing effort, so Stephanie and I sat down and figured out a better approach.

We decided to work together on the stories as they were developed. For some stories Stephanie was lead "tester," and sometimes I took that role. If I was lead, I'd create my test conditions and examples and Stephanie would use those as her basis for the documentation. When Stephanie was lead, she would write her documentation, and then I would use that to determine the test cases.

Doing it this way enabled the documentation to be tested and the tests to be challenged before they were ever executed. Working hand in hand like this proved to be a very successful experiment. The resulting documentation matched the software's behavior and was much more useful to the end users.

—Janet

Don't forget to check the help text too. Are the links to help text easily identifiable? Are they consistent throughout the user interface? Is the help text presented clearly? If it opens in a pop-up, and users block pop-ups in their browsers, what's the impact? Does the help cover all of the topics needed? On Lisa's projects, help text tends to be a low priority, so it often doesn't get done at all. That's a business decision, but if you feel an area of the application needs extra help text or documentation, raise the issue to your team and your customers.

Reports

Another system component that's often overlooked from a testing perspective is reports. Reports are critical to many users for decision-making purposes but are often left until the very end, and either don't get done or are poorly executed. Reports might be tailored to meet specific customer needs, but there are many third-party tools available for generating reports. Reports may be part of the application itself or be generated through a separate reporting system for end users.

We discuss testing reports along with the other Quadrant 3 test activities in order to critique the product, but we recommend that you also write Quadrant 2 report tests that will guide the coding and help the team understand the customer's needs as it produces reports. They can certainly be written test-first. Like documents, though, you need to look at a report to know if it's easy enough to read and presents information in an understandable way.

One of the biggest challenges when testing reports is not the formatting but getting the right data. When you try to create test data for reports, it can be difficult to get a good cross section of realistic data. It also is usually the edge cases that make the reports fail, so incorporating that extra data is not feasible. In most cases, it's best to use production data (or data copied from the production system into a test environment) to test the different reporting variations.

Lisa's Story

Our application includes a number of reports, many of which help companies meet governmental compliance requirements. While we have automated smoke tests for each report, any change to a report, or even an upgrade in the tool we use to generate reports, requires extensive manual and visual testing. We have to watch like hawks: Has a number been truncated by one character? Did a piece of text run over to the next page? Is the right data included? Wrong or missing data can mean trouble with the regulatory agency.

Another challenge is verifying the data contained in the report. If I were to use the same query that the report uses, it doesn't prove anything. I sometimes struggle to come up with my own SQL queries to compare the actual data with what shows up on a report. We budget extra time to test reports, even the simple-looking ones.

Because reports are so subjective, we find that different stakeholders have different preferences for how the data is presented. The plan administrator who has to explain a report to a user on the phone has a different idea of what's easy to understand than the company lawyer who decides what data needs to be on the report. Our product owner helps us get consensus from all areas of the business.

The contents and formatting of a report are important, of course, but for online reports, the speed at which they come up is critical too. Our plan administrators wanted complete freedom to specify any date range for some transaction history reports. Our DBA, who coded the reports, warned that for a large company's retirement plan, data for more than a few months worth of transactions could take several minutes to render. Over time, companies grew, they had more and more transactions, and eventually the user interface started timing out before it could deliver the report. When testing, try out worst-case scenarios, which could eventually become the most common scenario.

—Lisa

See Chapter 8, "Business-Facing Tests that Support the Team," for information about using thin slices.

If you're tackling a project that involves lots of reports, don't give in to the temptation to leave them to the end. Include some reports in each iteration if you can. One report could be a single story or maybe even broken up into a couple of stories. Use mock-ups to help the customers decide on report contents and formatting. Find the "thin slice" or "critical path" in the report, code that first, and show it to your customer before you add the next slice. Incremental development works as well with reports as it does with other software.

Sometimes your customers themselves aren't sure how a report should look or how to approach it incrementally. And sometimes nobody on the team anticipates how hard the testing effort will prove to be.

Lisa's Story

Like other financial accounts, retirement plans need to provide periodic statements to account holders that detail all of the money going into and out of the account. These statements show the change in value between the beginning and ending balances and other pertinent information, such as the names of account beneficiaries. Our company wanted to improve the account statements, both as a marketing tool and to reduce the number of calls from account holders who didn't understand their statements.

We didn't have access to our direct competitors' account statements, so the product owner asked for volunteers to bring in account statements from banks and other financial institutions in order to get ideas. Months of discussions and experimentation with mock-ups produced a new statement format, which included data that wasn't on the report previously, such as performance results for each mutual fund.

Stories for developing the new account statement were distributed throughout two quarters worth of iterations. During the first quarter, stories to collect new data were done. Testing proved much harder than we thought. We used FitNesse tests to verify capturing the different data elements, which lulled us into a false sense of security. It was hard to cover all of the variations, and we missed some with the automated tests. We also didn't anticipate that the changes to collect new data could have an adverse effect on the data that already displayed on the existing statements.

As a result, we didn't do adequate manual testing of the account statements. Subtle errors slipped past us. When the job to produce quarterly statements ran, calls started coming in from customers. We had a mad scramble to diagnose and fix the errors in both code and data. The whole project was delayed by a quarter while we figured out better ways to test and added internal checks and better logging to the code.

—Lisa

Short iterations mean that it can be hard to make time for adequate exploratory testing and other Quadrant 3 activities. Let's look at tools that might help speed up this testing and make time for vital manual and visual tests.

TOOLS TO ASSIST WITH EXPLORATORY TESTING

Exploratory testing is manual testing. Some of the best testing happens because a person is paying attention to details that often get missed if we are following a script. Intuition is something that we cannot make a machine learn. However, there are many tools that can assist us in our quest for excellence.

Tools shouldn't replace human interaction; they should enhance the experience. Tools can provide testers with more power to find the hard-to-reproduce bugs that often get filed away because no one can get a handle on them. Exploratory testing is unconventional, so why shouldn't the tools be as well? Think about low-effort, high-value ways that tools can be incorporated into your testing.

See the bibliography for references to Jonathan Kohl's writings on using human and automation power together for optimal testing.

Computers are good at doing repetitive tasks and performing calculations. These are two areas where they are much better than humans, so let's use them for those tasks. Because testing needs to keep pace with coding, any time advantage we can gain is a bonus.

In the next few sections, we'll look at some areas where automation can leverage exploratory testing. The ones we cover are test setup, test data generation, monitoring, simulators, and emulators.

Test Setup

Let's think about what we do when we test. We've just found a bug, but not one that is easily reproducible. We're pretty sure it happens as a result of interactions between components. We go back to the beginning and try one scenario after another. Soon we've spent the whole day just trying to reproduce this one bug.

Ask yourself how you can make this easier. We've found that one of the most time-consuming tasks is the test setup and getting to the right starting point for your actual test. If you use session-based testing, then you already know how much time you spend setting up the test, because you have been tracking that particular time waster. This is an excellent opportunity for some automation.

The tools used for business-facing tests that support the team described in Chapter 9 are also valuable for manual exploratory testing. Automated functional test scripts can be run to set up data and scenarios to launch exploratory testing sessions. Tests configured to accept runtime parameters are particularly powerful for setting up a starting point for evaluating the product.

Lisa's Story

Our Watir test scripts all accept a number of runtime parameters. When I need a retirement plan with a specific set of options, and specific types of participants, I can kick off a Watir script or two with some variables set on the command line. When the scripts stop, I have a browser session with all of the data I need for testing already set up. This is so fast that I can test permutations I'd never get to using all-manual keystrokes.

—Lisa

The test scripts you use for functional regression testing and for guiding development aren't the only tools that help take the tedium out of manual exploratory testing. There are other tools to help set up test data as well as to help you evaluate the outputs of your testing sessions.

Whatever tool you are using, think about how it can be adapted to run the scenario over and over with different inputs plugged in. Janet has also successfully used Ruby with Watir to set up tests to run multiple times to help identify bugs. Tools that drive the browser or UI in much the same way that an end user would makes your testing more reliable because you can play it back on your monitor and watch for anything that might not look as it should during the setup. When you get to the place where the test actually starts, you can then use your excellent testing abilities to track down the source of the bug.

Test Data Generation

PerlClip is an example of a tool that you can use to test a text field with different kinds of inputs. James Bach provides it free of charge on his website, www.satisfice.com, and it can be very helpful in validating fields. For example, if you have a field that will accept a maximum input of 200 characters, testing this field and its boundaries manually would be very tedious. Use PerlClip to create a string, put it in your automation library, and have your automation tool call the string to test the value.

Monitoring Tools

Tools like the Unix/Linux command `tail -f`, or James Bach's LogWatch, can help monitor log files for error conditions. IDEs also provide log analysis tools. Many error messages are never displayed on the screen, so if you're testing via the GUI, you never see them. Get familiar with tools like these, because they can make your testing more effective and efficient. If you are not sure where your system logs warnings and errors, ask your developers. They probably have lots of ideas about how you can monitor the system.

Simulators

See the "System Test" example in Chapter 12, "Summary of Testing Quadrants," to see how a simulator was critical to the testing the whole system.

Simulators are tools used to create data that represent key characteristics and behavior of real data for the system under test. If you do not have access to real data for your system, simulated data will sometimes work almost as well. The other advantage of using a simulator is for pumping data into a system over time. It can be used to help generate error conditions that are difficult to create under normal circumstances and can reduce time in boundary testing.

Setting up data and test scenarios is half of the picture. You also need to have a way to watch the outcomes of your testing. Let's consider some tools for that purpose.

Emulators

An emulator duplicates the functionality of a system so that it behaves like the system under test. There are many reasons to use an emulator. When you need to test code that interfaces with other systems or devices, emulators are invaluable.

Two Examples of Emulators

WestJet, a Canadian airline company, provides the capability for guests to use their mobile devices to check in at airports that support the feature. When testing this application, it is better for both the programmers and the testers to test various devices as early as possible. To make this feasible, they use downloadable emulators to test the Web Check-in application quickly and often during an iteration. Real devices, which are expensive to use, can then be used sparingly to verify already tested functionality.

The team also created another type of emulator to help test against the legacy system being interfaced with. The programmers on the legacy system have different priorities and delivery schedules, and a backlog of requests. To prevent this from holding up new development, the programmers on the web application have created a type of emulator for the API into the legacy system that returns predetermined values for specific API calls. They develop against this emulator, and when the real changes are available, they test and make any modifications then. This change in process has enabled them to move ahead much more quickly than was previously possible. It has proved to be a simple but very powerful tool.

Emulators are one tool that helps to keep testing and coding moving together hand-in-hand. Using them is one way for testing to keep up with development in short iterations. As you plan your releases and iterations, think about the types of tools that might help with creating production-like test scenarios. See if you can use the tools you're already using for automating tests to drive development as aids to exploratory testing.

Driving development with tests is critical to any project's success. However, we humans won't always get all of the requirements for desired system behavior entirely correct. Our business experts themselves can miss important aspects of functionality or interaction with other parts of the system when they provide examples of how a feature should work. We have to use techniques to help both the customer and developer teams learn more about the system so they can keep improving the product.

SUMMARY

A large part of the testing effort is spent critiquing the product from a business perspective. This chapter gave you some ideas about the types of tests you can do to make your testing efforts more effective.

- Demonstrate software to stakeholders in order to get early feedback that will help direct building the right stuff.
- Use scenarios and workflows to test the whole system from end to end.
- Use exploratory testing to supplement automation and to take advantage of human intellect and perceptions.
- Without usability in mind when testing and coding, applications can become shelfware. Always be aware of how the system is being used.
- Testing behind the GUI is the most effective way of getting at the application functionality. Do some research to see how you can approach your application.
- Incorporate all kinds of tests to make a good regression suite.
- Don't forget about testing documentation and reports.
- Automation tools can perform tedious and repetitive tasks, such as data and test scenario setup, and free up more time for important manual exploratory testing.
- Tools you're already using to automate functional tests might also be useful to leverage exploratory tests.

- Monitoring, resource usage, and log analysis tools built into operating systems and IDEs help testers appraise the application's behavior.
- Simulators and emulators enable exploratory testing even when you can't duplicate the exact production environment.
- Even when tests are used to drive development, requirements for desired behavior or interaction with other systems can be missed or misunderstood. Quadrant 3 activities help teams keep adding value to the product.

## Chapter 11

CRITIQUING THE PRODUCT USING TECHNOLOGY-FACING TESTS

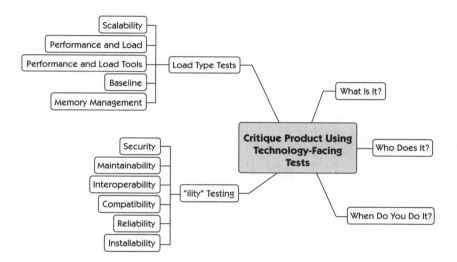

This chapter is focused on the bottom right corner of our testing quadrant. We've looked at driving development with both business-facing and technology-facing tests. After the code is written, we are no longer driving the development but are looking at ways to critique the product. In the previous chapter, we examined ways to critique from a business point of view. Now we look at ways to critique from a technology-facing point of view. These tests are an important means of evaluating whether our product delivers the right business value.

INTRODUCTION TO QUADRANT 4

Individual stories are pieces of the puzzle, but there's more to an application than that. The technology-facing tests that critique the product are more concerned with the nonfunctional requirements than the functional ones. We worry about deficiencies in the product from a technical point of view. Rather than using the business domain language, we describe requirements using a programming domain vocabulary. This is the province of Quadrant 4 (see Figure 11-1).

Nonfunctional requirements include configuration issues, security, performance, memory management, the "ilities" (e.g., reliability, interoperability, and scalability), recovery, and even data conversion. Not all projects are concerned about all of these issues, but it is a good idea to have a checklist to make sure the team thinks about them and asks the customer how important each one is.

Our customer should think about all of the quality attributes and factors that are important and make informed trade-offs. However, many customers focus

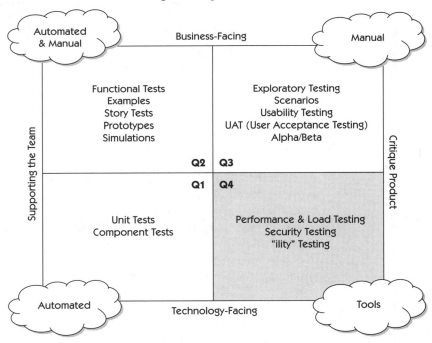

Figure 11-1   Quadrant 4 tests

on the business side of the application and don't understand the criticality of many nonfunctional requirements in their role of helping to define the level of quality needed for the product. They might assume that the development team will just take care of issues such as performance, reliability, and security.

We believe that the development team has a responsibility to explain the consequences of not addressing these nonfunctional or cross-functional requirements. We're really all part of one product team that wants to deliver good value, and these technology-oriented factors might expose make-or-break issues.

Many of these nonfunctional and cross-functional issues are deemed low-risk for many applications and so are not added to the test plan. However, when you are planning your project, you should think about the risks in each of these areas, address them in your test plan, and include the tools and resources needed for testing them in your project plan.

Lisa's Story

In the past, I've been asked by specialists in areas such as performance and security testing why they didn't hear much about "ility" testing at agile conferences or in publications about agile development. Like Janet, I've always seen these areas of testing as critical, so this wasn't my perception. But as I thought about it, I had to agree that this wasn't a much-discussed topic at the time (although that's changed recently).

Why would agile discussions not include such important considerations as load testing? My theory is that it's because agile development is driven by customers, from user stories. Customers simply assume that software will be designed to properly accommodate the potential load, at a reasonable rate of performance. It doesn't always occur to them to verbalize those concerns. If not asked to address them, programmers may or may not think to prioritize them. I believe that one area where testers have contributed greatly to agile teams is in bringing up questions such as, "How many concurrent users should the application support?" and "What's the average response time required?"

—Lisa

Because the types of testing in this quadrant are so diverse, we'll give examples of tools that might be helpful as we go along instead of a separate toolkit section. Tools, whether homegrown or acquired, are essential to succeed with Quadrant 4 testing efforts. Still, the people doing the work count, so let's consider who on an agile team can perform these tests.

WHO DOES IT?

All of the agile literature talks about teams being generalists; anyone should be able to pick up a task and do it. We know that isn't always practical, but the idea is to be able to share the knowledge so that people don't become silos of information.

However, there are many tasks that need specialized knowledge. A good example is security testing. We're not talking about security within an application, such as who has access rights to administer it. Because that type of security is really part of the functional requirements and will be covered by regular stories, verifying that it works falls within the first three quadrants. We're talking about probing for external security flaws and knowing the types of vulnerabilities in systems that hackers exploit. That is a specialized skill set.

Performance testing can be done by testers and programmers collaborating and building simple tools for their specific needs. Some organizations purchase load-testing tools that require team members who specialize in that tool to build the scripts and analyze and interpret the results. It can be difficult for a software development organization, especially a small one, to have enough resources to duplicate an accurate production-level load for a test, so external providers of performance testing may be needed.

Chapter 15, "Tester Activities in Release or Theme Planning," explains how to plan to work with external teams.

Larger organizations may have groups such as database experts that your team can use to help with data conversion, security groups that will help you identify risks to your application, or a production support team that can help you test recovery or failover. Build a close relationship with these specialists. You'll need to work together as a virtual team to gather the information you need about your product.

The more diverse the skill sets are in your team, the less likely you are to need outside consultants to help you. Identify the resources you need for each project. Many teams find that a good technical tester or toolsmith can take on many of these tasks. If someone already on the team can learn whatever specialized knowledge is required, great; otherwise, bring in the expertise you need.

Skills within the Team

Jason Holzer, Product Owner for Property Testing (performance, security, stability, and reliability) at Ultimate Software, tells us that a good programmer can write a multithreaded engine to call a function concurrently and test performance. Jason feels that agile teams do have the skills to do their own performance testing; they just may not realize it.

Performance testing does require a controlled, dedicated environment. Some specialized tools are needed, such as a profiler to measure code performance. But, in Jason's view, performance, stability, scalability, and reliability (PSR) tests can, and should, be done at the unit level. There's a mind-set that holds that these tests are too complex and require specialists when in fact the teams do possess the necessary skills.

Jason finds that awareness of the "PSR" aspects of code needs to be part of the team's culture.

If stakeholders place a high priority on performance, stability, scalability, and the like, Jason recommends that the team talk about ways to verify these aspects of the application. When teams understand the priority of qualities such as performance and reliability, they figure out how to improve their code to ensure them. They don't need to depend on an outside, specialized team. Jason explains his viewpoint.

> The potential resistance I see today to this plan is that someone believes that programmers don't know how to PSR test and that there will need to be a great deal of training. In my opinion, a more accurate statement is that programmers are not aware that PSR testing is a high priority and a key to quality. I don't think it has anything to do with knowing how to PSR test. PSR testing is a combination of math, science, analysis, programming, and problem solving. I am willing to bet that if you conducted a competition at any software development organization where you asked every team to implement a tree search algorithm, and the team with the fastest algorithm would win, that every team will do PSR testing and provide PSR metrics without teaching them anything new.

> PSR testing is really just telling me "How fast?" (performance), "How long?" (stability), "How often?" (reliability), and "How much?" (scalability). So, as long as the awareness is there and the organization is seriously asking those questions with everything they develop, then PSR testing is successfully integrated into a team.

Take a second look at the skills that your team already possesses, and brainstorm about the types of "ility" testing that can be done with the resources you already have. If you need outside teams, plan for that in your release and iteration planning.

Regardless of whether or not your team brings in additional resources for these types of tests, your team is still responsible for making sure the minimum testing is done. The information these tests provide may result in new stories and tasks in areas such as changing the architecture for better scalability or implementing a system-wide security solution. Be sure to complete the feedback loop from tests that critique the product to tests that drive changes that will improve the nonfunctional aspects of the product.

Just because this is the fourth out of four agile testing quadrants doesn't mean these tests come last. Your team needs to think about when to do performance, security, and "ility" tests so that you ensure your product delivers the right business value.

WHEN DO YOU DO IT?

As with functional testing, the sooner technology-facing tests that support the team are completed, the cheaper it is to fix any issues that are found. However, many of the cross-functional tests are expensive and hard to do in small chunks.

Technical stories can be written to address specific requirements, such as: "As user Abby, I need to retrieve report X in less than 20 seconds so that I can make a decision quickly." This story is about performance and requires specialized tests to be written, and it can be done along with the story to code the report, or in a later iteration.

Consider a separate row on your story board for tasks needed by the product as a whole. Lisa's team uses this area to put cards such as "Evaluate load test tools" or "Establish a performance test baseline." Janet has successfully used different colored cards to show that the story is meant for one of the expert roles borrowed from other areas of the organization.

Some performance tests might need to wait until much of the application is built if you are trying to baseline full end-to-end workflows. If performance and reliability are a top priority, you need to find a way to test those early in the project. Prioritize stories so that a steel thread or thin slice is complete early. You should be able to create a performance test that can be run and continue to run as you add more and more functionality to the workflow. This may enable you to catch performance issues early and redesign the system architecture for improvements. For many applications, correct functionality is irrelevant without the necessary performance.

The time to think about your nonfunctional tests is during release or theme planning. Plan to start early, tackling small increments as needed. For each iteration, see what tasks your team needs in order to determine whether the code design is reliable, scalable, usable, and secure. In the next section, we'll look at some different types of Quadrant 4 tests.

Performance Testing from the Start

Ken De Souza, a software developer/tester at NCR [2008], responded to a question on the agile-testing mailing list about when to do stress and performance testing in an agile project with an explanation of how he approaches performance testing.

> I'd suggest designing your performance tests from the start. We build data from the first iteration, and we run a simple performance test to make sure it all holds together. This is more to see that the functionality of the performance scripts holds together.
>
> I used JMeter because I can hook FTP, SOAP, HTTP, RegEx, and so on, all from a few threads, with just one instance running. I can test out my calls right from the start (or at least have the infrastructure in place to do it).
>
> My eventual goal is that when the product is close to releasing, I don't have to nurse the performance test; I just have to crank up the threads and let go. All my metrics and tasks have already been tested out for months, so I'm fairly certain that anyone can run my performance test.

Performance testing can be approached using agile principles to build the tools and test components incrementally. As with software features, focus on getting the performance information you need, one small chunk at a time.

"ILITY" TESTING

If we could just focus on the desired behavior and functionality of the application, life would be so simple. Unfortunately, we have to be concerned with qualities such as security, maintainability, interoperability, compatibility, reliability, and installability. Let's take a look at some of these "ilities."

Security

OK, it doesn't end in -ility, but we include it in the "ility" bucket because we use technology-facing tests to appraise the security aspects of the product. Security is a top priority for every organization these days. Every organization needs to ensure the confidentiality and integrity of their software. They want to verify concepts such as no repudiation, a guarantee that the message has been sent by the party that claims to have sent it and received by the party that claims to have received it. The application needs to perform the correct authentication, confirming each user's identity, and authorization, in order to allow the user access only to the services they're authorized to use. Testing so many different aspects of security isn't easy.

In the rush to deliver functionality, both business experts and development teams in newly started organizations may not be thinking of security first. They just want to get some software working so they can do business. Authorization is often the only aspect of security testing that they consider as part of business functionality.

Lisa's Story

My current team is a case in point. The business was interested in automating functionality to manage 401(k) plans. They did take pains to secure the software and data, but it wasn't a testing priority. When I "got religion" after hearing some good presentations about security testing at conferences, I bought a book on security testing and started hacking around on the site. I found some serious issues, which we fixed, but we realized we needed a comprehensive approach to ensuring security. We wrote stories to implement this. We also started including a "security" task card with every story so that we'd be mindful of security needs while developing and testing.

—Lisa

Budgeting this type of work has to be a business priority. There's a range of alternatives available, depending on your company's priorities and resources. Understand your needs and the risks before you invest a lot of time and energy.

Janet's Story

One team that I worked with has a separate corporate security team. Whenever functionality is added to the application that might expose a security flaw, the corporate team runs the application through a security test application and produces a report for the team. It performs static testing using a canned black-box probe on the code and has exposed a few weak areas that the developers were able to address. It does not give an overall picture of the security level for the application, but that was not deemed a major concern.

—Janet

Testers who are skilled in security testing can perform security risk-based testing, which is driven by analyzing the architectural risk, attack patterns, or abuse and misuse cases. When specialized skills are required, bring in what you need, but the team is still responsible for making sure the testing gets done.

There are a variety of automated tools to help with security verification. Static analysis tools, which can examine the code without executing the application, can detect potential security flaws in the code that might not otherwise show up for years. Dynamic analysis tools, which run in real time, can test for vulnerabilities such as SQL injection and cross-site scripting. Manual exploratory testing by a knowledgeable security tester is indispensable to detect issues that automated tests can miss.

See http://en .wikipedia.org/wiki/ Buffer_overflow and http://en .wikipedia.org/wiki/ Format_string_ vulnerabilities for more information.

See http://en .wikipedia.org/wiki/ List_of_tools_for_ static_code_analysis for a list of tools that can be used for static code analysis.

More resources on this subject can be found at: www .fuzzing.org/ category/fuzzing- book/ and www .fuzzing.org/fuzzing- software

Security Testing Perspectives

Security testing is a vast topic on its own. Grig Gheorghiu shares some highlights about resources that can help agile teams with security testing.

Just like functional testing, security testing can be done from two perspectives: from the inside out (white-box testing) and from the outside in (black-box testing). Inside-out security testing assumes that the source code for the application under test is available to the testers. The code can be analyzed statically with a variety of tools that try to discover common coding errors that can make the application vulnerable to attacks such as buffer overflows or format string attacks.

The fact that the testers have access to the source code of the application also means that they can map what some books call "the attack surface" of the application, which is the list of all of the inputs and resources used by the program under test. Armed with a knowledge of the attack surface, testers can then apply a variety of techniques that attempt to break the security of the application. A very effective class of such techniques is called fuzzing and is based on fault injection. Using this technique, the testers try to make the application fail by feeding it various types of inputs (hence the term *fault injection*). These inputs can be carefully crafted strings used in SQL injection attacks, random byte changes in given input files, or random strings fed as command line arguments.

The outside-in approach is the one mostly used by attackers who try to penetrate into the servers or the network hosting your application. As a security tester, you need to have the same mind-set that attackers do, which means that you have to use your creativity in discovering and exploiting vulnerabilities in your own application. You also need to stay up-to-date with the latest security news and updates related to the platform/ operating system your application runs on, which is not an easy task.

So what are agile testers to do when faced with the apparently insurmountable task of testing the security of their application? Here are some practical, pragmatic steps that anybody can follow:

1. Adopt a continuous integration (CI) process that periodically runs a suite of automated tests against your application.

2. Learn how to use one or more open source static code analysis tools. Add a step to your CI process that consists of running these tools against your application code. Mark the step as failed if the tools find any critical vulnerabilities.

3. Install an automated security vulnerability scanner such as Nessus (http://www.nessus.org/nessus/). Nessus can be run in a command-line, non-GUI mode, which makes it suitable for inclusion in a CI tool. Add a step to your CI process that consists of running Nessus against your application. Capture the Nessus output in a file and parse that file for any high-importance security holes found by the scanner. Mark the step as failed when any such holes are found.

4. Learn how to use one or more open source fuzzing tools. Add a step to your CI process that consists of running these tools against your application code. Mark the step as failed if the tools find any critical vulnerabilities.

As with any automated testing effort, running these tools is no guarantee that your code and your application will be free of security defects. However, running these tools will go a long way toward improving the quality of your application in terms of security. As always, the 80/20 rule applies. These tools will probably find the 80% most common security bugs out there while requiring 20% of your security budget.

To find the remaining 20% of the security defects, you're well advised to spend the other 80% of your security budget on high-quality security experts. They will be able to test your application security thoroughly by the use of techniques such as SQL injection, code injection, remote code inclusion, and cross-site scripting. While there are some tools that try to automate some of these techniques, they are no match for a trained professional who takes the time to understand the inner workings of your application in order to craft the perfect attack against it.

Security testing can be intimidating, so budget time to adopt a hacker mind-set and decide on the right approach to the task at hand. Use the resources Grig suggests to educate yourself. Take advantage of these tools and techniques in order to achieve security tests with a reasonable return on investment.

Just this brief look at security testing shows why specialized training and tools are so important to do a good job of it. For most organizations, this testing is absolutely required. One security intrusion might be enough to take a company out of business. Even if the probability were low, the stakes are too high to put off these tests.

Code that costs a lot to maintain might not kill an organization's profitability as quickly as a security breach, but it could lead to a long, slow death. In the next section we consider ways to verify maintainability.

Maintainability

Maintainability is not something that is easy to test. In traditional projects, it's often done by the use of full code reviews or inspections. Agile teams often use pair programming, which has built-in continual code review. There are other ways to make sure the code and tests stay maintainable.

We encourage development teams to develop standards and guidelines that they follow for application code, the test frameworks, and the tests themselves. Teams that develop their own standards, rather than having them set by some other independent team, will be more likely to follow them because they make sense to them.

The kinds of standards we mean include naming conventions for method names or test names. All guidelines should be simple to follow and make maintainability easier. Examples are: "Success is always zero and failure must be a negative value," "Each class or module should have only one single responsibility," or "All functions must be single entry, single exit."

Standards for developing the GUI also make the application more testable and maintainable, because testers know what to expect and don't need to wonder whether a behavior is right or wrong. It also adds to testability if you are automating tests from the GUI. Simple standards such as, "Use names for all GUI objects rather than defaulting to the computer assigned identifier" or "You cannot have two fields with the same name on a page" help the team achieve a level where the code is maintainable, as are the automated tests that provide coverage for it.

Maintainable code supports shared code ownership. It is much easier for a programmer to move from one area to another if all code is written in the same style and easily understood by everyone on the team. Complexity adds risk and also makes code harder to understand. The XP value of simplicity should be applied to code. Simple coding standards can also include guidelines such as, "Avoid duplication—Don't copy-paste methods." These same concepts apply to test frameworks and the tests themselves.

Maintainability is an important factor for automated tests as well. Test tools have lagged behind programming tools in features that make them easy to maintain, such as IDE plug-ins to make writing and maintaining test scripts simpler and more efficient. That's changing fast, so look for tools that provide easy refactoring and search-and-replace, and for other utilities that make it easy to modify the scripts.

Database maintainability is also important. The database design needs to be flexible and usable. Every iteration might bring tasks to add or remove tables, columns, constraints, or triggers, or to do some kind of data conversion. These tasks become a bottleneck if the database design is poor or the database is cluttered with invalid data.

Lisa's Story

A serious regression bug went undetected and caused production problems. We had a test that should have caught the bug. However, a constraint was missing from the schema used by the regression suite. Our test schemas had grown haphazardly over the years. Some had columns that no longer existed in the production schema. Some were missing various constraints, triggers, and indices. Our DBA had to manually make changes to each schema as needed for each story instead of running the same script in each schema to update it. We budgeted time over several sprints to recreate all of the test schemas so that they were identical and also matched production.

—Lisa

Plan time to evaluate the database's impact on team velocity, and refactor it just as you do production and test code. Maintainability of all aspects of the application, test, and execution environments is more a matter of assessment and refactoring than direct testing. If your velocity is going down, is it because parts of the code are hard to work on, or is it that the database is difficult to modify?

Interoperability

Interoperability refers to the capability of diverse systems and organizations to work together and share information. Interoperability testing looks at end-to-end functionality between two or more communicating systems. These tests are done in the context of the user—human or a software application—and look at functional behavior.

In agile development, interoperability testing can be done early in the development cycle. We have a working, deployable system at the end of each iteration so that we can deploy and set up testing with other systems.

In Chapter 20, "Successful Delivery," we discuss more about the importance of this level of testing.

Quadrant 1 includes code integration tests, which are tests between components, but there is a whole other level of integration tests in enterprise systems. You might find yourself integrating systems through open or proprietary interfaces. The API you develop for your system might enable your users to easily set up a framework for them to test easily. Easier testing for your customer makes for faster acceptance.

In one project Janet worked on, test systems were set up at the customer's site so that they could start to integrate them with their own systems early. Interfaces to existing systems were changed as needed and tested with each new deployment.

If the system your team works on has to work together with external systems, you may not be able to represent them all in your test environments except with stubs and drivers that simulate the behavior of the other systems or equipment. This is one situation where testing after development is complete might be unavoidable. You might have to schedule test time in a test environment shared by several teams.

Consider all of the systems with which yours needs to communicate, and make sure you plan ahead to have an appropriate environment for testing them together. You'll also need to plan resources for testing that your application is compatible with the various operating systems, browsers, clients, servers, and hardware with which it might be used. We'll discuss compatibility testing next.

Compatibility

The type of project you're working on dictates how much compatibility testing is required. If you have a web application and your customers are worldwide, you will need to think about all types of browsers and operating systems. If you are delivering a custom enterprise application, you can probably reduce the amount of compatibility testing, because you might be able to dictate which versions are supported.

As each new screen is developed as part of a user interface story, it is a good idea to check its operability in all supported browsers. A simple task can be added to the story to test on all browsers.

One organization that Janet worked at had to test compatibility with reading software for the visual impaired. Although the company had no formal test lab, it had test machines available near the team area for easy access. The testers made periodic checks to make sure that new functionality was still compatible with the third-party tools. It was easy to fix problems that were discovered early during development.

Having test machines available with different operating systems or browsers or third-party applications that need to work with the system under test makes it easier for the testers to ensure compatibility with each new story or at the end of an iteration. When you start a new theme or project, think about the resources you might need to verify compatibility. If you're starting on a brand new product, you might have to build up a test lab for it. Make sure your team gets information on your end users' hardware, operating systems, browsers, and versions of each. If the percentage of use of a new browser version has grown large enough, it might be time to start including that version in your compatibility testing.

When you select or create functional test tools, make sure there's an easy way to run the same script with different versions of browsers, operating systems, and hardware. For example, Lisa's team could use the same suite of GUI regression tests on each of the servers running on Windows, Solaris, and Linux. Functional test scripts can also be used for reliability testing. Let's look at that next.

Reliability

Reliability of software can be referred to as the ability of a system to perform and maintain its functions in routine circumstances as well as unexpected circumstances. The system also must perform and maintain its functions with consistency and repeatability. Reliability analysis answers the question, "How long will it run before it breaks?" Some statistics used to measure reliability are:

- **Mean time to failure:** The average or mean time between initial operation and the first occurrence of a failure or malfunction. In other words, how long can the system run before it fails the first time?
- **Mean time between failures:** A statistical measure of reliability, this is calculated to indicate the anticipated average time between failures. The longer the better.

In traditional projects, we used to schedule weeks of reliability testing that tried to run simulations that matched a regular day's work. Now, we should be able to deliver at the end of every iteration, so how can we schedule reliability tests?

We have automated unit and acceptance tests running on a regular basis. To do a reliability test, we simply need to use those same tests and run them over and over. Ideally, you would use statistics gathered that show daily usage, create a script that mirrors the usage, and run it on a stable build for however long your team thinks is adequate to prove stability. You can input random data into the tests to simulate production use and make sure the application doesn't crash because of invalid inputs. Of course, you might want to mirror peak usage to make sure that it handles busy times as well.

You can create stories in each iteration to develop these scripts and add new functionality as it is added to the application. Your acceptance tests could be very specific such as, "Functionality X must perform 10,000 operations in a 24-hour period for a minimum of 3 days."

Beware: Running a thousand tests without any serious problems doesn't mean you have reliable software. You have to run the right tests. To make a reliability test effective, think about your application and how it is used all day, every day, over a period of time. Specify tests that are aimed at demonstrating that your application will be able to meet your customers' needs, even during peak times.

Ask the customer team for their reliability criteria in the form of measurable goals. For example, they might consider the system reliable if ten or fewer errors occur for every 10,000 transactions, or the web application is available 99.999% of the time. Recovery from power outages and other disasters might be part of the reliability objectives, and will be stated in the form of Service Level Agreements. Know what they are. Some industries have their own software reliability standards and guidelines.

Driving development with the right programmer and customer tests should enhance the application's reliability, because this usually leads to better design and fewer defects. Write additional stories and tasks as needed to deliver a system that meets the organization's reliability standards.

Your product might be reliable after it's up and running, but it also needs to be installable by all users, in all supported environments. This is another area where following agile principles gives us an advantage.

Installability

One of the cornerstones of a successful agile team is continuous integration. This means that a build is ready for testing anytime during the day. Many teams choose to deploy one or more of the successful builds into test environments on a daily basis.

Automating the deployment creates repeatability and makes deployment a non-event. This is exciting to us because we have experienced weeks of trying to integrate and install a new system. We know that if we build once and deploy the same build to multiple environments, we have developed consistency.

Janet's Story

On one project I worked on, the deployment was automatic and was tested on multiple environments in the development cycle. However, there were issues when deploying to the customer site. We added a step to the end game so that the support group would take the release and do a complete install test as if it were the customer's site. We were able to walk through the deployment notes and eliminated many of the issues the customer would have otherwise seen.

—Janet

Chapter 20, "Successful Delivery," has more on installation testing.

As with any other functionality, risks associated with installation need to be evaluated and the amount of testing determined accordingly. Our advice is to do it early and often, and automate the process if possible.

"ility" Summary

There are other "ilities" to test, depending on your product's domain. Safety-critical software, such as that used in medical devices and aircraft control systems, requires extensive safety testing, and the regression tests probably would contain tests related to safety. System redundancy and failover tests would be especially important for such a product. Your team might need to look at industry data around software-related safety issues and use extra code reviews. Configurability, auditability, portability, robustness, and extensibility are just a few of the qualities your team might need to evaluate with technology-facing tests.

Whatever "ility" you need to test, use an incremental approach. Start by eliciting the customer team's requirements and examples of their objectives for that particular area of quality. Write business-facing tests to make sure the code is designed to meet those goals. In the first iteration, the team might do some research and come up with a test strategy to evaluate the existing quality level of the product. The next step might be to create a suitable test environment, to research tools, or to start with some manual tests.

As you learn how the application measures up to the customers' requirements, close the loop with new Quadrant 1 and 2 tests that drive the application closer to the goals for that particular property. An incremental approach is also recommended for performance, load, and other tests that are addressed in the next section.

PERFORMANCE, LOAD, STRESS, AND SCALABILITY TESTING

Performance, load, stress, and scalability testing all fall into Quadrant 4 because of their technology focus. Often specialized skills are required, although many teams have figured out ways to do their own testing in these areas. Let's talk about scalability first, because it is often forgotten.

Scalability

Scalability testing verifies the application remains reliable when more users are added. What that really means is, "Can your system handle the capacity of a growing customer base?" It sounds simple, but really isn't, and is a problem that an agile team usually can't solve by itself.

It is important to think about the whole system and not just the application itself. For example, the network is often the bottleneck, because it can't handle the increased throughput. What about the database? Will it scale? Will the hardware you are using handle the new loads being considered? Is it simple just to add new hardware, or is it the bottleneck?

Janet's Story

In one organization I was recently working in, their customer base had grown very quickly, and the solution they had invested in had reached its capacity due to hardware constraints. It was not a simple matter of adding a new server, because the solution was not designed that way. The system needed to be monitored to restart services during peak usage.

To grow, the organization had to actually change solutions to accommodate its future growth, but this was not recognized until problems started to happen.

Ideally, the organization would have replaced the old system before it was an issue. This is an example of why it is important to understand your system and its capability, as well as future growth projections.

—Janet

You will need to go outside the team to get the answers you require to address scalability issues, so plan ahead.

Performance and Load Testing

Performance testing is usually done to help identify bottlenecks in a system or to establish a baseline for future testing. It is also done to ensure compliance with performance goals and requirements, and to help stakeholders make informed decisions related to the overall quality of the application being tested.

Load testing evaluates system behavior as more and more users access the system at the same time. Stress testing evaluates the robustness of the application under higher-than-expected loads. Will the application scale as the business grows? Characteristics such as response time can be more critical than functionality for some applications.

Grig Gheorghiu [2005] emphasizes the need for clearly defined expectations to get value from performance testing. He says, "If you don't know where you want to go in terms of the system, then it matters little which direction you take (remember Alice and the Cheshire Cat?)." For example, you probably want to know the number of concurrent users and the acceptable response time for a web application.

Performance and Load-Testing Tools

See the bibliography for links to sites where you can research tools.

After you've defined your performance goals, you can use a variety of tools to put a load on the system and check for bottlenecks. This can be done at the unit level, with tools such as JUnitPerf, httperf, or a home-grown harness. Apache JMeter, The Grinder, Pounder, ftptt, and OpenWebLoad are more examples of the many open source performance and load test tools available at the time of this writing. Some of these, such as JMeter, can be used on a variety of server types, from SOAP to LDAP to POP3 mail. Plenty of commercial tool options are available too, including NeoLoad, WebLoad, eValid LoadTest, LoadRunner, and SOATest.

Use these tools to look for performance bottlenecks. Lisa's team uses JProfiler to look for application bottlenecks and memory leaks, and JConsole to analyze database usage. Similar tools exist for .NET and other environments, including .NET Memory Profiler and ANTS Profiler Pro. As Grig points out, there are database-specific profilers to pinpoint performance issues at the database level; ask your database experts to work with you. Your system administrators can help you use shell commands such as top, or tools such as PerfMon to monitor CPU, memory, swap, disk I/O, and other hardware resources. Similar tools are available at the network level, for example, NetScout.

You can also use the tools the team is most familiar with. In one project, Janet worked very closely with one of the programmers to create the tests. She helped him to define the tests needed based on customer's performance and load expectations, and he automated them using JUnit. Together they analyzed the results to report back to the customer.

Establishing a baseline is a good first step for evaluating performance. The next section explores this aspect of performance testing.

Baseline

Performance tuning can turn into a big project, so it is essential to provide a baseline that you can compare against new versions of the software on performance. Even if performance isn't your biggest concern at the moment, don't ignore it. It's a good idea to get a performance baseline so that you know later which direction your response time is headed. Lisa's company hosts a website that has had a small load on it. They got a load test baseline on the site so that as it grew, they'd know how performance was being affected.

Performance Baseline Test Results

Lisa's coworker Mike Busse took on the task of obtaining performance baselines for their web application that manages retirement plans. He evaluated load test tools, implemented one (JMeter), and set about to get a baseline. He reported the results both in a high-level summary and a spreadsheet with detailed results.

The tests simulated slowly increasing the load up to 100 concurrent users. Three test scripts, each for a common user activity, were used, and they were run separately and all together. Data gathered included:

- Maximum time of a transaction

- Maximum number of busy connections.

- A plot of the max time of a transaction against the number of users (see Figure 11-2 for an example of a chart)

- Number of users who were on the system when the max time of a transaction equaled eight seconds

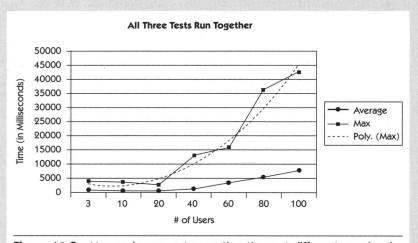

Figure 11-2   Max and average transaction times at different user loads.

An important aspect of reporting results was providing definitions of terms such as *transaction* and *connection* in order to make the results meaningful to everyone. For example, maximum time of a transaction is defined as the longest transaction of all transactions completed during the test.

Mike's report also included assumptions made for the performance test:

- Eight seconds is a transaction threshold that we would not like to cross.
- The test web server is equivalent to either of the two web servers in production.
- The load the system can handle, as determined by these tests, can be doubled in production because the load is distributed between two web servers.
- The distribution of tasks in the test that combines all three tests is accurate to a reasonable degree.

Mike also identified shortcomings with the performance baseline. More than one transaction can contribute to loading a page, meaning that the max page load time could be longer than the max time of a transaction. The test machine doesn't duplicate the production environment, which has two machines and load-balancing software to distribute the transactions.

The report ended with a conclusion about the number of concurrent users that the production system could support. This serves as a guideline to be aware of as the production load increases. The current load is less than half of this number, but there are unknowns, such as whether the production users are all active or have neglected to log out.

Make sure your performance tests adequately mimic production conditions. Make results meaningful by defining each test and metric, explaining how the results correlate to the production environment and what can be done with the results, and providing results in graphical form.

If there are specific performance criteria that have been defined for specific functionality, we suggest that performance testing be done as part of the iteration to ensure that issues are found before it is too late to fix them.

Benchmarking can be done at any time during a release. If new functionality is added that might affect the performance, such as complicated queries, re-run the tests to make sure there are no adverse effects. This way, you have time to optimize the query or code early in the cycle when the development team is still familiar with the feature.

Any performance, load, or stress test won't be meaningful unless it's run in an environment that mimics the production environment. Let's talk more about environments.

Test Environments

Final runs of the performance tests will help customers make decisions about accepting their product. For accurate results, tests need to be run on equipment that is similar to that of production. Often teams will use smaller machines and extrapolate the results to decide if the performance is sufficient for the business needs. This should be clearly noted when reporting test results.

Stressing the application to see what load it can take before it crashes can also be done anytime during the release, but usually it is not considered high-priority by customers unless you have a mission-critical system with lots of load.

One resource that is affected by increasing load is memory. In the next section, we discuss memory management.

Memory Management

Memory is usually described in terms of the amount (normally the minimum or maximum) of memory to be used for RAM, ROM, hard drives, and so on. You should be aware of memory usage and watch for leaks, because they can cause catastrophic failures when the application is in production during peak usage. Some programming languages are more susceptible to memory issues, so understanding the strengths and weaknesses of the code will assist you in knowing what to watch for. Testing for memory issues can be done as part of performance, load, and stress testing.

Garbage collection is one tool used to release memory back to the program. However, it can mask severe memory issues. If you see the available memory steadily decreasing with usage and then all of a sudden increasing to maximum available, you might suspect the garbage collection has kicked in. Watch for anomalies in the pattern or whether the system starts to get slow under heavy usage. You may need to monitor for a while and work with the programmers to find the issue. The fix might be something simple, such as scheduling the garbage collection more often or setting the trigger level higher.

When you are working with the programmers on a story, ask them if they expect problems with memory. You can test specifically if you know there might be a risk in the area. Watching for memory leaks is not always easy, but there are tools to help. This is an area where programmers should have tools easily available. Collaborate with them to verify that the application is free of memory issues. Perform the performance and load tests described in the previous section to verify that there aren't any memory problems.

You don't have to be an expert on how to do technology-facing testing that critiques the product to help your team plan for it and execute it. Your team can evaluate what tests it needs from this quadrant. Talk about these tests as you plan your release; you can create a test plan specifically for performance and load if you've not done it before. You will need time to obtain the expertise needed, either by acquiring it through identifying and learning the skills, or by bringing in outside help. As with all development efforts, break technology-facing tests into small tasks that can be addressed and built upon each iteration.

SUMMARY

In this chapter, we've explored the fourth agile testing quadrant, the technology-facing tests that critique the product.

- The developer team should evaluate whether it has, or can acquire, the expertise to do these tests, or if it needs to plan to bring in external resources.
- An incremental approach to these tests, completing tasks in each iteration, ensures time to address any issues that arise and avoid production problems.

- The team should consider various types of "ility" testing, including security, maintainability, interoperability, compatibility, reliability, and installability testing, and should execute these tests at appropriate times.
- Performance, scalability, stress, and load testing should be done from the beginning of the project.
- Research the memory management issues that might impact your product, and plan tests to verify the application is free of memory issues.

Chapter 12

SUMMARY OF
TESTING QUADRANTS

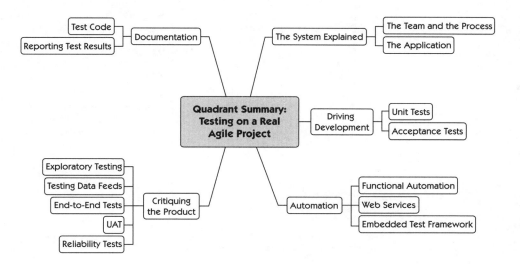

In Chapter 6, we introduced the testing quadrants, and in the chapters that followed we talked about how to use the concepts in your agile project. In this chapter, we'll bring it all together with an example of an agile team that used tests from all four quadrants.

REVIEW OF THE TESTING QUADRANTS

We've just spent five chapters talking about each of the quadrants (see Figure 12-1) and examples of tools you can use for the different types of testing. The next trick is to know which tests your project needs and when to do them. In this chapter, we'll walk you through a real-life example of an agile project that used tests from all four agile testing quadrants.

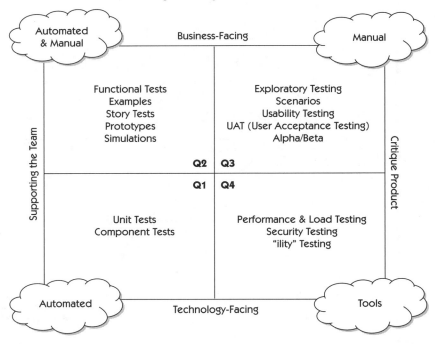

Figure 12-1   Agile Testing Quadrants

A SYSTEM TEST EXAMPLE

The following story is about one organization's success in testing its whole system using a variety of home-grown and open source tools. Janet worked with this team, and Paul Rogers was the primary test architect. This is Paul's story.

The Application

The system solves the problem of monitoring remote oil and gas production wells. The solution combines a remote monitoring device that can transmit data and receive adjustments from a central monitoring station using a proprietary protocol over a satellite communication channel.

Figure 12-2 shows the architecture of the Remote Data Monitoring system. The measurement devices on the oil wells, Remote Terminal Units (RTU), use a va-

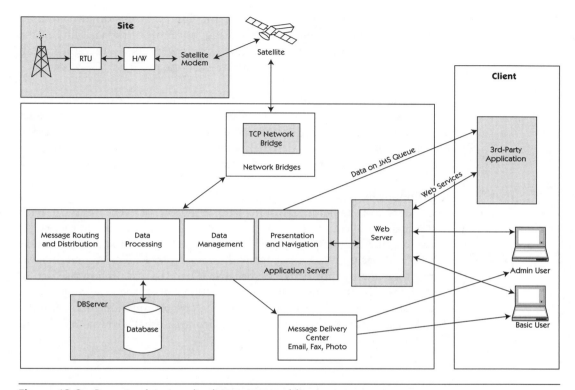

Figure 12-2   Remote data monitoring system architecture

riety of protocols to communicate with the measurement device. This data from each RTU is transmitted via satellite to servers located at the client's main office. It is then made available to users via a web interface. A notification system, via email, fax, or phone, is available when a particular reading is outside of normal operational limits. A Java Message Service (JMS) feed and web services are also available to help integration with clients' other applications.

The software application was a huge legacy system that had few unit tests. The team was slowly rebuilding the application with new technology.

The Team and the Process

The team consisted of four software programmers, two firmware programmers, three to four testers, a product engineer, and an off-site manager. The "real" customer was in another country. The development team uses XP practices, including pair programming and TDD. The customer team used the defect-tracking system for the backlog, but most of the visibility of the stories was through index cards. Story cards were used during iteration planning meetings, and the task board tracked the progress.

Scrum was used as the outside reporting mechanism to the organization and the customers. The team had two week iterations and released the product about every four months. This varied depending on the functionality being developed. Retrospectives were held as part of every iteration planning session, and action was taken on the top three priority items discussed.

Continuous integration through CruiseControl provided constant builds for the testers and the demonstrations held at the end of every iteration. Each tester had a local environment for testing the web application, but there were three test environments available to the system. The first one was to test new stories and was updated as needed with the latest build. The second one was for testing client-reported issues, because it had the last version released to the clients. The third environment was a full stand-alone test environment that was available for testing full deploys, communication links, and the firmware and hardware. It was on this environment that we ran our load and reliability tests.

TESTS DRIVING DEVELOPMENT

The tests driving development included unit test and acceptance tests.

Unit Tests

Chapter 7, "Technology-Facing Tests that Support the Team," explains more about unit testing and TDD.

Unit tests are technology-facing tests that support programming. Those that are developed as part of test-driven development not only help the programmer get the story right but also help to design the system.

The programmers on the Remote Data Monitoring project bought into Test Driven Development (TDD) and pair programming wholeheartedly. All new functionality was developed and tested using pair programming. All stories delivered to the testers were supported by unit tests, and very few bugs were found after coding was complete. The bugs that were found were generally integration-related.

However, when the team first started, the legacy system had few unit tests to support refactoring. As process changes were implemented, the developers decided to start fixing the problem. Every time they touched a piece of code in the legacy system, they added unit tests and refactored the code as necessary. Gradually, the legacy system became more stable and was able to withstand major refactoring when it was needed. We experienced the power of unit tests!

Acceptance Tests

The product engineer (the customer proxy) took ownership of creating the acceptance tests. These tests varied in format depending on the actual story. Although he struggled at first, the product engineer got pretty good at giving the tests to the programmers before they started coding. The team created a test template, which evolved over time, that met both the programmers' and the testers' needs.

The tests were sometimes informally written, but they included data, required setup if it wasn't immediately obvious, different variations that were critical to the story, and some examples. The team found that examples helped clarify the expectations for many of the stories.

The test team automated the acceptance tests as soon as possible, usually at the same time as the stories were being developed. Of course, the product engineer was available to answer any questions that came up during development.

See Chapter 8, "Business-Facing Tests that Support the Team," for more about driving development with acceptance tests.

These acceptance tests served three purposes. They were business-facing tests that supported development because they were given to the team before coding started. Secondly, they were used by the test team as the basis of automation that fed into the regression suite and provided future ideas for exploratory testing. The third purpose was to confirm that the implementation met the needs of the customer. The product engineer did this solution verification.

AUTOMATION

Automation involved the functional test structure, web services, and embedded testing.

The Automated Functional Test Structure

Ruby was used with Watir as the tool of choice for the functional automation framework. It was determined to have the most flexibility and opportunity for customization that was required for the system under test.

The automated test code included three distinct layers, shown in Figure 12-3. The lowest layer, Layer 1, included Watir and other classes, such as loggers that wrote to the log files.

The second layer, Layer 2, was the page access layer, where classes that contained code to access individual web pages lived. For example, in the application under test (AUT) there was a login page, a create user page, and an edit user page. Classes written in Ruby contained code that could perform certain functions in the AUT, such as a class that logs into the application, a class to edit a user, and a class to assign access rights to a user. These classes contained no data. For example, the log-in class didn't know what username to log in with.

The third and top layer, Layer 3, was the test layer, and it contained the data needed to perform a test. It called Layer 2 classes, which in turned called Layer 1.

For example, the actual test would call LogIn and pass Janet as the user name and Passw0rd as the password. This meant you could feed in many different data sets easily.

```
LogIn ('Janet', 'Passw0rd')
```

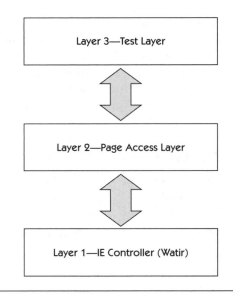

Figure 12-3   Functional test layers

Layer 2 also knew how to handle the error messages the application generated. For example, when an invalid username was entered on the login page, the login class detected the error message and then passed the problem back to the tests in Layer 3.

This means the same Layer 2 classes could be used for both happy path testing and for negative testing. In the negative case, Layer 3 would expect Layer 2 to return a failure, and would then check to see if the test failed for the correct reason by accessing the error messages that Layer Two scraped from the browser.

The functional tests used Ruby with Watir to control the DOM on the browser and could access almost all of the objects in the page. The automated test suite was run on nightly builds to give the team consistent feedback on high-level application behavior. This was a lifesaver as the team continued to build out the unit tests. This architecture efficiently accommodated the business-facing tests that support the team.

Web Services

Web services were used by clients to interface with some of their other applications. The development group used Ruby to write a client to test each service they developed. For these tests, Ruby's unit testing framework, Test::Unit, was used.

The web services tests were expanded by the test team to cover more than 1,000 different test cases, and took just minutes to run. They gave the team an amazing amount of coverage in a short period of time.

The team demonstrated the test client to the customers, who decided to use it as well. However, the customers subsequently decided it didn't work for them, so they started writing their own tests, albeit in a much more ad hoc fashion using Ruby.

They used IRB, the interactive interface provided by Ruby, and fed values in an exploratory method. It gave the customer an interactive environment for discovering what worked and what didn't. It also let them get familiar with Ruby and how we were testing, and it gave them much more confidence in our tests. Much of their User Acceptance Testing was done using IRB.

Three different slants on the web services tests served three different purposes. The programmers used it to help test their client and drive their development. The testers used it to critique the product in a very efficient automated manner, and the customers were able to test the web services delivered to them using IRB.

Embedded Testing

In addition to the web interface, the RDM system consisted of a small embedded device that communicated with measuring equipment using various protocols. Using Ruby, various tests were developed to test part of its administrative interface. This interface was a command-line system similar to FTP.

These data-driven tests were contained in an Excel spreadsheet. A Ruby script would read commands from Excel using the OLE interface and send them to the embedded device. The script would then compare the response from the device with the expected result, also held in the spreadsheet. Errors were highlighted in red. These automated tests took approximately one hour to run, while doing the same tests manually would take eight hours.

While this provided a lot of test coverage, it didn't actually test the reason the device was used, which was to read data from RTUs. A simulator was written in Ruby with a FOX (FXRuby) GUI. This allowed mock data to be fed into the device. Because the simulator could be controlled remotely, it was incorporated into automated tests that exercised the embedded device's ability to read data, respond to error conditions, and generate alarms when the input data exceeded a predetermined threshold.

Embedded testing is highly technical, but with the power provided by the simulator, the whole team was able to participate in testing the device. The simulator was written to support testing for the test team, but the programmer for the firmware found it valuable and used it to help with his development efforts as well. That was a positive unexpected side effect. Quadrant 2 tests that support the team may incorporate a variety of technologies, as they did in this project.

CRITIQUING THE PRODUCT WITH BUSINESS-FACING TESTS

The business-facing tests that critique the product are outlined in this section.

Exploratory Testing

The automated tests were simple and easy for everyone on the team to use. Individual test scripts could be run to set up specific conditions, allowing ef-

Exploratory testing, usability testing, and other Quadrant 3 tests are discussed in Chapter 10, "Business-Facing Tests that Critique the Product."

fective exploratory testing to be done without having to spend a lot of time manually entering data. This worked for all three test frameworks: functional, web services, and embedded.

The team performed exploratory testing to supplement the automated test suites and get the best coverage possible. This human interaction with the system found issues that automation didn't find.

Usability testing was not a critical requirement for the system, but the testers watched so that the interface made sense and flowed smoothly. The testers used exploratory testing extensively to critique the product. The product engineer also used exploratory testing for his solution verification tests.

Testing Data Feeds

As shown in Figure 12-2, the data from the system is available on a JMS queue, as well as the web browser. To test the JMS queue, the development group wrote a Java proxy. It connected to a queue and printed any arriving data to the console. They also wrote a Ruby client that received this data via a pipe, which was then available in the Ruby automated test system.

Emails were automatically sent when alarm conditions were encountered. The alarm emails contained both plain text email and email with attachments. The MIME attachments contained data useful for testing, so a Ruby email client that supported attachments was written.

The End-to-End Tests

Quadrant 3 includes end-to-end functional testing that demonstrates the desired behavior of every part of the system. From the beginning, it was apparent that correct operation of the whole Remote Data Monitoring system could only be determined when all components were used. Once the simulator, embedded device tests, web services tests, and application tests were written, it was a relatively simple matter to combine them to produce an automated test of the entire system. Once again, Excel spreadsheets were used to hold the test data, and Ruby classes were written to access the data and expected results.

The end-to-end tests were complicated by the unpredictable response of the satellite transmission path. A predefined timeout value was set, and if the test's actual value did not match the expected value, the test would cycle until it matched or the timeout was reached. When the timeout expired, the test was deemed to have failed. Most transmission issues were found and eliminated this way. It would have been highly unlikely that they would have been found with manual testing, because they were sporadic issues.

Because end-to-end tests such as these can be fragile, they may not be kept as part of the automated regression suite. If all of the components of the system are well covered with automated regression tests, automated end-to-end tests might not be necessary. However, due to the nature of this system, it wasn't possible to do a full test without automation.

User Acceptance Testing

User Acceptance Testing (UAT) is the final critique of the product by the customer, who should have been involved in the project from the start. In this example, the real customer was in France, thousands of miles from the development team. The team had to be inventive to have a successful UAT. The customer came to work with the team members a couple of times during the year and so was able to interact with the team a little easier than if they'd never met.

After the team introduced agile development, Janet went to France to facilitate the first UAT at the customer site. It worked fairly well, and the release was accepted after a few critical issues were fixed. The team learned a lot from that experience.

The second UAT sign-off was done in-house. To prepare, the team worked with the customer to develop a set of tests the customer could perform to verify new functionality. The customer was able to test the application throughout the development cycle, so UAT didn't produce any issues. The customer came, ran through the tests, and signed off in a day.

We cannot stress the importance of working with the customer enough. Even though the product engineer was the proxy for the customer, it was crucial to get face time with the actual customer. The relationship that had been built over time was critical to the success of the project. Janet strongly believes that the UAT succeeded because the customer knew what the team was doing along the way.

Reliability

Reliability, one of the "ilities" addressed by Quadrant 4 tests, was a critical factor of the system because it was monitoring remote sites that were often

See Chapter 10, "Business-Facing Tests that Critique the Product," for more about Quadrant 4 tests such as reliability testing.

inaccessible, especially in winter. The simulator that was developed for testing the embedded system was set up on a separate environment, and was run for weeks at a time measuring stability (yet another "ility") of the whole system. Corrections to the system design could be planned and coded as needed. This is a good example of why you shouldn't wait until the end of the project to do the technology-facing tests that critique the product.

DOCUMENTATION

The approach taken to documentation is presented in this section.

Documenting the Test Code

During development, it became clear that a formal documentation system was needed for the test code. The simplest solution was to use RDoc, similar to Javadoc, but for Ruby. RDoc extracted tagged comments from the source code and generated web pages with details of files, classes, and methods. The documents were generated every night using a batch file and were available to the complete team. It was easy to find what test fixtures were created.

The documentation of the test code helped to document the tests and make it easier to find what we were testing and what the tests did. It was very powerful and easy to use.

Reporting the Test Results

Although comprehensive testing was being performed, there was little evidence of this outside of the test team. The logs generated during automated tests provided good information to track down problems but were not suitable for a wider audience.

Chapter 16, "Hit the Ground Running," gives more examples of ways teams report test results.

To raise the visibility of the tests being performed, the test team developed a logging and reporting system using Apache, PHP, and mySQL. When a test ran, it logged the result into the database. A web front end allowed project stakeholders to determine what tests were run, the pass/failure rate, and other information.

Chapter 18, "Coding and Testing," also discusses uses of big visible charts.

We also believed in making our progress visible (good or bad) as much as possible. To this end we created charts and graphs along the way and posted them in common areas. Figure 12-4 shows some of the charts we created.

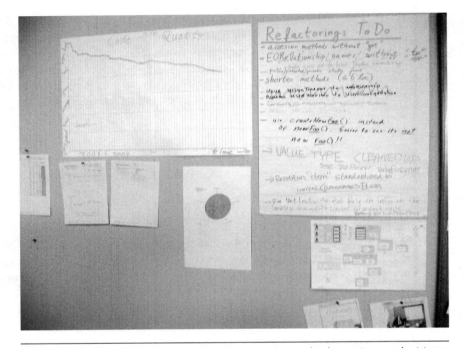

Figure 12-4   Big visible charts used by the remote monitoring system project team

Using the Agile Testing Quadrants

This example demonstrates how testing practices from all four agile testing quadrants are combined during the life of a complex development project to achieve successful delivery. The experience of this team illustrates many of the principles we have been emphasizing. The whole team, including programmers, testers, customer proxy, and the actual customer, contributed to efforts to solve automation problems. They experimented with different approaches. They combined their homegrown and open source tools in different ways to perform testing at all levels, from the unit level to end-to-end system testing and UAT. The success of the project demonstrates the success of the testing approach.

As you plan each epic, release, or iteration, work with your customer team to understand the business priorities and analyze risks. Use the quadrants to help identify all of the different types of testing that will be needed and when they should be performed. Is performance the most important criteria? Is the highest priority the ability to interface with other systems? Is usability perhaps the most important aspect?

Invest in a test architecture that accommodates the complexity of the system under test. Plan to obtain necessary resources and expertise at the right time for specialized tests. For each type of test, your team should work together to choose tools that solve your testing problems. Use retrospectives to continually evaluate whether your team has the resources it needs to succeed, and whether all necessary tests are being specified in time to serve their purpose, and automated appropriately.

Does end-to-end testing seem impossible to do? Is your team finding it hard to write unit tests? As Janet's team did, get everyone experimenting with different approaches and tools. The quadrants provide a framework for productive brainstorming on creative ways to achieve the testing that will let the team deliver value to the business.

SUMMARY

In this chapter, we described a real project that used tests from all four agile testing quadrants to overcome difficult testing challenges. We used examples from this project to show how teams can succeed with all types of testing. Some important lessons from the Remote Data Monitoring System project are:

- The whole team should choose or create tools that solve each testing problem.
- Combinations of common business tools such as spreadsheets and custom-written test scripts may be needed to accomplish complex tests.
- Invest time in building the right test architecture that works for all team members.
- Find ways to keep customers involved in all types of testing, even if they're in a remote location.
- Report test results in a way that keeps all stakeholders informed about the iteration and project progress.
- Don't forget to document . . . but only what is useful.
- Think about all four quadrants of testing throughout your development cycles.
- Use lessons learned during testing to critique the product in order to drive development in subsequent iterations.

## Part IV

AUTOMATION

Test automation is a core agile practice. Agile projects depend on automation. Good-enough automation frees the team to deliver high-quality code frequently. It provides a framework that lets the team maximize its velocity while maintaining a high standard. Source code control, automated builds and test suites, deployment, monitoring, and a variety of scripts and tools eliminate tedium, ensure reliability, and allow the team to do its best work at all times.

Automation is also a vast topic. It includes tasks like writing simple shell scripts, setting up session properties, and creating robust automated tests. The range and number of automated tools seem to grow exponentially as we learn about better ways to produce software. Happily, the number of excellent books that teach ways to automate appears to grow just as fast.

This book is focused on the tester's role in agile development. Because automation is key to successful agile development, we need to talk about it, but we can't begin to cover every aspect of the subject. What we do want to explain is why you, as a tester, must embrace automation, and how you and your team can overcome the many obstacles that can hamper your automation efforts. This section describes how you can apply agile values, principles, and practices to grow a practical automation strategy, overcome barriers, and get traction on test automation.

Chapter 13

WHY WE WANT TO AUTOMATE TESTS AND WHAT HOLDS US BACK

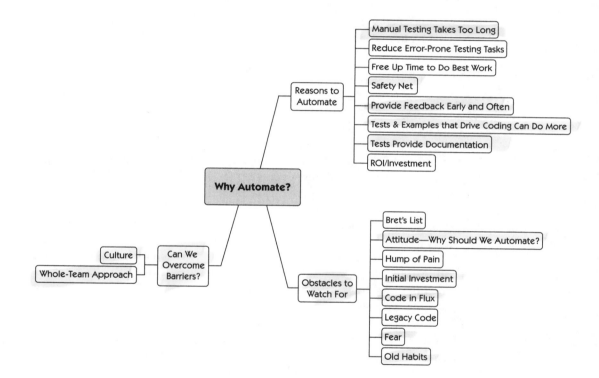

Why do we automate testing, the build process, deployment, and other tasks? Agile teams focus on always having working software, which enables them to release production-ready software as often as needed. Achieving this goal requires constant testing. In this chapter, we look at reasons we want to automate and the challenges that make it hard to get traction on automation.

WHY AUTOMATE?

There are multiple reasons to automate besides our saying you need to have automation to be successful using agile. Our list includes the following:

- Manual testing takes too long.
- Manual processes are error prone.
- Automation frees people to do their best work.
- Automated regression tests provide a safety net.
- Automated tests give feedback early and often.
- Tests and examples that drive coding can do more.
- Tests provide documentation.
- Automation can be a good return on investment.

Let's explore each of these in a little more detail.

Manual Testing Takes Too Long

The most basic reason a team wants to automate is that it simply takes too long to complete all of the necessary testing manually. As your application gets bigger and bigger, the time to test everything grows longer and longer, sometimes exponentially, depending on the complexity of the AUT (Application under test).

Agile teams are able to deliver production-ready software at the end of each short iteration by having production-ready software every day. Running a full suite of passing regression tests at least daily is an indispensable practice, and you can't do it with manual regression testing. If you don't have any automation now, you'll have to regression test manually, but don't let that stop you from starting to automate it.

If you execute your regression testing manually, it takes more and more time testing every day, every iteration. In order for testing to keep pace with coding, either the programmers have to take time to help with manual regression testing, or the team has to hire more testers. Inevitably, both technical debt and frustration will grow.

If the code doesn't even have to pass a suite of automated unit level regression tests, the testers will probably spend much of their time researching, trying to reproduce and report those simple bugs, and less time finding potentially serious system level bugs. In addition, because the team isn't doing test-first development, code design is more likely to be less testable and may not provide the functionality desired by the business.

Manually testing a number of different scenarios can take a lot of time, especially if you're keying inputs into a user interface. Setting up data for a variety of complex scenarios can be an overwhelming task if you have no automated way to speed it up. As a result, only a limited number of scenarios may be tested, and important defects can be missed.

Manual Processes Are Error Prone

Manual testing gets repetitive, especially if you're following scripted tests, and manual tests get boring very quickly. It's way too easy to make mistakes and overlook even simple bugs. Steps and even entire tests will be skipped. If the team's facing a tight deadline, there's a temptation to cut corners, and the result is a missed problem.

Because manual testing is slow, you might still be testing at midnight on the last day of the iteration. How many bugs will you notice then?

Automated builds, deployment, version control, and monitoring also go a long way toward mitigating risk and making your development process more consistent. Automating these scripted tests eliminate the possibility of errors, because each test is done exactly the same way every time.

The adage of "build once, deploy to many" is a tester's dream come true. Automation of the build and deploy processes allow you to know exactly what you are testing on any given environment.

Automation Frees People to Do Their Best Work

Writing code test-first helps programmers understand requirements and design code accordingly. Having continual builds run all of the unit tests and the functional regression tests means more time to do interesting exploratory testing. Automating the setup for exploratory tests means even more time to probe into potentially weak parts of the system. Because you didn't spend time executing tedious manual scripts, you have the energy to do a good job, thinking of different scenarios and learning more about how the application works.

If we're thinking constantly about how to automate tests for a fix or new feature, we're more likely to think of testability and a quality design rather than a quick hack that might prove fragile. That means better code and better tests.

Automating tests can actually help with consistency across the application.

Janet's Story

See Chapter 9, "Toolkit for Business-Facing Tests that Support the Team," Chapter 12, "Summary of Testing Quadrants," and Chapter 14, "An Agile Test Automation Strategy," for more information about Ruby and Watir.

Jason (one of my fellow testers) and I were working on some GUI automation scripts using Ruby and Watir, and were adding constants for button names for the tests. We quickly realized that the buttons on each page were not consistently named. We were able to get them changed and resolved those consistency issues very quickly, and had an easy way to enforce the naming conventions.

—Janet

Books such as *Pragmatic Project Automation* [2004] can guide you in automating daily development chores and free your team for important activities such as exploratory testing.

Giving Testers Better Work

Chris McMahon described the benefits he's experienced due to regression test automation in a posting to the agile-testing mailing list in November 2007:

> Our UI regression test automation has grown 500% since April [of 2007]. This allows us to focus the attention of real human beings on more interesting testing.

Chris went on to explain, "Now that we have a lot of automation, we have the leisure to really think about what human tests need doing. For any testing that isn't trivial, we have just about institutionalized a test-idea brainstorming session before beginning execution." Usually, Chris and his teammates pair either two testers or one tester and a developer. Sometimes a tester generates ideas and gets them reviewed, via a mind-map, a wiki page, or a list in the release notes. Chris observed, "We almost always come up with good test ideas by pairing that wouldn't have been found by either individual independently."

Referring to their frequent releases of significant features, Chris says, "Thanks to the good test automation, we have the time to invest in making certain that the whole product is attractive and functional for real people. Without the automation, testing this product would be both boring and stupid. As it is, we testers have significant and interesting work to do for each release."

We agree with Chris that the most exciting part of test automation is the way it expands our ability to improve the product through innovative exploratory testing.

Projects succeed when good people are free to do their best work. Automating tests appropriately makes that happen. Automated regression tests that detect changes to existing functionality and provide immediate feedback are a primary component of this.

Automated Regression Tests Provide a Safety Net

Most practitioners who've been in the software business for a few years know the feeling of dread when they're faced with fixing a bug or implementing a new feature in poorly designed code that isn't covered by automated tests. Squeeze one end of the balloon here and another part of it bulges out. Will it break?

Knowing the code has sufficient coverage by automated regression tests gives a great feeling of confidence. Sure, a change might produce an unexpected effect, but we'll know about it within a matter of minutes if it's at the unit level, or hours if at a higher functional level. Making the change test-first means thinking through the changed behavior before writing the code and writing a test to verify it, which adds to that confidence.

Janet's Story

I recently had a conversation with one of the testers on my team who questioned the value of automated tests. My first answer was "It's a safety net" for the team. However, he challenged that premise. Don't we just become reliant on the tests rather than fixing the root cause of the problem?

It made me think a bit more about my answer. He was right in one sense; if we become complacent about our testing challenges and depend solely on automated tests to find our issues, and then just fix them enough for the test to pass, we do ourselves a disservice.

However, if we use the tests to identify problem areas and fix them the right way or refactor as needed, then we are using the safety net of automation in the right way. Automation is critical to the success of an agile project, especially as the application grows in size.

—Janet

When they don't have an automated suite of tests acting as a safety net, the programmers may start viewing the testers themselves as a safety net. It's easy to imagine that Joe Programmer's thought process goes like this: "I ought to go back and add some automated unit tests for formatEmployeeInfo, but I know Susie Tester is going to check every page where it's used manually. She'll see if anything is off, so I'd just be duplicating her effort."

It's nice that a programmer would think so highly of the tester's talents, but Joe is headed down a slippery slope. If he doesn't automate these unit tests, which other tests might he skip? Susie is going to be awfully busy eyeballing all those pages.

Teams that have good coverage from automated regression tests can make changes to the code fearlessly. They don't have to wonder, "If I change this formatEmployeeInfo module, will I break something in the user interface?" The tests will tell them right away whether or not they broke anything. They can go lots faster than teams relying exclusively on manual testing.

Automated Tests Give Feedback, Early and Often

After an automated test for a piece of functionality passes, it must continue to pass until the functionality is intentionally changed. When we plan changes in the application, we change the tests to accommodate them. When an automated test fails unexpectedly, a regression defect may have been introduced by a code change. Running an automated suite of tests every time new code is checked in helps ensure that regression bugs will be caught quickly. Quick feedback means the change is still fresh in some programmer's mind, so troubleshooting will go more quickly than if the bug weren't found until some testing phase weeks later. Failing fast means bugs are cheaper to fix.

Automated tests run regularly and often act as your change detector. They allow the team an opportunity to know what has changed since the last build. For example, were there any negative side effects with the last build? If your automation suite has sufficient coverage, it can easily tell far-reaching effects that manual testers can never hope to find.

More often than not, if regression tests are not automated, they won't get run every iteration, let alone every day. The problem arises very quickly during the end game, when the team needs to complete all of the regression tests. Bugs that would have been caught early are found late in the game. Many of the benefits of testing early are lost.

Tests and Examples that Drive Coding Can Do More

In Chapter 7, "Technology-Facing Tests that Support the Team," we talked about using tests and examples to drive coding. We've talked about how important it is to drive coding with both unit and customer tests. We also want to stress that if these tests are automated, they become valuable for a different reason. They become the base for a very strong regression suite.

Lisa's Story

After my team got a handle on unit tests, refactoring, continuous integration, and other technology-facing practices, we were able to catch regression bugs and incorrectly implemented functionality during development.

Of course, this didn't mean our problems were completely solved; we still sometimes missed or misunderstood requirements. However, having an automation framework in place enabled us to start focusing on doing a better job of capturing requirements in up-front tests. We also had more time for exploratory testing. Over time, our defect rate declined dramatically, while our customers' delight in the delivered business value went up.

—Lisa

The bibliography contains an article by Jennitta Andrea [2008] on team etiquette for TDD.

TDD and SDD (story test-driven development) keep teams thinking test-first. During planning meetings, they talk about the tests and the best way to do them. They design code to make the tests pass, so testability is never an issue. The automated test suite grows along with the code base, providing a safety net for constant refactoring. It's important that the whole team practices TDD and consistently writes unit tests, or the safety net will have holes.

The team also doesn't accrue too much technical debt, and their velocity is bound to be stable or even increase over time. That's one of the reasons why the business managers should be happy to let software teams take the time to implement good practices correctly.

Tests Are Great Documentation

In Part III, we explained how agile teams use examples and tests to guide development. When tests that illustrate examples of desired behavior are automated, they become "living" documentation of how the system actually works. It's good to have narrative documentation about how a piece of functionality works, but nobody can argue with an executable test that shows in red and green how the code operates on a given set of inputs.

It's hard to keep static documentation up to date, but if we don't update our automated tests when the system changes, the tests fail. We need to fix them to keep our build process "green." This means that automated tests are always an accurate picture of how our code works. That's just one of the ways our investment in automation pays off.

ROI and Payback

All of the reasons just presented contribute to the bottom line and the payback of automation. Automation provides consistency to a project and gives the team opportunity to test differently and push the limits of the application. Automation means extra time for testers and team members to concentrate on getting the right product out to market in a timely manner.

An important component of test automation payback is the way defects are fixed. Teams that rely on manual tests tend to find bugs long after the code containing the bug is written. They get into the mode of fixing the "bug of the day," instead of looking at the root cause of the bug and redesigning the code accordingly. When programmers run the automated test suite in their own sandbox, the automated regression tests find the bugs before the code is checked in, so there's time to correct the design. That's a much bigger payback, and it's how you reduce technical debt and develop solid code.

BARRIERS TO AUTOMATION—THINGS THAT GET IN THE WAY

Back in 2001, Bret Pettichord [2001] listed seven problems that plague automation. They are still applicable, but are intended for teams that do not incorporate automation as part of their development. And of course, because you are doing agile, you are doing that, right?

We would like to think that everyone has included automation tasks as part of each story, but the reality is that you probably wouldn't be reading this section if you had it all under control. We've included Bret's list to show what problems you probably have if you don't include automation as part of the everyday project deliverables.

Bret's List

Bret's list of automation problems looks like this:

- Only using spare time for test automation doesn't give it the focus it needs.
- There is a lack of clear goals.
- There is a lack of experience.
- There is high turnover, because you lose any experience you may have.
- A reaction to desperation is often the reason why automation is chosen, in which case it can be more of a wish than a realistic proposal.

- There can be a reluctance to think about testing; the fun is in the automating, not in the testing.
- Focusing on solving the technology problem can cause you to lose sight of whether the result meets the testing need.

We think there are some other problems that teams run into when trying to automate. Even if we do try to include automation in our project deliverables, there are other barriers to success. In the next section, we present our list of obstacles to successful test automation.

Our List

Our list of barriers to successful test automation is based on the experiences we've had with our own agile teams as well as that of the other teams we know.

- Programmers' attitude
- The "Hump of Pain"
- Initial investment
- Code that's always in flux
- Legacy systems
- Fear
- Old habits

Programmers' Attitude—"Why Automate?"

Programmers who are used to working in a traditional environment, where some separate, unseen QA team does all of the testing, may not even give functional test automation a lot of thought. Some programmers don't bother to test much because they have the QA team as a safety net to catch bugs before release. Long waterfall development cycles make testing even more remote to programmers. By the time the unseen testers are doing their job, the programmers have moved on to the next release. Defects go into a queue to be fixed later at great expense, and nobody is accountable for having produced them. Even programmers who have adopted test-driven development and are used to automating tests at the unit level may not think about how acceptance tests beyond the unit level get done.

Lisa's Story

I once joined an XP team of skilled programmers practicing test-driven development that had a reasonable suite of unit tests running in an automated build process. They had never automated any business-facing tests, so one day I started a discussion about what tools they might use to automate functional business-facing regression tests. The programmers wanted to know why we needed to automate these tests.

At the end of the first iteration, when everyone was executing the acceptance tests by hand, I pointed out that there would be all these tests to do again in the next iteration as regression tests, in addition to the tests for all of the new stories. In the third iteration, there would be three times as many tests. To a tester, it seems ridiculously obvious, but sometimes programmers need to do the manual tests before they understand the compulsion to automate them.

—Lisa

Education is the key to getting programmers and the rest of the team to understand the importance of automation.

The "Hump of Pain" (The Learning Curve)

It's hard to learn test automation, especially to learn how to do it in a way that produces a good return on the resources invested in it. A term we've heard Brian Marick use to describe the initial phase of automation that developers (including testers) have to overcome is the "hump of pain" (see Figure 13-1). This phrase refers to the struggle that most teams go through when adopting automation.

New teams are often expected to adopt practices such as TDD and refactoring, which are difficult to learn. Without good coaching, plenty of time to master new skills, and strong management support, they're easily discour-

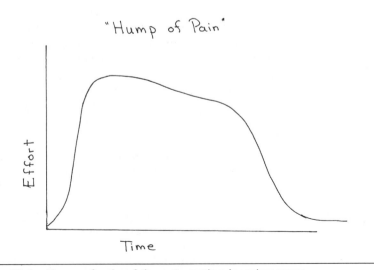

Figure 13-1 Hump of pain of the automation learning curve

aged. If they have extra obstacles to learning, such as having to work with poorly designed legacy code, it may seem impossible to ever get traction on test automation.

Lisa's Story

My team at ePlan Services originally tried to write unit tests for a legacy system that definitely wasn't written with testing in mind. They found this to be a difficult, if not impossible, task, so they decided to code all new stories in a new, testable architecture. Interestingly, about a year later, they discovered it wasn't really that hard to write unit tests for the old code. The problem was they didn't know how to write unit tests at all, and it was easier to learn on a well-designed architecture. Writing unit-level tests became simply a natural part of writing code.

—Lisa

The hump of pain may occur because you are building your domain-specific testing framework or learning your new functional test tool. You may want to bring in an expert to help you get it set up right.

You know your team has overcome the "hump" when automation becomes, if not easy, at least a natural and ingrained process. Lisa has worked on three teams that successfully adopted TDD and functional test automation. Each time, the team needed lots of time, training, commitment, and encouragement to get traction on the practices.

Initial Investment

Even with the whole team working on the problem, automation requires a big investment, one that may not pay off right away. It takes time and research to decide on what test frameworks to use and whether to build them in-house or use externally produced tools. New hardware and software are probably required. Team members may take a while to ramp up on how to use automated test harnesses.

Many people have experienced test automation efforts that didn't pay off. Their organization may have purchased a vendor capture-playback tool, given it to the QA team, and expected it to solve all of the automation problems. Such tools often sit on a shelf gathering dust. There may have been thousands of lines of GUI test scripts generated, with no one left who knows what they do, or the test scripts that are impossible to maintain are no longer useful.

Janet's Story

I walked into an organization as a new QA manager. One of my tasks was to evaluate the current automated test scripts and increase the test coverage. A vendor tool had been purchased a few years earlier, and the testers who had developed the initial suite were no longer with the organization. One of the new testers hired was trying to learn the tool and was adding tests to the suite.

The first thing I did was ask this tester to do an assessment on the test suite to see what the coverage actually was. She spent a week just trying to understand how the tests were organized. I started poking around as well and found that that the existing tests were very poorly designed and had very little value.

We stopped adding more tests and instead spent a little bit of time understanding what the goal was for our test automation. As it turned out, the vendor tool could not do what we really needed it to do, so we cancelled the licenses and found an open source tool that met our needs.

We still had to spend time learning the new open source tool, but that investment would have been made if we'd stayed with the original vendor tool anyhow, because no one on the team knew how to use the original tool.

—Janet

Test design skills have a huge impact on whether automation pays off right away. Poor practices produce tests that are hard to understand and maintain, and may produce hard-to-interpret results or false failures that take time to research. Teams with inadequate training and skills might decide the return on their automation investment isn't worth their time.

Good test design practices produce simple, well-designed, continually refactored, maintainable tests. Libraries of test modules and objects build up over time and make automating new tests quicker. See Chapter 14 for some hints on and guidelines for test design for automation.

We know it's not easy to capture metrics. For example, trying to capture the time it takes to write and maintain automated tests versus the time it takes to run the same regression tests manually is almost impossible. Similarly, trying to capture how much it costs to fix defects within minutes of introducing them versus how much it costs to find and fix problems after the end of the iteration is also quite difficult. Many teams don't make the effort to track this information. Without numbers showing that automating requires less effort and provides more value, it's harder for teams to convince management that an investment in automation is worthwhile. A lack of metrics that demonstrate automation's return on investment also makes it harder to change a team's habits.

Code that's Always in Flux

Automating tests through the user interface is tricky, because UIs tend to change frequently during development. That's one reason that simple record and playback techniques are rarely a good choice for an agile project.

If the team is struggling to produce a good design on the underlying business logic and database access, and major rework is done frequently, it might be hard to keep up even with tests automated behind the GUI at the API level. If little thought is given to testing while designing the system, it might be difficult and expensive to find a way to automate tests. The programmers and testers need to work together to get a testable application.

In Chapter 14, "An Agile Test Automation Strategy," we'll look at ways to organize automated tests.

Although the actual code and implementation, like the GUI, tends to change frequently in agile development, the intent of code rarely changes. Organizing test code by the application's intent, rather than by its implementation, allows you to keep up with development.

Legacy Code

In our experience, it's much easier to get traction on automation if you're writing brand new code in an architecture designed with testing in mind. Writing tests for existing code that has few or no tests is a daunting task at best. It seems virtually impossible to a team new to agile and new to test automation.

It is sometimes a Catch-22. You want to automate tests so you can refactor some of the legacy code, but the legacy code isn't designed for testability, so it is hard to automate tests even at the unit level.

If your team faces this type of challenge and doesn't budget plenty of time to brainstorm about how to tackle it, it'll be tough to start automating tests effectively. Chapter 14 gives strategies to address these issues.

Fear

Test automation is scary to those who've never mastered it, and even to some who have. Programmers may be good at writing production code, but they might not be very experienced at writing automated tests. Testers may not have a strong programming background, and they don't trust their potential test automation skills.

Non-programming testers have often gotten the message that they have nothing to offer in the agile world. We believe otherwise. No individual tester should need to worry about how to do automation. It's a team problem, and there are usually plenty of programmers on the team who can help. The trick is to embrace learning new ideas. Take one day at a time.

Old Habits

When iterations don't proceed smoothly and the team can't complete all of the programming and testing tasks by the end of an iteration, team members may panic. We've observed that when people go into panic mode, they fall into comfortable old habits, even if those habits never produced good results.

So we may say, "We are supposed to deliver on February 1. If we want to meet that date, we don't have time to automate any tests. We'll have to do whatever manual tests can be done in that amount of time and hope for the best. We can always automate the tests later."

This is the road to perdition. Some manual tests can get done, but maybe not the important manual exploratory tests that would have found the bug that cost the company hundreds of thousands of dollars in lost sales. Then, because we didn't finish with our test automation tasks, those tasks carry over to the next iteration, reducing the amount of business value we can deliver. As iterations proceed, the situation continues to deteriorate.

CAN WE OVERCOME THESE BARRIERS?

See Chapter 3, "Cultural Challenges," for some ideas on making changes to the team culture in order to facilitate agile practices.

The agile whole-team approach is the foundation to overcoming automation challenges. Programmers who are new to agile are probably used to being rewarded for delivering code, whether it's buggy or not, as long as they meet deadlines. Test-driven development is oriented more toward design than testing, so business-facing tests may still not enter their consciousness. It takes leadership and a team commitment to quality to get everyone thinking about how to write, use, and run both technology-facing and business-facing tests. Getting the whole team involved in test automation may be a cultural challenge.

In the next chapter, we show how to use agile values and principles to overcome some of the problems we've described in this chapter.

SUMMARY

In this chapter, we analyzed some important factors related to test automation:

- We need automation to provide a safety net, provide us with essential feedback, keep technical debt to a minimum, and help drive coding.
- Fear, lack of knowledge, negative past experiences with automation, rapidly changing code, and legacy code are among the common barriers to automation.
- Automating regression tests, running them in an automated build process, and fixing root causes of defects reduces technical debt and permits growth of solid code.
- Automating regression tests and tedious manual tasks frees the team for more important work, such as exploratory testing.
- Teams with automated tests and automated build processes enjoy a more stable velocity.
- Without automated regression tests, manual regression testing will continue to grow in scope and eventually may simply be ignored.
- Team culture and history may make it harder for programmers to prioritize automation of business-facing tests than coding new features. Using agile principles and values helps the whole team overcome barriers to test automation.

Chapter 14

AN AGILE TEST
AUTOMATION STRATEGY

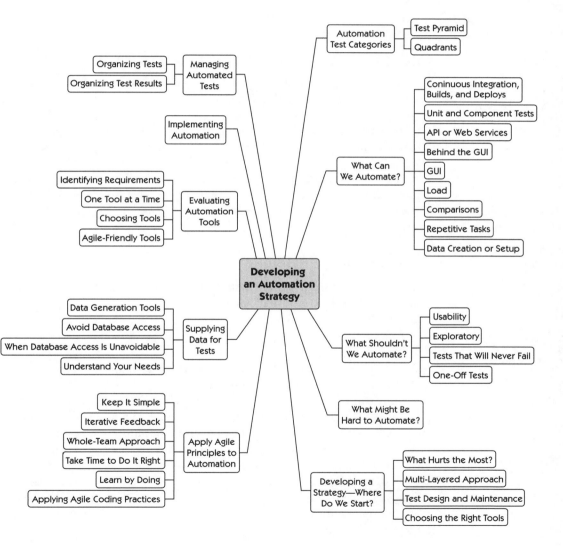

As we explored each of the Agile Testing Quadrants in Part III, we gave examples of tools that can help those different testing efforts succeed. Many of those tools are for automating tests. As we described in the previous chapter, teams face plenty of obstacles in their quest for successful test automation. Better tools become available all the time, but the trick is to choose the right tools and learn to use them effectively. Test automation requires thoughtful investment and incremental improvement. In this chapter, we explain how you can apply agile values and principles to get traction in starting or improving your automation efforts.

AN AGILE APPROACH TO TEST AUTOMATION

Here you are, reading this chapter on how to get your test automation strategy working, maybe hoping for that silver bullet, or an answer to all your questions. We hate to disappoint you, but we need to tell you right up front, there is no silver bullet. There is no one answer that works for every team. Don't lose heart though, because we have some ideas to help you get started.

First, we suggest approaching your automation problems as you would any problem. Define the problem you are trying to solve. To help you figure that out, we first talk about some basics of test automation and reintroduce some terms.

Automation Test Categories

In Part III, we introduced the Agile Testing Quadrants and talked about each quadrant and the purpose of the tests in each quadrant. In this section, we look at the quadrants in a different light. Let's look carefully at the quadrants (see Figure 14-1).

You can see that we've labeled both quadrants that support the team (Q1 and Q2) as using automation. In Quadrant 4, the tools used for critiquing the product from a technology point of view also usually require automated tools. In Chapter 9, "Toolkit for Business-Facing Tests that Support the Team," we discussed some of the tools that can be used for automating business-facing tests in the quest for supporting the team. In fact, the only quadrant that is not labeled as using automation is Quadrant 3—the business-facing tests that critique the product. However, as we discussed in Chapter 10, "Business-Facing Tests that Critique the Product," tools may be useful for some of that testing. For example, automation can help set up test data and user scenarios, and analyze logged activity.

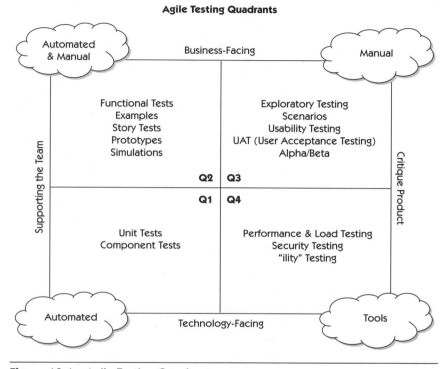

Figure 14-1   Agile Testing Quadrants

See Chapter 8, "Business-Facing Tests that Support the Team," for more about Wizard of Oz testing.

Use the quadrants to help you identify the different types of automation tools you might need for each project, even for each iteration. We find it helpful to go through each quadrant and make a checklist of what tools might be needed. Let's say we're about to redesign a UI. We look at Quadrant 1. How can it be coded test-first? Do we know how to unit test our presentation layer? Do we need a new tool to help with that? Now on to Quadrant 2. We'll need to do some prototyping; should we just use paper, or should we plan a Wizard of Oz type activity? What tool will we use to create executable business-facing tests to guide development? Do we have regression test scripts that will need updating or replacing? We know that one of our Quadrant 3 activities will be usability testing. That takes some advance planning. We might want tools to help track the users' activities so we can analyze them further. Thinking about Quadrant 4, we realize that we have load test scripts that use the old UI, so we have to budget time to update them for the new one.

As we emphasized in Part III, "Using the Agile Testing Quadrants," the order of quadrants doesn't relate to the order in which we do the testing. As we make our checklist of tools needed for each type of test, we think about when we want to test so we know when to have our automation tools ready. For example, a team designing a new architecture would plan to do a spike and run scalability test against it as soon as possible. They will need to spend time during the first iteration of the project finding and implementing a performance test tool.

The quadrants help us figure out what tools we might need, but with so many different automation options at different levels, a strategy for where to do which types of testing and how to organize the tests is essential. To deliver value quickly and often, our automation efforts need a high ROI. The test pyramid helps us optimize our test investment.

Test Automation Pyramid

Figure 14-2 illustrates the "test automation pyramid." We like the version that Mike Cohn introduced, which shows the foundation layer made up of technology-facing unit and component tests. We recognize that many teams will struggle with this idea, because it seems the opposite of what many teams currently have. Many test teams have been taught the "V" model of testing, where activities such as component, system, and release testing are done in sequence after coding activities. Other teams have an inverted pyramid, with the majority of the tests in the functional or presentation layer.

The agile test automation pyramid shows three different layers of automated tests. The lowest tier is the foundation that supports all of the rest. It's mainly made up of robust unit tests and component tests, the technology-facing tests that support the team. This layer represents the bulk of the automated tests. They're generally written in the same language as the system under test, using the xUnit family of tools. After a team has mastered the art of TDD, these tests are by far the quickest and least expensive to write. They provide the quickest feedback, too, making them highly valuable. They have the biggest ROI by far of any type of test.

See Chapter 7, "Technology-Facing Tests that Support the Team" for more about unit and component tests.

In agile development, we try to push as many tests as possible to this layer. While business-facing tests tend to go in one of the higher levels, we implement them at the unit level when it makes sense. If they're tests the customers don't have to be able to read, and they can be coded much more quickly as unit tests, it's a good option. Other types of technology-facing tests such as performance tests may also be possible at the unit level.

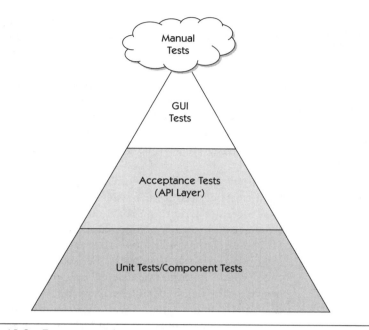

Figure 14-2 Test automation pyramid

See Chapter, 8, "Business-Facing Tests that Support the Team," for more about business-facing tests that support the team.

The middle tier in the pyramid is the layer that includes most of the automated business-facing tests written to support the team. These are the functional tests that verify that we are "building the right thing." The tests in this layer may include "story" tests, "acceptance" tests, and tests that cover larger sets of functionality than the unit test layer. These tests operate at the API level or "behind the GUI," testing the functionality directly without going through the GUI. We write test cases that set up inputs and fixtures that feed the inputs into the production code, accept the outputs, and compare them to expected results. Because these tests bypass the presentation layer, they are less expensive to write and maintain than tests that use the interface.

We try to write them in a domain-specific language that the customers can understand, so they take more work than unit-level tests. They also generally run more slowly, because each test covers more ground than a unit test and may access the database or other components. The feedback they provide is not as quick as the unit-level tests, but it is still much faster than we could get operating through the user interface. Therefore, their ROI is not as high as the tests that form the base of the pyramid, but it's higher than the top layer.

■————
We have more
about these tests
in Chapter 8,
"Business-Facing
Tests that Support
the Team," and
Chapter 9, "Toolkit
for Business-Facing
Tests that Support
the Team," where
we discuss the
business-facing
tests that support
the team and the
tools that effec-
tively capture
these tests.

Fit and FitNesse are examples of tools used for the middle layer of the pyramid. Home-grown test harnesses that use spreadsheets or other business-friendly means for defining test cases are also common.

The top tier represents what should be the smallest automation effort, because the tests generally provide the lowest ROI. These tests are the ones done through the GUI, the ones that actually operate and manipulate the presentation layer. They are written after the code is completed, and so are usually written to critique the product and go directly to the regression suite.

These tests are traditionally more expensive to write, although there are new tools that help reduce the investment needed. Because components of the user interface tend to be changed often, these tests are much more brittle than tests that work at a functional or unit level. For example, just renaming HTML elements could cause a test script to fail. Operating through the user interface also slows these tests down, compared to tests in the lower levels of the pyramid that operate directly on production code. The tests in the top layer do provide important feedback, but a suite of GUI tests may take hours to run rather than the few minutes required for unit-level test suites. We want to minimize the number of tests at this layer, so they should only form the tip of the pyramid.

No matter how many automated tests they have, most systems also need manual testing activities, such as exploratory testing and user acceptance testing. We don't want to forget these, so we've illustrated them with the little cloud at the tip of the pyramid. The bulk of our regression testing must be automated or our manual testing won't give us a good return on investment either.

Patrick Wilson-Welsh [2008] adds a descriptive dimension to the test automation pyramid with a "three little pigs" metaphor. The bottom foundation layer is made of bricks. The tests are solid, and not vulnerable to the huffing and puffing of the Big Bad Wolf. The middle layer is made of sticks. They need rearranging more often than the brick layer to stay strong. The tests in the top layer are made of straw. It's hard to get them to stay in place, and the wolf can easily blow them around. If we have too many tests made out of straw, we're going to spend lots of time putting them back into shape.

Most new agile teams don't start with this shape pyramid—it's usually inverted, a left-over from previous projects. GUI test tools are often easier to learn, so teams start out with a lot of tests in their top "straw" layer. As we mentioned in the previous chapter, the "hump of pain" that most programmers have to overcome to master unit test automation means that the team

See the bibliography for a link to Patrick Wilson-Welsh's discussion of "flipping the test pyramid" right-side up.

may start out with only a few bricks. The fixtures that automate functional tests in the middle layer are easy to write if the system is designed with those tests in mind, so the sticks might pile up faster than the bricks. As teams master TDD and unit test automation, the bottom layer starts to grow. When they get traction, a team using TDD will quickly build out the brick foundation of the test pyramid.

The testing pyramid is a good place to start looking at how test automation can help an agile team. Programmers tend to focus on the bottom of the pyramid, and they need plenty of time and training to get over the "hump of pain" and get to the point where TDD is natural and quick. In traditional teams, testers usually have no choice but to automate tests at the GUI level. The whole-team approach used by agile teams means that testers pair with programmers and help them get better at writing tests, which in turn solidifies that brick foundation layer of the pyramid. Because tests drive development, the whole team is always designing for maximum testability, and the pyramid can grow to the right shape.

Programmers pair with testers to automate functional-level tests, filling out the middle layer. For example, a tester and customer may prepare a 400-row spreadsheet of test cases for a web services application. The programmer can help figure out a way to automate those tests. Different team members may have expertise in areas such as generating test data or using tools such as Excel macros, and all that knowledge spreads around the team. Working together, the team finds the best combinations of tools, test cases, and test data.

Involving the programmers in finding cost-effective ways to automate the top-level GUI tests has multiple benefits. These efforts may give programmers a better understanding of the system's "big picture," and testers can learn how to create more pliable, less straw-like GUI tests.

The more a team can work together and share knowledge, the stronger the team, the application, and the tests will become. The Big Bad Wolf won't stand a chance. Let's start by looking at what kind of tests we can automate and then at what we shouldn't even try.

What Can We Automate?

Most types of testing you can think of benefit from automation. Manual unit tests don't go far toward preventing regression failures, because performing a suite of manual tests before every check-in just isn't practical. You can't design code test-first through manual unit tests either. When programmers can't run tests quickly at the touch of a button, they may not be motivated enough to run tests at all. We could manually test that different units of code work together correctly, but automated component tests are a much more effective safety net.

Manual exploratory testing is an effective way to find functional defects, but if we don't have enough automated business-facing regression tests, we probably spend all of our time madly trying to keep up with manual regression testing. Let's talk about all of the different kinds of testing that can be done well with automation.

To run automated tests, you need some kind of automated framework that allows programmers to check in code often, run tests on that code, and create deployable files. Let's consider this first.

Continuous Integration, Builds, and Deploys

See Chapter 7, "Technology-Facing Tests that Support the Team," for examples of build automation tools.

Any tedious or repetitive task involved in developing software is a candidate for automation. We've talked about the importance of an automated build process. You can't build your automated test pyramid without this. Your team needs the immediate feedback from the unit-level tests to stay on track. Getting automated build emails listing every change checked in is a big help to testers because they know when a build is ready to test without having to bother the programmers.

Peril: Waiting for Tuesday's Build

In a traditional environment, it is normal for testers to wait for a stable build, even if that means waiting until next Tuesday. In an agile environment, if testers don't keep up with the developers, the stories get tested late in the game. If the developers don't get the feedback, such as suggestions and bugs, the testers can lose credibility with the developers. Bugs won't be discovered until the developers are already on another story and do not want to be interrupted to fix them until later.

Bugs pile up, and automation suffers because it can't be completed. Velocity is affected because a story cannot be marked "done" until it is tested. This makes it harder to plan the next iteration. At the end of the release cycle, your story testing runs into the end game and you may not have a successful release. At the very least, you will have a stressful release.

An automated deployment process also speeds up testing and reduces errors. In fact, the day Janet was editing this chapter, she messed up the deployment because it was a manual process. It was pretty simple, but she was new to the project and moved the file to the wrong place. Getting an automated deployment process in place went on Janet's list of things to get done right away. Lisa's team implemented its continuous integration and build framework first thing, and found it fairly easy and quick to do, although it requires continual care and feeding. Other teams, especially those with large, complex systems, face much bigger hurdles.

We've talked with teams who had build times of two hours or more. This meant that a programmer would have to wait for two hours after checking in code to get validation that his check-in didn't break any preexisting functionality. That is a long time to wait.

Most agile teams find an ongoing build longer than eight to ten minutes to be unworkable. Even 15 minutes is much too long to wait for feedback, because check-ins will start stacking up, and testers will wait a long time to get the latest, greatest build. Can you imagine how the developers working with a build that takes two hours feel as they approach the end of an iteration or release cycle? If they break any functionality, they'll have to wait two more hours to learn whether or not they had fixed it.

Many times, long builds are the result of accessing the database or trying to test through the interface. Thousands of tests running against a large codebase can tax the resources of the machine running the build. Do some profiling of your tests and see where the bottleneck is. For example, if it is the database access that is causing most of the problems, try mocking out the real database and use an in-memory one instead. Configure the build process to distribute tests across several machines. See if different software could help manage resources better. Bring in experts from outside your team to help if needed.

The key to speeding up a continuous integration and build process is to take one small step at a time. Introduce changes one at a time so that you can measure each success separately and know you are on the right track. To start with, you may want to simply remove the most costly (in terms of time) tests to run nightly instead of on every build.

A fast-running continuous integration and build process gives the greatest ROI of any automation effort. It's the first thing every team needs to automate.

See the bibliography for links to build automation tools and books with more information about improving the build process.

Chapter 7, "Technology-Facing Tests that Support the Team," goes into detail about some of the tools that can be used.

When it's in place, the team has a way to get quick feedback from the automated tests. Next, we look at different types of tests that should be automated.

Unit and Component Tests

We can't overemphasize the importance of automating the unit tests. If your programmers are using TDD as a mechanism to write their tests, then they are not only creating a great regression suite, but they are using them to design high-quality, robust code. If your team is not automating unit tests, its chances of long-term success are slim. Make unit-level test automation and continuous integration your first priority.

API or Web Services Testing

Testing an API or web services application is easiest using some form of automation. Janet has been on teams that have successfully used Ruby to read in a spreadsheet with all of the permutations and combinations of input variables and compare the outputs with the expected results stored in the spreadsheets. These data-driven tests are easy to write and maintain.

One customer of Janet's used Ruby's IRB (Interactive Ruby Shell) feature to test the web services for acceptance tests. The team was willing to share its scripts with the customer team, but the business testers preferred to watch to see what happened if inputs were changed on the fly. Running tests interactively in a semiautomated manner allowed that.

Testing behind the GUI

See Chapter 9, "Toolkit for Business-Facing Tests that Support the Team," for specific tool examples.

Testing behind the GUI is easier to automate than testing the GUI itself. Because the tests aren't affected by changes to the presentation layer and work on more stable business logic code, they're more stable. Tools for this type of testing typically provide for writing tests in a declarative format, using tables or spreadsheets. The fixtures that get the production code to operate on the test inputs and return the results can generally be written quickly. This is a prime area for writing business-facing tests, understandable to both customers and developers that drive development.

Testing the GUI

Even a thin GUI with little or no business logic needs to be tested. The fast pace of agile development, delivering new functionality each iteration, mandates some automated regression tests at the GUI level for most projects.

Tool selection is key for successful GUI automation. The automated scripts need to be flexible and easy to maintain. Janet has used Ruby and Watir very successfully when the framework was developed using good coding practices, just as if it were a production application. Time was put into developing the libraries so that there was not a lot of rework or duplication in the code, and changes needed could be made in one place. Making the code easy to maintain increased the ROI on these tests.

See Chapter 9, "Toolkit for Business-Facing Tests that Support the Team," for examples of GUI test frameworks.

A point about testability here—make sure the programmers name their objects or assign IDs to them. If they rely on system-generated identifiers, then every time a new object is added to the page, the IDs will change, requiring changes to the tests.

Keep the tests to just the actual interface. Check things like making sure the buttons really work and do what they are supposed to. Don't try to try to test business functionality. Other types of tests that can be automated easily are link checkers. There is no need for someone to manually go through every link on every page to make sure they hit the right page. Look for the low-hanging fruit, automate the things that are simple to automate first, and you'll have more time for the bigger challenges.

Load Tests

See Chapter 11, "Critiquing the Product Using Technology-Facing Tests," for examples of load test automation tools.

Some types of testing can't be done without automation. Manual load tests aren't usually feasible or accurate, although we've all tried it at one time or another. Performance testing requires both monitoring tools and a way to drive actions in the system under test. You can't generate a high-volume attack to verify whether a website can be hacked or can handle a large load without some tool framework.

Comparisons

Read more about source code management tools and IDEs in Chapter 7, "Technology-Facing Tests that Support the Team."

Visually checking an ASCII file output by a system process is much easier if you first parse the file and display it in a human-readable format. A script to compare output files to make sure no unintentional changes were made is a lot faster and more accurate than trying to compare them manually. File comparison tools abound, ranging from the free diff to proprietary tools such as WinDiff. Source code management tools, and IDEs have their own built-in comparison tools. These are essential items in every tester's toolbox. Don't forget about creating scripts for comparing database tables when doing testing for your data warehouse or data migration projects.

Repetitive Tasks

As we work with our customers to better understand the business and learn what's valuable to them, we might see opportunities to automate some of their tasks. Lisa's company needed to mail several forms with a cover letter to all of their clients. The programmers could not only generate the forms but could also concatenate them with the cover letter and greatly speed up the mailing effort. Lisa's fellow tester, Mike Busse, wrote a spreadsheet macro to do complex calculations for allocating funds that the retirement plan administrators had been doing manually. A lot of manual checklists can be replaced with an automated script. Automation isn't just for testing.

Data Creation or Setup

Another useful area for automation is data creation or setup. If you are constantly setting up your data, automate the process. Often, we need to repeat something multiple times to be able to recreate a bug. If that can be automated, you will be guaranteed to have the same results each time.

Lisa's Story

Many of our test schemas, including the ones used for automated regression suites, use canonical data. This canonical or "seed" data was originally taken from production. Some tables in the database, such as lookup tables, don't change, so they never need to be refreshed with a new copy. Other tables, such as those containing retirement plan, employee, and transaction information, need to start from Ground Zero whenever a regression suite runs.

Our database developer wrote a stored procedure to refresh each test schema from the "seed" schema. We testers may specify the tables we want refreshed in a special table called REFRESH_TABLE_LIST. We have an ant target for each test schema to run the stored procedure that refreshes the data. The automated builds use this target, but we use it ourselves whenever we want to clean up our test schema and start over.

Many of our regression tests create their own data on top of the "seed" data. Our Watir tests create all of the data they need and include logic that makes them re-runnable no matter what data is present. For example, the script that tests an employee requesting a loan from his or her retirement plan first cancels any existing loans so a new one can be taken out.

FitNesse tests that test the database layer also create their own data. We use a special schema where we have removed most constraints, so we don't have to add every column of every table. The tests only add the data that's pertinent to the functionality being tested. Each test tears down the data it created, so subsequent tests aren't affected, and each test is independent and rerunnable.

—Lisa

Cleaning up test data is as important as generating it. Your data creation toolkit should include ways to tear down the test data so it doesn't affect a different test or prevent rerunning the same test.

We've looked at major areas where automation is required or at least useful. Our opinion is that whenever you need to do a test or some testing-related activity, first decide whether it can be aided by automation. In some cases, automation won't be appropriate. Let's look at some of those.

WHAT SHOULDN'T WE AUTOMATE?

Some testing needs human eyes, ears, and intelligence. Usability and exploratory testing are two that fall into that category. Other tests that may not justify the automation investment are one-off tests and those that will never fail.

Usability Testing

We discuss some logging and monitoring tools in Chapter 10, "Business-Facing Tests that Critique the Product."

Real usability testing requires someone to actually use the software. Automation might be helpful in setting up scenarios to subsequently examine for usability. Observing users in action, debriefing them on their experiences, and judging the results is a job for a person who understands that usability aspects of software cannot be automated. Logging user actions is helpful for usability testing.

Janet's Story

We had evaluated several GUI tools but decided to use Ruby with Watir. We kept our tests limited to GUI functions only. One of our tests was checking to make sure that correct validation messages were displaying on the screen. I was running the tests and happened to be watching the screen because I hadn't seen this particular test that one of the other testers created. My eyes caught something weird, but the test passed, so I replayed it again. One of the programmers had added a "$" to the screen, and the error message was displayed offset because of it. The correct message was displayed, just not in the right place. In this instance, the value in watching the tests run was huge because we were preparing to release fairly soon, and we probably wouldn't have caught that particular problem.

—Janet

It is possible to automate tests that make sure the GUI never changes, but you need to ask yourself whether it's worth the cost. Do you really care that a button has changed positions by one pixel? Do the results justify the effort? We don't think you should automate "look and feel" testing, because an automated script can only look for what you tell it to see. Automation would miss visual problems that would jump out at a human.

Exploratory Testing

See Chapter 10, "Business-Facing Tests that Critique the Product," for more on exploratory testing and tools that can facilitate it.

Similarly, exploratory testing may be speeded up with scripts to create test data and jump through some setup steps, but it requires a skilled tester to design and execute the tests. One major goal of exploratory testing is to learn more about the product by doing, and then use that information to improve future development. Automated scripts won't do that for you. However, as we've said before, you won't have time for exploratory testing without a lot of other automated tests.

Tests that Will Never Fail

We've heard an argument that tests that will never fail don't need to be automated. If a requirement is so obvious that there's only one way to implement it, and no programmer will ever look at that code later without knowing exactly what it should do, the chances of someone introducing a defect in that code are next to nothing. Let's say we have a form with address fields. Do we need an automated regression test to verify that the second street address line is not required? After we've verified it manually, how likely is it that someone will accidentally change it to a required field later? Even if someone did, it wouldn't be a catastrophic event. Someone else would notice it and people could work around it easily until it was fixed.

Then again, a test for it would be easy to include. And programmer tricks such as copy/paste errors happen all the time. If you feel comfortable that one-time manual testing does the job and that the risk of future failures doesn't justify automating regression tests, don't automate them. If your decision turns out to be wrong, you'll get another chance to automate them later. If you aren't sure, and it's not terribly difficult to automate, go for it.

See Chapter 18, "Coding and Testing," for more about risk analysis and how it relates to testing.

If you're testing a life-critical system, even a very small risk of a regression failure is too much. Use risk analysis to help decide what tests should be automated.

One-Off Tests

Most times, manually executing a one-off test is sufficient. If automating a test doesn't have payoff, why do it? Sometimes automation is worth doing for a one-off test.

Lisa's Story

We recently did a story to pop up a warning message dialog when posting a payroll, but the message should only come up during the first two weeks of January. Automating a test for this functionality would require some way to simulate that the current date was between January 1 and January 15. That's not terribly hard to do, but the consequences of a failure were fairly trivial, and we had more critical stories to deliver that iteration. Automating that test at that time just didn't have enough value to justify the cost, and the risk factor was low. We decided to test it manually.

There are other cases where doing a one-off test seems the most intuitive but automation is a better choice. We host sites for different business partners, and each one has unique content, look, and feel. Values in the database drive the correct behavior and content for each brand. Some of the data, such as fee schedules based on asset values and numbers of participants, are highly complex. It's much easier and much more accurate to verify this data using FitNesse tests. We have a set of fixtures that let us specify keys for the partner "brand" that we want to test. We can easily plug in the appropriate expected results from the spreadsheets that the business development staff creates for each new partner. These tests aren't part of our regression suite. They're used one time only to validate the new brand.

—Lisa

Tedious tasks may be worth automating, even if you don't do them often. Weigh the automation cost against the amount of valuable time eaten up by manually doing the test. If it's easy to do manually, and automating wouldn't be quick, just keep it manual.

WHAT MIGHT BE HARD TO AUTOMATE?

When code isn't written test-first, or at least with test automation in mind, it's much harder to automate. Older systems tend to fall into this category, but no doubt plenty of new code with the same untestable characteristics is still being produced.

If you're faced with working on existing code that doesn't already have automated tests, you're in for an uphill battle, but a winnable one. Legacy code may have I/O, database access, as well as business logic and presentation code intertwined. It may not be clear where to hook into the code to automate a test. How do you get started automating tests on such a system? You certainly can't plan on automating everything below the GUI, because much of the logic is in the presentation layer.

There are at least a couple of different approaches that work well. The "hump of pain" we talked about in Chapter 13, "Why We Want to Automate Tests and What Holds Us Back," is intimidating, but it can be overcome, and then test automation will become much easier. Michael Feathers' *Working Effectively With Legacy Code* [2004] explains how to build a test harness around existing code bases and refactor them to accommodate automation. Even with legacy code, you can write tests to protect against introducing new problems. This approach can work even on systems that lack structure or aren't object-oriented.

Lisa's team decided on a different but equally effective approach. The team members started "strangling" the legacy code by writing all new features in a new test-friendly architecture. They're gradually replacing all of the old code with code written test-first. When they do work on old code to fix bugs, or in the cases where the old code needs updating, they simply add unit tests for all of the code they change. A GUI smoke test suite covers the critical functions of the rest of the legacy system that has no unit tests.

As with any automation project, approach the hard-to-automate code one piece at a time, and address the highest risk areas first. Solve the testability problem and find a way to write unit-level tests. The effort will pay off.

> Chapter 7, "Technology-Facing Tests that Support the Team," goes into more detail about different agile approaches to legacy code.

DEVELOPING AN AUTOMATION STRATEGY—WHERE DO WE START?

A simple, step-by-step approach sounds incompatible with an automation strategy, but in agile testing we try to understand the problem first. Deciding where and how to start with automation requires a bit of thought and discussion. As your team looks at testing challenges, you'll need to consider where automation is appropriate. Before you start searching for a particular automation tool, you'll want to identify your requirements.

You need to understand what problem you are trying to solve. What are you trying to automate? For example, if you have no test automation of any kind, and you start by buying an expensive commercial test tool thinking it will automate all your functional tests, you may be starting in the wrong place.

We suggest you start at the beginning. Look for your biggest gain. The biggest bang for the buck is definitely the unit tests that the programmers can do. Instead of starting at the top of the test pyramid, you may want to start at the bottom, making sure that the basics are in place. You also need to consider the different types of tests you need to automate, and when you'll need to have tools ready to use.

In this section, we assume you have automated Quadrant 1 unit and component tests in place, and are looking to automate your business-facing tests in Quadrants 2 and 3, or your Quadrant 4 technology-facing tests that critique the product. We'll help you design a good strategy for building your automation resources.

Think about the skills and experience on your team. Who needs the automation, and why? What goals are you trying to achieve? Understanding some of these issues may affect your choice of tools and what effort you expend. There is a section on evaluating tools at the end of this chapter.

Automation is scary, especially if you're starting from scratch, so where do we begin?

Where Does It Hurt the Most?

To figure out where to focus your automation efforts next, ask your team, "What's the greatest area of pain?" or, for some teams, "What's the greatest area of boredom?" Can you even get code deployed in order to test it? Do team members feel confident about changing the code, or do they lack any safety net of automated tests? Maybe your team members are more advanced, have mastered TDD, and have a full suite of unit tests. But they don't have a good framework for specifying business-facing tests, or can't quite get a handle on automating them. Perhaps you do have some GUI tests, but they're extremely slow and are costing a lot to maintain.

Peril: Trying to Test Everything Manually

If you're spending all your time retesting features that you've tested before, not getting to new features, and needing to add more and more testing, you're suffering from a severe lack of test automation. This peril means that testers don't have time to participate in design and implementation discussions, regression bugs may creep in unnoticed, testing can't keep up anymore with development, and testers get stuck in a rut. Developers aren't getting involved in the business-facing testing, and testers don't have time to figure out a better way to solve the testing problems.

Your team can fix this by developing an automation strategy, as we describe in this chapter. The team starts designing for testability and chooses and implements appropriate automation tools. Testers get an opportunity to develop their technical skills.

Chapter 18, "Coding and Testing," has more information on a simple approach to risk analysis.

Wherever it hurts the most, that's the place to start your automation efforts. For example, if your team is struggling to even deliver deployable code, you need to implement an automated build process. Nothing's worse than twiddling your thumbs while you wait for some code to test.

But, if performance puts the existence of your organization in danger, performance testing has to be the top priority. It's back to understanding what problem you are trying to solve. Risk analysis is your friend here.

Janet's Story

I worked on a legacy system that was trying to address some quality issues as well as add new features for our main customer. There were no automated unit or functional tests for the existing application, but we needed to refactor the code to address the quality issues. The team members decided to tackle it one piece at a time. As they chose a chunk of functionality to refactor, the programmers wrote unit tests, made sure they passed, and then rewrote the code until the tests passed again. At the end of the refactoring, they had testable, well-written code and the tests to go with them. The testers wrote the higher-level functional tests at the same time. Within a year, most of the poor-quality legacy code had been rewritten, and the team had achieved good test coverage just by tackling one chunk at a time.

—Janet

Test automation won't pay off unless other good development practices are in place. Continuous integration running a robust suite of unit tests is a first step toward automating other tests. Code that's continually refactored for maintainability and good design will help increase the ROI on automation. Refactoring can't happen without that good unit test coverage. These development practices also need to be applied to the automated functional test scripts.

Multi-Layered Approach

While we recommend mastering one tool at a time, don't expect too much out of any one tool. Use the right tool for each need. The tool that works best for unit tests may or may not be appropriate to automate functional tests. GUI, load, performance, and security testing may each require a different tool or tools.

Mike Cohn's test pyramid concept (see Figure 14-2) has helped our teams put their automation efforts where they do the most good. We want to maximize the tests that have the best ROI. If the system architecture is designed for testability, test automation will be less expensive, especially at the unit level.

Tests that go through the user interface usually have the lowest ROI, because they're expensive to maintain, but we do need them. They make up the small tip of our pyramid We may choose to automate some of these tests, but the majority of GUI tests are defined in business terms and probably are best left as human interaction tests (i.e., manual tests).

The middle layer represents the functional tests that work directly with production code, without a GUI or other layer in between. While they're not as inexpensive to automate as unit-level tests, and provide feedback a bit more slowly, the right tools allow them to have a good ROI. The fact that these tests can be written in a language the business experts understand adds to their value.

There are many different layers in the application that can be tested independently. In his book *xUnit Test Patterns* [2007], Gerard Meszaros refers to this as the Layer Test pattern. He cautions that when trying to test all of the layers of the application separately, we still have to verify that the layers are hooked up correctly, and this may require at least one test of the business logic through the presentation layer.

Lisa's Story

As my team built our automation framework one step at a time, we gathered an arsenal of tools. After implementing a continuous build framework with Ant and CruiseControl, we mastered JUnit for unit testing. We knew that unit test automation is the quickest and cheapest way to automate, and provides the fastest feedback to the programmers.

Our legacy system had no automated tests, so we built a GUI regression test suite with Canoo WebTest. This provided good payback because the WebTest scripts were specified, not programmed. They were quick to write and easy to maintain.

After JUnit and WebTest were in place, we experimented with FitNesse and found it worked well for functional testing behind the GUI. We found automating with FitNesse to go relatively quickly. Although FitNesse tests are significantly more expensive to produce and maintain than unit tests, their value in driving development and promoting collaboration among customers, programmers, and testers kept the ROI high.

All of these tools were easy to learn, implement, and integrate with the build process, and provided continual feedback about our regression issues. They were important considerations when we were deciding on our test automation strategy.

—Lisa

When evaluating the payback of your automation efforts, consider less tangible aspects such as whether the tool promoted collaboration between the technical and customer teams. A primary reason to write tests is to help guide development. If the process of writing your automated acceptance tests results in a thorough understanding of business requirements, that's plenty of payback, even if the tests never find a single regression bug later on.

Think about Test Design and Maintenance

Think about all of the manual test scripts you've written in your life. Don't you just wish those all would have been automated? Wouldn't your life have been a lot easier? We believe that all scripted tests should be automated. Let's get started converting those manual scripted tests.

After you get started, it can be quite easy to automate tests. For example, when you have a working FitNesse fixture, adding more test cases requires little effort. This is great when you have a lot of different permutations to test. You'll probably test more conditions than you would if all your testing was done manually. When Lisa's team members rewrote their retirement plan's loan system, they could test hundreds of different possibilities for loan payment processing via FitNesse tests. What happens when three loan payments are processed on the same day? If someone doesn't make any payments for three months, and then sends in a large payment, is the interest calculated and applied correctly? It was easy to write automated tests to find out.

That's a great advantage, but it has a down side. Now the team has dozens, or even hundreds, of test cases to maintain. What if the rules about calculating the amount of interest for a loan payment change a year from now? This could require updating every test. If your test tool doesn't easily accommodate making changes to existing tests, your big suite of automated tests can turn into a headache.

End-to-end tests are particularly tricky to automate because they have the most potential to need maintenance as business rules change. How do we balance the need for automation with the cost?

Test Design

Chapter 8, "Business-Facing Tests that Support the Team," explains more about thin slices.

Remember to start with the thin slice or steel thread of the feature you're testing. Approach automation just as programmers approach coding. Get one small unit of the steel thread working, and then move on to the next. After you've covered the whole thin slice, go back and flesh it out.

See Chapter 9, "Toolkit for Business-Facing Tests that Support the Team," for more information about effective test design.

Choose your test pattern thoughtfully. Automate all of the test cases you need, but no more, and automate them at the lowest level that you can. Limit the scope of each test case to one test condition or one business rule. Understand the purpose of the test. Avoid dependencies between tests, because they quickly increase complexity and maintenance expense.

Consider Options

As we've mentioned before, the lower the level at which you automate a test, the better the ROI. Push test automation as far down the pyramid as you can. If you have good coverage in your unit and code integration tests, you don't need to automate as many functional tests. With solid coverage at the lower levels, it might be enough to do end-to-end tests manually to verify the system's behavior. Use risk analysis to help you decide.

User Interface

The user interface does need to be tested. In some situations, test automation at the GUI level is critical. Perhaps your team is using third-party GUI controls, and you aren't sure how they will behave. If your risk and ROI analysis supports a lot of automation at the GUI level, make the investment.

If you do automate at the higher levels, don't go overboard and automate every possible path through the system. You don't have to keep every automated test created during the development phase in the regression suite; consider tradeoffs of build time and the chance of finding defects. Focus your efforts on covering every important path through the code at the unit, code integration, and functional levels. You'll get a much better payback.

Strike a Balance

Striking a balance isn't an agile principle, it's just common sense. You need a good-enough solution right now, but it doesn't have to be perfect. Does the tool provide the results you need right now? Does it provide an adequate return on the resources needed to use it for automation? If so, go ahead and use it, and budget time later to look for alternatives. You can improve your automation framework over time. The most important factor is whether your automation tools fit your particular situation right now.

Don't slide the other way, and think, "OK, we can generate a bunch of scripts with this record tool, get our immediate testing done, and refactor the scripts later to make them maintainable." While you don't need to keep searching for the perfectly ideal automation solution, you do need a solution that doesn't add to your team's technical debt. Find a balance between "It finds the bugs we need to know about and doesn't cost too much to maintain" and "This is the most elegant and cool solution we can find."

Choosing the Right Tools

It's cool that we have so many tools available to help us solve our automation problems. Don't go for more sophistication than you need. Lisa's coworkers have found that a spreadsheet that retrieves data from the database and performs calculations independently of the system is a powerful tool, both for driving development and for verifying the application's calculations.

We usually minimize test automation at the GUI layer, but there are situations where more GUI automation is appropriate. If the user makes a change at X, what else changes? Some problems only manifest themselves at the GUI level. Lisa tested a bug fix that addressed a back-end problem when retirement plan participants requested a distribution of money from their accounts. The change was surrounded by unit tests, but it was a GUI regression test that failed when the distribution form failed to pop up upon request. Nobody anticipated that a back-end change could affect the GUI, so they probably wouldn't have bothered to test it manually. That's why you need GUI regression tests, too.

We've talked about some disadvantages of record/playback tools, but they're appropriate in the right situation. You may be using a record/playback tool for a good reason: Maybe your legacy code already has a suite of automated tests created in that tool, your team has a lot of expertise in the tool, or your management wants you to use it for whatever reason. You can use recorded scripts as a starting point, then break the scripts into modules, replace hard-coded data with parameters where appropriate, and assemble tests using the modules as building blocks. Even if you don't have much programming experience, it's not hard to identify the blocks of script that should be in a module. Login, for example, is an obvious choice.

Record/playback may also be appropriate for legacy systems that are designed in such a way that makes unit testing difficult and hand-scripting tests from scratch too costly. It's possible to build a record and playback capability into the application, even a legacy application. With the right design, and the use of some human-readable format for the recorded interaction, it's even possible to build playback tests before the code is built.

GUI Test Automation: From the Dark Ages to Successful Automation in an Agile Environment

Pierre Veragen, SQA Lead at iLevel by Weyerhaeuser, explains how his team used a tool that provided both record/playback and scripting capability productively in a waterfall environment, and then leveraged it when the company adopted agile development.

Back in our waterfall development days, in 2000, we started doing GUI test automation using a record-playback approach. We quickly accumulated tens of thousands of lines of recorded scripts that didn't meet our testing needs. When I took over 18 months later, I quickly became convinced that the record-playback approach was for the dinosaurs.

When we had a chance to obtain a new test automation tool at the end of 2003, we carefully evaluated tools with these criteria in mind: record capability to help us understand the scripting language, and the ability to build an object-oriented library to cover most of our needs, including test reporting. At the time, TestPartner from CompuWare fulfilled all of our requirements.

We started using TestPartner on a highly complex, CAD-with-engineering application, built in Visual Basic 6, still using a waterfall process. Before we started automating tests, our releases were quickly followed by one or more patches. We focused our automation efforts toward checking the engineering calculations through the GUI, and later, the actual position of the CAD details. These tests included hundreds of thousands of individual verification points, which could never have been done by hand. Within a year, having added a solid set of manual tests of the user interaction, in addition to our automated tests, we were releasing robust software without the usual follow-up patches. We felt confident about our combination of manual and automated tests, which didn't include a single line of recorded scripts.

In 2004, our group moved to Visual Basic .NET. I spent several months adapting our TestPartner library to activate .NET controls. In 2006, we adopted an Agile methodology. Building on lessons previously learned in the non-Agile world, we achieved astonishing results with test automation. By the end of 2006, team members were able to produce maintainable GUI test scripts and library components after just a few days of training. At the same time, the team embraced unit testing with NUnit and user acceptance tests with FitNesse.

As of this writing, issues are caught at all three levels of our automated testing: Unit, FitNesse, and GUI. The issues found by each of the three testing tiers are of a different nature. Because everything is automated and triggered automatically, issues are caught really fast, in true Agile fashion. Each part of our test automation is bringing value.

Some people feel resources would be better spent on architecture and design, so that GUI test automation isn't needed. In our development group, each team made its own decision about whether to automate GUI tests.

In case you decide to use GUI test automation, here's some advice: Stay away from recorded scripts, invest in maintainability, and minimize the required GUI testing with a good architecture of the application. It is my experience that investing in good GUI test automation practices will always pay off.

Pierre's advice reflects well how good development practices, especially those followed in agile development projects, apply to automated test development as well as to production code development.

Built-In Record & Playback

Gerard Meszaros, agile coach and author of *xUnit Test Patterns* [2007], describes a situation where the simplest approach turned out to be record/playback. We've mentioned drawbacks to record/playback tools, but if you design your code to support them, they can be the best approach.

I was asked to help a team that was porting a "safety sensitive" application from OS2 to Windows. The business was very concerned about the amount of time it would take it to retest the ported system and the likelihood that the team would miss important bugs. The system was designed to only offer the user valid choices that would not compromise safety. They considered using a test recording tool to record tests on the old system and play them back on the new system, but there were no test recording tools available for both OS2 and Windows that could deal with windows drawn using ASCII characters. After reviewing the architecture of the system, we determined that writing xUnit tests would not be a cost-effective way to test the system because much of the business logic was embedded in the user interface logic, and refactoring the code to separate them would be too risky and time-consuming. Instead, we proposed building a Record & Playback test capability right into the system before we ported it.

Even though the rest of the project was milestone-driven, we developed the built-in test mechanism in a very agile way. Each screen required at least one new hook and sometimes several. We started with the most frequently used screens, adding the necessary hooks to record the user's actions and the systems responses to them into an XML file. We also added the hooks to play back the XML and determine the test results. Initially, we focused our efforts on proving the concept by hooking only the screens we needed to record and then playing back a simple but realistic test. After everyone was convinced the approach would work, we prioritized the screens with respect to how much benefit it would provide. We implemented the hooks one by one until we could automate a significant portion of the tests. We also built an XSLT stylesheet that would format the XML in a Fit-like way, with green cells indicating acceptable results and red cells indicating a failed test step.

In the meantime, the client was identifying the test scenarios that needed test cases. As we finished enough screens to record a particular test, the client would "acceptance test" our hooks by recording and playing back (still on OS2) the test(s) that were waiting for those hooks. When all of the hooks were in place, we could go ahead and port the code, including the test hooks, from OS2 to Windows. After verifying successful playback on OS2, the client would move the XML test files over to Windows and run them against the ported version of the code. The client found this quite easy to do and was able to record a large number of tests in a relatively short period of time. Because the tests were recording actions and responses in business terms, the tests were fairly easy to understand. The client loved the capability, and still raves about how much effort it saved and how much more confidence it has in the product. "Not only did this save tens of man-years of testing effort, but it even uncovered hidden unknown bugs in the legacy system, which we had considered to be the gold standard."

In Gerard's story, the team worked together to retrofit testability onto a system that wasn't designed for testability. They gave their customers a way to capture their test scenarios on one platform and play them back on both platforms to verify the successful port. This is a stellar example of the whole-team approach. When everyone on the team collaborates on a test automation solution, there's a much better chance it's going to succeed.

See more examples of specific tools for business-facing tests in Chapter 9, "Toolkit for Business-Facing Tests that Support the Team."

Some agile teams get value from commercial or open source test tools, while others prefer a completely customized approach. Many testers find value writing simple scripts in a scripting language such as Ruby, or a shell, to automate mundane but necessary tasks, generate test data, or drive other tools. Books such as *Everyday Scripting with Ruby for Teams, Testers, and You* give a roadmap for this approach. If you're a tester without a strong programming background, we encourage you to pick up a book, find an online tutorial, or take a class on a scripting language, and see how easy it can be to write useful scripts.

What we're trying to tell you is that you can use many different tools. Look at the problem you are trying to solve and decide as a team the easiest and most effective way to solve it. Every so often, step back and take a look at the tools you're using. Is everyone on the team happy with them? Are you missing problems because you don't have the right tools? Budget time to explore new tools and see if they might fill gaps or replace a tool that isn't paying off.

If your team is new to agile development, or working on a brand-new project, you might be faced with choosing tools and setting up test environments during the early iterations, when you also might be working on high-risk stories. Don't expect to be able to deliver much business value if you're still creating your test infrastructure. Plan in lots of time for evaluating tools, setting up build processes, and experimenting with different test approaches.

APPLYING AGILE PRINCIPLES TO TEST AUTOMATION

Every team, every project, and every organization has a unique situation with unique automation challenges. Each has its own culture, history, resources, business pressures, products, and experience. No matter what your team's situation, you can use the agile principles and values discussed in Chapter 2 to help you find solutions. Concepts such as courage, feedback, simplicity, communication, continuous improvement, and responding to change aren't just agile ideas—they're qualities that are common to all successful teams.

Keep It Simple

The agile maxim of "do the simplest thing that could possibly work" applies to tests as well as code. Keep the test design simple, keep the scope minimal, and use the simplest tool that will do the job.

Simplicity is a core agile value for a good reason. The best place to start is the simplest approach you can think of. However, doing the simplest thing doesn't mean doing the easiest thing. It involves really thinking about what you need now and taking baby steps to get there. By keeping things simple, if you do make a bad choice, you won't go too far off track before realizing the error of your ways.

It's easy to get involved in a task and slip away from the basics into some intriguing challenge. Weigh the ROI of every automation task before you do it. Automation is fun (when you get past the scary part of getting started). It's tempting to try something difficult just because you can. Like all other aspects of testing in an agile development project, the only way to keep up is to do only the minimum required.

Use the simplest tool you can get away with. Remember the test pyramid. If a customer-facing test can be most easily automated at the unit level, do it there. Lisa sometimes writes test cases in FitNesse, only to learn the programmers can automate them much faster as JUnit tests. Conversely, sometimes the programmers use FitNesse for TDD instead of JUnit, because the code they're writing lends itself to testing in one of the FitNesse fixture formats.

Iterative Feedback

Short iterations allow us to experiment with various automation approaches, evaluate results, and change course as quickly as needed. Commit to an automation effort, such as developing a test framework in-house or implementing an open source tool for at least a couple of iterations. After each iteration, look at what's working and what's not working. Think of ideas to overcome problems, and try those in the next iteration. If it's not the right solution, try something else for a few iterations. Don't get sucked into a quagmire where you've put so many resources into a tool, and have so many tests that use it, that you feel you can't switch tools. Between the many open source and commercial tools, plus programmers' ability to write home-grown test tools, there's no reason to settle for less than the optimum tool.

Lisa's Story

One of my early XP teams struggled to find a good way to automate customer-facing acceptance tests for a Java-based web application. This was back when there were far fewer tool options for agile teams. First, we tried an open source tool that simulated a browser, but it lacked the features we required. It just wasn't quite robust enough. We discussed this at the next retrospective.

We decided to try using the unit testing tool for testing behind the GUI for the next two iterations. By committing to two iterations, we felt we were giving ourselves enough time to give the tool a good try, but not so much time that we would have too much invested if it weren't the right solution. The customers found the unit tests hard to read, and there was logic in the GUI we couldn't test with this tool.

After another discussion during our retrospective, we then committed to two iterations of using a vendor GUI test tool I had used extensively on previous projects. The Java programmers found it slow going because the tool used a proprietary scripting language, but it worked well enough to do the minimum automation needed. After two iterations, we decided that it wasn't ideal, but at the time there weren't a lot of other options, and it was the best one we had.

In hindsight, we should have kept looking for a better option. Perhaps we could have developed our own test harness. We were able to automate about 60% of the regression tests above the unit level using the vendor tool, which seemed great at the time. If we had pushed ourselves a little more, we might have done a lot better.

—Lisa

Use iterations to your advantage. They facilitate a step-wise approach. If your idea's a dud, you'll know quickly and have a chance to try a different one. Don't be afraid to keep looking, but don't keep looking for the perfect solution if one you try performs adequately.

Whole-Team Approach

Agile development can't work without automation. Fortunately, the whole-team approach, which we explored in Chapter 1, means that a wider range of skills and resources are available to find and implement a useful automation strategy. Attacking the problem as a team means it's more likely that code will be designed for testability. Programmers, testers, and other team members will collaborate to automate tests, bringing multiple viewpoints and skill sets to the effort.

The whole-team approach helps overcome the fear barrier. Automation tasks can be overwhelming to start with. Knowing there are other people with different skills and experience to help gives us courage. Being able to ask for and receive help gives us confidence that we can achieve adequate coverage with our automated tests.

Lisa's Story

My current team made a commitment to automating regression tests at all levels where it made sense. Here are some examples of where I've asked for help to succeed with automation.

Early on, when we had no automated tests at all and the developers were trying to master test-driven development, we settled on Canoo WebTest for the GUI smoke tests. I needed a bit of help understanding how to configure WebTest to run in our environment, and I needed a lot of help to run the tests from the automated build process. I asked our system administrator (who was also one of the programmers) to help. We quickly got a suite of tests running in the build.

Later, I really wanted to try FitNesse for functional testing behind the GUI. I had to be patient while the programmers were still getting traction with the automated unit tests. The team agreed to try the tool, but it was hard to find time to start using it. I picked a story that seemed suited to FitNesse tests, and asked the programmer working on the story if I could pair with him to try some FitNesse tests. He agreed, and we got some tests automated in FitNesse. The programmer found it easy and worthwhile, and gave a good report to the rest of the team.

After that, it wasn't hard to approach each programmer, suggest writing FitNesse tests for the story he was working on, and let him see the results. The FitNesse tests found test cases the programmer hadn't thought of, and they saw the benefit right away. When everyone on the team had some experience with the tool, they were not only happy to automate the tests, but started designing code in a way that would make writing FitNesse fixtures easier.

When our Ruby expert, who designed most of our Watir test suite, left the company, I was quite concerned about maintaining our huge suite of tests as well as being able to code new ones. My Ruby expertise was not as good as his (plus, we were down to just one tester, so time was an issue). Every programmer on the team went out, bought a book on Ruby, and helped when I had problems updating scripts to work when the code changed. One programmer even wrote a new script to test a new story when I didn't have time for that task. When we hired a new tester, he and I were able to handle the care and feeding of the Watir scripts, so the programmers no longer needed to take on those tasks.

I know I can ask teammates for help with automation issues, and the entire team sees automation as a priority, so the programmers always think about testability when designing the code. This is an example of the whole-team approach at work.

—Lisa

Chapter 11, "Critiquing the Product Using Technology-Facing Tests," talks about technology-facing tests such as these and different approaches to handling them.

Specialized technology-facing tests such as security or load testing might require bringing in experts from outside the team. Some companies have specialist teams that are available as shared resources to product teams. Even while taking advantage of these resources, agile teams should still take responsibility for making sure all types of testing are done. They may also be surprised to find that team members may have the skills needed if they take a creative approach.

Some organizations have independent test teams that do post-development testing. They may be testing to ensure the software integrates with other systems, or conducting other specialized testing such as large-scale performance testing. Development teams should work closely with these other teams, using feedback from all testing efforts to improve code design and facilitate automation.

Taking the Time to Do It Right

Solving problems and implementing good solutions takes time. We must help our management understand that without enough time to do things the right way, our technical debt will grow, and our velocity will slow. Implementing solutions the "right" way takes time up front but will save time in the long term. Consider the time it takes for brainstorming ideas, solutions, formal training, and for on-the-job learning.

Your organization's management is understandably interested in producing results as quickly as possible. If management is reluctant to give the team time to implement automation, explain the trade-offs clearly. Delivering some features in the short term without automated regression tests to make sure they keep working will have a big cost down the line. As your team accumulates technical debt, you'll be less able to deliver the business value management needs. Work toward a compromise. For example, cut the scope of a feature but keep the essential value, and use automation to deliver and maintain a better product.

We always have deadlines, and we always feel pressed for time. The temptation to just go back to doing things the way we always have, like executing regression tests manually and hoping for the best, is always there even though we know that doesn't work. There is never enough time to go back and fix things. During your next planning meeting, budget time to make meaningful progress on your automation efforts.

Lisa's Story

Our team focuses on taking time for good design, a strong set of automated tests, and ample time for exploratory testing. Quality, not speed, has always been our goal. Our production problems cost a lot to fix, so the whole company is on board to take the time to prevent them. Sometimes we don't pick the right design, and we aren't afraid to rip it out and replace it when we realize it.

Naturally there are business tradeoffs, and the business decides whether to proceed with known risks. We work to explain all of the risks clearly and give examples of potential scenarios.

Here are a couple of recent examples of taking the time to do things right. We started a theme to make major changes to the account statements for the retirement plans. One of the programmers, Vince Palumbo, took on the task of collecting additional data to be used for the statements. He decided to write robust unit tests for the data collection functionality, even though this meant the story would have to continue on to the next iteration. Writing the unit tests took a great deal of time and effort, and even with the tests, the code was extremely complex and difficult to do. A couple of iterations later, another programmer, Nanda Lankalapalli, picked up another story related to the data collection and was pleasantly surprised to find new unit tests. He was able to make his changes quickly, and the testing effort was greatly reduced because the unit tests were in place.

Later, we found we had missed an edge case where some calculations for the change in account value were incorrect. The combination of automated unit tests and a great deal of exploratory testing were not enough to catch all of the scenarios. Still, having the tests meant Vince could write his corrected code test-first and feel more confident that the code was now correct.

Another recent example concerned processing of incoming checks. The business wanted to shorten the two-step process to one step, which meant the money would be invested in the retirement plan accounts two days earlier than was then possible. The existing process was all written in legacy code, without unit tests. We discussed whether to rewrite the processing in the new architecture. Our product owner was concerned about the amount of time this might take. We felt it would take just as long to change the existing code as to completely rewrite it, because the old code was difficult to understand and had no unit tests at all. We decided on the rewrite, which not only reduced the risk of problems in this critical functionality but also gave us the opportunity to provide a couple of extra features at little extra cost. So far, this strategy has proven worthwhile.

—Lisa

Allow yourself to succeed. Work at a sustainable pace. Take the time to refactor as you go or you'll end up with a mess eventually. As testers, we always have many different tasks to do. If you're learning a new tool or trying to automate new tests, don't multitask. Find a big block of time and focus. This is hard, but switching gears constantly is harder.

If business stakeholders are impatient for your team to "just get it done," analyze the problem with them. What are the risks? How much will a production problem cost? What are the benefits of releasing a quick hack? How much technical debt will it add? What's the long-term return on investment of a solid design supported with automated tests? How will each approach affect company profitability and customer satisfaction? What about the intangible costs, such as the effect that doing poor-quality work has on team morale? Sometimes the business will be right, but we're betting that you'll usually find that up-front investment pays off.

Learn by Doing

Everyone learns in different ways, but when you've decided how you're going to automate a test, jump in and start doing it. In *Everyday Scripting with Ruby for Teams, Testers, and You* [2007], Brian Marick advises to learn to program by writing a program. Make mistakes! The more problems you have, the more you'll learn. Getting someone to pair with you will help speed up learning, even if neither one of you is familiar with the tool or the language.

If you don't have anyone to pair with, talk to the "rubber ducky": Imagine you're describing the problem to a coworker. The process of explaining can often make the cause of the problem jump into view. Simply reading a test aloud to yourself can help you find the weaknesses in it.

Apply Agile Coding Practices to Tests

Tests are just as valuable as production code. In fact, production code isn't much without tests to support it. Treat your tests the same way you treat all code. Keep it in the same source code control tool as your production code.

You should always be able to identify the versions of test scripts that go with a particular version of code.

Pairing, refactoring, simple design, modular and object-oriented design, good standards, keeping tests as independent as possible—all of the qualities of good code are also qualities of good automated tests. Agile development is sometimes perceived by the uninformed to be chaotic or lax, when in fact it is highly disciplined. Undertake your automation tasks with the greatest discipline, proceeding in small steps, checking in each step that succeeds. If you're programming automated scripts, write them test-first, just as any agile programmer would write production code. Keep simplicity in mind, though. Don't write fancy test scripts with lots of logic unless there's a good ROI. Those tests need testing and cost more to maintain. Specify tests when you can instead of coding them, and always go with the simplest approach possible.

We can't emphasize it enough: Test automation is a team effort. The varying experience, skills, and perspectives of different team members can work together to come up with the best approach to automation. Innovate—be creative. Do what works for your unique situation, no matter what the "common wisdom" says.

Automation tools are just one piece of the puzzle. Test environments and test data are essential components. Let's look at test data next.

SUPPLYING DATA FOR TESTS

No matter what tool we use to automate tests, the tests need data to process. Ideally, they need realistic data that matches production data. However, production databases usually contain lots and lots of data, and they can be highly complex. Also, database access slows down tests exponentially. Like so much of agile testing, it's a balancing act.

Data Generation Tools

As we write this book, there are several cool tools available to generate test data for all kinds of input fields and boundary conditions. Open source and commercial tools such as Data Generator, databene benerator, testgen, Datatect, and Turbo Data are available to generate flat files or generate data directly to database tables. These tools can generate huge varieties of different types of data, such as names and addresses.

It's also fairly easy to generate test data with a home-grown script, using a scripting language such as Ruby or Python, a tool such a Fit or FitNesse, or a shell script.

Lisa's Story

Our Watir scripts create randomized test data inputs, both to ensure they are re-runnable (they're unlikely to create an employee with the same SSN twice), and to provide a variety of data and scenarios. The script that creates new retirement plans produces plans with about 200 different combinations of options. The script that tests taking out a loan randomly generates the frequency, reason, and term of the loan, and verifies that the expected payment is correct.

We have utility scripts to create comma-separated files for testing uploads. For example, there are several places in the system that upload census files with new employee information. If I need a test file with 1,000 new employees with random investment allocations to a retirement plan, I can simply run the script and specify the number of employees, the mutual funds they're investing in, and the file name. Each record will have a randomly generated Social Security Number, name, address, beneficiaries, salary deferral amounts, and investment fund allocations. Here's a snippet of the code to generate the investment calculations.

```
# 33% of the time maximize the number of funds chosen, 33% of the time
# select a single fund, and 33% of the time select from 2-4 funds
    fund_hash = case rand(3)
      when 0: a.get_random_allocations(@fund_list.clone)
      when 1: a.get_random_allocations(@fund_list.clone, 1)
when 2: a.min_percent = 8;
a.get_random_allocations(@fund_list.clone, rand(3) + 2)
    end
    emp['fund_allocations'] = fund_hash_to_string(fund_hash)
```

Scripts like these have dual uses, both as regression tests that cover a lot of different scenarios and exploratory test tools that create test data and build test scenarios. They aren't hard to learn to write (see the section "Learning by Doing" earlier in this chapter).

—Lisa

Scripts and tools to generate test data don't have to be complex. For example, PerlClip simply generates text into the Windows clipboard so it can be pasted in where needed. Any solution that removes enough tedium to let you discover potential issues about the application is worth trying. "The simplest thing that could possibly work" definitely applies to creating data for tests. You want to keep your tests as simple and fast as possible.

Avoid Database Access

Your first choice for testing should try to have tests that can run completely in-memory. They will still need to set up and tear down test data, but the data won't store in a database. Each test is independent and runs as quickly as any test could. Database access means I/O and disks are inherently slow. Every read to the database slows down your test run. If your goal is to give fast feedback to the team, then you want your tests to run as quickly as possible. A fake object such as an in-memory database lets the test do what it needs to do and still give instant feedback.

One of our build processes runs only unit-level tests, and we try to keep its runtime less than eight minutes, for optimum feedback. The tests substitute fake objects for the real database in most cases. Tests that are actually testing the database layer, such as persisting data to the database, use a small schema with canonical data originally copied from the production database. The data is realistic, but the small amount makes access faster.

At the functional test level, our FitNesse test fixtures build data in-memory wherever possible. These tests run quickly, and the results appear almost instantaneously. When we need to test the database layer, or if we need to test legacy code that's not accessible independently of the database layer, we usually write FitNesse tests that set up and tear down their own data using a home-grown data fixture. These tests are necessary, but they run slowly and are expensive to maintain, so we keep them to the absolute minimum needed to give us confidence. We want our build that runs business-facing tests to provide feedback within a couple of hours in order to keep us productive.

—Lisa

Because it's so difficult to get traction on test automation, it would be easy to say "OK, we've got some tests, and they do take hours to run, but it's better than no tests." Database access is a major contributor to slow tests. Keep taking small steps to fake the database where you can, and test as much logic as possible without involving the database. If this is difficult, reevaluate your system architecture and see if it can be organized better for testing.

If you're testing business logic, algorithms, or calculations in code, you're interested in the behavior of the code itself given certain inputs; you don't care where the data comes from as long as it accurately represents real data. If this is the case, build test data that is part of the test and can be accessed in memory, and let the production code operate from that. Simulate database access and objects, and focus on the purpose of the test. Not only will the tests run faster, but they'll be easier to write and maintain.

When generating data for a test, use values that reflect the intent of the test, where possible. Unless you're completely confident that each test is independent, generate unique test values for each test. For example, use timestamps as part of the field values. Unique data is another safety net to keep tests from infecting each other with stray data. When you need large amounts of data, try generating the data randomly, but always clean it up at the end of the test so that it doesn't bleed into the next test. We recognize that sometimes you need to test very specific types of data. In these cases, randomly generated data would defeat the purpose of the test. But you may be able to use enough randomization to ensure that each test has unique inputs.

When Database Access Is Unavoidable or Even Desirable

If the system under test relies heavily on the database, this naturally has to be tested. If the code you're testing reads from and/or writes to the database, at some point you need to test that, and you'll probably want at least some regression tests that verify the database layer of code.

Setup/Teardown Data for Each Test

Our preferred approach is to have every test add the data it needs to a test schema, operate on the data, verify the results in the database, and then delete all of that test data so the test can be rerun without impacting other subsequent tests. This supports the idea that tests are independent of each other.

Lisa's Story

We use a generic data fixture that lets the person writing the test specify the database table, columns, and values for the columns in order to add data. Another generic data lookup fixture lets us enter a table name and SQL where clause to verify the actual persisted data. We can also use the generic data fixture to delete data using the table name and a key value. Figure 14-3 shows an example of a table that uses a data fixture to build test data in the database. It populates the table

Data Fixture	all_fund			
ticker	name	share_price	class_id	addRow?
BOGUS	Fund ABC	15.786	6	true
BOGEY	Fund DEF	2.413	2	true
BENNY	Fund BEN	1	2	true
WHAAT	Fund What	27.4	3	true
WHYYY	Fund Why	1	6	true
WHERE	Fund Where	1.431	1	true

Figure 14-3 Example of a table using a data fixture to build test data in the database "all fund" with the specified columns and values. It's easy for those of us writing test cases to populate the tables with all of the data we need.

Note that the schemas we use for these tests have most of their constraints removed, so we only have to populate the tables and columns pertinent to the functionality being tested. This makes maintenance a little easier, too. The downside is that the test is a bit less realistic, but tests using other tools verify the functionality with a realistic environment.

The downside to creating test data this way is that whenever a change is made in the database, such as a new column with a required value, all of the data fixture tables in the tests that populate that table will have to be changed. These tests can be burdensome to write and maintain, so we only use them when absolutely needed. We try to design the tests to keep maintenance costs down. For example, the data fixture in Figure 14-3 is in an "include" library and can be included into the tests that need it. Let's say we add a new column, "fund_category." We only need to add it to this "include" table, rather than in 20 different tests that use it.

—Lisa

Canonical Data

Another alternative is having test schemas that can quickly be refreshed with data from a canonical or seed database. The idea is that this seed data is a representative sample of real production data. Because it's a small amount of data, it can be quickly rebuilt each time a suite of regression tests needs to be run.

This approach also increases the time it takes to run tests, but it's just a few minutes at the start of the regression suite rather than taking time out of each individual test. The tests will still be slower than tests that don't access the database, but they'll be faster than tests that have to laboriously populate every column in every table.

Canonical data has many uses. Testers and programmers can have their own test schema to refresh at will. They can conduct both manual and automated tests without stepping on anyone else's testing. If the data is carefully chosen, the data will be more realistic than the limited amount of data each test can build for itself.

Of course, as with practically everything, there's a downside. Canonical data can be a pain to keep up. When you need new test scenarios, you have to identify production data that will work, or make up the data you need and add it to the seed schema. You have to scrub the data, mask real peoples' identifying characteristics, making it innocuous for security reasons. Every time you add a table or column to the production database, you must update your test schemas accordingly. You might have to roll date-sensitive data forward every year, or do other large-scale maintenance. You have to carefully select which tables should be refreshed and which tables don't need refreshing, such as lookup tables. If you have to add data to increase test coverage, the refresh will take longer to do, increasing the time of the build process that triggers it. As we've been emphasizing, it's important that your automated builds provide feedback in a timely manner, so longer and longer database refreshes lengthen your feedback cycle. You also lose the test independence with canonical data, so if one test fails, others may follow suit.

Lisa's team members run their GUI test suites and some of their functional regression tests against schemas refreshed each run with canonical data. On rare occasions, tests fail unexpectedly because of an erroneous update to the seed data. Deciding whether to "roll" data forward, so that, for example, 2008's rows become 2009's rows, gets to be a headache. So far, the ROI on using canonical data has been acceptable for the team. Janet's current team also uses seed data for its "middle layer" testing on local builds. It works well for fast feedback during the development cycle. However, the test environment and the staging environments use a migrated copy of production data. The downside is that the regression tests can only be run on local copies of the build. The risk is low because they practice "build once, deploy to many."

Production-Like Data

The ability to test a system that is as much like production as possible is essential to most software development teams. However, running a suite of automated regression tests against a copy of a production database would probably run too slowly to be useful feedback. Besides, you couldn't really depend on any data remaining stable as you bring over new copies to stay up-to-date. Generally, when you're talking about functional or end-to-end testing, a clone of the production database is most useful for manual exploratory testing.

Stress, performance, and load testing, which are automation–intensive, need an environment that closely simulates production in order to provide results that can translate to actual operations. Usability, security, and reliability are other examples of testing that needs a production-like system, although they may not involve much automation.

There is always a trade-off; your production database might be huge, so it is expensive and slow, but it provides the most accurate test data available. If your organization can afford hardware and software to store multiple copies of production data for testing purposes, this is ideal. Small companies may have resource constraints that might limit the amount of data that can be stored in test and staging environments. In this case, you'll need to decide how much test data you can support and plan how to copy enough relevant data to make the test representative of what's used in "real life." Or you may consider making the investment in hardware, which is getting less expensive every day, to support a real production style environment. Otherwise, your test results might be misleading. As we mentioned with the canonical data, you may need to scrub the data before using it.

Data Migration

Data migration needs to be tested against a real database. The database upgrade scripts need to be run against real data and against the last known release of the database schema.

Testing a Database Migration

Paul Rogers, an automation test architect, tells this story of testing an eye-opening database migration [2008]:

> Just yesterday, I ran a Rails migration against my test database. The developers had written it, tested it, and checked it using their development databases. My test database was probably 20,000 times larger. The migration for them took seconds. For me, well, I stopped it after three hours, at probably 10% complete. The programmers needed to redo their migration strategy.
>
> I doubt this would have shown up on an in-memory database, so for me, a real database in this instance was definitely the right choice. In fact, this is likely to feed into things we need to consider before releasing, such as how long does a deployment take, or how long does the database update take. We can then use this to estimate how much down time we will need for the actual upgrade.

This is another example of how we must strike a balance between tests that deliver quick feedback and tests that realistically reflect events that might occur in production.

Understand Your Needs

If you understand the purpose of your tests, you can better evaluate your needs. For example, if you don't need to test stored procedures or SQL queries directly for speed, consider tools such as in-memory databases, which work just like real databases but greatly speed up your tests. When you need to simulate the actual production environment, make a copy of the entire production database, if necessary. Quick feedback is the goal, so balance testing realistic scenarios with finding defects as efficiently as possible.

EVALUATING AUTOMATION TOOLS

The first step in choosing an automation tool is to make a list of everything the tool needs to do for you. Let's consider how you can decide on your test tool requirements.

Identifying Requirements for Your Automation Tool

After deciding on the next automation challenge to tackle, think about your tool needs. What tools do you already have? If you need additional ones, you probably want something that integrates well with your existing testing and development infrastructure. Do you need a tool to easily integrate into the continuous build process? Will your existing hardware support the automation you need to do? Setting up a second build process to run functional tests may require additional machinery.

Who's going to use the test tool you're hoping to implement? Will non-programmers be writing test cases? Do your programmers want a tool they feel comfortable with as well? Do you have distributed team members who need to collaborate?

Who will be automating and maintaining the tests? The skills already on your team are important. How much time do you have to get a tool installed and learn how to use it? If your application is written in Java, a tool that uses Java for scripting may be the most appropriate. Do team members have experience with particular tools? Is there a separate test team with expertise in a certain tool? If you're starting the transition to agile development and you already have a team of test automators, it may make sense to leverage their expertise and keep using the tools they know.

Your tool requirements are dependent on your development environment. If you're testing a web application, and the tool you choose doesn't support SSL or AJAX, you may have a problem. Not every test tool can test web services applications. Embedded system testing can need different tools again. The case study in Chapter 12, "Summary of Testing Quadrants," shows one way to use Ruby to test an embedded application.

Of course, the type of testing you're automating is key. Security testing probably needs highly specialized tools. There are many existing open source and vendor tools for performance, so the job of selecting one isn't overwhelming. As you master one challenge, you'll be better prepared for the next. It took Lisa's team a couple of years to develop robust regression test suites at the unit, integration, and functional levels. Performance testing was their next area of pain. Lessons learned from the earlier automation efforts helped them do a better job of identifying requirements for a test tool, such as ease of reporting results, compatibility with existing frameworks, and scripting language.

Write a checklist that captures all your tool requirements. Some of them might conflict with or contradict each other—"The tool needs to be easy enough so that customers can specify tests" or "The tests should be easy to automate." Write them down so you can find the right balance. Then start doing your research.

One Tool at a Time

You're going to need different tools to serve different purposes. Implementing new tools and learning the best way to use them can get overwhelming pretty quickly. Try one tool at a time, addressing your greatest area of pain. Give it enough time for a fair trial and evaluate the results. If it's working for you, master that tool before you go on to the next area of pain and the next tool. Multitasking might work for some situations, but new technology demands full attention.

When you've settled on a tool to address a particular need, take a step back and see what else you need. What's the next automation challenge facing your team? Will the tool you just selected for another purpose work for that need, too, or do you need to start a new selection process?

The bibliography contains websites that help with tool searches and evaluation.

If you've decided to look outside your own organization for tools, the first step is to find time to try some out. Start with some basic research: Internet searches, articles and other publications about tools, and mailing lists are good places to get ideas. Compile a list of tools to consider. If your team uses a wiki or online forum tool, post information about tools and start a discussion about pros and cons.

Budget time for evaluating tools. Some teams have an "engineering sprint" or "refactoring iteration" every few months where, rather than delivering stories prioritized by the business, they get to work on reducing technical debt, upgrading tool versions, and trying out new tools. If your team doesn't have these yet, make a case to your management to get them. Reducing your technical debt and establishing a good testing infrastructure will improve your velocity in the future and free time for exploratory testing. If you never have time to make code easier to maintain or upgrade tools, technical debt will drag down your velocity until it comes to a halt.

When you have a list of tools that may meet your requirements, narrow the possibilities down to one or two, learn how to use each one well enough to try it, and do a spike: Try a simple but representative scenario that you can throw away. Evaluate the results against the requirements. Use retrospectives to consider pros and cons.

What resources do you need to implement and use the tool? What impact will the tool have on the team's productivity and velocity? What risks does it pose? What will it allow you to do in the long term that you can't do now?

Pick your top candidate and commit to trying it for some period of time—long enough to get some competency with it. Make sure you try all your mission-critical functionality. For example, if your application uses a lot of Ajax, make sure you can automate tests using the tool. In retrospectives, look at what worked and what didn't. Be open to the idea that it might not be right and that you have to throw it out and start over. Don't feel you have to keep on with the tool because you have so much invested in it already.

We all know that there's no "silver bullet" that can solve all your automation problems. Lower your expectations and open your mind. Creative solutions rely on art as much as science.

Lisa's Story

Chapter 11, "Critiquing the Product Using Technology-Facing Tests," shows an example of the results produced by the performance test tool chosen, JMeter.

When conducting the performance test tool search, we turned to an agile testing mailing list for suggestions. Many people offered their experiences, and some even offered to help learning and implementing a tool. We searched for a tool that used Java for scripting, had a minimal learning curve, and presented results in a useful graphical format. We listed tools and their pros and cons on the team wiki. We budgeted time for trial runs. Lisa's coworker, Mike Busse, tried the top two candidates and showed highlights to the rest of the team. A tool was chosen by team consensus and has proven to be a good fit.

—Lisa

Choosing Tools

We're lucky to have an already vast range and ever-growing set of tools to choose from: home-grown, open source, vendor tools, or a combination of any, are all viable alternatives. With so many choices, the trick is knowing where to look and finding time to try tools out to see if they fit your requirements. Because we can't predict the future, it may be hard to judge the ROI of each potential solution, but an iterative approach to evaluating them helps get to the right one.

Should You Grow Your Own?

Does your application present unique testing challenges, such as embedded software or integration with outside systems? Do team members have the skills, time, and inclination to write their own test framework or build one on top of an existing open source tool? If so, home-grown test tools may be the best fit.

A happy result (or perhaps a major success factor) of agile development is that many programmers are "test infected." Today's development tools and languages make automation frameworks easier to build. Ruby, Groovy, Rails, and many languages and frameworks lend themselves to automation. Existing open source tools such as Fit and HtmlUnit can be leveraged, with custom frameworks built on top of them.

Home-grown tools have many advantages. They're definitely programmer-friendly. If your team is writing its own automation frameworks, they'll be precisely customized to the needs of your development and customer teams, and integrated with your existing build process and other infrastructure—and you can make them as easy to execute and interpret results as you need.

Home-grown doesn't mean free, of course. A small team may not have the bandwidth to write and support tools as well as develop production code. A large organization with unique requirements may be able to put together a team of automation specialists who can collaborate with testers, customers, programmers, and others. If your needs are so unique that no existing tool supports them, home-grown may be your only option.

Open Source Tools

Many teams who wrote their own tools have generously made them available to the open source community. Because these tools were written by test-infected programmers whose needs weren't met by vendor tools, they are usually lightweight and appropriate for agile development. Many of these tools are developed test-first, and you can download the test suite along with the source code, making customization easier and safer. These tools have a broad appeal, with features useful to both programmers and testers. The price is right, although it's important to remember that purchase price is only a fraction of any tool's cost.

Not all open source tools are well documented, and training can be an issue. However, we see seminars and tutorials on using these tools at many conferences and user group meetings. Some open source tools have excellent user manuals and even have online tutorials and scheduled classes available.

See Chapter 9, "Toolkit for Business-Facing Tests that Support the Team," for more about open source test automation tools.

If you're considering an open source solution, look for an active developer and user community. Is there a mailing list with lots of bandwidth? Are new features released often? Is there a way to report bugs, and does anyone fix them? Some of these tools have better support and faster response on bugs than vendor tools. Why? The people writing them are also using them, and they need those features to test their own products.

Vendor Tools

Commercial tools are perceived as a safe bet. It's hard to criticize someone for selecting a well-known tool that's been around for years. They're likely to come with manuals, support, and training. For testers or other users who lack a technical background, the initial ramp-up might be faster. Some are quite robust and feature-rich. Your company may already own one and have a team of specialists who know how to use it.

Although they are changing with the times, vendor tools are historically programmer-unfriendly. They tend to use proprietary scripting languages that programmers don't want to spend time learning. They also tend to be heavy-weight. The test scripts may be brittle, easily broken by minor changes to the application, and expensive to maintain. Most of these tools are recording scripts for subsequent playback. Record/playback scripts are notoriously costly from a maintenance perspective.

See the bibliography for a full discussion by Elisabeth Hendrickson on this subject.

Elisabeth Hendrickson [2008] points out that specialized tools such as these may create a need for test automation specialists. Silos such as these can work against agile teams. We need tools that facilitate test-first, rather than test-last development. Test tools shouldn't stand in the way of change.

If you have people already expert in a vendor tool, and a use for a tool that might be used only by a subset of the development team or a team separate from development, a vendor tool could make lots of sense. Lisa's first two XP teams used a vendor tool with some degree of success.

As of this writing, better functional test tools and IDEs are emerging. These facilitate test maintenance tasks with features such as global search/replace. Twist is an example of a tool implemented as a collection of plug-ins to the Eclipse IDE, so it can take advantage of powerful editing and refactoring features.

Agile-Friendly Tools

Part III, "Using Agile Testing Quadrants," and particularly Chapter 9, "Toolkit for Business-Facing Tests that Support the Team," contain examples of test automation tools that work well on agile projects.

Elisabeth Hendrickson [2008] lists some characteristics of effective agile test automation tools. These tools should:

- Support starting the test automation effort immediately, using a test-first approach
- Separate the essence of the test from the implementation details
- Support and encourage good programming practices for the code portion of the test automation
- Support writing test automation code using real languages, with real IDEs
- Foster collaboration

IMPLEMENTING AUTOMATION

While you're evaluating tools, think about how quickly your top priority automation need must be addressed. Where will you get the support to help implement it? What training does the team need, and how much time will be available to devote to it? How quickly do you have to ramp up on this tool?

Keep all of these constraints in mind when you're looking at tools. You might have to settle for a less robust tool than you really want in order to get vital automation going in the short term. Remember that nothing's permanent. You can build your automation effort step-by-step. Many teams experience unsuccessful attempts before finding the right combination of tools, skills, and infrastructure.

Selenium at Work

Joe Yakich, a software engineer with test automation experience, describes how a team he worked with implemented a test automation effort with Selenium, an open source test automation tool.

The software company I worked for—let's call it XYZ Corp—had a problem. The product, an enterprise-level web-based application, was a powerful, mature offering. Development projects were managed using

Agile and Scrum, and a talented stable of engineers churned out new features quickly. The company was growing steadily.

So, what was the problem? XYZ was facing a future where software testing efforts might not be able to keep pace with the development effort. Software quality issues might slow adoption of the product or—worse yet—cause existing customers to look elsewhere.

Test automation seemed like an obvious way to mitigate these risks, and XYZ was fully aware of it. In fact, they had attempted to create a test automation suite twice before, and failed.

The third time, XYZ chose to use Selenium RC, driven by the Ruby programming language. Selenium RC—the RC is for "Remote Control"—is a tool for test automation. Selenium RC consists of a server component and client libraries. The Java server component acts as an HTTP proxy, making the Selenium Core JavaScript appear to originate from the web-server of the application under test (AUT). The server can start and stop browser sessions (supported browsers include nearly all modern browsers, including Internet Explorer, Firefox, and Safari) and interpret commands to interact with elements such as buttons, links, and input fields. The client libraries allow test scripts to be written in Java, .NET, Perl, Python, and Ruby.

Our team chose Ruby because it's a purely object-oriented, dynamic, interpreted language with a syntax that is elegant, expressive, and tersely powerful. Most importantly, Ruby is an ideal tool for the creation of a Domain Specific Language (DSL). Ruby is malleable enough for the programmer to first choose the structure and syntax of the DSL and then craft an implementation, as opposed to a more rigid language that might impose constraints on that freedom. One of our goals was to create an automation framework—a DSL—hiding complex detail. We wanted to be able to say things like

```
editor.save
```

in our tests instead of

```
s.click("//table[@class='edit']/tbody/tr[0]//img[@src='save.gif']")
```

Not only is the former more readable, it's also far more maintainable. The XPath expression in the latter can be put in a library method to be called as needed. Using a DSL that employs the nouns and verbs of the application allows an engineer writing a test to focus on the test, not the underlying complexity of interacting with on-screen controls.

XYZ created an automation team to build the framework and tests. Creating the framework itself was a time-consuming, technically challenging task. Some of the framework classes themselves were complicated enough to warrant unit tests of their own. After a sufficient amount of test framework was constructed, we began work on actual application tests, using the Ruby RSpec library. RSpec is itself a DSL for test specifications. One of its strengths is the use of simple declarative statements to describe behavior and expectations. One might, for example, write a test using the statement

"A user should be able to save data in an editor by clicking Save"

filling in the body of the test with calls to the Selenium-based test framework we had created.

Nearly a year later, we had automated nearly two thousand test cases. Although the majority of the application was covered by automation, other portions of the application required manual testing—we had been forced to make choices and prioritize our efforts. Every week the test suite took longer to run than the preceding week; it now took nearly six hours to complete, and we had begun to think about running tests in parallel. We had not yet managed to expand our testing across all of the browsers supported by the application. The enthusiasm that automation generated had waned somewhat, and we found it necessary to carefully manage expectations, both with upper management and with other engineers. Despite these issues, Selenium was a clear win, for had we not invested heavily in test automation, testing at XYZ would have required hiring an army of test engineers (which would have been prohibitively expensive even had we been able to find enough qualified applicants).

Not everything can be automated, because of budgetary or technical reasons. In addition, exploratory testing is invaluable and should not be neglected. It should be noted, however, that these drawbacks are shared by every other test automation tool currently available, and most of the other automation tools that can rival Selenium's automation prowess are commercial products that cannot match its price: free.

Good development practices are key to any automation effort. Use an object-oriented approach. As you build your library of test objects, adding new tests becomes easier. A domain specific language helps make business-facing tests understandable to customers, while lowering the costs of writing and maintaining automated test scripts.

Good object-oriented design isn't the only key to building a suite of maintainable automated tests that pay off. You also need to run the tests often enough to get the feedback your team needs.. Whatever tools we choose must be integrated with our build process. Easy-to-interpret results should come to us automatically.

The tools we choose have to work on our platforms, and must share and play well with our other tools. We have to continually tweak them to help with our current issues. Is the build breaking every day? Maybe we need to hook our results up to an actual traffic light to build team awareness of its status. Did a business-facing test fail? It should be plain exactly what failed, and where. We don't have extra time to spend isolating problems.

These concerns are an essential part of the picture, but still only part of the picture. We need tools that help us devise test environments that mimic production. We need ways to keep these test environments independent, unaffected by changes programmers might be making.

Building test infrastructure can be a big investment, but it's one our agile team needs to make to get a jump on test automation. Hardware, software, and tools need to be identified and implemented. Depending on your company's resources, this might be a long-term project. Brainstorm ways to cope in the short term, while you plan how to put together the infrastructure you really need to minimize risk, maximize velocity, and deliver the best possible product.

MANAGING AUTOMATED TESTS

Let's say we need a way to find the test that verifies a particular scenario, to understand what each test does, and to know what part of the application it verifies. Perhaps we need to satisfy an audit requirement for traceability from each requirement to its code and tests. Automated tests need to be maintained and controlled in the same way as production source code. When you tag your production code for release, the tests that verified that functionality need to be part of the tag.

Here's an example where that comes in handy. We just found a problem in the code under development. Is it a new problem, or has it been lurking in the code for a while and somehow missed by the test? We can deploy the tag that's in production, try to reproduce the problem, and investigate why the tests didn't catch it. Lisa's team recently had a situation where the regression suite missed a bug because a database constraint was missing in the test schema. That kind of problem is hard to pinpoint if you aren't tying your test code versions to your production code versions.

Organizing Tests

Many tools come with their own means of organization. For example, FitNesse comes with its own wiki, with a hierarchical organization, and built-in version control. As of this writing, FitNesse is starting to provide support for source code control tools such as Subversion. Scripts written in other test tools, such as Watir and Canoo WebTest, can and should be maintained within the same source code control system as production code, just as the unit tests are.

Organizing Tests with the Project under Test

We asked some agile testing experts how they manage tests. Dierk König, founder and project manager of Canoo WebTest, explained how his teams have managed their automated tests to satisfy the needs of both the development and customer teams.

> We always organize our tests alongside the project under test. That is, test sources are stored together with the project sources in the exact same repository, using the same mechanisms for revision control, tagging, and sharing the test base.
>
> WebTest comes with a standard layout of how to organize tests and test data in directories. You can adapt this to any structure you fancy, but the "convention over configuration" shows its strength here. In large projects, every sub-project maintains its own test base in a "webtest" subdirectory that follows the convention.
>
> Whenever a client did not follow this approach, the experience was very painful for all people involved. We have seen huge databases of test descriptions that did not even feature a proper revision control (i.e., where you could, for example, see diffs to old releases or who changed which test for what reason).
>
> Keep in mind that tests are made up from modules so that you can eliminate duplication of test code; otherwise the maintenance will kill you. And before changing any module, you need to know where it is used.
>
> In short: Make sure the master of your tests and your test data is in a text format that is versioned together with your code under test.
>
> Nontechnical personnel (for example, management, QA) may require more high-level information about test coverage, latest test results, or even means of triggering a test run. Don't let these valid requirements undermine the engineering approach to test automation. Instead, write little tools, for example, web-based report applications, that address these needs.

The ability of customers to access information about tests is as important as the ability to keep test and production code coordinated. As Dierk pointed out, you might not be able to do all this with the same tool.

Test management helps your team answer questions such as the following:

- Which test cases have been automated?
- Which still need automating?
- Which tests are currently running as part of a regression suite?
- Which tests cover what functional areas?
- How is feature XYZ designed to work?
- Who wrote this test case? When? Who changed it last?
- How long has this test been part of the regression suite?

Because one of the primary reasons we write tests is to guide development, we need to organize tests so that everyone on the team can find the appropriate tests for each story and easily identify what functionality the tests cover. Because we use tests as documentation, it's critical that anyone on either the development or customer team can find a particular test quickly when there's a question about how the system should behave. We might need multiple tools to satisfy different test management goals.

It's easy to lose control of test scripts. When a test fails, you need to pinpoint the problem quickly. You may need to know what changes have been made recently to the test script, which is easy with the history available in a source code control system. Your customer team also needs a way to keep track of project progress, to understand how much of the code is covered with tests, and possibly to run tests themselves. Test management systems, like the tests themselves, should promote communication and collaboration among team members and between different teams.

Test Transparency

Declan Whelan, a software developer and agile coach, uses a test management approach designed to keep tests visible to testers, developers, managers, and other teams.

We treat all test artifacts the same as source code from an organizational and revision control perspective. We use Subversion, and anyone who wants to run or edit the tests simply checks them out.

The latest Fit tests are available on a Confluence Wiki. We did this to support collaboration (team is distributed) and to leverage the strong capabilities of Confluence. Having the tests visible on the wiki was also helpful to others such as managers and other teams who did not want to check it out from the repository.

Prior to this, the QA team maintained test cases on a drive that was not accessible to anyone outside of QA. This meant that developers could not easily see what was being tested. Making the tests visible, transparent, and supported by a version control system (Subversion) really helped to break down barriers between developers and testers on the team.

Make sure your tests are managed with solid version control, but augment that with a way for everyone to use the tests in ways that drive the project forward and ensure the right value is delivered.

Organizing Test Results

Everyone involved with delivering software needs easy access to tests and test results. Another aspect of managing tests is keeping track of what tests are from prior iterations and need to keep passing, versus tests that are driving development in the current iteration and may not be passing yet. A continuous integration and build process runs tests for quick feedback on progress and to catch regression failures. Figure 14-4 shows an example of a test result report that's understandable at a glance. One test failed, and the cause of the failure is clearly stated.

If you're driving development with tests, and some of those tests aren't passing yet, this shouldn't fail a build. Some teams, such as Lisa's, simply keep new tests out of the integration and build process until they pass for the first time. After that, they always need to pass. Other teams use rules in the build process itself to ignore failures from tests written to cover the code currently being developed.

As with any test automation tool, you can solve your test management problems with home-grown, open source, or commercial systems. The same criteria we described in the section on evaluating test tools can be applied to selecting a test management approach.

Test management is yet another area where agile values and principles, together with the whole-team approach, applies. Start simple. Experiment in small steps until you find the right combination of source code control, repositories, and build management that keeps tests and production code in synch. Evaluate your test management approach often, and make sure it accommodates all of the different users of tests. Identify what's working and what's missing, and plan tasks or even stories to try another tool or process to fill any gaps. Remember to keep test management lightweight and maintainable so that everyone will use it.

Home Testcases Testsets Testsets Results Admin Preferences Status Search Tools Logout Goto [   ] [Testcase] [Test Set]

Viewing all results for testcase: Ideal - Declined deposit

Pass: 248
Fail: 129
Not Run: 0
Invalid: 0

Result	Environment	Build	Comments	Bugs	Test Date/time	Details	Parent Test Set
Pass			Member_Login (Member_Ideal_transactions.rb:56): Everything was good Member_NordeaDeposit (Member_Ideal_transactions.rb:57): correctly received a TRANSACTION_DECLINED exception		01-Aug-2008 08:36	view	view
Pass			Member_Login (Member_Ideal_transactions.rb:56): Everything was good Member_NordeaDeposit (Member_Ideal_transactions.rb:57): correctly received a TRANSACTION_DECLINED exception		31-Jul-2008 17:45	view	view
Pass			Member_Login (Member_Ideal_transactions.rb:56): Everything was good Member_NordeaDeposit (Member_Ideal_transactions.rb:57): correctly received a TRANSACTION_DECLINED exception		31-Jul-2008 13:17	view	view
Fail			Member_Login (Member_Ideal_transactions.rb:56): Everything was good Member_NordeaDeposit (Member_Ideal_transactions.rb:57): received RuntimeError which was completely unexpected		30-Jul-2008 14:11	view	view
Pass			Member_Login (Member_Ideal_transactions.rb:56): Everything was good Member_NordeaDeposit (Member_Ideal_transactions.rb:57): correctly received a TRANSACTION_DECLINED exception		28-Jul-2008 17:42	view	view
Pass			Member_Login (Member_Ideal_transactions.rb:56): Everything was good Member_NordeaDeposit (Member_Ideal_transactions.rb:57): correctly received a TRANSACTION_DECLINED exception		28-Jul-2008 16:10	view	view
Pass			Member_Login (Member_Ideal_transactions.rb:56): Everything was good Member_NordeaDeposit (Member_Ideal_transactions.rb:57): correctly received a TRANSACTION_DECLINED exception		26-Jul-2008 16:41	view	view
Pass			Member_Login (Member_Ideal_transactions.rb:56): Everything was good Member_NordeaDeposit (Member_Ideal_transactions.rb:57): correctly received a TRANSACTION_DECLINED exception		25-Jul-2008 16:42	view	view

Figure 14-4   Test results from a home-grown test management tool

Managing Tests For Feedback

Megan Sumrell, an agile trainer and coach, describes how her team coordinates its build process and tests for optimum feedback.

We create a FitNesse test suite for each sprint. In that suite, we create a subwiki for each user story that holds its tests. As needed, we create a setup and teardown per test or suite. If for some reason we don't complete a user story in the sprint, then we move the tests to the suite for sprint in which we do complete the story.

We scripted the following rule into our build: If any of the suites from the previous sprint fail, then the build breaks. However, if tests in the current sprint are failing, then do not fail the build.

Each test suite has a lengthy setup process, so when our FitNesse tests started taking longer than 10 minutes to run, our continuous integration build became too slow. We used symbolic links to create a suite of tests that serve as our smoke tests, running as part of our continuous integration build process. We run the complete set of FitNesse tests on a separate machine. We set it up to check the build server every five minutes. If a new build existed, then it would pull the build over and run the whole set of FitNesse tests. When it was done, it would then check the build server again every five minutes and after a new build existed, it would repeat the process.

Megan's team took advantage of features built into their tools, such as symbolic links to organize FitNesse test suites for different purposes—one for a smoke test, others for complete regression testing. The team members get immediate feedback from the smoke tests, and they'll know within an hour whether there's a bug that the smoke tests missed.

GO GET STARTED

Don't be afraid to get something—anything—in place, even if it's somewhat deficient. The most important factor in success is to just get started. Many, if not most, successful teams have started with a poor process but managed to turn an inadequate process into something truly essential to the team's success, one piece at a time. As with so many aspects of agile testing, improving in tiny increments is the key to success.

If you don't start somewhere, you'll never get traction on automation. Get the whole team together and start an experiment. Without the right level of test automation, your team can't do its best work. You need the right test automation to deliver business value frequently. A year or two from now, you'll wonder why you thought test automation was so hard.

SUMMARY

In this chapter, we considered how to apply agile values, principles, and practices to develop an automation strategy. We discussed the following subjects related to automation:

- Use the agile testing quadrants to help identify where you need test automation, and when you'll need it.
- The test automation pyramid can help your team make the right investments in test automation that will pay off the most.

- Apply agile values, principles, and practices to help your team get traction on test automation.
- Repetitive tasks, continuous integration and build processes, unit tests, functional tests, load tests, and data creation are all good candidates for automation.
- Quadrant 3 tests such as usability testing and exploratory testing may benefit from some automation to set up test scenarios and analyze results, but human instincts, critical thinking, and observation can't be automated.
- A simple, whole-team approach, using iterative feedback, and taking enough time can help you get started on a good solution.
- When developing an automation strategy, start with the greatest area of pain, consider a multi-layered approach, and strive for continuously revisiting and improving your strategy rather than achieving perfection from the start.
- Consider risk and ROI when deciding what to automate.
- Take time to learn by doing; apply agile coding practices to tests.
- Decide whether you can simply build inputs in-memory, or whether you need production-style data in a database.
- Supply test data that will allow tests to be independent, rerunnable, and as fast as possible.
- Take on one tool need at a time, identify your requirements, and decide what type of tool to choose or build that fits your needs.
- Use good development practices for test automation, and take time for good test design.
- Automated tools need to fit into the team's development infrastructure.
- Version-control automated tests along with the production code that they verify.
- Good test management ensures that tests can provide effective documentation of the system and of development progress.
- Get started on test automation today.

Part V

AN ITERATION IN
THE LIFE OF A TESTER

Whenever we do tutorials, webinars, or Q&A sessions with participants who are relatively new to agile development, we're always asked questions such as "What do testers do during the first part of an iteration before anything's ready to test?" or "Where does user acceptance testing fit into an agile release cycle?" It's easy to expound on theories of who should do what and when, in an agile process, but we find giving concrete examples from our own experience is the best help we can give agile newbies. Through our talking to many different agile teams, we've learned that there's a lot of commonality in what works well for agile development and testing.

In this part of the book, we'll follow an agile tester's life throughout an iteration. Actually, we'll explore more than just an iteration. We'll start with what testers do during release or theme planning, when the team looks at the work it will do for several upcoming iterations. We'll give examples of what testers can do to help the team members hit the ground running when they start the iteration. We'll show how coding and testing are part of one integrated process of delivering software, and we'll describe how testers and programmers work closely and incrementally. We'll explain different ways that testers can help their teams stay on track and gauge progress, including useful approaches to metrics and handling defects. We'll look at testing-related activities involved in wrapping up an iteration and finding ways to improve for the next one. Finally, we'll examine a tester's role in a successful release, including the end game, UAT, packaging, documentation, and training.

The activities described in this slice-of-life look at agile testing can be performed by anyone on the team, not only testing specialists. On some teams, all team members can, and do, perform any task, be it development, testing, database, infrastructure, or other tasks. For simplicity, in this section we'll assume we're following someone whose primary role is testing as they help to deliver high-quality software.

## Chapter 15

TESTER ACTIVITIES IN RELEASE OR THEME PLANNING

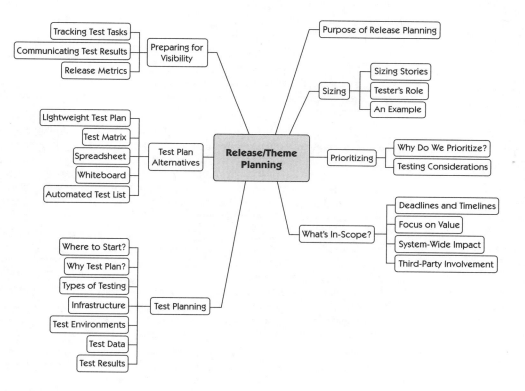

Agile development teams complete stories and deliver production-ready software in every iteration but plan the big picture or a larger chunk of functionality in advance. A theme, epic, or project may encompass several iterations. In this chapter, we look at what testers do when their team takes time to plan their release. We also consider ways to track whether our development is proceeding as anticipated, or if course corrections are needed.

THE PURPOSE OF RELEASE PLANNING

One reason software teams try agile development is because they know long-range plans don't work. Most business environments are volatile, and priorities change every week, or even every day. Agile development is supposed to avoid "big design up front." Most of us have experienced making plans that turned out to be a waste of effort. But we have to have some understanding of what our customer is looking for and how we might deliver it in order to get off to a good start. Fortunately, an agile approach can make planning a useful way to give us a head start on knowing how we will deliver the product.

Agile Planning Applied

Janet's sister, Carol Vaage, teaches first grade when she isn't directing conferences. She relates her first experience with using agile practices to organize a conference:

> My table is loaded with binders and to-do lists, and a feeling of being overwhelmed freezes me into inaction. I am Conference Director and the task right now seems onerous. When my sister offers to help me, I agree, because I am desperate to get this planning under control. I welcome Janet to my clutter, show her my pages of hand-written lists of things that need to get done, explain the huge tasks waiting for my attention, and share how my committee works.
>
> Janet showed me in simple language how to separate each task onto a sticky note and use color coordination for different responsibilities and different individuals. She explained about the columns of "To Do," "In Progress," "To Review," and "Done." I had never heard of the word iteration before but fully understood about a timeline. She recommended two-week blocks of time, but I chose one-week iterations. We set up a wall for my planning board, and Janet left me to pull it together and to add the tasks needed.
>
> In the six days since Janet has been here, ten tasks have been moved from the To-Do column to In-Progress. Three tasks are Done, and specific time-related tasks have been blocked by the correct time period. The most positive thing is that as I add more tasks in the To-Do column, I am not feeling overwhelmed. I understand that all I need to do is initiate the steps to start it, and then the job becomes easier. The feeling of chaos is gone; I see progress and understand that there is still much work to be done. The timeline is clear, the tasks are discrete and concrete. And the most difficult task of all, finding a way to coordinate the video conference for our keynote speaker has been tackled. This system works!

Agile planning and tracking practices are useful for more than software development. A little time carefully invested, and simple tools used in organizing and planning the testing activities and resources for a release, will help the team deliver high-quality software.

XP teams may take a day every few months for release planning. Other agile teams do advance planning when getting ready to start on a theme, epic, or major feature, which we think of as a related group of stories. They work to understand the theme or release at a high level. What is the customer's vision of what we should be delivering? What's the purpose of the release? What's the big picture? What value will it deliver to the business, to the customers? What other teams or projects are involved and require coordination? When will UAT take place? When will code be released to staging, to production? What metrics do we need to know if we're on track? These general questions are addressed in release planning.

Some teams don't spend much time doing release planning activities. Priorities change quickly, even within a particular theme of features. Nobody wants to do too much work up front that ends up being wasted. Some teams just look at the first couple of stories to make sure they can get a running start. At the very least, teams want to know enough to get their system architecture pointed in the right direction and get started on the first few stories.

These planning meetings aren't intended to plan every iteration of the release in detail. And we know we can't predict exactly how many stories we can complete each iteration. However, we do have an idea of our average velocity, so we can get a general idea of the possible scope of the release. The team talks about the features and stories, trying to get a 20,000-foot view of what can go into the release and how many iterations it might take to complete. Both of us like Mike Cohn's approach to release planning in his book *Agile Estimating and Planning* [2005]. Stories that the business wants to include are sized relative to each other, and then features are prioritized according to the value they deliver. The team may identify "thin slices" through the features to determine what stories absolutely have to be done, what's in scope, what "nice-to-haves" could be put off until later. They look at dependencies between stories, relative risk, and other factors that determine the order in which features should be coded. The order in which stories are coded is as important, or sometimes more important, than the size of the stories. Teams want to deliver value the first iteration of the release.

Release planning is a chance for the developers and customers to consider the impact of the planned features on the larger system, clarify assumptions, and look at dependencies that might affect what stories are done first. They may think about testing at a high level and whether new resources such as test environments and software will be needed.

Let's follow our agile tester through release planning activities and see how she contributes value through her unique perspective and focus.

Sizing

Agile teams estimate the relative size of each story. Some teams size as they go, delaying the estimation until the iteration where they'll actually complete the story. Others have meetings to estimate stories even in advance of release planning. Some developer and customer teams sit together to write and estimate the size of stories all at one time. The goal of sizing is for the programmers to give the business an idea of the cost of each story and to help them prioritize and plan the first few iterations. High-functioning teams who've worked together for years may take a less formal approach. For new agile teams, learning to size stories takes a lot of practice and experience. It's not important to get each story sized correctly but to be close enough to give customers some idea of how big the stories are so they can prioritize with better information. Over time, variations on individual story sizing will average out, and we find that a theme or related group of stories takes about the amount of time expected.

How to Size Stories

As far as how to calculate story size, different teams use different techniques, but again, we like Mike Cohn's approach to determining story size. We size in story points, ideal days, or simply "small, medium, large." The relative size of each story to others is the important factor. For example, adding an input field to an existing user interface is obviously much smaller than developing a brand new screen from scratch.

If the business knows the average velocity (the number of story points the team completes each iteration) and has the initial size estimates of each story it wants to get done, it has an idea of how long it might take to implement a given theme. As with any other development methodology, there are no guarantees, because estimates are just that. Still, the business can plan well enough to conduct its usual activities.

Our teams use planning poker (explained in Mike Cohn's book *Agile Estimating and Planning*) to estimate story size. In planning poker, each team member has a deck of cards. Each card has a number of points on it. The process begins with the customer or product owner reading a story and explaining its purpose and the value it will deliver. He might list a few conditions of satisfaction or high-level test cases. After a brief discussion, team members each hold up a point card that represents how "big" they think the story is from their perspective. They discuss any big differences in point value and estimate again until they reach consensus. Figure 15-1 shows team members talking about

Figure 15-1   Planning poker. Used with permission of Mike Thomas. Copyright 2008.

the point values they each just displayed. This needs to be a quick process—long discussions about details don't result in more accurate size estimates.

Some teams figure the relative sizes of stories by how many people are needed to complete a given story in a set amount of time. Others estimate how many ideal days one person would need to finish it. Use a measurement that makes sense to all team members and one that provides consistency among estimates.

The Tester's Role in Sizing Stories

One of our favorite sayings is, "No story is done until it's tested." However, we've run across teams where testing wasn't included in estimates of story size. In some cases, testing a piece of functionality might take longer than coding it.

In our experience, testers usually have a different viewpoint than other team members. They often have a broad understanding of the domain and can quickly identify "ripple effects" that one story might have on the rest of the system. They also tend to think of activities not directly related to development that might need to be done, such as training users on a new or changed interface.

Lisa's Story

What does a tester do during the story sizing process? I think quickly about the story from several viewpoints. What business problem is the story solving, or what business value does it deliver? If this isn't clear, I ask the product owner questions. How will the end user actually use the feature? If it's still not clear, I ask the product owner for a quick example. I might ask, "What's the worst thing that could go wrong with it?" This negative approach helps gauge the story's risk. What testing considerations might affect the story's size? If test data will be hard to obtain or the story involves a third party, testing might take longer than coding. I try to quickly flush out any hidden assumptions. Are there dependencies or special security risks? Will this part of the application need to handle a big load?

Many stories aren't big enough to warrant that much thought. Usually, we don't need much detail to get an idea of relative size. However, your team can really get burned if a story is underestimated by a factor of five or ten. We once gave a relatively small estimate to a story that ended up being at least ten times the size. These are the disasters we want to avoid by asking good questions.

—Lisa

Testers need to be part of the sizing process. Some teams think that only programmers should participate, but when testers are active participants, they can help to get a much more accurate story sizing, which is in the best interests of the whole team.

An Example of Sizing Stories

Let's imagine we have the story in Figure 15-2 to size up.

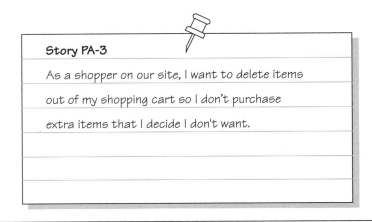

Figure 15-2   Story to delete items

After the product owner reads the story, the following discussion ensues:

Product Owner: "We just want some easy way for users to delete items, but we don't have a specific implementation in mind."

Tester: "Should they be able to delete several items at once?"

Product Owner: "Oh, yes, just make it as easy as possible."

Tester: "What if they accidentally delete an item they wanted to buy?"

Product Owner: "Is there some way the deleted items can be saved for later retrieval?"

Programmer: "Sure, but you should write a new story for that. For now, we should start with the basic delete functionality."

Tester: "Last release we implemented a wish list feature. Do you want users to be able to move items from their shopping basket to their wish list? That would be a new story also."

Product Owner: "Yes, those are two more stories we want to do, for sure. I'll write those down, we can size them also. But we could definitely put them off until the next release, if we have to."

Tester: "What's the worst thing that could happen with this feature?"

Product Owner: "If they can't figure out how to delete, they might just abandon their whole shopping basket. It has to be really easy and obvious."

The ScrumMaster calls for an estimate. The team understands they're sizing only the basic story for deleting items, not for doing something else with the deleted items. They quickly agree on a point value.

Let's look at another story. (See Figure 15-3.)

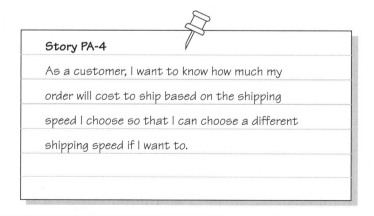

Story PA-4

As a customer, I want to know how much my order will cost to ship based on the shipping speed I choose so that I can choose a different shipping speed if I want to.

Figure 15-3 Story on shipping speed

Tester: "What are the shipping speeds the user can choose?"

Product Owner: "Standard 5-day, 2-day, and next-day."

Programmer: "We should probably start by only offering one speed, and calculating that cost. Then we can easily implement the other two speeds."

Product Owner: "It's fine to break it up like that."

Tester: "Will we use BigExpressShipping's API to calculate cost based on weight and destination?"

Programmer: "That would be the easiest."

The team holds up their point cards. The tester and one of the programmers hold up an 8; the other developers hold up a 5.

ScrumMaster: "Why did you two choose 8?"

Tester: "We've never used BigExpressShipping's cost API before, and I'm not sure how that will impact our testing. We have to find out how to access their system for testing."

Other Programmer with 8: "I agree, I think the testing effort is more intense than the coding effort for this story."

The team agrees to size the story as eight points.

This sizing process may occur before the planning meeting, and if the stories were sized or estimated a long time ago, the team might want to make sure they feel comfortable with the story sizes. Teams may have changed or may be more experienced. Either of those factors can make a team change the estimates.

There are many times when a story will have a large testing component, and the coding effort is small. At other times, the reverse will be true. It's important to consider all perspectives.

Lisa's Story

Our team grew to dread story sizing meetings, because we got into overly long discussions about details, and the meetings always lasted long past the scheduled time. Since then, our ScrumMaster has found ways to keep us on track. She uses an egg timer to time discussions, and stops them each time the sand runs out to see if we think we really need more time to ask questions. Our product owner has also learned what information we need for estimating and usually has what we need. We also learned to only work on stories that were likely to come up in the next few iterations.

With all of our meetings, little traditions have grown to make the meetings more fun. Someone always brings treats to iteration planning meetings. In stand-up meetings, we pass around a combination penlight and laser pointer, so each of us holds it as we report on what we're working on. We always end story sizing meetings with a competition to see who can throw his or her deck of planning poker cards into the small plastic tub where they live. Figure 15-4 shows this goofy but fun meeting-ending activity. Always remember the agile value of enjoyment and have some fun with your meetings.

—Lisa

Figure 15-4   A meeting-ending tradition. Used with permission of Mike Thomas. Copyright 2008.

PRIORITIZING

The purpose of the release planning meeting is also to get an idea of what stories the team will try to finish by the release date. The customers prioritize the stories, but there may be dependencies, so it makes sense to do certain stories first, even if they aren't the highest priority. It is important that the team understands the possibility that not all of the stories will get completed by the release date. One of the basic premises of agile is to deliver working software, so it is important to have the highest-value stories completed first so that the software we do deliver meets the customer's needs.

Why We Prioritize Stories

Everyone's goal is to deliver real value in each iteration. Testers can help the team pick out the core functionality that has to work. In Chapter 8, we explained the "thin slice" or "steel thread" concept, identifying one path through the functionality to code and test first, and adding more features after the first critical path works. This concept applies at the release level, too. The order of the stories is critical. Lisa's team will sometimes break up a story and pull out a core part of a feature to do in the first iteration.

Some teams that don't do full-blown release planning do take time to look at the stories and decide which two or three should be first. That way, they deliver business value in the very first iteration of the release.

Let's look at an example.

> If our theme is providing the ability for an online shopper to choose shipping options and then calculate the shipping cost based on weight, shipping speed, and destination, it may be a good idea to complete simple stories or even subsets of stories so that the checkout process can proceed end-to-end. Start by only allowing standard 5-day shipping, items less than 10 pounds, and destinations in the continental United States. When the user can get the shipping cost for that scenario and check out, the team can decide the next priorities. They may include heavyweight items, faster shipping speeds, shipping to Hawaii and Alaska, and shipping to Canada and Mexico.

By providing this thin slice first, the testers have something to start testing immediately. The programmers have also tested their design and code integration steps and so have a solid idea of how things will work when the whole feature is complete.

Testing Considerations While Prioritizing

It is important that the team understands the big picture or theme. In our example, team members know the stories for shipping outside the continental United States will come later. This knowledge may affect how they implement the first story. This doesn't mean they have to plan for every eventuality, but if they know they need more shipping options, they may implement a drop-down list rather than a basic text field. No need to make more work or rework than necessary.

During release planning, we also consider the relative risk of the stories. If certain stories have many unknowns, it might be best to include them in an early iteration, so there's time to recover if a story "blows up" and takes much more time than estimated. The same may apply to a story which, if not completed or implemented incorrectly, would have a costly negative impact. Scheduling it early will leave more time for testing.

If new technology or software is needed, it might be good to learn it by developing a straightforward story and plan more difficult ones for later iterations. This new technology may or may not affect your test automation. You may want more time to check out the impact. If the features are all brand new and the team needs more time to understand how they should work, plan to do less than your average velocity for the first iteration. That way, you'll have more time to write tests that will correctly guide development. Identify risks and decide what approach makes the most sense from a testing perspective as well as a development perspective. This is one of the reasons it is important to include the whole team in the planning sessions.

Looking at the stories from a testing viewpoint is essential. This is where testers add the most value. The team needs to develop in small, testable chunks in order to help decide what stories are tentatively planned for which iteration. The key here is testable. Many new agile teams think small chunks means doing all of the database work first, or all of the configuration stuff. Testable doesn't necessarily mean it needs a GUI either. For example, the algorithm that calculates shipping cost is an independent piece of code that can be tested independently of any user interface but requires extensive testing. That might be a good story for the first iteration. It can be tested as freestanding code and then later tested in combination with the UI and other parts of the system.

The testers may lobby for getting an end-to-end tracer bullet through the code quickly, so they can build an automation framework, and then flesh it out as the story development proceeds. If there are stories that present a big testing challenge, it might be good to do those early on. For example, if the release includes implementing a new third-party tool to create documents from templates and dynamic data, there are many permutations to test. If the team is unfamiliar with the tool, the testers can ask the team to consider doing those stories in the first iteration of the release.

WHAT'S IN SCOPE?

Agile teams continually manage scope in order to meet business deadlines while preserving quality. High-value stories are the first priority. Stories that are "nice-to-haves" might be elbowed out of the release.

Lisa's Story

Our team's customers list their stories in priority order and then draw a line between the stories that must be done before the release can occur, and the ones that could safely be put off. They call the less important stories "below the line," and those stories may never get done.

For example, when we undertook the theme to allow retirement plan participants to borrow money from their retirement accounts, there was a "below the line" story to send emails to any participants whose loans are changing status to "pending default" or "default." When the loan is in "default" status, the borrower must pay taxes and penalties on the balance. The email would be extremely helpful to the borrowers, but it wasn't as important to our business as the software to request, approve and distribute loans, or process loan payments.

The email story didn't make it into the release. It wasn't done until more than two years later, after enough complaints from people who didn't know their loans were going into default until it was too late.

—Lisa

Janet worked with a team whose customers were under the misplaced assumption that all of the features would get into their release and that when they were prioritizing, they were just picking which stories got done first. When the rest of the team realized the misunderstanding, they also implemented the idea of stories above and below the line. It helped to track progress as well as make the stories that were dropped below the line very visible.

Deadlines and Timelines

Many domains revolve around fixed dates on the calendar. Retail businesses make most of their profit during the holiday season. An Internet retail site is smart to have all new features implemented by October 1. Implementing a new feature close to the peak buying period is risky. Lisa's company's customers must complete government-required tasks during certain periods of the year. When it's too late for a feature to get released this year, it often gets put off for the next year, because more urgent priorities must be addressed. Regulatory changes have specific timelines, and organizations have no choice about the timeline.

Janet's Story

While working on this book, I was planning a release with my team at WestJet. We had several possible stories and worked with the customers to decide what the release would look like. We had one regulatory change that was light work for the programmers, but heavy for the testers. It needed to be in production by a certain date, so the other stories we were considering for the release took that into consideration.

We decided to create a small maintenance release with just that one major feature, along with a few bugs from the backlog so the release of the regulatory change would not be jeopardized. While the testers completed their testing, the rest of the team started some of elaboration stories for the next release.

An alternative plan could have been that the programmers chip in and help test and fit in more features. However, the whole team decided that this plan would work the best with the least amount of risk.

—Janet

Focus on Value

It's rather easy for a team to start discussing a complex story and lose sight of what value the features actually deliver. Release planning is the time to start asking for examples and use cases of how the features will be used, and what value they'll provide. Drawing flowcharts or sample calculations on the whiteboard can help pinpoint the core functionality.

Lisa's Story

Our product owner wrote a story to provide a warning if an employer overrides the date a participant becomes eligible to contribute to a retirement account after the participant has already made contributions.

The warning needed to be incorporated into the legacy UI code, which didn't easily accommodate it. The team discussed how it might be implemented, but every option was fairly costly. Not only would coding be tricky, but a lot of time was needed to test it adequately and update existing automated tests. This feature wouldn't provide much value to the business, just a bit of help to the end users. The release was already pretty close to the limit on features.

One of the programmers suggested providing a report of participants who met the criteria so the plan administrators could simply call the employers who may need to make corrections. The report story was much smaller than the warning story, could easily fit into the release, and was acceptable to the customer.

—Lisa

There is no guarantee that these initial "guesstimates" at what will be in a given release will hold up over time. That is why customers needs to understand their priorities, take checkpoints at the end of every iteration, and re-evaluate the priorities of remaining stories.

System-Wide Impact

We talked about the "ripple effects" in Chapter 8, "Business Facing Tests that Support the Team."

One of our jobs as testers is to keep the big picture in mind. The agile tester thinks about how each story might affect the system as a whole, or other systems that ours has to work with. For example, if the toy warehouse makes a change to its inventory software, and the new code has a bug that overstates the number of items in stock, the website might sell more of the hot new doll than there are available, disappointing thousands of children and their parents at Christmas. When risk is high, listing areas of the system that might be affected for a theme or group of stories might be a worthwhile exercise even during release planning.

Contact points between our system and that of partners or vendors always merit consideration. Even a minor change to a csv or xml file format could have a huge impact if we don't communicate it correctly to partners who ftp files to us. Stories that mean changes for third parties need to be done early enough in the release cycle to let the third parties make necessary changes.

Figure 15-5 shows a simplified diagram of a new system that touches many pieces of the existing system. Different tools might be needed to test the integrations.

Testers who have worked with some of the other systems or understand what testing needs to happen on those systems can offer valuable insight into the impact of a new story. Often, stories will need to be delayed until a future release if the impact has not been explored. This is a good time to recall previous releases that didn't end so well.

Third-Party Involvement

Working with vendor tools, partners, or other contractor teams on a big project complicates release planning. If anyone outside your team is responsible for some part of the project, that's one piece that's out of your control. If

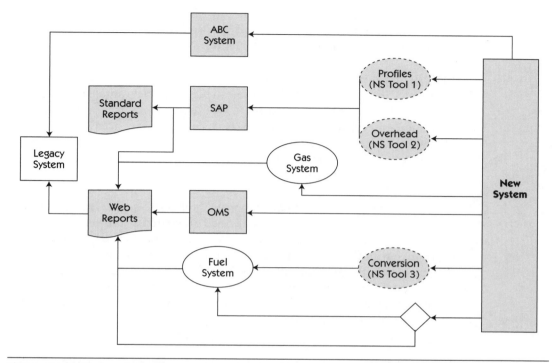

Figure 15-5 System impacts

you need to coordinate with others, including possible new users of the system, it's best to start early.

Lisa's team has written several interfaces to allow users to upload data to their systems. In each case, they had to get the proposed file format out to the users early to make sure it would work for them. Other projects involved sending data to partners or vendors. These required extra planning to arrange testing with their test systems and getting their feedback on whether data was valid and correctly formatted.

If you're using a third-party product as part of your solution, you might assume it has been tested, but that might be a poor assumption. You will need to budget extra time to test your application in conjunction with the vendor software. If there's a problem in the other company's software, it might take a long time to resolve. Lisa's team uses third-party software for critical tasks such as document creation. If a theme includes modifying or creating new documents, they plan extra time to upgrade the software if needed, and extra time for testing in case fixes are needed. If possible, bring the third-party software into the project early, and start end-to-end testing. The more you can work with the interface, the better off you'll be.

Other third-party software that we often forget about until it's too late is our own testing environments. Sometimes a team will incorporate new code that takes advantages of new features in their chosen language. For example, if team members are using AJAX or JavaScript, they may need to upgrade the software development kit they're using. This means that a team will have to upgrade its production runtime environment as well, so take that into consideration and test early.

Clients or partners might have concerns about a release that isn't within your own team's scope. Lisa's team was once prevented at the very last minute from releasing a new feature because a partner didn't have time to okay the change with their legal advisors. The programmers had to quickly devise a way to turn the functionality off without requiring extensive additional testing. Interestingly, partners who aren't using agile development sometimes have trouble meeting their own deadlines. They might be unprepared when your team meets the deadline.

Janet's Story

I worked on a project to implement a feature that required a new piece of hardware for scanning a new 2D bar code. The team decided to implement in stages because it was not known when the scanners would be available for full testing, but the customer wanted the code ready for when the scanners arrived.

The initial phase was programmer-intensive because there was a lot of research to be done. After they determined how they would implement the feature, the story was created to add it into the code. However, we knew we couldn't thoroughly test it until the scanners were available. The code was ready to test, but instead of backing it all out, we only needed to worry about testing that the feature could be turned off for the release. The next release would require more testing, but only if the scanners were available. The testing of the story was kept in the product backlog so we would not forget to do it.

—Janet

If you'll be working with other teams developing different components of the same system, or related systems, budget time to coordinate with them. It's a good idea to designate a member from each team to coordinate together.

Release planning is the time to identify extra roles you need on your team, additional resources, and time needed for out-of-the-ordinary circumstances.

TEST PLANNING

Chapter 8,
"Business-Facing
Tests that Support
the Team," ex-
plains how to
identify steel
threads or thin
slices in a story
or theme.

We can't expect to plan the iterations in a release at a detailed level. We can get an idea of the theme's steel threads, prioritize stories, and make a guess at what stories will be in which iteration. Detailed test planning needs to wait for iteration planning. Still, we need to think about testing at a high level, and try to budget enough time for it. We might even take time separately from the release planning meeting to strategize our testing for the release. In Chapter 8, Business-Facing Tests that Support the Team, we mentioned one of the perils of agile testing: "forgetting the big picture." Test Planning will help you with that problem.

Where to Start

During release planning, it's helpful to know the business conditions of satisfaction for each story or high-level user acceptance test case. When stories need clarification, agile testers ask for examples. At this stage, examples will be high-level, covering just the basics, but enough to be able to size and prioritize the story. Drawing flowcharts or writing calculations on the whiteboard and discussing them helps us identify project-specific testing issues.

At a minimum, the team needs to understand the top-priority stories that are scheduled to be performed first. Lightweight planning might involve only looking at those core stories with the understanding that more time will be needed for defining additional tests.

As we get a sense of which stories will probably be included in the release, we can start thinking about the scope of the testing. What assumptions have been made that might affect testing? Use of third-party software, such as the example of using a shipping company's shipping calculation API, affects test planning. Are there any unusual risks in this release that will impact testing? If we have stories to implement batch jobs, and we've never had any batch processing in the system before, there are probably new frameworks that impact testing. We need to budget time to learn them.

Why Write a Test Plan?

In release planning, we talk about the purpose of the release, what's in scope, and what assumptions we're making. We do some quick risk analysis and plan our test approach to address those risks. We consider automation and what we need for test environments and test data. We certainly want to identify milestones and deliverables. Hmmm, this is starting to sound like . . . a test plan!

See Chapter 5, "Transitioning Typical Processes," for more about test plans and test strategies.

If, like ourselves, you spent time working in a traditional waterfall environment, you might have wasted time writing bulky test plans that nobody read and nobody bothered to maintain. In agile development, we want our test plans to serve our needs. Your customer might require a test plan for each release for compliance reasons. Even if it's not a required deliverable, it can be useful. Keep it concise and lightweight. It only has to serve your purposes during this release. Address the testing issues that are specific to this release or project. Include your risk analysis and identify assumptions. Outline the critical success factors that your customer has identified. Think about what people need to know related to testing, and remove anything extraneous.

Even if you don't create a formal test plan, be sure you have made note of all these different testing factors involved in the release. You'll want to keep them in mind during every iteration planning session. The biggest benefit in test planning is the planning itself. It allows you to consider and address issues such as test data requirements, infrastructure, or even what test results are required. Test planning is a risk mitigation strategy. Let's consider some of these issues.

Types of Testing

In Part III, we covered the four quadrants of testing and talked about all of the different types of testing you can do during your project. Release planning is a good time to consider these different needs. Do you need to plan to bring in a load test tool, or will there be the need to build some kind of specialty test harness?

It could be that your next release is just an extension of your last, and you will just carry on creating your examples, automating your story tests, and doing the rest of the testing as you've been doing. You are one of the lucky ones. For those of you who are starting a brand new project with no previous processes in place, now is the time to consider what testing you will need. We don't mean you have to decide how to test each story, but look at the big picture and think about the quadrants. Will you need to plan for a special UAT, or will the iteration demos be enough? It is important to raise these issues early so the team can plan for them.

Infrastructure

While you are doing your test planning, you need to consider your infrastructure. Infrastructure can mean your continuous integration setup, test environments, and test database. It can mean how you promote your builds to your test environments. It might mean your test lab, if you have one, or having a separate server to run all your automation tests. These are generally pieces of infrastructure that need some lead time to get in place. This is the time to make a plan.

Lisa's Story

Some types of testing might require extra effort. My team had a tool to do performance testing and some scripts, but we lacked a production-style environment where we could control all of the variables that might affect performance. For example, the test database was shared by testers, programmers, and two build processes. Slower performance might simply mean someone was running database-intensive tests. We used our staging environment to get a baseline, but it was missing some of the components of production. We set a six-month goal to acquire hardware and software for a proper test environment and get it set up. We wrote a task card or two each iteration to establish the environment step by step.

—Lisa

Whatever your needs are, make sure you understand them and can plan for what you need. If you don't have the right infrastructure, then you will waste time trying to get it together and cause a bottleneck in mid-iteration.

Test Environments

As we look at the types of features in the next release, we might see the need for a whole new test environment. Think about specialized test environments you may need as well. Will you need more tools? Do you need to expand your test lab so that you can test with different browsers and operating systems? This is the time to think about all testing considerations.

If you're planning your first release, test environments are a key consideration. You might need a story or iteration just to set up the infrastructure you need. We've started more than one project where the only place we could test was the development environment. We found that doesn't work very well, because the environment is never stable enough for effective testing.

Just as programmers have their own sandboxes to work and test in, it works well if each tester has that same availability and control. We recognize that not all applications lend themselves to this, but at the very least, you need to know what build you're testing. You also need test data that others will not walk over with their tests. If you don't have a testing sandbox that's under your own control, take time to plan what you need to establish for your test environments. Brainstorm with your team about how you can obtain the necessary hardware and software. It might take time, so develop a Plan B for getting something done while waiting for the infrastructure you need.

If you're working on a large system, you may have to queue up along with other teams to get time on a test or staging environment that includes all of the various pieces of software with which yours must work. This staging environment should mimic your production system as much as possible. If your organization doesn't have someone responsible for creating environments, your team might need extra roles dedicated to obtaining the test environments you need. These roles might involve working with other teams as well. Release planning is the time to consider all of these testing infrastructure requirements.

Test Data

Release or theme planning is also a good time to think about what test data you might need during the project.

Using test data that closely resembles real data is generally a good practice. Plan for the data you need. We've had the opportunity in several organizations to use a copy of production data. Real data provides a good base for different scenarios for exploratory testing. Production data may need to be "scrubbed" before it's used for testing in order to remove any sensitive information such as identification or bank account numbers. The data needs to be altered to hide the original values but remain valid so that it doesn't violate database restrictions. Because it takes time for database experts to port production data to a test environment, be sure they're included in your planning.

Janet's Story

In one of the organizations I was working with, we used two different baseline test data schemes. For our individual test environments, we used Fit fixtures to load predefined data. We tried to make this data as close to production as possible, but we also seeded it with some very specific test data. Every time we checked out a new version of code, we were able to reload a base set of data. In this way, we also tested the database schema as well to see if anything had changed.

For our more stable test environment where we wanted data persisted, we used the data migration scripts that the programmers developed as they made database changes. These migration scripts were eventually used for the initial cut over from production and by then we were pretty certain they were correct.

—Janet

Enlist your customers' support in obtaining meaningful test data. If you're working on a story that involves sending a file to a third-party vendor, your business expert can find out what data the vendor expects in the file. Lisa's team developed features to allow retirement plan brokers to offer their customers portfolios of mutual funds. They asked the product owner to provide samples of portfolios, including a name, description, and set of funds for each. This helped them test with realistic data.

Test data tends to get stale and out of date over time. Older data, even if it came from production, may no longer accurately reflect current production data. A "passing" test using data that's no longer valid gives a misleading sense of confidence. Continually review your test data needs. Refresh data or create it using a new approach, as needed.

Chapter 14, "An Agile Test Automation Strategy," explores different approaches to obtaining test data

Test data requirements vary according to the type of testing. Regression tests can usually create their own data or run against a small representational set of data that can be refreshed to a known state quickly. Exploratory testing may need a complete replica of production type data.

Test Results

Different teams have different requirements for test result reporting. Think about how you are going to report test results at this stage of the game so that you can do so effectively when the time comes to do the actual reporting. Your organization may have audit compliance requirements, or maybe your customer just wants to know how you tested. Understand your needs so that you can choose the approach that is right for your team.

There are many ways to report test results. There are vendor tools that will record both automated and manual results. Your team may find a way to persist the results from tools such as Fit, or you may just choose to keep a big visible manual chart.

The approach that a few teams have taken is to create home-grown test result applications. For example, a simple Ruby application written with Ruby on Rails for the database or a MySQL database with a PHP front end can make a very simple but easy-to-use test management system.

A tool such as this can be very simple or can include added complexity such as the capability to categorize your tests. The important thing is the test results. If your automated tests record their pass or fail result along with the error, you have some history to help determine fragility of the test.

Your team can configure your automated build process to provide test results from each build, by email, or a feedback utility or web interface that team members can view online. Results over time can be summarized in a variety of formats that make progress visible. One of Lisa's teams produced a daily graph of tests written, run, and passing that was posted in the team's work area. Another produced a daily calendar with the number of unit tests passing every day. Even simple visual results are effective.

We talk about some of the metrics you can use later in this chapter.

TEST PLAN ALTERNATIVES

We've talked about why to test plan and what you should consider. Now we talk about some of the alternatives to the heavy test plans you may be used to. Whatever type of test plan your organization uses, make it yours. Use it in a way that benefits your team, and make sure you meet your customer's needs. As with any document your team produces, it should fulfill a purpose.

Lightweight Test Plans

If your organization or customer insists on a test plan for SOX compliance or other regulatory needs, consider a lightweight test plan that covers the necessities but not any extras. Do not repeat items that have already been included in the Project Plan or Project Charter. A sample Test Plan might look something like the one shown in Figure 15-6.

A test plan should not cover every eventuality or every story, and it is not meant to address traceability. It should be a tool to help you think about testing risks to your project. It should not replace face-to-face conversation with your customer or the rest of your team.

Using a Test Matrix

Janet uses release planning to work with the testers and customers to develop a high-level test matrix. A test matrix is a simple way to communicate the big picture concerning what functionality you want to test. It gives your team a quick overview of the testing required.

A test matrix is just a list of functionality down the side and test conditions across the top. When thinking about test conditions and functionality, consider the whole application and any impact the new or changed functionality

Project ABC Test Plan
Prepared by: Janet Gregory and Lisa Crispin

Introduction
The Test Plan is intended as a baseline to identify what is deemed in and out of scope for testing, and what the risks and assumptions are.

Resourcing

Tester	% Committed
Janet	100%
Lisa	50%

In Scope
Testing includes all new functionality, identified high-risk regression suite functionality, UAT, and Load Testing. Localization is part of this project. Manual regression tests deemed low priority will be run if time permits.

Out of Scope
Actual translation testing is outsourced, so it is not part of this test plan.

New Functionality
The following functionality is being changed in this release.

Feature Description	Depth of Testing
Adding new toggle for language selection on home page	Testing all 5 languages (English, Spanish, French, Italian, and German). Testing that we are able to dynamically switch languages.

Performance & Load Testing
Load testing will concentrate on the following areas. Load testing details will be found in the Load Test Plan document [link to Load Test Plan].

UAT (User Acceptance Testing)
UAT will be performed and coordinated with the Paris office as well as the Calgary office. Users will be chosen for their expertise in select areas and transactions as well as being fluent in one of the following languages: German, Italian, Spanish, or French.

Infrastructure Considerations
The test lab will need all 5 languages installed and available for testing.

Assumptions
Translation has been tested before being delivered to project team.

Risks
The following risks have been identified and the appropriate action identified to mitigate their impact on the project. The impact (or severity) of the risk is based on how the project would be affected if the risk was triggered.

#	Risk	Impact	Mitigation Plan
1	Users aren't ready for UAT	High	

Figure 15-6 Sample Test Plan

might have on the rest of the application. Testers sitting with customers and thinking about test conditions is what is important.

It can also be a mechanism to track coverage and can be as detailed as you like. A high-level test matrix can be used by the team to show the customer team or management what has been tested already and what is left. A more detailed test matrix can be used by the team to show what is planned for testing and track the progress of the testing. After the matrix has been created, it becomes easy to fill in the squares when testing is done. Keep it simple. Because we like big visible charts that are easy to read, we recommend colors that mean something to your team. For example, green (G) means testing is done and the team is happy with it, while yellow (Y) might mean some testing has been done but more exploratory testing is needed if there is time. Red (R) means something is broken. A white square means it hasn't been tested yet, and a gray (not applicable) square means it doesn't need to be tested.

Let's look at an example. We have a small release we want to put out that calculates shipping costs. In Figure 15-7, different pieces of functionality are represented on one axis, and properties of the shipment are represented on the other. Individual cells are color-coded to show which cases are tested and which need more attention. All of the cells for "<= 2 lbs" are finished, the top three cells for > 4 lbs are done but need more exploratory testing, and the "Ship to Alaska"/">4 lbs" cell denotes a possible issue.

Shipping Test Matrix										
	Test Conditions									
Functionality	Single Destination	Multiple Destinations	Physical Address	<= 2 lbs	2 – 4 lbs	> 4 lbs	Same Day	Next Day	< 5 Business Days	Shipping Estimates
Ship within US			G	G		Y				
Ship to Canada				G		Y				
Ship to Hawaii				G		Y				
Ship to Alaska				G		R				
Shipping estimates				G						n/a

Figure 15-7 A sample test matrix

Janet's Story

I had an unexpected side effect from using a test matrix in one project I was on. The customers and testers put the test matrix together, and had thought of all affected functionality for the project and the high-level test conditions they would need. As expected, the act of planning brought a lot of issues out that would have been missed until later.

When they hung the matrix on the wall in their team area, Dave, the developer team lead, expressed an interest. One of the testers explained the matrix to him, and I was surprised when he said it was very useful for them as well. Dave said "I didn't know that this functionality would affect this area. We need to make sure our unit tests touch on this as well."

Looking back on this, I shouldn't have been surprised, but I had never had that experience with the programmers before.

—Janet

A test matrix is a very powerful tool and can be used to help address traceability issues if your team has those problems. Think about what makes sense for your team and adapt it for your team and what makes sense to you.

Test Spreadsheet

Janet has also seen a spreadsheet format used with some success. For example, at WestJet, the first tab in a workbook was a high-level list of functionality that existed in the application. For each row, the team determined if the project affected that piece of functionality. If so, they gave a rating of the expected impact. After the impact of the changes had been determined, decisions about test environments, test data, or UAT could then be made.

Tabs were used for risks and assumptions but could be used for anything your team may need. A flexible format such as a spreadsheet means you can tailor it to work for you.

This information can be used in a number of different ways. It can be used to determine where to concentrate your exploratory testing efforts, or maybe to help create a high-level test matrix to make sure you touch on all of the areas during your testing.

A Whiteboard

If your team is informal and has small releases, any kind of documentation may be too much. Sometimes it's enough to list the risks and assumptions on a whiteboard or on index cards. Janet has used a whiteboard to manage risks, and it worked quite well. If a risk actually became an issue, the result was documented and crossed off. It was easy to add new risks and mitigation strategies, and the list was visible to the whole team. This could also be done on a wiki page.

We cannot stress enough that you need to know your team and its needs.

Automated Test List

Sometimes you may be required to present more information to your customers, such as a list of test cases. If your team has a tool from which you could extract a list of test case names, you could provide this list easily to anyone who needed it. This would present more of a traditional type detailed test plan but wouldn't be available until after tests were actually written. We don't recommend spending any time on this because we don't see added value, but sometimes this list may be required for risk assessment or auditability.

PREPARING FOR VISIBILITY

If your team is just getting started with agile development, make sure you have necessary infrastructure in place for your early iterations. You may change the way you are tracking progress as you go along, and your retrospectives will help you bring these issues to light. If you're having problems completing the work planned for each iteration, maybe you need more visible charts or visual aids to help you gauge progress and make mid-iteration adjustments. Do your customers have some way to know how the iteration is progressing and which stories are done? Take time before the each iteration to evaluate whether you're getting the right kind of feedback to keep track of testing.

Tracking Test Tasks and Status

The effective agile teams we know all follow this simple rule: "No story is done until it's tested." This rule can be expanded to say that not only must the story be tested, the code must be checked in, it must have automated tests that are run by a continual build process, it must be documented, or whatever your team's "doneness" criteria are. At any time during an iteration, you need to be able to quickly assess how much testing work remains on each story, and which stories are "done." Story or task boards are ideal for this purpose, especially if they use color-coding to denote test tasks vs. development and other types of tasks. Cork boards, steel sheets with magnets, poster-sized sticky notes, or whiteboards all work fine. Give each story its own row, and order them by priority. Have columns for "to do," "work in progress," "verify," and "done."

Janet's Story

I started with team members who had been doing agile for a few months with only a couple of programmers and one tester. They had been using XPlanner to track their tasks and stories, and it was working ok for them. At the same time I came on board, a couple of new programmers were added, and the stand-ups became less effective; the team was not completing the stories it had planned. I suggested a storyboard, and although they were skeptical about keeping two sets of "tasks," they said they would try it.

We took an open wall and used stickies to create our story board. We started having stand-ups in front of the story board and our discussion became more specific. It provided a nice visible way of knowing when the tasks were done and what was left to do. After a couple of months, the team grew again and we had to move the story board into an office. We also moved our stand-ups and our test result charts there. However, the constant visibility was lost, and programmers and testers stopped moving their tasks.

We had to reevaluate what we wanted to do. One size does not fit all teams. Make sure you plan for what is right for your team.

—Janet

Some teams use different colored index cards for the different types of tasks: green for testing, white for coding, yellow and red for bugs. Other teams use one card per development task, and add different colored stickers to show that testing is in progress or show that there are bugs to resolve. Use any method that lets you see at a quick glance how many stories are "done," with all coding, database, testing, and other tasks completed. As the iteration progresses, it's easy to see if the team is on track, or if you need to pull a story out or have programmers pitch in on testing tasks.

Janet's Story

Our story board (shown in Figure 15-8) wasn't very big, and we didn't have a lot of wall space to expand to have the regular column-type task board. Instead, we decided to use stickers to designate the status.

White cards, such as those shown in the first row of Figure 15-8, were regular tasks, blue cards designated technical stories such as refactoring or spikes, and pink cards, shown toward the right-hand side of the board as the darkest color, were bugs that need to be addressed. It is easy to see that this picture was taken at the beginning of an iteration because there are no colored circles on each card. In the top right-hand corner, you can see the legend. Blue stickers meant it has been coded, green would indicate done (tested), and red meant the task has been deemed not completed or a bug was rejected as not fixed. As a task or story was completed (i.e., green sticker), it was moved to the right of the board.

—Janet

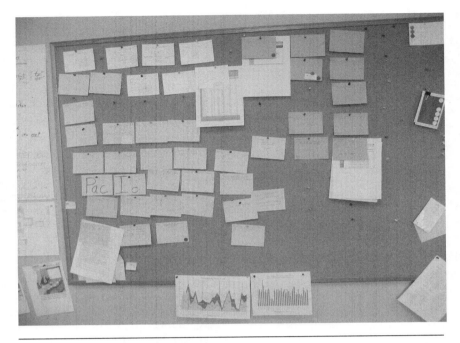

Figure 15-8   Example story board

Lisa's Story

For more than four years, our story board was a couple of sheets of sheet metal, painted in company colors, using color-coded index cards attached to the board with magnets. Figure 15-9 shows a picture of it early in an iteration. Our task cards were also color-coded: white for development tasks, green for coding tasks, yellow and red for bugs, and striped for cards not originally planned in the iteration. The board was so effective in indicating our progress that we eventually stopped bothering with a task burndown chart. It let us focus on completing one story at a time. We also used it to post other big visible charts, such as a big red sign showing the build had failed. We loved our board.

Then, one of our team members moved overseas. We tried using a spreadsheet along with our physical story board, but our remote teammate found the spreadsheet too hard to use. We tried several software packages designed for Scrum teams, but they were so different from our real story board that we couldn't adjust to using them. We finally found a product (Mingle) that looked and worked enough like our physical board that everyone, including our remote person, could use it. We painted our old story board white, and now we can project the story board on the wall during stand-up meetings.

—Lisa

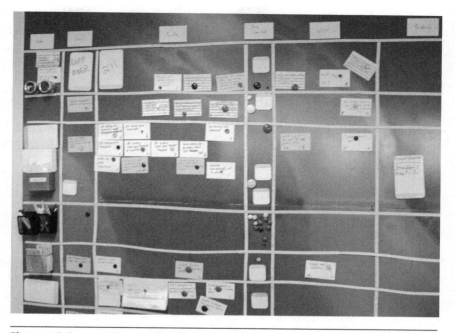

Figure 15-9   Another sample story board. Used with permission of Mike Thomas. Copyright 2008.

Distributed teams need some kind of online story board. This might be a spreadsheet, or specialized software that mimics a physical story board as Mingle does.

Communicating Test Results

Earlier, we talked about planning how to track test results. Now we want to talk about effectively communicating them. Test results are one of the most important ways to measure progress, see whether new tests are being written and run for each story, and whether they're all passing. Some teams post big visible charts of the number of tests written, run, and passed. Others have their build process email automated test results to team members and stakeholders. Some continuous integration tools provide GUI tools to monitor builds and build results.

We've heard of teams that have a projector hooked up to the machine that runs FitNesse tests on a continuous build and displays the test results at all times. Test results are a concrete depiction of the team's progress. If the number of tests doesn't go up every day or every iteration, that might indicate a problem. Either the team isn't writing tests (assuming they're developing test-first), or they aren't getting much code completed. Of course, it's possible they are ripping out old code and the tests that went with it. It's important to analyze why trends are going the wrong way. The next section gives you some ideas about the types of metrics you may want to gather and display.

However your team decides they want to communicate your progress, make sure you think about it up front and everyone gets value from it.

Release Metrics

We include this section here, because it is important to understand what metrics you want to gather from the very beginning of a release. These metrics should give you continual feedback about how development is proceeding, so that you can respond to unexpected events and change your process as needed. Remember, you need to understand what problem you are trying to solve with your metrics so that you can track the right ones. The metrics we talk about here are just some examples that you may choose to track.

Number of Passing Tests

Many agile teams track the number of tests at each level: unit, functional, story tests, GUI, load, and so on. The trend is more important than the number. We get a warm fuzzy feeling seeing the number of tests go up. A number without context is just a number, though. For example, if a team says it has 1000 tests, what does that mean? Do 1000 tests give 10% or 90% coverage? What happens when code that has tests is removed?

Tracking the number of tests written, running, and passing at a story level is one way to show a story's status. The number of tests written shows progress of tests to drive development. Knowing how many tests aren't passing yet gives you an idea of how much code still needs to be written.

After a test passes, it needs to stay "green" as long as the functionality is present in the code. Graphs of the number of tests passing and failing over time show whether there's a problem with regression failures and also show the growth of the code base. Again, it's the trend that's important. Watch for anomalies.

These types of measurements can be reported simply and still be effective.

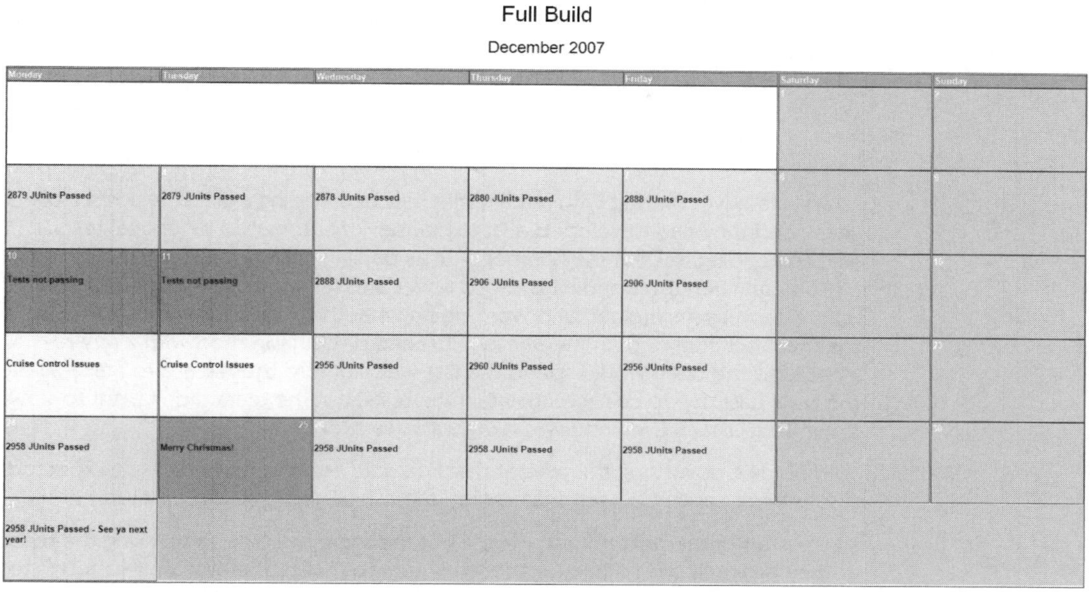

Full Build

December 2007

Monday	Tuesday	Wednesday	Thursday	Friday	Saturday	Sunday
2879 JUnits Passed	2879 JUnits Passed	2878 JUnits Passed	2880 JUnits Passed	2888 JUnits Passed		
Tests not passing	Tests not passing	2888 JUnits Passed	2906 JUnits Passed	2906 JUnits Passed		
Cruise Control Issues	Cruise Control Issues	2956 JUnits Passed	2960 JUnits Passed	2956 JUnits Passed		
2958 JUnits Passed	Merry Christmas!	2958 JUnits Passed	2958 JUnits Passed	2958 JUnits Passed		
2958 JUnits Passed - See ya next year!						

Figure 15-10   Full build result email from Lisa's team

Lisa's Story

My team emails a color-coded calendar out every day showing whether the "full build" with the full suite of regression tests passed each day (see Figure 15-10). Two "red" days in a row (the darkest color) are a cause for concern and noticed by management as well as the development team. Seeing the visual test results helps the organization pull together to fix the failing tests or any other problems causing the build to not run, such as hardware or database issues.

—Lisa

There are different ways to measure the number of tests. Choose one and try to stay consistent across the board with all types of tests, otherwise your metrics may get confusing. Measuring the number of test scripts or classes is one way, but each one may contain multiple individual test cases or "asserts," so it may be more accurate to count those.

If you're going to count tests, be sure to report the information so that it can be used. Build emails or build status UIs can communicate the number of tests run, passed, and failed at various levels. The customer team may be content to see this information only at the end of each sprint, in the sprint review, or an email.

Whatever metrics you choose to gather, be sure the team buys into them.

Janet's Story

I started a new contract with a team that had been doing agile for a couple of years, and they had developed a large number of automated functional tests. I started keeping track of the number of tests passing each day. The team didn't see a problem when the trending showed fewer and fewer tests were passing. The unit tests were maintained and were doing what they were supposed to do, so the team felt confident in the release. It seemed this happened with every release, and the team would spend the last week before the release to make all of the tests pass. It was costly to maintain the tests, but the team didn't want to slow down to fix them. Everyone was okay with this except me.

I did not see how fixing the tests at that late date could ensure the right expected results were captured. I felt that we ran the risk of getting false positives.

At the start of the next release cycle, I got the team to agree to try fixing the tests as they broke. It didn't take long for the team to realize that it wasn't so tough to fix the tests as soon as we knew they were broken, and we found a lot of issues early that hadn't usually been caught until much later. The team soon set a goal of having 95% of the tests passing at all times.

We also realized how brittle the tests were. The team made a concerted effort to refactor some of the more complex tests and eliminate redundant ones. Over time, the number of high-level tests was reduced, but the quality and coverage was increased.

We started out measuring passing rates, but we ended up with far more.

—Janet

Don't get so caught up in the actual measurements that you don't recognize other side effects of the trending. Be open to adjusting what you are measuring if the need is there.

Code Coverage

Code coverage is another traditional metric. How much of our code is exercised by our tests? There are excellent commercial and open source code coverage tools available, and these can be integrated into your build process so that you know right away if coverage has gone up or down. As with most metrics, the trend is the thing to watch. Figure 15-11 shows a sample code coverage report.

GHIDRAH

Overall Coverage Summary

Name	Class, %	Method, %	Block, %	Line, %
all classes	95% (1727/1809)	77% (13605/17678)	72% (201131/279707)	75% (43454.5/58224)

Overall Stats Summary

total packages:	240
total executable files:	1329
total classes:	1809
total methods:	17678
total executable lines:	58224

WHITNEY

Overall Coverage Summary

Name	Class, %	Method, %	Block, %	Line, %
all classes	15% (109/737)	8% (669/8760)	4% (16292/363257)	5% (3713.7/80358)

Overall Stats Summary

total packages:	46
total executable files:	655
total classes:	737
total methods:	8760
total executable lines:	80358

Figure 15-11 Sample code coverage report from Lisa's team. "Ghidrah" is the new architecture; "Whitney" is the legacy system.

Figures 15-12 and 15-13 are two examples of trends that work together. Figure 15-12 shows a trend of the total number of methods each iteration. Figure 15-12 is the matching code coverage. These examples show why graphs need to be looked at in context. If you only look at the first graph showing the number of methods, you'll only get half the story. The number of methods is increasing, which looks good, but the coverage is actually decreasing. We do not know the reason for the decreased coverage, but it should be a trigger to ask the team, "Why?"

Remember that these tools can only measure coverage of the code you've written. If some functionality was missed, your code coverage report will not

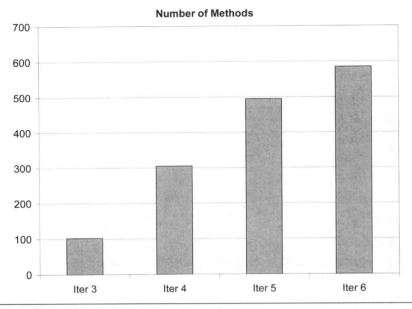

Figure 15-12 Number of methods trend

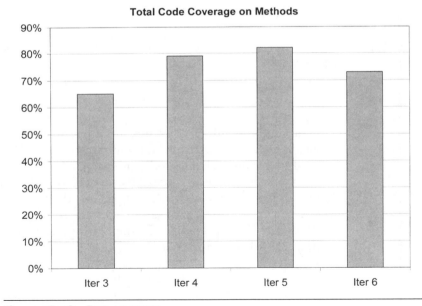

Figure 15-13 Test coverage

bring that to light. You might have 80% code coverage with your tests, but you're missing 10% of the code you should have. Driving development with tests helps avoid this problem, but don't value code coverage statistics more than they deserve.

Know What You Are Measuring

Alessandro Collino, a computer science and information engineer with Onion S.p.A. who works on agile projects, told us about an experience where code coverage fell suddenly and disastrously. His agile team developed middleware for a real-time operating system on an embedded system. He explained:

> A TDD approach was followed to develop a great number of good unit tests oriented to achieve good code coverage. We wrote many effective acceptance tests to check all of the complex functionalities. After that, we instrumented the code with a code coverage tool and reached a statement coverage of 95%.

> The code that couldn't be tested was verified by inspection, leading them to declare 100% of statement coverage after ten four-week sprints.

> After that, the customer required to us to add a small feature before we delivered the software product. We implemented this request and applied the code optimization of the compiler.

> This time, when we ran the acceptance tests, the result was disastrous; 47% of acceptance tests failed, and the statement coverage had fallen down to 62%!

What happened? The problem turned out to be due to enabling compiler optimization but with an incorrect setting. Because of this, a key value was read once as the application started up and was stored in a CPU register. Even when the variable was modified in memory, the value in the CPU register was never replaced. The routine kept reading this same stale value instead of the correct updated value, causing tests to fail.

Alessandro concludes, "The lesson learned from this example is that the enabling of the compiler optimization options should be planned at the beginning of the project. It's a mistake to activate them at the final stages of the project."

Good metrics require some good planning. Extra effort can give you more meaningful data. Pierre Veragen's team members use a break-test baseline technique to learn if their code coverage metric is meaningful. They manually introduce a flaw into each method and then run their tests to make sure the tests catch the problem. Some tests just make sure the code returns some value, any value. Pierre's team makes sure the tests return the *correct* value. In this way, they can determine whether their test coverage is good enough.

Code coverage is just one small part of the puzzle. Use it as such. It doesn't tell you how good your tests are but only if a certain chunk of code was run during the test. It does not tell you if different paths through the application were run, either. Understand your application and try identifying your highest risk areas, and set a coverage goal that is higher for those areas than for low-risk areas. Don't forget to include your functional tests in the coverage report as well.

Defect Metrics

As your team sets goals related to defects, use appropriate metrics to measure progress toward those goals. There are trends that you will want to monitor for the whole release, and there are ones that are iteration-specific. For example, if you're trying to achieve zero defects, you may want to track the open bugs at the end of each iteration, or how many bugs were found after development but before release. Most of us are interested in knowing how many defects have been reported after the code is in production, which is something completely different altogether. These issues will tell you after the fact how well your team did on the last release, but not how well you are doing on the current release. They may give you some indication of what processes you need to change to reduce the number of defects. Lisa's team is more concerned with production defects found in the "new" code that was rewritten in the new architecture. They're working hard to produce this new code with zero defects, so they need to know how well they're doing. They expect that bugs will be found fairly often in the legacy system, where only the most critical functionality is covered by automated GUI smoke tests, and there are few automated unit and behind-the-GUI tests.

Knowing the defect rate of legacy code might be good justification for refactoring or rewriting it, but the team's top priority is doing a good job with the new code, so they group bugs by "new" and "old" code, and focus on the "new" bugs.

More on defect tracking systems can be found in Chapter 5, "Transitioning Traditional Processes."

Make sure your bug database can track what you want to measure. You may have to make some changes in both the database and your process to get the data you need. For example, if you want to measure how many defects were found in production after a release, you have to make sure you have environment and version as mandatory fields, or make sure that people who enter bugs always fill them in.

Because defect tracking systems are often used for purposes besides tracking bugs, be sure not to muddle the numbers. A request for a manual update to the database doesn't necessarily reflect an issue with the existing code. Use your defect tracking tool properly to ensure that your metrics are meaningful.

Lisa's Story

Periodically evaluate the metrics you're reporting and see if they're still relevant. Figure 15-14 shows two defect reports that Lisa's team used for years. When we first transitioned to agile, managers and others looked at these reports to see the progress that resulted from the new process. Four years later, our ScrumMaster found that nobody was reading these reports anymore, so we quit producing them. By that time, rates of new defects had reduced dramatically, and nobody really cared about the old defects still hanging about in the legacy code.

—Lisa

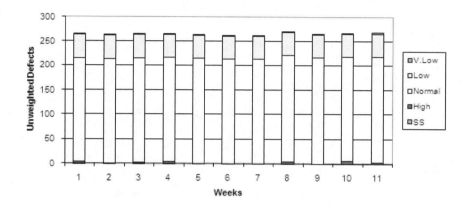

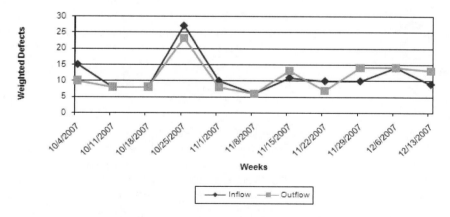

Figure 15-14   Sample defect reports used (and no longer used) by Lisa's team

Release planning is a good time to evaluate the ROI of the metrics you've been tracking. How much effort are you spending to gather and report the metrics? Do they tell you what you need to know? Does the code you release meet your team's standards for internal quality? Is the code coverage percentage going up? Is the team meeting its goals for reducing the number of defects that get out to production? If not, was there a good reason?

Metrics are just one piece of the puzzle. Use your release, theme, or project planning meetings to refocus on delivering business value when the business needs it. Take some time to learn about the features you're about to develop. Don't get caught up with committing to your plans—the situation is bound to change. Instead, prepare for doing the right activities and getting the right resources in time to meet the customers' priorities.

SUMMARY

As your team puts together its plan for a new theme or release, keep the main points of this chapter in mind.

- When sizing a story, consider different viewpoints, including business value, risk, technical implementation, and how the feature will be used. Ask clarifying questions, but don't get bogged down in details.
- Testers can help identify the "thin slice" or "critical path" through a feature set to help prioritize stories. Schedule high-risk stories early if they might require extra testing early.
- The size of testing effort for a story helps determine whether that story is in scope for the release.
- Testers can help the team think about how new stories will impact the larger system.
- Plan for extra testing time and resources when features may affect systems or subsystems developed by outside teams.
- As the team identifies the scope of the release, evaluate the scope of testing and budget enough time and resources for it.
- Spend some time during release planning to address infrastructure, test environment, and test data concerns.
- A lightweight, agile test plan can help make sure all of the testing considerations are addressed during the life of the release or project.
- Consider alternatives to test plans that might be more appropriate for your team; test matrices, spreadsheets, or even a whiteboard may be sufficient.

- Formal release planning may not be appropriate for your situation. In the absence of release planning, consider identifying and discussing at least the first few stories that should be done first.
- Plan for what metrics you want to capture for the life of the release; think about what problem you are trying to solve and capture only those metrics that are meaningful for your team.

Chapter 16

HIT THE GROUND RUNNING

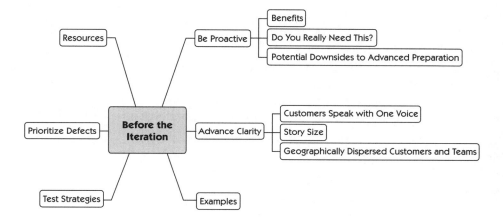

In agile development, we generally like to do tasks "just in time." We can't see around the curves in the road ahead, so we focus on the activities at hand. Then again, we want to hit the ground running when we start each new iteration. That may require a little preparation. Baking is a good analogy here. You decide you want to bake cookies because someone is coming over. Before you start, you make sure you have the right ingredients. If you don't, you either go buy what you need, or you choose a different kind to make.

Don't go overboard—if a pre-iteration activity doesn't save time during the iteration, or help you do a better job, don't do it before the iteration. Do what is appropriate for your team, and keep experimenting. Maybe you'll do some of these activities after the iteration starts instead. Here are some ideas to think about that might help you "bake quality in" to your product.

BE PROACTIVE

In Chapter 2, "Ten Principles of an Agile Tester," we explained how agile testers have to shift their mind-set. Instead of waiting for work to come to us, we develop a proactive attitude where we get up and go look for ways to contribute. With the fast and constant pace of agile development, it's easy to get immersed in the current iteration's stories. We are so busy making sure we've covered the features with up-front tests, performing exploratory testing to be sure we've understood the business requirements, and automating adequate regression tests, it's hard to think of anything else. However, it's sometimes appropriate to take a bit of time to help our customers and our team prepare for the next iteration. When our team is about to break new ground, or work on complex and risky stories, some work before the iteration can help maximize our team's velocity and minimize frustration.

We sure don't want to spend all our time in meetings, or planning for stories that might be re-prioritized. However, if we can make our iteration planning go faster, and reduce the risk of the stories we're about to undertake, it's worth doing some research and brainstorming before we start the iteration.

Benefits

Working on stories in advance of the iteration may be especially useful for teams that are split across different geographic locations. By working ahead, there's time to get information to everyone and give them a chance to give their input.

The problem is that we're so busy during each short agile iteration that it's hard to find time to meet about the next iteration's stories, much less start writing test cases. If your iterations always go smoothly, with stories delivered incrementally and plenty of time to test, and the delivered software matches customer expectations, you may not need to take time to prepare in advance. If your team has trouble finishing stories, or ends up with big mismatches between actual and desired behavior of features, a little advance planning may save you time during the iteration.

Lisa's Story

Our team used to feel we didn't have time to plan in advance for the next iteration. After many experiences of misunderstanding stories and having them far exceed estimations, and finding most "bugs" were missed requirements, we decided to budget time in the iteration to start talking about the next one. Now the whole team, including the product owner and other customers as needed, meet for an hour or less the day before the planning meeting for our next sprint.

We laughingly call this the "pre-planning" meeting. We go over the stories for the next iteration. The product owner explains the purpose of each story. He goes over the business conditions of satisfaction and other items in his story checklists, and gives examples of desired behavior. We brainstorm about potential risks and dependencies, and identify steel threads where appropriate.

Sometimes it's enough to spend a few minutes listening to the product owner's explanation of the stories. At other times, we take time to diagram thin slices of a story on the whiteboard. Figure 16-1 shows an example diagram where we got into both the details of the UI flow and the database tables. Note the numbers for the "threads." Thread #1 is our critical path. Thread #2 is the second layer, and so on. We upload photos of these diagrams to the wiki so our remote developer can see them too.

We can start thinking about what task cards we might write the next day and what approach we might take to each story. For some reason, being able to ruminate about the stories overnight makes us more productive in the actual iteration planning meeting the next day. After doing this for a few iterations, we were spending less time overall in planning the iteration, even though we had two meetings to do it.

Sometimes we pull in other customers to discuss stories that affect them directly. If they aren't available right then, we still have time before our iteration planning meeting to talk to them to clarify the story.

In one pre-planning meeting, our product owner introduced a story about obtaining performance data for mutual funds. We would send a file to the vendor containing a list of mutual funds, and the vendor would provide an XML file on a website with all the latest performance information for those funds. We would then upload that data into our database.

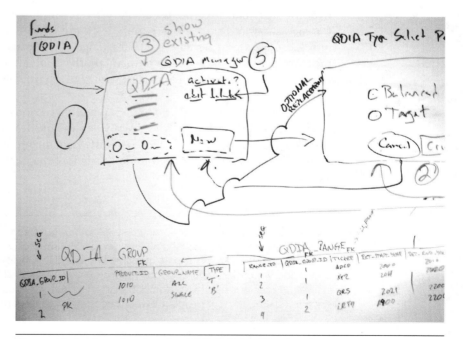

Figure 16-1 Sample planning whiteboard diagram

In the pre-planning meeting, we asked questions such as, "What's the format of the file we send the vendor?" "Is the 'as-of' date for each fund always the last day of the month?" "Is there any security on the website that contains the XML?" "Will we ever get a record for the same fund and "as-of" date that has new data, or can we ignore records with a date we already have in our database?"

By the next day's iteration planning meeting, the product owner had obtained answers to all our questions. Writing task cards went quickly, and coding could proceed with correct assumptions.

Often, we find a much simpler solution to a story when we discuss it in the pre-iteration planning discussion. We found that to go fast, we needed to slow down first.

—Lisa

Do You Really Need This?

Your team may not need much or any advance preparation. Pierre Veragen and Erika Boyer described to Lisa how their teams at iLevel by Weyerhaeuser write user acceptance tests together at their iteration kickoff meeting.

These tests, which were written on a wiki page or some similar tool along with the story narrative, are used later when team members write task cards for each story and start writing more tests and code. Examples are turned into executable tests. Because the tests change as the team learns more about the story, the team may opt not to maintain the original ones that were written at the start. Keep it simple to start with, and dig into details later.

Lisa subsequently observed one of their planning sessions and saw first-hand how effective this technique was. Even when the product manager provides concrete examples, turning them into tests may flush out missing requirements. Their team did not need to do this before the iteration planning session, but it is not the case with all teams.

Lisa's Story

My team liked the practice of writing tests together, but because we were writing task cards during iteration planning, we decided to write user acceptance tests together during the pre-planning meeting. We found this kept our discussions focused and we understood each story more quickly. We also did a better job of delivering exactly what the customer had in mind. Our customers noticed a difference in quality, and our product owner encouraged us to continue this practice.

—Lisa

Experiment with short pre-iteration discussions and test-writing sessions. It'll take you several iterations to find your team's rhythm, and find out if advance story discussions make you more productive during the iteration.

Potential Downsides to Advance Preparation

There's a risk to "working ahead." You could spend time learning more details about a feature only to have the business people re-prioritize at the last minute and put that feature off indefinitely. Invest preparation time when it's appropriate. When you know you have a complex theme or story coming up, and it has a hard deadline such as Lisa's team had with the statement story, consider spending some time up front checking out different viewpoints. The only reason to discuss stories in advance is to save time during iteration planning and during development. A deeper understanding of the feature behavior can speed up testing and coding, and can help make sure you deliver the right functionality.

If your situation is so dynamic that stories might be re-prioritized the day that the iteration starts, it isn't worth trying to do this planning. Instead, make sure you budget time for these discussions during your planning meeting.

ADVANCE CLARITY

Lisa's product owner, Steve Perkins, came up with the term "advance clarity." Different parts of each organization have different priorities and agendas. For example, Business Development is looking for new features to attract new business, while Operations is prioritizing features that would reduce the number of phone calls from users. The development team tries to understand the range of business needs and get a feel for each individual's job.

With many different agendas, someone needs to decide what stories should be implemented in the next iteration. Because there are many ways to implement any given story, someone has to decide the specific requirements and capture them in the form of examples, conditions of satisfaction, and test cases. Steve gets everyone together to agree on the value they want from each story, and to provide "advance clarity."

Customers Speak with One Voice

Scrum provides the helpful role of the product owner to help all the customers "Speak with One Voice." Whether or not you're on a Scrum team, find some way to help your customers agree on the priority of the stories and how the components of each story ought to be implemented. Management support is crucial, because any person in this role needs time and authority to get everyone on the same page.

Other teams use business analysts to help flesh out the stories before the next iteration. In one organization Janet worked with, the customers were not available full-time to answer questions, but each team had a business analyst that worked with the customers to flesh out the requirements before the iteration planning meeting. If there were any questions that she could not answer at the meeting, the team either called the customer directly or the analyst followed up immediately after the meeting.

As a tester, you want to sit in on story writing and prioritization meetings. Ask questions that help the customers focus on the core functionality, the critical business value they need. Help participants stay focused on concrete examples that crystallize the meaning of the stories. In meetings that involve multiple customers, it is critical to have a strong facilitator and a method for determining consensus.

As with code, stories are best if they have the bare minimum. For example, an Internet shopping cart needs some way to delete unwanted items, but the ability to move items from the cart to a "save for later" list can probably wait. It may be helpful to talk about this before the iteration, so that the team is clear on what tasks need to be planned. Focus on the simplest thing first and use an example to make it clear.

Get All Viewpoints

Getting requirements from different customers for a story, each of whom has a different agenda, might create chaos. That's why it's essential for someone on the customer team to get consensus and coordinate all points of view. This doesn't mean we shouldn't get input from different customers. As a tester, you're considering each story from multiple points of view. It helps to know what the story means to people in different roles.

Lisa's Story

When my company decided to redesign the retirement plan participants' quarterly account statements, different people on the business side wanted changes for different reasons. The plan administrators wanted a clearly understandable layout that would minimize the number of calls from confused participants to customer support.

For example, they wanted the statement to show the date and amount of the participant's most recent contribution. This helps the participant know whether her employer is late in posting contributions to the accounts. Business development wanted jazzy new features that they could sell to potential customers, such as graphs of performance by fund category. Our legal person needed some new text and data on the statement to satisfy federal regulations.

While the product owner balanced all the different needs and presented the final statement layout, it was still important for our team to understand the purpose behind each new piece of information. We needed to talk directly to business experts in the plan administration, business development, and legal areas, and to the product owner. A tester and a programmer met with each group to gather the different viewpoints. By doing this before starting on stories to gather and display data, we understood the requirements much more clearly and even made suggestions to produce the information more efficiently.

—Lisa

Make sure you are as efficient as possible in collecting this data. Sometimes it is important for the whole team to understand the need, and sometimes it is sufficient for one or two of the team members to do the research.

Story Size

As you discuss stories for the next iteration with the customer team members, ask questions to help them make sure each story delivers the value needed. This is a good time to identify new stories they might need to write. Even though the team sized the stories previously, you might find a story is bigger than previously thought. You might even discover that a feature can be implemented more simply than planned, and the story can be smaller.

Sometimes assumptions are made when the story is sized and on further investigation turn out to be false. Even simple stories deserve a closer look. It's hard for any one person to remember all the details of an application.

Lisa's Story

Here are some examples of stories that turned out to be significantly bigger or smaller than originally thought.

1. The story was to produce a file of account statements for all participants in a given company retirement plan, which was to be sent to a vendor who would print and mail the statements. It was originally sized with the assumption that all statements were exactly three pages long. Upon further investigation, we discovered that some participants had four-page statements, but the vendor required that all statements be the same length. Our business experts had to decide whether to have a feature to flag any plans whose participants had four-page statements and deal with those manually, or change the statements to make them all four pages long. That's a much bigger effort than the original

story. After we started developing the story, the customers revealed another requirement: If any participant's address was missing or invalid, the statement should be mailed to the employer instead. It's reasonable, but we didn't know about it when we sized the story.

2. Our customers wanted to start displaying the sales phone number in various locations in the UI. There is a different sales phone number for each partner's site, and at the time there were about 25 different partner sites. This sounded like such a straightforward story that it wasn't even given to the team to size. The development manager just assigned it a small point value, and it was just "added" to the iteration. He had assumed the phone number was stored in the database, when in fact it was hard-coded in the HTML of each partner's "contact" page. Storing the correct number for each partner in the database, and changing the code to retrieve the value, made the story twice as big, and there wasn't room for it in that iteration, so it did not get done.

3. We sized a story for the user interface to allow administrators to submit a request for a batch job to rebalance participant accounts that met a certain condition. It included a confirmation page displaying the number of participants affected. Because the request was queued to run as an asynchronous batch job, the code to determine which participants were affected was in the batch job's code. Refactoring the code to obtain the number of participants at request time was a big job. After we started working on the story, we asked the primary user of the feature whether he really needed that number upon submitting the request, and he decided it wasn't necessary. The story became much smaller than originally thought. We always ask questions to find out the true business value that the customers want and eliminate components that don't have a good ROI.

—Lisa

These stories show that a few questions up front might save time during the iteration that could be spent figuring out what to do with new discoveries. However, we recognize that not all discoveries can be found early. For example, on the first story, a simple question about statement size may have prevented last-minute confusion about how to handle four-page statements, but the inaccurate address issue may not have been considered until it was being coded or tested.

We know there will always be discoveries along the way, but if we can catch the big "gotchas" first, that will help the team work as effectively as possible.

Geographically Dispersed Teams

Some preparation for the next iteration may be useful for teams that are split across different locations. Teams that are distributed in multiple locations may do their iteration planning by conference call, online meeting, or teleconference. One practice, which a team of Lisa's used, is to assign each team a subset of the upcoming stories and have them write task cards in advance. During the planning meeting, everyone can review all the task cards and make changes as needed. The up-front work enhances communication, makes the stories and tasks visible to everyone, and speeds up the planning process.

Of course, this assumes that the team is using an electronic story or task board. Lisa's team uses Thoughtwork's Mingle, but there are many other products out there that serve this purpose.

Coping with Geographic Diversity

We talked to a team we know at a software company that has customers, developers, and testers spread all over the globe. Not only are the customers far away from the technical team but they don't have bandwidth to be available to answer the development team's questions. Instead, the team relies on functional analysts who understand both the business side of the application at a detailed level and the technical implementation of the software. These functional analysts act as liaisons between the business and technical teams.

Patrick Fleisch and Apurva Chandra are consultants who were working with this company and served as functional analysts on a project to develop web-based entitlement software, because they are experts in this domain. They traveled between locations to facilitate communication between stakeholders and developers.

The functional analysts worked in advance of the iteration, sizing and getting stories ready to size, helping the technical team to understand the stories. They entered stories into an online tool and built on them by defining test cases, edge conditions, and other information that helped the technical team understand the story. They documented high-level functionality on a wiki aimed at the business users.

Apurva and Patrick played a key role in making the decisions that the technical team needed to get started with the new stories. Their deep business and technical understanding allowed them to provide the team with requirements they needed to get coding, because the actual customers weren't available to them. David Reed, a tester and automation engineer, told us how he relied on Apurva and Patrick for the information he needed to perform and automate tests. While agile principles say to collaborate closely with the customer, in some situations you have to be creative and find another way to get clear business requirements.

If customers aren't readily available to answer questions and make decisions, other domain experts who are accessible at all times should be empowered to guide the team by determining priorities and expressing desired system behavior with examples. Testers and business analysts are often called upon to do these activities.

EXAMPLES

You may notice that we talk about examples in just about every chapter of this book. Examples are an effective way to learn about and illustrate desired (and undesired) functionality; it's worth using them throughout your development cycle. Our motto was coined by Brian Marick: "An example would be handy right about now." (See Figure 16-2.) Start your discussions about features and stories with a realistic example. The idea has taken off, so that at a recent workshop for functional testing we were discussing ideas around calling it "Example-Driven Development."

When Lisa's team members meet with their product owner to talk about the next iteration, they ask him for examples of desired behavior for each story. This keeps the discussion at a concrete level and is a fast way to learn how the new features should work. Have a whiteboard handy while you do this, and start drawing. If some team members are in a distant location, consider using tools that allow everyone to see whiteboard diagrams and participate in the discussion. Go through real examples with your customers or their proxies. As during release planning, consider different points of view: the business, end users, developers, and business partners. Unlike release planning, you are looking at far more detail because these are the stories you are planning for the next iteration.

Using examples, you can write high-level tests to flesh out each story a bit more. You may not need to do this before the iteration starts, but for com-

Figure 16-2   Brian Marick's example sticker

plex stories, it can be a good idea to write at least one happy path and one negative path test case in advance. Let's consider the story in Figure 16-3.

Story PA-3

As a shopper on our site, I want to delete items

out of my shopping cart, so I don't purchase extra

items I don't want.

Figure 16-3   Story for deleting items from shopping cart

The product owner sketches out the desired UI on the whiteboard. There's a "delete" checkbox next to each item and an "update cart" button. The user can select one or more items and click the button to remove the items. The high-level tests might be:

- When the user clicks the delete checkbox next to the item and clicks the "update cart" button, the page refreshes showing the item is no longer in the cart.
- When the user clicks the delete checkboxes next to every item in the cart and clicks the "update cart" button, the page refreshes showing an empty cart. (This will generate questions—should the user be directed to another page? Should a "keep shopping" button display?)
- When the user clicks the "update cart" button without checking an item for delete, the page is refreshed and nothing is removed from the cart.

Ask your customers to write down examples and high-level test cases before the iteration. This can help them think through the stories more and help define their conditions of satisfaction. It also helps them identify which features are critical, and which might be able to wait. It also helps to define when the story is done and manage expectations among the team.

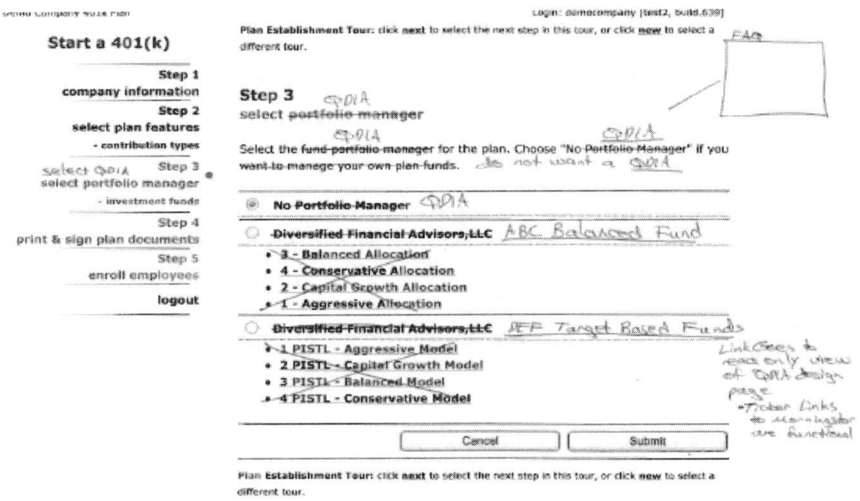

Figure 16-4   Sample customer mock-up

Figure 16-4 shows a sample mock-up, where the product owner marked changes on the existing page. Be careful about using an existing screenshot from an old system, because you will run the risk of having a new system look exactly like the old one even if that is not what you wanted.

Mock-ups are essential for stories involving the UI or a report. Ask your customers to draw up their ideas about how the page should look. Share these ideas with the team. One idea is to scan them in and upload them on the wiki so everyone has access. Use those as a starting point and do more paper prototypes, or draw them on the whiteboard. These can be photographed and uploaded for remote team members to see.

TEST STRATEGIES

As you learn about the stories for the next iteration, think about how to approach testing them. Do they present any special automation challenge? Are any new tools needed?

Lisa's Story

Recently, our company needed to replace the voice response unit hardware and interactive voice interface software. A contractor was to provide the software to operate the voice application, but it needed to interact via stored procedures with the database.

This was a big departure from any software we'd worked on before, so it was helpful to have an extra day to research how other teams have tested this type of application before the first iteration planning that involved a story related to this project. During the iteration planning session, we were able to write tasks that were pertinent to the testing needed and give better estimates.

—Lisa

Chapter 9, "Toolkit for Business-Facing Tests that Support the Team," Chapter 10, "Business-Facing Tests that Critique the Product," and Chapter 11, "Critiquing the Product Using Technology-Facing Tests," provide examples of tools for different types of testing.

When your team embarks on a new type of software, you may decide to do a development spike to see what you can learn about how to develop it. At the same time, try a test spike to help make sure you'll know how to drive the development with tests and how to test the resulting software. If a major new epic or feature is coming up, write some cards to research it and hold brainstorming meetings an iteration or two in advance. That helps you know what stories and tasks to plan when you actually start coding. One idea is to have a "scout" team that looks at what technical solutions might work for upcoming stories or themes.

PRIORITIZE DEFECTS

In our ideal world, we want zero defects at the end of each iteration and definitely at the end of the release. However, we recognize that we don't live in an ideal world. Sometimes we have legacy system defects to worry about, and sometimes fixing a defect is just not high enough value for the business to fix. What happens to these defects? We'll talk about strategies in Chapter 18, "Coding and Testing," but for now, let's just consider that we have defects to deal with.

Before the next iteration is an ideal time to review outstanding issues with the customer and triage the value of fixing versus leaving them in the system. Those that are deemed necessary to be fixed should be scheduled into the next iteration.

RESOURCES

Another thing to double-check before the iteration is whether your team has all the resources you need to complete any high-risk stories. Do you need any experts who are shared with other projects? For example, you may need a security expert if one of the stories poses a security risk or is for a security feature. If load testing will be done, you may need to have a special tool, or have help from a load testing specialist from another team, or even a vendor who provides load testing services. This is your last chance to plan ahead.

Summary

Your team may or may not need to do any preparation in advance of an iteration. Because priorities change fast in agile development, you don't want to waste time planning stories that may be postponed. However, if you're about to implement some new technology, embark on a complex new theme, hope to save time in iteration planning, or your team is divided into different locations, you might find some up-front planning and research to be productive. As a tester, you can do the following:

- Help the customers achieve "advance clarity"—consensus on the desired behavior of each story—by asking questions and getting examples.
- Be proactive, learn about complex stories in advance of the iteration, and make sure they're sized correctly.
- You don't always need advance preparation to be able to hit the ground running in the next iteration. Don't do any preparation that doesn't save time during the iteration or ensure more success at meeting customer requirements.
- Coordinate between different locations and facilitate communication. There are many tools to help with this.
- Obtain examples to help illustrate each story.
- Develop test strategies in advance of the next iteration for new and unusual features.
- Triage and prioritize existing defects to determine whether any should be scheduled for the next iteration.
- Determine whether any necessary testing resources not currently at hand need to be lined up for the next iteration.

Chapter 17

ITERATION KICKOFF

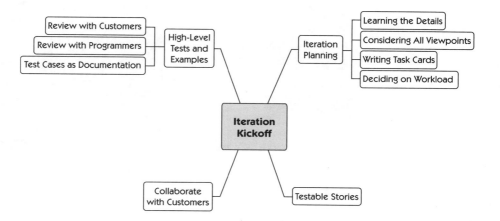

Agile testers play an essential role during iteration planning, helping to plan testing and development tasks. As the iteration gets under way, testers actively collaborate with customers and developers, writing the high-level tests that help guide development, eliciting and illustrating examples, making sure stories are testable. Let's take a closer look at the agile tester's activities at the beginning of each iteration.

ITERATION PLANNING

Most teams kick off their new iteration with a planning session. This might be preceded by a retrospective, or "lessons learned" session, to look back to see what worked well and what didn't in the previous iteration. Although the retrospective's action items or "start, stop, continue" suggestions will affect the iteration that's about to start, we'll talk about the retrospective as an end-of-iteration activity in Chapter 19, "Wrap Up the Iteration."

While planning the work for the iteration, the development team discusses one story at a time, writing and estimating all of the tasks needed to implement

Figure 17-1   Iteration planning meeting. Used with permission of Mike Thomas. Copyright 2008.

that story. If you've done some work ahead of time to prepare for the iteration, this planning session will likely go fairly quickly.

Teams new to agile development often need a lot of time for their iteration planning sessions. Iteration planning often took a whole day when Lisa's team first started out. Now they are done in two or three hours, which includes time for the retrospective. Lisa's team uses a projector to display user acceptance test cases and conditions of satisfaction from their wiki so that everyone on the team can see them. They also project their online story board tool, where they write the task cards. Another traditional component of their planning meetings is a plate of treats that they take turns providing. Figure 17-1 shows an iteration planning meeting in progress.

Learning the Details

Ideally, the product owner and/or other customer team members participate in the iteration planning, answering questions and providing examples describing requirements of each story. If nobody from the business side can attend, team members who work closely with the customers, such as analysts and testers, can serve as proxies. They explain details and make decisions on behalf of the customers, or take note of questions to get answered quickly. If your team went over stories with the customers in advance of the iteration, you may think you don't need them on hand during the iteration planning session. However, we suggest that they be available just in case you do have extra questions.

As we've emphasized throughout the book, use examples to help the team understand each story, and turn these examples into tests that drive coding. Address stories in priority order. If you haven't previously gone over stories with the customers, the product owner or other person representing the customer team first reads each story to be planned. They explain the purpose of the story, the value it will deliver, and give examples of how it will be used. This might involve passing around examples or writing on a whiteboard. UI and report stories may already have wire frames or mock-ups that the team can study.

A practice that helps some teams is to write user acceptance tests for each story together, during the iteration planning. Along with the product owner and possibly other stakeholders, they write high-level tests that, when passing, will show that the story is done. This could also be done shortly in advance of iteration planning as part of the iteration "prep work."

Stories should be sized so they'll take no more than a few days to complete. When we get small stories to test on a regular basis, we do not have them all finished at once and stacked up at the end of the iteration waiting to be tested. If a story has made it past release planning and pre-iteration discussions and is still too large, this is the final chance to break it up into smaller pieces. Even a small story can be complex. The team may go through an exercise to identify the thin slices or critical path through the functionality. Use examples to guide you, and find the most basic user scenarios.

Agile testers, along with other team members, are alert to "scope creep." Don't be afraid to raise a red flag when a story seems to be growing in all directions. Lisa's team makes a conscious effort to point out "bling," or "nice to have" components, which aren't central to the story's functionality. Those can be put off until last, or postponed, in case the story takes longer than planned to finish.

Considering All Viewpoints

As a tester, you'll try to put each story into the context of the larger system and assess the potential of unanticipated impacts on other areas. As you did in the release planning meeting, put yourself in the different mind-sets of user, business stakeholder, programmer, technical writer, and everyone involved in creating and using the functionality. Now you're working at a detailed level.

In the release planning chapter, we used this example story:

> *As a customer, I want to know how much my order will cost to ship based on the shipping speed I choose, so I can change if I want to.*

We decided to take a "thin slice" and change this story to assume there is only one shipping speed. The other shipping speeds will be later stories. For this story, we need to calculate shipping cost based on item weight and destination, and we decided to use BigExpressShipping's API for the calculation. Our story is now as shown in Figure 17-2.

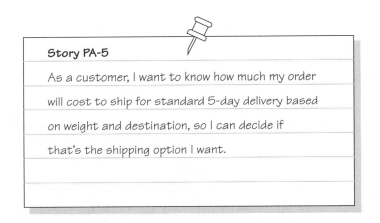

Figure 17-2   Story shipping speed for 5-day delivery

The team starts discussing the story.

Tester: "Does this story apply for all items available on the site? Are any items too heavy or otherwise disqualified for 5-day delivery?"

Product Owner: "5-day ground is available for all our items. It's the overnight and 2-day that are restricted to less than 25 lbs."

Tester: "What's the goal here, from the business perspective? Making it easy to figure the cost to speed up the checkout? Are you hoping to encourage them to check the other shipping methods—are those more profitable?"

Product Owner: "Ease of use is our main goal, we want the checkout process to be quick, and we want the user to easily determine the total cost of the order so they won't be afraid to complete the purchase."

Programmer: "We could have the 5-day shipping cost display as a default as soon as the user enters the shipping address. When we do the stories for the other shipping options, we can put buttons to pop up those costs quickly."

Product Owner: "That's what we want, get the costs up front. We're going to market our site as the most customer friendly."

Tester: "Is there any way the user can screw up? What will they do on this page?"

Product Owner: "When we add the other shipping options, they can opt to change their shipping option. But for now, it's really straightforward. We already have validation to make sure their postal code matches the city they enter for the shipping address."

Tester: "What if they realize they messed up their shipping address? Maybe they accidentally gave the billing address. How can they get back to change the shipping address?"

Programmer: "We'll put buttons to edit billing and shipping addresses, so it will be very easy for the user to correct errors. We'll show both addresses on this page where the shipping cost displays. We can extend this later when we add the multiple shipping addresses option."

Tester: "That would make the UI easy to use. I know when I shop online, it bugs me to not be able to see the shipping cost until the order confirmation. If the shipping is ridiculously expensive and I don't want to continue, I've already wasted time. We want to make sure users can't get stuck in the checkout process, get frustrated, and just give up. So, the next page they'll see is the order confirmation page. Is there any chance the shipping cost could be different when the user gets to that page?"

Programmer: "No, the API that gives us the estimated cost should always match the actual cost, as long as the same items are still in the shopping cart."

Product Owner: "If they change quantities or delete any items, we need to make sure the shipping cost is immediately changed to reflect that."

As you can see by the conversation, a lot of clarification came to light. Everyone on the team now has a common understanding of the story. It's important to talk about all aspects of the story. Writing user acceptance tests as a group is a good way to make sure the development team understands the customer requirements. Let's continue monitoring this conversation.

Tester: "Let's just write up some quick tests to make sure we get it right."

Customer: "OK, how's this example?

> *I can select two items with a 5-day shipping option and see my costs immediately.*

Tester: "Great start, but we won't know where to ship it to at that point. How about a more generic test like:

> *Verify the 5-day shipping cost displays as the default as soon as the user enters a shipping address.*

Customer: "That works for me."

Considering All of the Facets

Paul Rogers recounts a situation during an iteration planning meeting, where a performance issue came up for a story that appeared to be straightforward and quick.

> During our iteration meeting, one of the stories we were discussing was for adding some new images to part of a web application. This discussion ensued.
>
> > Product Owner: "I'd like to also get in the story for additional images."
> >
> > Developer 1: "OK, who has ideas on how long it will take?"
> >
> > Developer 2: "It's fairly quick, maybe half a day."
> >
> > Developer 3: "But what about the database changes?"
> >
> > Developer 2: "I included those in the estimate."
> >
> > Developer 1: "OK, let's go with half a day."
> >
> > Me: "Hang on. We looked at some performance issues last iteration. If we add all those images, we will be taking a performance hit.

> Developer 1: "OK, we should think about that some more. Maybe there are other ways of implementing it.
>
> Developer 2: "Why don't we do a quick spike, add the mock images, and run another performance test?"
>
> It was really good that this discussion before even starting on a story gave us some ideas of what problems we may encounter.
>
> Anyone who's uncertain about either the impact of a story on the rest of the system or the difficulty of developing the functionality can, and should, raise an issue during iteration planning. It's better to address uncertainty early on and then do more research or a spike to get more information.

Asking questions based on different viewpoints will help to clarify the story and allow the team to do a better job.

Writing Task Cards

When your team has a good understanding of a story, you can start writing and estimating task cards. Because agile development drives coding with tests, we write both testing and development task cards at the same time.

If you have done any pre-planning, you may have some task cards already written out. If not, write them during the iteration planning meeting. It doesn't matter who writes the task cards, but everyone on the team should review them and get a chance to give their input. We recognize that tasks may be added as we begin coding, but recognizing most of the tasks and estimating them during the meeting gives the team a good sense of what is involved.

Lisa's Story

When our team is ready to start writing task cards, programmers usually come up with the coding task cards. The testers write testing task cards at the same time.

I usually start with a card to write high-level test cases. I ask the programmers whether the story can be tested behind the GUI, and write testing task cards accordingly. This usually means a test card to "Write FitNesse test cases" and a developer task card to "Write FitNesse fixture," unless the fixtures already exist. Sometimes all of the behind-GUI tests can be covered more easily in unit tests, so it is always good to ask whether this is the case.

We put anything the team needs to remember during the iteration on a task card. "Show UI to Anne" or "Send test files to Joe" go up on the story board along with all of the other tasks.

I estimate the testing task cards as I go, and ask the team for feedback on the cards and the estimates. Sometimes we divide into groups, and each group takes some stories and writes task cards for them. We always review all cards together, along with the estimated time. If development time is relatively low compared to testing time, or vice versa, that provokes a discussion. We reach a consensus as to whether we think all aspects of the story have been covered with task cards. If there are still some unknowns, we simply postpone writing the task cards until we have the information.

The testing and development cards all go on the story board in the "to do" column. Anyone on the team can sign up for any card. Some testing task cards move to the "work in progress" or "done" column before coding cards start to move, so that programmers have some tests to guide their coding. As coding task cards are moved to the "done" column, the cards for testing the "done" functionality are moved into "work in progress."

—Lisa

Janet uses an approach similar to this, but the programmer's coding card stays in the "To Test" column until the testing task has been completed. Both cards move at the same time to the "Done" column.

Three test cards for Story PA-5 (Figure 17-2), displaying the shipping cost for 5-day delivery based on weight and destination, that Lisa's team might write are:

- Write FitNesse tests for calculating 5-day ship cost based on weight and destination.
- Write WebTest tests for displaying the 5-day ship cost.
- Manually test displaying the 5-day delivery ship cost.

Some teams prefer to write testing tasks directly on the development task cards. It's a simple solution, because the task is obviously not "done" until the testing is finished. You're trying to avoid a "mini-waterfall" approach where testing is done last, and the programmer feels she is done because she "sent the story to QA." See what approach works best for your team.

If the story heavily involves outside parties or shared resources, write task cards to make sure those tasks aren't forgotten, and make the estimates generous enough to allow for dependencies and events beyond the team's control. Our hypothetical team working on the shipping cost story has to work with the shipper's cost calculation API.

Tester: "Does anyone know who we work with at BigExpressShipping to get specs on their API? What do we pass to them, just the weight and postal code? Do we already have access for testing this?"

Scrum Master: "Joe at BigExpressShipping is our contact, and he's already sent this document specifying input and output format. They still need to authorize access from our test system, but that should be done in a couple of days."

Tester: "Oh good, we need that information to write test cases. We'll write a test card just to verify that we can access their API and get a shipping cost back. But how do we know the cost is really correct?"

Scrum Master: "Joe has provided us with some test cases for weight and postal code and expected cost, so we can send those inputs and check for the correct output. We also have this spreadsheet showing rates for some different postal codes."

Tester: "We should allow lots of time for just making sure we're accessing their API correctly. I'm going to put a high estimate on this card to verify using the API for testing. Maybe the developer card for the interface to the API should have a pretty conservative estimate, too."

When writing programmer task cards, make sure that coding task estimates include time for writing unit tests and for all necessary testing by programmers. A card for "end-to-end" testing helps make sure that programmers working on different, independent tasks verify that all of the pieces work together. Testers should help make sure all necessary cards are written and that they have reasonable estimates. You don't want second-guess estimates, but if the testing estimates are twice as high as the coding estimates, it might be worth talking about.

Some teams keep testing tasks to a day's work or less and don't bother to write estimated hours on the card. If a task card is still around after a day's work, the team talks about why that happened and writes new cards to go forward. This might cut down on overhead and record-keeping, but if you are entering tasks into your electronic system, it may not. Do what makes sense for your team.

Estimating time for bug fixing is always tricky as well. If existing defects are pulled in as stories, it is pretty simple. But what about the bugs that are found as part of the iteration?

Janet's Story

With new agile teams, I found that they always seem to end up with time spent on bugs that wasn't allotted as part of their estimates for the stories. Over time, programmers learn how much time they typically spend fixing bugs from a story, and can just add half a day or a couple hours to their tasks for that purpose. Retesting bug fixes adds time to tester's estimates as well.

Until the team members get a handle on this, it may be appropriate to track the time spent on fixing and testing bugs separately. My current team adds a story in XPlanner with tasks for fixing and testing those bugs that didn't get caught immediately. We are tracking the time so we can better estimate down the road.

—Janet

However your team chooses to estimate time spent for fixing defects during the iteration, whether it is included in the story estimate or tracked separately, make sure it is done consistently.

Another item to consider when estimating testing tasks is test data. The beginning of an iteration is almost too late to think about the data you need to test with. As we mentioned in Chapter 15, "Tester Activities in Release or Theme Planning," think about test data during release planning, and ask the customers to help identify and obtain it. Certainly think about it as you prep for the next iteration. When the iteration starts, whatever test data is missing must be created or obtained, so don't forget to allow for this in estimates.

Lisa's Story

We worked on a theme related to quarterly account statements for participants in retirement plans. We were modifying a monthly job that takes a "snapshot" of each participant's account on the specified date. The snapshot relies on a huge amount of data in the production database, including thousands of daily transactions. We planned ahead.

For the first iteration, we did a few stories in the theme knowing we could only test a few cases using some individual retirement plans for which we had data in the test database. We also knew we needed a larger-scale test, with all of the retirement plans in the database and at least an entire month's worth of data. We wrote a task card to copy enough production data to produce one monthly "snapshot" and made sure the data was scrubbed to protect privacy.

Then we planned the full-blown test in the next iteration. This data enabled the testers to find problems that were undetectable earlier when only partial data was available. It was a nice balance of "just enough" data to do most of the coding and the full amount available in time to verify the complete functionality. Because the team planned ahead, the bugs were fixed in time for the critical release.

—Lisa

Deciding on Workload

We, as the technical team, control our own workload. As we write tasks for each story and post them on our (real or virtual) story board, we add up the estimated hours or visually check the number of cards. How much work can we take on? In XP, we can't exceed the number of story points we completed in the last iteration. In Scrum, we commit to a set of stories based on the actual time we think we need to complete them.

Lisa's current team has several years of experience in their agile process and finds they sometimes waste time writing task cards for stories they may not have time to do during the iteration. They start with enough stories to keep everyone busy. As people start to free up, they pull in more stories and plan the related tasks. They might have some stories ready "on deck" to bring in as soon as they finish the initial ones. This sounds easy, but it is difficult to do until you've learned enough to be more confident about story sizes and team velocity, and know what your team can and cannot do in a given amount of time and in specific circumstances.

Your job as tester is to make sure enough time is allocated to testing, and to remind the team that testing and quality are the responsibility of the whole team. When the team decides how many stories they can deliver in the iteration, the question isn't "How much coding can we finish?" but "How much coding and testing can we complete?" There will be times when a story is easy to code but the testing will be very time consuming. As a tester, it is important that you only accept as many stories into the iteration as can be tested.

If you have to commit, commit conservatively. It's always better to bring in another story than to have to drop one. If you have high-risk stories that are hard to estimate, or some tasks are unknown or need more research, write task cards for an extra story or two and have them ready on the sidelines to bring in mid-iteration.

As a team, we're always going to do our best. We need to remember that no story is done until it's tested, so plan accordingly.

TESTABLE STORIES

When you are looking at stories, and the programmers start to think about implementation, always think how you can test them. An example goes a long way toward "testing the testability." What impact will it have on my testing? Part III, "The Agile Testing Quadrants," gives a lot of examples of how to design the application to enable effective testing. This is your last opportunity to think about testability of a story before coding begins.

Janet's Story

One team I worked with told me about issues they had in the previous release. The team was rewriting the first step of a multistep process. What they didn't anticipate was that when the development on the new step started, the rest of the process broke. No testing could be done on any other changes in that iteration until the whole first step was finished.

Testability had not been considered when planning the story. In the next release, when they decided to rewrite the second step, they learned from their previous mistake. The programmers created an extra button on the page that allowed the testers to either call the new page (in flux) or the old page to allow them test other stories.

Remember to ask, "How can we test this?" if it is not obvious to you.

—Janet

During iteration planning, think about what kind of variations you will need to test. That may drive other questions.

Janet's Story

During one iteration planning meeting that I was in, the programmers started talking about implementation and drawing pictures on the whiteboard to show what they were thinking.

I thought about it for a bit and asked the question, "Can it be done more simply? The permutations and combinations for testing your proposed implementation will make testing horrendous."

The programmers thought about it for a couple of minutes and suggested an alternative that not only met the customer's needs, but was simpler and easier to test. It was a win-win combination for everyone.

—Janet

When testability is an issue, make it the team's problem to solve. Teams that start their planning by writing test task cards probably have an advantage here, because as they think about their testing tasks, they'll ask how the story can be tested. Can any functionality be tested behind the GUI? Is it possible to do the business-facing tests at the unit level? Every agile team should be thinking test-first. As your team writes developer task cards for a story, think about how to test the story and how to automate testing for it. If the programmers aren't yet in the habit of coding TDD or automating unit tests, try writing a "XUnit" task card for each story. Write programming task cards for any test automation fixtures that will be needed. Think about application changes that could help with testing, such as runtime properties and APIs.

Lisa's Story

The application that I work on has many time- and date-dependent activities. The programmers added a runtime server property to the web application to set the server date. I can specify a date and time override, and when the server starts up, it behaves accordingly. This allows kicking off monthly or quarterly processes with a simple override. This property has helped in testing a wide variety of stories.

Markus Gärtner [2008] told us his team has a similar property, a "DATE_OFFSET" counted in "days to advance." However, this was only used by the Java components of the application where the business logic lives. The back-end systems in C and C++ don't use the date offset, which caused a problem.

—Lisa

If you have similar issues because other teams are developing parts of the system, write a task card to discuss the problem with the other team and come up with a coordinated solution. If working with the other team isn't an option, budget time to brainstorm another solution. At the very least, be mindful of the limitations, and adjust testing estimates accordingly and manage the associated risk.

Lisa's Story

We started a project to replace our company's interactive voice response (IVR) system, which allows retirement plan participants to obtain account information and manage accounts by phone. We contracted with another company to write the system in Java, with the intention that our team would maintain it after a certain time period.

We spent some time brainstorming what testing would be needed and how to do it. Presumably, the contractor would test things like the text-to-speech functionality, but we had to supply stored procedures to retrieve appropriate data from the database.

Our first step was to negotiate with the contractor to deliver small chunks of features on an iteration basis, so they could be tested as the project progressed and the work would be spread out evenly over the life of the contract. We decided to test the stored procedures using FitNesse fixtures, and explored the options. We settled on PL/SQL to access the stored procedures. A programmer was tasked with getting up to speed on PL/SQL to tackle the test automation.

The team aimed for a step-by-step approach. By allocating plenty of time for tasks at the start, we allowed for the steep learning curves involved.

Interestingly, the contractor delivered an initial build for the first iteration but was not able to deliver the increments of code for the next few iterations. We ended up canceling the contract and postponing the project until we could find a better solution. By forcing the contractor to work in increments, we discovered right away that it couldn't deliver. What if we had let them take six months to write the whole application? It probably wouldn't have ended well. We put what we learned to good use in researching a better approach.

—Lisa

When you're embarking on something new to the team, such as a new templating framework or reporting library, remember to include it as a risk in your test plan. Hopefully, your team considered the testability before choosing a new framework or tool, and selected one that enhanced your ability to test. Be generous with your testing task estimates with everything new, including new domains, because there are lots of unknowns. Sometimes new domain knowledge or new technology means a steep learning curve.

COLLABORATE WITH CUSTOMERS

Working closely with customers, or customer proxies such as functional analysts, is one of our most important activities as agile testers. As you kick off the iteration, your customer collaboration will also kick into high gear. This is the time to do all those good activities described in Chapter 8, "Business-Facing Tests that Support the Team." Ask the customers for examples, ask open-ended questions about each story's functionality and behavior, have discussions around the whiteboard, and then turn those examples into tests to drive coding.

Even if your product owner and/or other customers explained the stories before and during iteration planning, it's sometimes helpful to go over them briefly one more time as the iteration starts. Not everyone may have heard it before, and the customer may have more information.

Lisa's Story

We start writing high-level acceptance tests the first day of the iteration. Because we go over all stories with the product owner the day before the iteration and write user acceptance tests as a team for the more complex stories, we have a pretty good idea of what's needed. However, the act of writing more test cases often brings up new questions. We go over the high-level tests and any questions we have with the product owner, who has also been thinking more about the stories.

One example of this was a story that involved a file of monetary distributions to plan participants who withdraw money from their retirement accounts. This file is sent to a partner who uses the information to cut checks to the participant. The amounts in some of the records were not reconciling correctly in the partner's system, and the partner asked for a new column with an amount to allow them to do a reconciliation.

After the iteration planning meeting, our product owner became concerned that the new column wasn't the right solution and brought up his misgivings in the story review meeting. He and a tester studied the problem further and found that instead of adding a new amount, a calculation needed to be changed. This was actually a bigger story, but it addressed a core issue with the distributions. The team discussed the larger story and wrote new task cards. It was worth taking a little time to discuss the story further, because the initial understanding turned out to be wrong.

—Lisa

Good communication usually takes work. If you're not taking enough opportunities to ask questions and review test cases, go ahead and schedule regular meetings to do so. If there's not much to discuss, the meetings will go quickly. Time in a meeting for an insightful discussion can save coding and testing time later, because you're more certain of the requirements.

HIGH-LEVEL TESTS AND EXAMPLES

We want "big picture" tests to help the programmers get started in the right direction on a story. As usual, we recommend starting with examples and turning them into tests. You'll have to experiment to see how much detail is appropriate at the acceptance test level before coding starts. Lisa's team has found that high-level tests drawn from examples are what they need to kick off a story.

High-level tests should convey the main purpose behind the story. They may include examples of both desired and undesired behavior. For our earlier Story PA-5 (Figure 17-2) that asks to show the shipping cost for 5-day delivery based on the order's weight and destination, our high-level tests might include:

- Verify that the 5-day shipping cost displays as the default as soon as the user enters a shipping address.
- Verify that the estimated shipping cost matches the shipping cost on the final invoice.

- Verify that the user can click a button to change the shipping address, and when this is done, the updated shipping cost displays.
- Verify that if the user deletes items from the cart or adds items to the cart, the updated shipping option is displayed.

See the bibliography for links to more information on graphical tests and model-driven development.

Don't confine yourself to words on a wiki page when you write high-level tests. For example, a test matrix such as the one shown in Figure 15-7 might work better. Some people express tests graphically, using workflow drawings and pictures. Brian Marick [2007] has a technique to draw graphical tests that can be turned into Ruby test scripts. Model-driven development provides another way to express high-level scope for a story. Use cases are another possible avenue for expressing desired behavior at the "big picture" level.

A Picture Is Worth a Thousand Words

The saying "A picture says a thousand words" can also be applied to test cases and test validations.

Paul Rogers [2008] has been experimenting with some cool ideas around this and explains his team's approach to its problem in the following sidebar. Figure 17-3 shows the UI model he describes.

> The application I work on is very graphical in its nature. It allows a user to modify a web page by adding "photo enhancements" such as glasses, hats, or speech bubbles to images, or by highlighting the text in the web page with a highlighter pen effect.
>
> There is a complex set of business rules as to what additions can be applied to images, how and where they are affixed, and how they can be rotated. To explain the tests for these rules, it was much simpler to draw a sketch of a typical web page with the different types of additions and add small notes to each picture.
>
> Text highlighting also posed many challenges. Most problematic were the areas where text highlighting covered only part of an HTML tag. To describe what should be expected in many different situations, we created different web pages and printed them out.
>
> Using real pen highlighters, we highlighted the areas we expected to show as highlighted after starting and ending in certain areas. This way, we had an easy-to-read regression test.

Low-tech tools can take the mystery out of complex application design. Find ways to express business rules as simply as possible, and share those with the entire team.

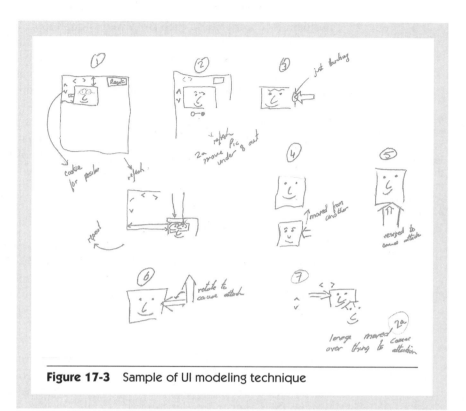

Figure 17-3 Sample of UI modeling technique

See the sample mock-up of UI changes in Chapter 16, "Hit the Ground Running."

Mock-ups can convey requirements for a UI or report quickly and clearly. If an existing report needs modifying, take a screenshot of the report and use highlighters, pen, pencil, or whatever tools are handy. If you want to capture it electronically, try the Windows Paint program or other graphical tool to draw the changes and post it on the wiki page that describes the report's requirements.

See Chapter 9, "Toolkit for Business-Facing Tests that Support the Team," for some ideas on tools to gather and communicate requirements.

Distributed teams need high-level tests available electronically, while co-located teams might work well from drawings on a whiteboard, or even from having the customer sit with them and tell them the requirements as they code.

What's important as you begin the iteration is that you quickly learn the basic requirements for each story and express them in context in a way that works for the whole team. Most agile teams we've talked to say their biggest problem is to understand each story well enough to deliver exactly what the customer wanted. They might produce code that's technically bug-free but doesn't quite match the customer's desired functionality. Or they may end up doing a lot of rework on one story during the iteration as the customer clarifies requirements, and run out of time to complete another story as a result.

See Chapter 8, "Business-Facing Tests that Support the Team," for more about what makes up a requirement.

Put time and effort into experimenting with different ways to capture and express the high-level tests in a way that fits your domain and environment. Janet likes to say that a requirement is a combination of the story + conversation + a user scenario or supporting picture if needed + a coaching test or example.

Reviewing with Customers

Earlier in this chapter we talked about the importance of constant customer collaboration. Reviewing high-level tests with customers is a good opportunity for enforced collaboration and enhanced communication, especially for a new agile team. After your team is in the habit of continually talking about stories, requirements, and test cases, you might not need to sit down and go over every test case.

If your team is contracting to develop software, requirements and test cases might be formal deliverables that you have to present. Even if they aren't, it's a good idea to provide the test cases in a format that the customers can easily read on their own and understand.

Reviewing with Programmers

You can have all of the diagrams and wiki pages in the world, but if nobody looks at them, they won't help. Direct communication is always best. Sit down with the programmers and go over the high-level tests and requirements. Go over whiteboard diagrams or paper prototypes together. Figure 17-4 shows a tester and a programmer discussing a diagram of thin slices or threads through a user workflow. If you're working with a team member in another location, find a way to schedule a phone conversation. If team members have trouble understanding the high-level tests and requirements, you'll know to try a different approach next time.

Programmers with good domain knowledge may understand a story right away and be able to start coding even before high-level tests are written. Even so, it's always a good idea to review the stories from the customer and tester perspective with the programmers. Their understanding of the story might

Figure 17-4   A whiteboard discussion. Used with permission of Mike Thomas. Copyright 2008.

Chapter 2, "Ten Principles for Agile Testers," introduces the "Power of Three" rule.

be different than yours, and it's important to look at mismatches. Remember the "Power of Three" rule and grab a customer if there are two opinions you can't reconcile. The test cases also help put the story in context with the rest of the application. Programmers can use the tests to help them to code the story correctly. This is the main reason you want to get this done as close to the start of the iteration as you can—before programmers start to code.

Don't forget to ask the programmers what they think you might have missed. What are the high-risk areas of the code? Where do they think the testing should be focused? Getting more technical perspective will help with designing detailed test cases. If you've created a test matrix, you may want to review the impacted areas again as well.

One beneficial side effect of reviewing the tests with the programmers is the cross-learning that happens. You as a tester are exposed to what they are thinking, and they learn some techniques for testing that they would not have otherwise encountered. As programmers, they may get a better understanding of what high-level tests they hadn't considered.

Test Cases as Documentation

High-level test cases, along with the executable tests you'll write during the iteration, will form the core of your application's documentation. Requirements will change during and after this iteration, so make sure your executable test cases are easy to maintain. People unfamiliar with agile development often have the misconception that there's no documentation. In fact, agile projects produce usable documentation that contains executable tests and thus is always up to date.

The great advantage of having executable tests as part of your requirements document is that it's hard to argue with their results.

Lisa's Story

Frequently, product owners, plan administrators, or business development managers will come and ask me a question such as, "What's the system supposed to do if someone submits a loan payment for zero dollars?" or "Why didn't everyone in this plan get a 3% nonelective contribution?"

Showing them a FitNesse test that replicates the scenario is much more powerful than just showing them narrative requirements. Maybe the system wasn't designed the way it should have been, but the test illustrates how it actually works, because we can clearly see the results of the inputs and operations. This has saved a lot of arguments on the level of "I thought it worked this way."

If they decide the functionality, as implemented, is incorrect, we can change the expected outputs of the test and write a story to implement code to make the test pass again with the new expectations. You can't do that with a requirements document.

—Lisa

Organizing the test cases and tests isn't always straightforward. Many teams document tests and requirements on a wiki. The downside to a wiki's flexibility is that you can end up with a jumble of hierarchies. You might have trouble finding the particular requirement or example you need.

Chapter 14, "An Agile Test Automation Strategy," has more on test management.

Lisa's team periodically revisits its wiki documentation and FitNesse tests, and refactors the way they're organized. If you're having trouble organizing your requirements and test cases, budget some time to research new tools that might help. Hiring a skilled technical writer is a good way to get your valuable test cases and examples into a usable repository of easy-to-find information.

SUMMARY

The iteration planning session sets the tone for the whole iteration. In this chapter, we looked at what agile testers do to help kick off the iteration to a good start.

- During iteration planning, testers help the team learn about the stories by asking questions and considering all viewpoints.
- Task cards need to be written along with development task cards and estimated realistically.
- Another way of tackling testing tasks is to write them directly on the developer task cards.
- Teams should commit to the work for which they can complete all of the testing tasks, because no story is done until it's fully tested.
- The start of an iteration is the last chance to ensure that the stories are testable and that adequate test data is provided.
- Testers collaborate with customers to explore stories in detail and write high-level test cases to let programmers kick off coding.
- Testers review high-level tests and requirements with programmers to make sure they are communicating well.
- Tests form the core of the application's documentation.

## Chapter 18

CODING AND TESTING

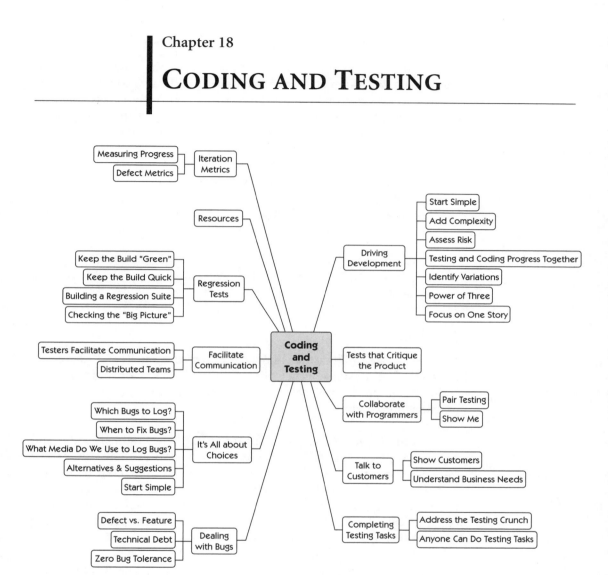

Our agile tester has helped plan the release, size stories appropriately, and make sure they're testable. She, along with colleagues on the customer and development team, has turned examples of desired behavior for each story into high-level user acceptance tests. She and her team have lined up the resources and infrastructure needed to deliver business value. Now, team members have picked up task cards and started writing code. What do testers do next, especially before any stories are ready to test?

DRIVING DEVELOPMENT

The beginning of coding is a good time to start writing detailed tests. The high-level tests written before the iteration, or in the first couple days of it, provide enough information for the programmers to start their own test-driven development. So now we have a bit of breathing room, but if we don't move quickly, coding could get way ahead of testing and go off in the wrong direction.

Now's the time to start writing executable tests that illustrate the details about a story in order to keep development moving forward smoothly and help testing keep pace with coding. Like the high-level tests, we base detailed tests on examples provided by the customers.

At this point, we're mainly writing tests that will be automated, but we're also thinking ahead to the important exploratory testing we need to do as coding is completed.

Start Simple

As testers, we're easily distracted by interesting code smells and edge cases. However, if we're using tests to guide coding, we have to start with the basics. Write the simplest happy path test you can in order to show that the core functionality works.

Chapter 14, "An Agile Automation Strategy," gives pointers for selecting the right tools.

Why executable tests? We're working on an extremely tight schedule, and neither the programmers nor the testers have time to stop and run manual tests over and over. They do have time to click a button and run an automated test. That test needs to fail in a way that makes the cause as obvious as possible. Ideally, we would give these tests to the programmers so that they could execute them as they code. That is one reason why picking the right automation framework is so important.

For some stories, automating the tests might take a long time. By keeping the first test simple, you keep the focus on designing the automation solution. When the simple test works, it's worth putting time into more complex test cases.

We stress the importance of automation, but Janet has worked with teams that have successfully used manual tests in the form of checklists or spreadsheets to give the programmers the information they need to start. However, to be successful in the long run, these tests do need to be automated.

Add Complexity

As soon as the happy path test works, start adding more test cases. Add boundary and edge conditions. The tests may show that the programmers misunderstood a requirement, or they may show that a tester did, or maybe the requirement's true meaning eluded everyone. The important thing is that everyone talks about it and gets on track.

As testers think of new scenarios to validate with executable tests, they also think about potential scenarios for manual exploratory testing. Make a note of these for later pursuit.

Remember the purpose of these tests. They should provide examples that tell the programmers what code to write. As the code evolves, your tests can challenge it more, but resist the temptation to immediately follow smells into edge cases. Get the basics working first. If you think of more cases based on some risk analysis, you can always add extra tests later.

Assess Risk

Testers have used risk analysis to help prioritize testing for a long time, and consideration for risk is already built into agile development. High-risk stories may get higher size estimates, and teams consider risk as they prioritize stories during release and iteration planning.

Some quick risk analysis can help you decide what testing to do first and where to focus your efforts. We never have time to test everything, and we can use risk analysis to figure out how much testing is just enough.

If you have a really complex story, you may want to start by listing all of the potential risks related to the story. These aren't limited to functionality. Consider security, performance, usability, and other "ilities." Next, for each item, rate the impact on the business if it were to occur, using a scale of 1 to 5 (or whatever scale works for you): 1 being a low impact, 5 being a critical negative impact.

Now, consider the likelihood of each item occurring, using the same scale: 1 for not at all likely to happen, and 5 for items that probably will come up. Multiply the two ratings together to get the total risk rating for each item. This makes it easy to pick out the areas where your team should focus its testing efforts first. Low-risk items can be left for last, or, because their impact is low or they're highly unlikely to occur, may not be addressed at all.

Your domain makes a huge difference here. If you're testing software that runs in heart pacemakers, you probably need to cover all risks with your testing no matter how low or unlikely they are. If you're testing an internal company web application to be used by a few trained subject matter experts, you may be able to skip over scenarios that are unlikely or have an obvious workaround.

Consider the story in Figure 18-1.

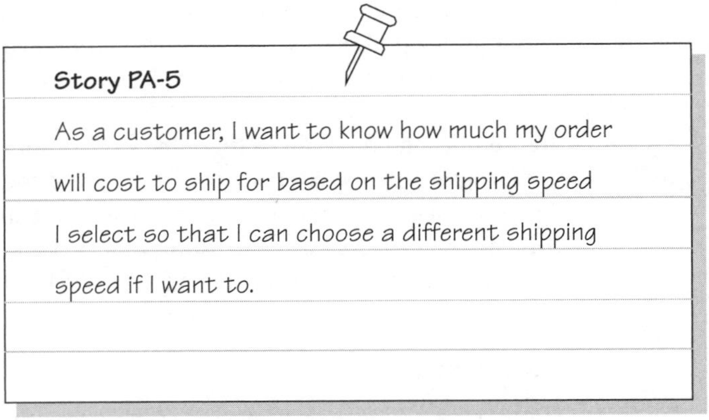

Story PA-5

As a customer, I want to know how much my order

will cost to ship for based on the shipping speed

I select so that I can choose a different shipping

speed if I want to.

Figure 18-1   Story on shipping speeds

Figure 18-2 shows a possible risk assessment for this shipping cost story.

#	Item	Impact	Probability	Risk
1	Incorrect cost displayed	4	2	8
2	User can't choose different shipping option	5	1	5
3	Item isn't eligible for selected shipping option, but selection allowed	3	2	6
4	Estimated cost doesn't match actual cost at checkout	3	4	12
5	Invalid postal code entered and not caught by validation	4	1	4
6	User can't understand shipping option rules	2	3	6
7	User can't change shipping address	5	2	10
8	User changes shipping address, but cost doesn't change accordingly	5	4	20

Figure 18-2   Sample risk assessment

Item 8 is the highest-risk item, so we'd want to be sure to test changing shipping addresses and verify the updated costs. We might want to automate an end-to-end test with this scenario. We're not too worried about item 5; maybe we have already tested our postal code validation and feel good about it, so we don't need to test it more. You may even have a very low-risk item that you chose not to test.

History is usually a good teacher. Take note of past issues and make sure they don't happen again.

Coding and Testing Progress Together

At this point in the iteration, coding and testing continue hand in hand. Testers, programmers, database experts, and other team members collaborate to develop the stories, following the guidelines provided by examples and tests. Different team members may contribute their particular expertise, but all of them feel responsible for making sure each story is finished. All of them learn about the story and learn from each other as work progresses.

Let's look at how a team might work on the shipping cost story in Figure 18-1. Patty Programmer picks up a task card to code the estimated shipping cost calculations. She already understands the story pretty well from earlier discussions, but she may look at the wiki pages or back of the story card where the testers wrote down some narrative describing the purpose of the story, some examples of how it should work, and some high-level tests to make sure she has a good idea of where to start. Tammy Tester sees that coding work has begun and starts to write behind-the-GUI test cases for the cost calculations.

The team had agreed during planning to start by calculating the 5-day shipping cost based on the shipping address and item weight. Items can only be shipped within continental North America, but that validation will be done in the presentation layer, so the cost calculation tests can assume only valid destinations are considered for input. They're using a cost calculation API provided by the shipping partner, and Tammy asks Patty where to find the algorithms so she can figure the cost herself in order to write the tests. Tammy writes the simplest test case she can think of in their behind-the-GUI test tool. We show it as a simple table in Figure 18-3.

Weight	Destination Postal Code	Cost
5 lbs	80104	7.25

Figure 18-3   Simple happy path test

Patty hasn't finished the code that would make this test pass yet, so Tammy starts working on another testing task for the story, setting up the test environment to work with the shipping partner's test system.

Identify Variations

Because this story and the test are so straightforward, Patty and Tammy don't discuss the test design and tweak it as they might on more complex stories. They also haven't needed to ask the product owner more questions yet. Patty calls Tammy over to show her that the simple test is now working. Tammy writes up more test cases, trying different weights and destinations within the United States. Those all work fine. She tries a Canadian postal code, and the test gets an exception. She shows this to Patty, who realizes that the API defaults to U.S. postal codes, and requires a country code for codes in Canada and Mexico. She hadn't written any unit tests yet for other countries. They revise the test inputs, and Patty pairs with Paul Programmer to change the code that calls the API. Now the test looks something like Figure 18-4.

Weight	Destination Postal Code	Coutry Code	Cost
5 lbs	80104	US	7.25
5 lbs	T2J 2M7	CA	9.40

Figure 18-4   Revised happy path test

This simple example illustrates the iterative back-and-forth between coding and testing. Different teams take different approaches. Patty and Tammy might pair on both the coding and testing. Tammy might pair with Paul to write the fixture to automate the test. Tammy might be in a remote office, using an online collaboration tool to work with Patty. Patty might write the executable story tests herself and then write the code to make them work, practicing true story test-driven development. The point is that testing and coding are part of one development process in which all team members participate.

Tammy can continue to identify new test cases, including edge cases and boundary conditions, until she feels all risk areas have been covered by the minimum amount and variety of test cases. She might test with the heaviest item available on the website sent to the most expensive destination. She might test having a large quantity of the same item. Some edge cases may be so unlikely that she doesn't bother with them, or she decides to run a test but after it passes doesn't include it in the regression suite. Some tests might be better done manually after a UI is available.

Power of Three

Patty has written unit tests with Hawaii as the shipping destination, but Tammy believes that only continental destinations are acceptable. Neither of them is sure whether military post office box destinations are acceptable. They go see Polly Product-Owner to ask what she thinks. They're using the Power of Three. When disagreements or questions arise, having three different viewpoints is an effective way to make sure you get a good solution and you won't have to rehash the issue later. If one of the participants in the discussion isn't familiar with the topic, the others will have to organize their thoughts to explain it clearly, which is always helpful. Involving people in different roles helps make sure that changes to requirements don't fly under the radar and surprise team members later.

When unexpected problems arise, as they always do, the Power of Three rule is a great place to start. You may need to pull in more people, or even the whole team, depending on the severity or complexity of the issue. What if the shipping partner's API proves to be so slow that the response time on the website will be unacceptable? Both the development team and the customer team need to quickly explore alternative solutions.

Focus on One Story

Paul looks for a programming task to work on. Although the UI tasks for the estimated shipping cost story are still in the "to do" column on the task board, he's more interested in the story to delete items out of the shopping cart, so he picks up one of those cards. Nobody has time to start writing the executable tests for that story, so he plunges ahead on his own.

Now the team has two stories going. They don't really know how much time it will take to finish either story. A much better approach would be for Paul to start working on a UI task for the first story so that story can be finished sooner. When a story's done (meaning all of the code is written and tested), you know exactly how much work is left to do on it: zero. If disaster struck and no other stories got finished this iteration, there is at least one completed story to release.

Completing the whole story isn't a testing concept, but it's one that testers should promote and follow. If a programmer has started coding on a story, make sure someone has also started working on testing tasks for that story. This is a balancing act. What if nobody has written even high-level tests for the delete items story? Maybe that's the highest testing priority? Usually, finishing a story should be the goal before the team can move on to the next story.

Unless the team is very small, there is always more than one story in progress at any given time. It might be more difficult, but try to focus on finishing one story at a time. Patty is about to wrap up the shipping cost story, and Paul has moved on to the delete items story. Patty runs into a snag, and she isn't sure how to solve it. Paul helps her to finish the code so that Tammy can finish her exploratory testing and they can mark the story "done." Now they have a better idea of how much they have left to finish this iteration (or at least, how much they don't still have to work on).

Sometimes, several different stories can be done at the same time if a programmer and tester pair up to complete each story together. This works if the stories are small and independent. What you don't want to see is programmers starting coding without testing tasks being completed at the same time.

TESTS THAT CRITIQUE THE PRODUCT

As soon as testable chunks of code are available, and the automated tests that guided their coding pass, take time to explore the functionality more deeply. Try different scenarios and learn more about the code's behavior. You should have task cards for tests that critique the product, both business- and technology-facing. The story's not "done" until all of these types of tests are complete.

This becomes more important when all tasks except testing are complete for a story. Now you should be able to test from one end of the story's thread to the other end, with all of the variations in between. Don't put this testing off. You may find requirements that were in the story but were missed with the tests that drove development and are thus missing in the code. Now's the time to write those missing tests and code. Fill in all of the gaps and add more value while the team is still focused on the story. Doing this later will cost much more.

Be aware that some of what you learn in testing the final story may be considered "nice to have," perhaps making the functionality easier to use or faster, items that weren't part of the original story. Consult with your customer. If there's time to add it in the iteration, and the business can use the extra value, go ahead. These additions are much cheaper to add now. But don't jeopardize other stories by spending too much time adding "bling" that doesn't have a big ROI.

If your exploratory testing leads the team and the customers to realize that significant functionality wasn't covered by the stories, write new stories for future iterations. Keep a tight rein on "scope creep" or your team won't have time to deliver the value you planned originally.

Chapter 10, "Business-Facing Tests that Critique the Product," and Chapter 11, "Tecnology-Facing Tests that Critique the Product," will help you make sure you cover all of the necessary tests that critique the product.

Technology-facing tests to critique the product are often best done during coding. This is the time to know if the design doesn't scale, or if there are security holes.

COLLABORATE WITH PROGRAMMERS

Our vignette describing a team writing and using detailed tests to drive coding shows how closely testers and programmers collaborate. This continues as coding and testing proceed. Working together enhances the team's ability to deliver the right product and provides many opportunities to transfer skills. Programmers learn new ways of testing, and they'll be better at testing their own code as they write it. Testers learn more about the process of coding and how the right tests might make it easier.

Pair Testing

Paul Programmer has completed the user interface for the estimated shipping options story, but he hasn't checked it in yet. He asks Tammy to come sit with him and demonstrates how the end user would enter the shipping address during the checkout process. The estimated shipping cost displays right away. Tammy changes the shipping address and sees the new cost appear. She enters a postal code that doesn't match the rest of the address and sees the appropriate error message appear. The UI looks good to both of them, so Paul checks in the code, and Tammy continues with her exploratory manual testing of it.

Janet likes to have the programmer "drive" during these pair testing sessions while she watches what happens. She finds that it is far more effective than taking control of the keyboard and mouse while the programmer watches.

"Show Me"

Tammy is especially concerned with changing the shipping address and having the estimated cost recalculate, because they identified that as a risky area. She finds that if she displays the estimated cost, goes ahead to the billing address page, and then comes back to change the shipping address, the estimated costs don't change properly. She gets Paul to come observe this behavior. He realizes there is a problem with session caching and goes back to fix it.

Showing someone a problem and working through it together is much more effective than filing a bug in a defect tracking system and waiting for someone to have time to look at it. It's harder to do if the team isn't co-located. If team members are working in vastly different time zones, it's even harder. Stick to the most direct communication available to you. One of Lisa's teammates is in a time zone 12½ hours ahead. He works late into his nighttime, and when needed, he calls Lisa and they work through test results and examples together.

The bibliography contains references for further reading on this subject.

The simple act of showing the GUI to another person may help Paul realize he's implemented some erroneous behavior. Similarly, if Tammy is having trouble getting her GUI test script to work, explaining the problem might be enough for her to realize what's causing it. If there is nobody available to look at what you've just coded or help you debug a problem, it sometimes helps to explain it out loud to yourself. "Rubber Ducking" and "Thinking Out Loud" are surprisingly effective ways to solve your own problems. Janet likes to have her own little rubber duck sitting on her desk to remind herself to think before she asks.

TALK TO CUSTOMERS

It's shockingly easy for development team members to get their heads down cranking out stories and forget to keep customers in the loop. In addition to consulting business experts when we have questions, we need to show them what we've delivered so far.

Hopefully, you were able to review test cases with customers, or with someone who could represent the customer, before coding began. If not, it's never too late. For situations where customers need to be more involved with the details of the executable tests, be sure to find test tools that work for them as well as for technical team members.

As we described in the last two chapters, you may have already gone over mock-ups or paper prototypes with your customers. If tasks to mock up a report or interface remain in the iteration plan, remember to keep the process simple. For example, don't code an HTML prototype when drawing on a whiteboard will do just as well. We want to keep the process as simple as possible; simplicity is a core value.

Show Customers

As soon as a coded user interface or report is ready, even if it's still rudimentary, lacking all features or displaying hard-coded data, show it to the appropriate customers. Nobody can explain exactly what they want ahead of time. They need to see, feel, and use the application to know if it's right. You may not be able to implement big changes mid-iteration, but if you start early, there may be time for minor tweaks, and your customers will know what to expect.

The iteration review meeting is a great opportunity to show what the team delivered and get feedback for the next iteration, but don't wait until then to get input from customers. Keep them involved throughout the iteration.

Understand the Business

Although we get caught up in the fast pace of iterations, we also need to stop and take time to understand the business better. Spend some time talking to business people about their jobs and what aspects might be enhanced with new software features. The better you understand your customer's business, the better you can be at providing a good product.

Lisa's Story

My team budgets time for each development team member to sit with the retirement plan administration team members as they do their daily work. Not only do we understand those jobs better, but we often identify small changes in the application that will make the administrator's work easier.

Simple additions such as a bit of extra data provided, an additional search filter, or changing the order of a display can make a big difference to a tedious and detailed process. We also document what we learn with flow charts and wiki pages so that other team members can benefit.

—Lisa

Some teams actually sit with the business people permanently so that they are involved with the actual business on a daily basis.

COMPLETING TESTING TASKS

Agile testers are proactive. We don't sit and wait for work to come to us. Testers who are accustomed to a waterfall process may feel there's nothing to do until a story is 100% complete. That's rarely true during an agile iteration. Work with programmers so that they produce some testable piece of code early on. The shipping cost algorithm presented earlier is a good example. It can be tested completely in isolation, without needing to access the database or the user interface. Alternatively, the user interface could be stubbed out with hard-coded data before the services accessing the real data are complete, and the behavior of the presentation layer can be tested by itself.

Peril: The Testing Crunch

Even experienced agile teams often experience a testing crunch at the end of an iteration. Maybe a story or two turned out to take much longer than expected, or a production problem took time away from development. What happens when tomorrow is the end of your iteration and your task board (real or virtual) is still full of testing cards?

If you see this, recognize it as a bad smell. Work with the team to determine what the problem may be. Are the programmers not working closely enough with the testers? Were there too many interruptions?

The way to address this peril is to involve the whole team. Remember that anyone on the team can sign up for testing tasks. In your daily stand-up, you can evaluate whether the team is on track to finish all of the stories. If multiple stories are in danger of not being completed, choose a story to drop, or reduce the scope on one or more stories. Focus on completing one story at a time. As the end of the iteration approaches, programmers may have to stop working on new features and start picking up testing tasks instead. Missing some functionality from a release is better than missing the entire release because testing couldn't be completed on all or most stories.

The programmers on Lisa's team regularly automate behind-the-GUI tests in addition to unit and integration tests. They also often write the functional behind-the-GUI test cases. Sometimes they write the initial happy path executable test so they can coordinate test and code design; then a tester adds more test cases. Occasionally, they write all of the functional test cases, because the testers don't have the bandwidth to cover all of the test-intensive stories.

Everyone on the team also must be willing to take on manual testing tasks. If your team is just starting and hasn't been able to address automation needs yet, the whole team should plan time to execute manual regression test scripts as well as manually testing new features. As Lisa's team can attest, this task provides great motivation for learning how to design the application to facilitate test automation. Other teams tell us this worked for them as well.

DEALING WITH BUGS

We've known many teams that struggle with the question of how to track bugs, or whether to track them at all. As Tom and Mary Poppendieck write in their book *Implementing Lean Software Development: From Concept to Cash* [2006], defect queues are queues of rework and thus collection points for waste. Some teams simply fix bugs as soon as they're discovered. They write a unit test to reproduce the bug, fix the code so the test passes, check in the test and the bug fix, and go on. If someone breaks that piece of code later, the test will catch the regression.

Chapter 5, "Transitioning Typical Processes," talks about why your team may or may not want to use a Defect Tracking System.

Other teams find value in documenting problems and fixes in a defect tracking system (DTS), especially problems that weren't caught until after code was released. They may even look for patterns in the bugs that got to production and do root cause analysis to learn how to prevent similar issues from recurring. Still, defect systems don't provide a good forum for face-to-face communication about how to produce higher-quality code.

Lisa and her fellow testers prefer to talk to a programmer as soon as a problem is found. If the programmer can fix it immediately, there's no need to log the bug anywhere. If no programmer is available immediately to work on the problem, and there's a possibility the bug might be forgotten, they write a card for it or enter it into their DTS.

We've added this section to this chapter because this is when you run into the problem. You have been writing tests first, but are finding problems as you work with the programmer. Do you log a bug? If so, how? You've been doing your exploratory testing and found a bug from a story that was marked done. Do you log a bug for that? Let's discuss more about defects and consider options that are open to you and your team.

Is It a Defect or Is It a Feature?

First, let's talk about defects versus features. The age-old question in software development is, "What is a bug"? Some answers we've heard are: It's a deviation from the requirements or it's behavior that is not what was expected. Of course, there are some really obvious defects such as incorrect output or incorrect error messages. But what really matters is the user's perception of the quality of the product. If the customer says it is a defect, then it is a defect.

In agile, we have the opportunity to work with customers to get things fixed to their satisfaction. Customers don't have to try to think of every possible feature and detail up front. It is okay for them to change their minds when they see something.

In the end, does it really matter if it is a bug or a feature if it needs to be fixed? The customer chooses priorities and the value proposition. If software quality is a higher priority for the customer than getting all of the new features, then we should try to fix all defects as we find them.

Customers on the team use their knowledge to give the best advice they can to the team on day-to-day development. However, when a product goes to UAT and is exposed to a larger customer base, there will always be requests in the form of bugs or new enhancements.

Technical Debt

Chapter 6, "The Purpose of Testing," explains how tests help manage technical debt.

One way of thinking about defects is as technical debt. The longer a defect stays in the system and goes undetected, the greater the impact. It also is true that leaving bugs festering in a code base has a negative effect on code quality, system intuitiveness, system flexibility, team morale, and velocity. Fixing one defect in buggy code may reveal more, so maintenance tasks take longer.

Zero Bug Tolerance

Janet encourages teams that she works with to strive for "zero tolerance" toward bug counts. New agile teams usually have a hard time believing it can be done. In one organization Janet was working with, she challenged each of the five project teams to see how close they could come to zero bugs outstanding at the end of each iteration, and zero at release time.

Zero Bug Iterations

Jakub Oleszkiewicz, the QA manager at NT Services [2008], recounts how his team learned how to finish each iteration with no bugs carried over to the next one.

I think it really comes down to exceptional communication between the testers, the developers, and the business analysts. Discipline was also key, because we set a goal to close off iterations with fully developed, functional, deployable, and defect-free features while striving to avoid falling into a waterfall trap. To us, avoiding waterfall meant we had to maintain alignment with code and test activities; we tried to plan an iteration's activities so that a given feature's test cases were designed and automated at the same time as that feature's code was written. We quickly found that we were practicing a form of test-driven development. I don't think it was pure TDD, because we weren't actually executing the tests until code was checked in, but we were developing the tests as developers wrote code, and developers were asking us how our tests were structured and what our expected results were.

Conversely, we regularly asked the developers how they were implementing a given feature. This kind of two-way questioning often elevated inconsistencies in how requirements were interpreted and ultimately highlighted defects in our interpretations before code was actually committed.

Every morning during our Scrum, we further ensured parity between the functional groups within the team through simple dialogue. Communication was ridiculously good—we sat close to each other, often even at the same computer. When a defect was discovered, the developer was right there observing, taking notes, and talking through the requirements. A business analyst was always nearby to further validate our thinking. Often within minutes a resolution was checked-in, deployed to the test environment, and verified.

Both developers and testers had to be committed to this approach or it wouldn't have worked. Without discipline, the developers could have easily moved forward onto more features and let the bugs slide until the end of the project, risking an incomplete iteration. If we were not co-located as we were, communication would have suffered; likely a bug tracking system or email would have become our primary means of communicating defects, resulting in longer turn-around times and an increased probability of rework.

As part of any development, you will always need to make trade-offs. Your team may decide to release with some outstanding bugs because it is deemed more important to get new functionality out the door than to fix low-level bugs.

IT's ALL ABOUT CHOICES

Teams have solved the problem of how to handle defects in many different ways. Some teams put all of their bugs on task cards. Other teams have chosen to write a card, estimate it, and schedule it as a story. Still others suggest adding a test for every bug—that way you don't have to record the defect, just the test.

Is there one right way? Of course not! But, how do you know what is right for your team? We have some suggestions to help you choose and decide what is right for you. Think about your team and your product and what might work in your situation. First, we'll talk about what defects we should log, then we'll talk a bit about when you should fix them, and finally we'll look at what media to choose. The right combination will depend on how far along your team is in its agile journey and how mature your product is.

Decide Which Bugs to Log

Not all bugs need to be logged, but teams often struggle with which ones should be recorded and which ones don't need to be. We recommend that you avoid creating a defect report if possible. Have a conversation with a real person first, and only produce a defect report if it is truly a real problem that demands a change to the product or the programmers just can't get to it right away.

Unit Test Failures

Don't log unit test failures. If you are part of a team that is practicing TDD (test-driven development) and has good coverage with its unit tests, you know that failed tests during the build should not be logged. A failed test during the continuous integration build is a signal for the programmers to address the problem right away. Logging these bugs would be redundant and a waste of time.

Failures in Higher-Level Regression Tests

Many teams have builds that run regression tests above the unit level, such as tests behind the GUI and tests through the GUI. When one of these builds fails, should you log the bug in a DTS?

Lisa's Story

We have two builds, an "ongoing build" that runs only unit tests, and a "full build" that runs the functional tests behind and through the GUI. When the "full build" breaks, if a developer investigates and tackles the problem right away as sometimes happens, usually no bug is logged. The problem is fixed quickly. At other times, the failure is not straightforward. One of the testers investigates, narrows down the problem, and files a bug that either states the name of the failing test or provides manual steps to recreate the problem.

In either case, tests are written that reproduce the bug, and the code is fixed to make the tests pass. The tests become part of one of the builds.

—Lisa

Failing tests in themselves are a type of recorded bug. But sometimes, as in Lisa's case, more information needs to be added to allow for an effective and clean fix, so logging the defect is warranted.

Story Bugs within the Current Iteration

Don't log bugs that can be fixed immediately, especially if you would otherwise record them in an electronic DTS. If your team is working closely with the programmers and is practicing pair testing as soon as a story is completed, we strongly recommend that you don't log those bugs as long as the programmer addresses them right away. As you notice issues, talk them over with the programmer and decide whether they are real issues or not. Talk to the customer if you need to, but make a couple of notes so you remember what you saw so you can adjust your tests if needed.

If you are using index cards to log bugs, you may want to put an index card up on the task board (or a card on your electronic board) just as a reminder.

Post-Iteration Bugs (Or Those that Can't Be Fixed Immediately)

Do log bugs that can't be fixed right away. We stress testing early in order to catch as many bugs as possible while the programmers are still working on the story. We know it is cheaper to fix them when caught early; however, sometimes we just don't catch them right away. The programmer has moved on to another story and can't drop everything to fix it now. Those are the ones that are good candidates for logging. Sometimes a "bug" is really a missed requirement and needs to be handled as a story—estimated and prioritized for a future iteration.

From the Legacy System

Do log bugs that occur in the legacy system. If your product has been around a long time, it likely has a number of bugs that have been lurking in the background just waiting to be discovered. When you find them, you have a couple of choices. If your product owner thinks it is worthwhile to fix them, then log the bugs and they can be prioritized as part of the product backlog. However, if they have been around a long time and cause no issues, your product owner may decide it is not worth fixing them. In this case, *don't* bother logging them. They will never get addressed anyhow, so don't waste your time.

Found in Production

Do log all production bugs. When your application is in production, all bugs found by the customer should be logged. Depending on their severity, these bugs may be fixed immediately, at the time of the next release, or they'll be estimated, prioritized, and put in your product backlog.

Choose When to Fix Your Bugs

There are three options. All bugs you find need to be triaged to determine if you fix them now, fix them later, or don't fix them at all. This triage may be as simple as a discussion with the programmer to determine if they are really bugs in the story he is working on. The triage may be a discussion with the product owner to determine if there should be another story for the next iteration. The triage may also be a formal process with the customers to prioritize which bugs to fix.

Fix Now

The more bugs you can fix immediately, the less technical debt your application generates and the less "defect" inventory you have. Defects are also cheaper to fix the sooner they are discovered. In an article in *iSixSigma Magazine*, Mukesh Soni [2008] quotes a report from IBM that the cost to fix an error found after product release was four to five times as much as one uncovered during design, and up to 100 times more than one identified in the maintenance phase (see Figure 18-5).

Figure 18-5 shows a statistic based on phased methodology, but the statistic still holds true for agile development. It is cheaper to fix bugs that are found during development than after.

If a defect is found while developing a new feature, or is a side effect from another bug fix, it should be automatically fixed. But, as usual, this is to be applied with prudence. For example, if a bug is found that the programmers say will be difficult to fix and may destabilize the product, it should be taken to the customers to prioritize.

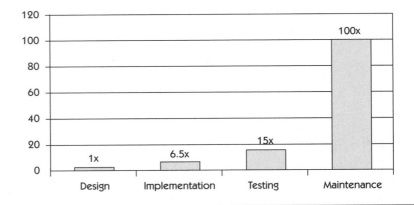

Figure 18-5   Relative costs to fix software defects (*Source:* IBM Systems Sciences Institute)

If you fix the bugs during development, you lessen the presence of bugs later in the process. Your team velocity can include time to fix bugs. Over time, your team members will get a good idea of how long they spend on fixing bugs found by the testers for a story. Hopefully, there are few. If your team is a new agile team, there may be quite a few bugs that escape development, but as the team gets more comfortable with the tools and the processes, the number of bugs found will lessen. To start, try making the estimate for a story to include two hours or half a day for fixing associated bugs.

Fix Later

Different teams have different ways of handling defects. Some teams believe that all defects found should be prioritized by the customers before they get put on the list to fix. They believe it is completely up to the customer to determine whether they really are defects, and if so, whether they should be fixed.

Never Fix

Your team has recognized a defect, but know it won't get fixed. Perhaps that section of code needs a complete rewrite later because the functionality will change, or perhaps it is just such a low-priority issue or so obscure that your customers may never find it. There are a multitude of reasons why it won't get fixed. If your triage determines this is the case, we suggest you just close the bug. Don't keep it open pretending that you will fix it someday.

Choose the Media You Should Use to Log a Bug

When we talk about media, we mean the variety of ways you can log a bug. It could be a defect tracking system or index cards, or maybe you choose to have no physical record at all.

Index Cards

Index cards (whether real or virtual cards in an online planning and tracking system) don't leave a lot of room for a lot of clerical details, but they do give great visibility to outstanding issues when they are pinned on the story board, especially if they are in another color. Some teams use screen prints and staple them to the back of the card or write the details in a text file, or even record steps in audio form on a hand-held voice recorder.

There are lots of options, but we would suggest that you pick one that contains enough information to guide someone to reproduce a problem or to focus a discussion when the programmer is ready to fix it. The card is tangible. Five hundred bugs in a DTS are just a number. A stack of 500 cards is impressive.

Use cards in the following circumstances:

- You are a disciplined agile team and are fixing all bugs within an iteration.
- You want to make bugs visible to the team.

There is nothing stopping you from having both index cards and a DTS.

Defect Tracking System

Use a DTS in the following circumstances:

- Your team is distributed.
- You need to track bugs for audit purposes or to capture them in release notes.
- You have bugs that escape an iteration and you need to remember to fix them later.
- You have a legacy system with a large number of defects.

One way or the other, you will likely want to have some kind of DTS to log some of the bugs. This does not mean you need to log them all. Be smart about which ones you do log.

None at All

Why wouldn't you log a bug? Most teams that we have worked with have set rules for themselves that no bug is fixed without a unit test. If you also have a functional automation suite, then you can catch the larger bugs with those. The argument is that if there is a test that will catch the bug, you have no need to log the bug. Anything learned from fixing the bug was captured in the test and the code. However, you need to recognize that not all tests are easy to automate.

Use tests to capture bugs in the following circumstance:

- Your team is disciplined and writes tests for every bug found.

Alternatives and Suggestions for Dealing with Bugs

As teams mature, they find procedures that work for them. They eliminate redundant tasks. They become more practiced at using story cards, story boards, and project backlogs. They use tests effectively, and learn which bugs to log and what metrics make sense to their team. In this section, we'll share some ideas that other teams have found work for them.

Set Rules

Set rules like, "The number of pink cards (bugs) should never get higher than ten at any one time." Revisit these each time you have a team retrospective. If your defect rate is going down, no worries. If the trend is the opposite, spend time analyzing the root cause of bugs and create new rules to mitigate those.

Fix All Bugs

Don't forget to fix low-priority bugs found during the iteration as well, because they have an effect on future development. In our experience, there seems to be a strong correlation between "low priority" and "quick to fix," although we don't have hard facts to support that. We suggest stopping small, isolated bugs before they become large, tangled bugs.

Combine Bugs

If you find a lot of bugs in one area, think about combining them into an enhancement or story.

Janet's Story

When I first started working at WestJet, I found a lot of small issues with the mobile application. The application worked correctly, but I was confused about the flow. I only found these issues because I was new and had no previous perceptions.

The team decided to group the issues I had raised and look at the whole issue as a new story. After studying the full problem with all of the known details, the final outcome was a solid feature. If the bugs had been fixed piecemeal, the effect would not have been so pretty.

—Janet

Treat It as a Story

If a "bug" is really missed functionality, choose to write a card for the bug and schedule it as a story. These stories are estimated and prioritized just like any other story. Be aware that bug stories may not receive as much attention as the new user stories in the product backlog. It also takes time to create the story, prioritize, and schedule it.

The Hidden Backlog

Antony Marcano, author of www.TestingReflections.com, points out that while user stories and their acceptance tests describe desired behavior, defect reports describe misbehavior. Behind each misbehavior is a desired behavior, often not previously defined. Thus, behind every defect report may be a hidden user story. He explains his experiences.

In Chapter 5, "Transitioning Typical Processes," we mentioned Antony Marcano's blog post about defect tracking systems being a hidden backlog in agile teams. Antony shares his ideas about how to bring that secret out into the open.

XP publications suggest that if you find a bug you should write an automated test reproducing it. Many teams file a bug report and then write a separate automated test. I've found that this results in duplication of effort—and therefore waste. When we write a bug report, we state the steps, what should have happened (expectation), and what actually happened (anti-expectation). An automated test tells you the same things—steps, expectation, and running it for the first time should demonstrate the anti-expectation. When you are able to write an automated acceptance test as easily as you write a bug-report *and* the test communicates as much as the bug report does *and* your backlogs and story boards allow you to manage the work involved in fixing it, then why write a separate bug report?

Bug metrics are all that remain. Bug metrics are traditionally used to help predict when software would be ready for release or highlight whether quality is improving or worsening. In test-first approaches, rather than telling us if quality is improving or worsening, it tells us how good we were at predicting tests—that is, how big the gaps were in our original thinking. This is useful information for retrospectives and can be achieved simply by tagging each test with details of when it was identified—story elaboration, post-implementation exploration, or in production. As for predicting when we will be able to release—when we are completing software of "releasable quality" every iteration—this job is handled by burn-down/burn-up charts and the like.

With one new project I was working on, I suggested that we start using a bug-tracking system when the need for one was compelling. We captured the output of exploratory testing performed inside the iteration as automated tests rather than bug reports. We determined whether the test belonged to the current story, another story, or whether these tests inspired new stories. We managed these stories as we would any other story and used burn-down charts to predict how much scope would be done by the end of the iteration. We never even set up a bug-tracking system in the end.

There is a difference between typical user stories and bug-inspired user stories, however. Previously our stories and tests only dealt with missing behaviors (i.e., features we know we want to implement in the future).

Now, they also started to represent *misbehaviors*. We found it useful to include summary information about the misbehavior in our proposed user story to help the customer prioritize it better. For example:

> *As a registered user, I want to be prevented from accessing the system if my password is entered using the incorrect case, so that I can feel safer that no one else can guess my password, **rather than** being allowed to access the system.*

The "rather than" was understood by the customer to mean "that's something that happens currently"— which is a misbehavior rather than merely a yet-to-be-implemented behavior.

Using this test-only approach to capturing bugs, I've noticed that bug-inspired stories are prioritized more as equals to the new-feature user stories, whereas before they often gave more attention to the "cool new features" in the product backlog than the misbehaviors described in the bug tracking. That's when I realized that bug-tracking systems are essentially hidden, or *secret backlogs.*

On some teams, however, the opposite is true. Fix-all-bugs policies can give more attention to bugs at the expense of perhaps more important new features in the main backlog.

Now, if I'm coaching a team mid-project, I help them to find better and faster ways of writing automated tests. I help them use those improvements in writing bug-derived automated tests. I help them find the appropriate story—new or existing—and help them harness the aggregate information useful to retrospectives. Eventually, they come to the same realization that I did: Traditional bug tracking starts to feel wasteful and redundant. That's when they decide that they no longer want or need a hidden backlog.

If bugs are simply logged in a DTS, important information might be effectively lost from the project. When we write acceptance tests to drive development, we tend to focus on desired behavior. Learning about undesired behavior from a defect, and turning that into stories is a vital addition to producing the right functionality.

Blue, Green, and Red Stickers

Each team needs to determine the process that works for it, and how to make that process easily visible. The following story is about one process that worked for Janet.

Janet's Story

A few years ago, I worked on a legacy system with lots of bugs already logged against the system before agile was introduced. One of the developers was adamant that he would not use a defect-tracking system. He firmly believed they were a waste of time. However, the testers needed the defects logged because there were so many.

The team worked out a compromise that worked for everyone. Bugs that were found during pair testing with the programmers were not recorded, because they were fixed right away. All others were logged in the DTS. Bugs that needed to be fixed in the current iteration were recorded on pink cards with the summary and bug number and then put on the story board. All others became part of the product backlog.

The programmers could look at details in the system but also asked testers for more information, if required. Because the issues were on the story board, they became part of the daily stand-ups and discussions. When a bug was fixed, the programmers wrote the fix and any extra information on the back of the card. They put a blue sticker on the card so the testers knew it was ready for testing. A green sticker meant it had been verified as fixed, and a red sticker meant it wasn't fixed and needed more work. Of course, there were lots of conversations between the testers and the programmers. James, one of the programmers, and I had a lot of fun with one bug that just wouldn't stay fixed. By the end, the card looked like it had a caterpillar on it—blue, red, blue, red, blue, and finally green. We were all quite excited when that bug was squashed.

The testers closed bugs and did most of the administration, because the DTS was their requirement. After a while, the programmers started entering what they fixed into the defect-tracking system because it was easier than writing on the card. The team still continued to use the cards because of the visibility. It was easy to see at a glance how many outstanding bugs there were in the iteration or on the backlog.

—Janet

This approach worked for this team because there was a lot of discipline in the team, and most new bugs were fixed in the iteration if they were part of the new or changed functionality. The only bugs that went into the backlog were legacy bugs that were deemed low risk.

Start Simple

We suggest using as simple a system as possible and applying complexity as required. Code produced test-first is, in our experience, fairly free of bugs by the time it's checked in. If you're finding a lot of bugs in new code, your team needs to figure out why, and take action. Try to shorten the cycle of coding, integrating and testing so that programmers get immediate feedback about code quality. Perhaps some buggy section of legacy code needs to be redesigned before it mires your team in technical debt. Maybe you need to work more closely with the business experts to understand the desired functionality.

More on retrospectives in Chapter 19, "Wrap Up the Iteration."

Another idea might be to create an ongoing "start, stop, continue" list so that you can remember some of the issues during the iteration retrospective.

FACILITATE COMMUNICATION

The daily stand-up helps teams maintain the close communication they need. Everyone on the team learns the current status of tasks and stories, and can help each other with obstacles. Often, hearing programmers describe tasks they're working on provides a clue that they may have misunderstood the customer's requirements. That signals the need for a group discussion after the stand-up. If a tester needs help with a testing issue that's come up, she might ask the team to stay after the stand-up to talk about it. Missed tasks are often identified during stand-ups, and new cards can be written on the spot.

The stand-up is a good time to look at progress. Use big, visible charts such as story boards, burndown charts, and other visual cues to help keep focus and know your status. If the end of the iteration is drawing near, and coding on a story seems "stuck," raise a red flag and ask the team what can be done about it. Perhaps some pairing or extra help will get things going. Lisa has often noted when there's a lot of testing left to do and time is running out. She asks for help to pick up the slack. The whole team focuses on what needs to be done to complete each story and talks about the best approach.

When teams use an electronic medium for keeping track of stories, there is a tendency to forget the story board. Janet finds that having both may seem like a duplication of effort, but the visibility of progress to the team far outweighs the extra overhead of writing up the task cards and moving them as they are completed. Having the story board gives your team focus during the stand-ups or when you are talking to someone outside the team about your progress.

Testers Facilitate Communication

Testers can help keep the iteration progressing smoothly by helping make sure everyone is communicating enough. Talk to programmers when they start working on a story, and make sure they understand it. Lisa finds that she can write all of the tests and examples she wants on the team wiki, but if nobody bothers to read them, they don't help. When in doubt, she goes over requirements and tests with the programmer who picks up the task cards.

Programmers will always have questions as they develop a story, even if they understand the business and the story well. It's best if a customer is available to answer questions, because that is the most direct communication. Testers shouldn't get in the way of that; however, we've observed that business experts sometimes have trouble explaining a requirement, or a programmer simply gets the wrong idea and can't get on the same page with the customer. The Power of Three applies here. Testers can help customers and programmers find a common language.

A Little Friendly Competition

Gerard Meszaros, well-known agile coach and author of *xUnit Test Patterns* [2007], shared this story about a team he was working with and how a game solved a communication issue.

> We were having trouble getting the developers to talk to the business people about their assumptions. When they did talk, the tester often got left out of the loop. The tester would sometimes discuss something with the business but never pass it on to the developer. Our project manager, Janice, decided to try to change the behavior through friendly competition.
>
> All of the developers were given blue poker chips with a "D" written on them. All of the testers got a red chip with a "T" on them, and the business people got yellow chips with a "B" on them. Whenever someone met with a counterpart from another area, he or she could exchange one chip with each person. The goal was to get the most complete sets of chips: T-B-D. The winner got a custom-made T-B-D trophy decorated with the three kinds of chips. The end result was that everyone was much keener to meet with each other because they would get more chips!

Find creative ways to get the business experts and programmers to talk and agree upon requirements. If a poker chip game gets them talking, embrace it.

Facilitating communication usually involves drawing on a whiteboard, mocking up interfaces, listing other areas that might be affected, or working through real examples. Whenever communication appears to reach a dead end, or confusion is rampant, ask for a new example and focus on that.

Lisa's Story

When retirement plan participants want to withdraw money from their accounts, many complex vesting rules and government regulations come into play. It gets worse if the participant has withdrawn money in the past. Working on a story to calculate a participant's vested balance, my team members all had different ideas on the correct algorithm, even though the product owner had worked through several examples at the beginning of the iteration. My fellow tester, Mike, asked the product owner to work through a new example, and several programmers and testers joined the session. It took a couple of rather tortuous hours of writing numbers and flowcharts on a whiteboard, but eventually they arrived at the correct formula, and everyone was on the same page.

—Lisa

Work through as many examples as you need until the team understands enough different aspects of the system. Try a different format if it's not working. For example, if pictures drawn on the whiteboard aren't sufficient to understand the story, try spreadsheets or some other format that's familiar to the business experts.

Distributed Teams

As we've noted in other chapters, having team members in different locations and different time zones means you have to work harder at communication. Phones, email, and instant messaging form the basics of communication, but better collaboration tools are developed all the time.

Chapter 9, "Toolkit for Business-Facing Tests that Support the Team," talks about some tools that can help distributed teams

Lisa's Story

One of the programmers on our team, who is also a manager, moved to India. Nanda works late into the evening there, so he's available for the Denver team in the mornings. He has a cell phone with a local Denver phone number, so it's easy to talk to him by phone as well as by instant message and email. We schedule meetings where we discuss stories, such as estimating meetings, brainstorming sessions, and iteration planning, early in the morning so he can participate. Although the team can't be as productive as we were when we were co-located, we're still able to benefit from Nanda's domain expertise and deep knowledge of the software.

If Nanda hires more team members in India, we may have to address more complex issues, such as coordinating integration and builds. We may consider more sophisticated technical solutions to communication problems.

—Lisa

You will need to experiment to see what works for your distributed team. Use retrospectives to evaluate whether collaboration and communication need improving, and brainstorm ways to improve. You, as a tester, may have a lot of experience in helping with process improvement projects. Just think about improving communication as one of those continual improvement needs.

A Remote Tester's Story

Sometimes, the testers are the remote team members. Erika Boyer of iLevel by Weyerhaeuser lives on the East Coast and works with a team in Denver. She's a tester by profession, but on her team all tasks are up for grabs. She might write fixtures to automate a FitNesse test or pair with a programmer to write production code. Being able to get in touch with people when she needs them is an issue. If she doesn't get a response when she instant-messages a coworker, she phones; every work area in the Denver office has a phone. It's not foolproof, because everyone could be in the break room at a going-away party and forgot to tell her. Teams in different locations have to make a special effort to keep each other informed.

Because Erika starts working a few hours before the team's daily stand-up, she needs work she can do alone during that time. She works with any team members who come in early in Denver and converses with other programmers late in the day about work she'll do the next morning.

Erika is able to see the team's tasks using a tool on their intranet that shows each task, its status, and its percentage complete. With a few extra accommodations, the team (which has other remote members) is able to keep up good communication.

Even from a distance, Erika has been able to transfer testing skills to the programmers but has found they think differently than testers. Her team uses these varying perspectives to their advantage by rotating all types of tasks among all of the team members.

Successful teams keep remote members "in the loop" and share skills and expertise. Distributed teams face extra challenges in successfully completing testing activities, but some minor adjustments, thoughtfulness on the part of all team members, and good communication tools help ensure that remote testers can be productive.

We all need to be able to communicate well with each other for our projects to succeed. When teams are in diverse geographic locations, they might have to work twice as hard to stay in constant touch.

REGRESSION TESTS

Unless you're on a team that's just starting its automation efforts, you have automated regression tests covering stories from previous iterations. Hopefully, these are running as part of a continual build process, or at least part of a daily build process. If they aren't, ask your team to make implementing this critical infrastructure a priority, and brainstorm with them how this might be done. Plan time in the next iteration to start a build process.

Keep the Build "Green"

Programmers should run all automated unit tests before checking in new code. However, unit tests may fail in the continual build, either because someone forgot to run them before check-in, or because of a difference in runtime environment or IDE. We have unit tests for a reason, so whenever one fails, the team's highest priority (apart from a showstopper production issue) should be to fix it and get the build working again.

Teams take different approaches to make sure their build stays "green." Lisa's team has a build process that emails results after every build. If the build fails, the person who checked in the failure usually fixes it right away. If it's not clear why the build failed, team members will get together to investigate. Their ScrumMaster has a stuffed toy that she puts on the desk of the person who "broke the build," as a visual reminder that it has to be fixed right away.

Some teams use a traffic light, ambient orb, GUI build monitoring tool, or other electronic visual way to show the build status. When the lights turn red, it's time to stop new development and fix the build. Another technique is to have a screen pop up in everyone's IDE showing that the build has failed, and the popup won't go away until you click "Ok, I'll fix the build." Have some fun with it, but keeping the build running is serious business.

In extreme cases, you may have to *temporarily* comment out a failing test until it can be diagnosed, but this is a dangerous practice, especially for a novice team. Everyone on the team should stop what they're doing if necessary until the build works again.

Keep the Build Quick

The build needs to provide immediate feedback, so keep it short. If the build takes longer than the average frequency of code check-ins, builds start to stack up, and testers can't get the code they need to test. The XP guideline for build time is ten minutes [Fowler, 2006]. Lisa's team tries to keep the build less than eight minutes, because they check in so often.

Tests that take too long, such as tests that update the database, functional tests above the unit level, or GUI test scripts, should run in a separate build process. If the team is limited in hardware, they might have to run the "full" build with the full suite of tests at night and the "ongoing" build that has only unit tests continually during working hours. Having a separate, continual "full" build with all of the regression test suites is worth the investment. Lisa's team gets feedback every 90 minutes from their "full" build, and this has proven invaluable in heading off regression issues. This secondary suite of tests does not stop a programmer from checking in their code.

Building a Regression Suite

During the iteration, you're automating new tests. As soon as these pass, add them to the regression suite, as appropriate. You may not need every edge case or permutation included in the regression suite, and you want to keep the regression suites fast enough to provide timely feedback. As each story is completed, tests that confirm its functionality should be included in the regression suite and be part of the regular build cycle.

The regression tests themselves must be under some form of version control. It's best to keep them in the same source code control system as the production code. That way, when you tag the code for production release, the tag also contains all of the versions of the tests that worked with the code. At minimum, keep a daily backup of the test code.

When tests have been added to the regression suite, their purpose changes. They no longer exist to help drive development, and they are not expected to find new bugs. There sole purpose in life is to detect unexpected changes or side effects in the system.

Checking the "Big Picture"

Hopefully, you wrote task cards to test the story in the context of the larger application and regression test other parts of the system to ensure the new story hasn't had a negative effect. You may have automated some of those end-to-end tests like the example in Chapter 12, "Summary of Testing Quadrants."

But sometimes, even if you have a large suite of regression tests, manual exploratory testing can be appropriate. The story isn't "done" until you've completed these tasks as well.

RESOURCES

As you start the iteration, make sure that test environments, test data, and test tools are in place to accommodate testing this iteration's stories. Hopefully you've anticipated these needs, but some requirements might only become obvious when you start working on a story. Collaborate with database experts, system administrators, and other team members to set up any additional infrastructure needed.

You may have brought in outside resources for this iteration to help with performance, usability, security, or other forms of testing. Include them in stand-ups and discussions with the customers as needed. Pair with them and help them understand the team's objectives. This is an opportunity to pick up new skills.

ITERATION METRICS

Chapter 15, "Tester Activities in Release or Theme Planning," talks about useful metrics to keep.

In Chapter 5, "Transitioning Typical Processes," we talked a bit about the purpose of metrics, but because metrics are critical to understanding how your coding and testing activities are progressing, we'll delve into them more here. Know what problem you are trying to solve before you start measuring data points and going to all the work of analyzing the results. In this section, we'll cover some of the typical measurements that teams gather through the iteration.

Measuring Progress

You need some way to know how much work your team has completed at any point in the iteration and an idea of how much work is left to do. You need to know when it becomes obvious that some stories can't be completed and the team needs a Plan B. Iteration burndown charts and estimated versus actual time for tasks are examples used to measure team progress. They may or may not provide value for your particular team.

Story or task boards are a good visual way to know the iteration's status, especially if color coding is used. If too many test task cards are still in the "to do" column or not enough coding task cards have been moved to "Done" or "Tested," it's time for the team to think of ways to make sure all of the testing is completed. Maybe some team members need to stop coding and start taking on testing tasks, or maybe one story or a less critical part of a story needs to be put off until the next iteration so that testing for all the other stories can be finished.

This can be accomplished with virtual story boards as well as physical ones. Get creative with your visual effects so that problems are instantly visible. Remember that no story is "done" until it's tested at all appropriate levels. Teams may have other criteria for when a story is "done," such as whether it has been peer reviewed or the automated regression tests are completed. On the story board shown in Figure 18-6, the "Done" column for each story row is the rightmost column. The column just to the left of it is the "Verify" column. The story isn't considered "done" until all the cards, including testing task cards, are in that "Done" column. A glance at the board is enough to know which stories are finished.

Even teams that don't track burndown at the task level can do so at the story level. Knowing how much work the team can do each iteration (its velocity) helps with the overall release plan, and the reprioritizing for each iteration. It simply may be enough to know the number of stories completed in an iteration if they tend to average out to the same size. Although plans are tentative at best, it's helpful to get an idea of about how many stories can be

Figure 18-6 Story board showing iteration stories and tasks. Used with permission of Mike Thomas. Copyright 2008.

completed by a hard release date or what stories might get done in the up-coming quarter.

Defect Metrics

We talked about defect metrics in Chapter 15, "Tester Activities in Release or Theme Planning" giving you some high level ideas about what to track. Gathering metrics on defects can be very time consuming so always consider the goal before you start to measure. What is the purpose of the metrics you would like to gather? How long will you need to follow the trend before you know if they are useful?

Defect containment is always a favorite metric to capture. When was the defect found? In traditional projects, it is much easier as you have "hard" requirements and coding phases. When the whole team is responsible for quality, and everyone is working together throughout, it is much harder to determine "when" the defect was injected into the system.

We would like to challenge the idea of this type of metric as not necessary in agile development. However, if you find a lot of bugs are slipping through, you may want to start tracking what type of bugs they are so you can address the root cause. For example, if the bugs could have been caught with unit tests, then maybe the programmers need more training on writing unit tests. If the bugs are missed or misunderstood requirements, then maybe not enough time is spent in iteration planning, or acceptance tests aren't detailed enough.

If you are practicing zero tolerance for defects, then you probably have no need to be tracking defects during coding and testing. A simple card on the story board will give you all the information you need.

Whatever metrics you choose to measure, go for simplicity.

Janet's Story

In one organization I was with, we tracked the number of defects logged in the DTS over several releases. These were defects that escaped the iteration or were found in the legacy system. Figure 18-7 shows the trend over a year and a half.

At the beginning, the number of issues found right after it was released to QA for final testing was high (33 issues found in one month). The customers found even more issues during UAT which lasted over two months because they were not

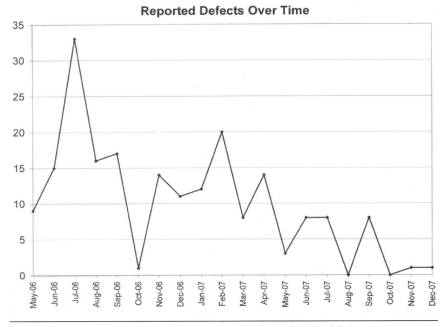

Figure 18-7   Sample Defect Trend (but stopped after a while)

confident in the quality of the release. In the month that zero defects were re-ported, we were just starting a new release so there was no new functionality to test. Over the next year, fewer and fewer defects were logged and it becomes im-possible to tell where an actual release happened by just looking at the trend.

This graph was used to show customers that the team was becoming consistent with their testing and their releases. Once the team and customers had faith the numbers were not going up, the metrics were no longer needed and were dropped.

—Janet

Don't be afraid to stop using metrics when they are no longer useful. If the problem they were initially gathered for no longer exists, there is no reason to keep gathering them.

Your team may have to provide metrics to upper managers or a Project Man-agement Office (PMO), especially if you work for a large organization. Patrick Fleisch, an Accenture Consultant who was working as a functional analyst at a

Useful Iteration Metrics

Coni Tartaglia, a software test manager at Primavera Systems, Inc., explains some ways she has found to achieve useful iteration metrics.

Collecting metrics at the end of the iteration is particularly useful when many different teams are working on the same product releases. This helps ensure all teams end the iteration with the same standard for "done." The teams should agree on what should be measured. What follows are some standards for potentially shippable software [Schwaber 2004], and different ways of judging the state of each one.

- Sprint deliverables are refactored and coded to standards.

Use a static analysis tool. Focus on data that is useful and actionable. Decide each sprint if corrective action is needed. For example, use an open source tool like FindBugs, and look for an increase each sprint in the number of priority one issues. Correct these accordingly.

- Sprint deliverables are unit tested.

For example, look at the code coverage results each sprint. Count the number of packages with unit test coverage falling into ranges of 0%–30% (low coverage), 31%–55% (average coverage), and 56%–100% (high) coverage. Legacy packages may fall into the low coverage range, while coverage for new packages should fall into the 56%–100% range, if you are practicing test driven development. An increase in the high coverage range is desirable.

- Sprint deliverables have passing, automated acceptance tests.

Map automated acceptance tests to requirements in a quality management system. At the end of the iteration, generate a coverage report showing that all requirements selected as goals for the iteration have passing tests. Requirements that do not show passing test coverage are not complete. The same approach is easily executed using story cards on a bulletin board. The intent is simply to show that the agreed-upon tests for each requirement or story are passing at the end of the sprint.

- Sprint deliverables are successfully integrated.

Check the continuous integration build test results to ensure they are passing. Run other integration tests during the sprint. Make corrections prior to the beginning of the next iteration. Hesitate to start a new iteration if integration tests are failing.

- Sprint deliverables are free of defects.

Requirements completed during the iteration should be free of defects.

- Can the product ship in [30] days?

> Simply ask yourself this question at the end of each iteration, and proceed into the next iteration according to the answer.
>
> Metrics like this are easy to collect and easy to analyze, and can provide valuable opportunities to help teams correct their course. They can also confirm the engineering standards the teams have put in place to create potentially shippable software in each iteration.

software company during the time we wrote this book, gave us the following examples of metrics his team provides to their PMO.

- Test execution numbers by story and functional area
- Test automation status (number of tests automated vs. manual)
- Line graph of the number of tests passing/failing over time
- Summary and status of each story
- Defect metrics

Gathering and reporting metrics such as these may result in significant overhead. Look for the simplest ways to satisfy the needs of your organization.

SUMMARY

At this point in our example iteration, our agile tester works closely with programmers, customers, and other team members to produce stories in small testing-coding-reviewing-testing increments. Some points to keep in mind are:

- Coding and testing are part of one process during the iteration.
- Write detailed tests for a story as soon as coding begins.
- Drive development by starting with a simple test; when the simple tests pass, write more complex test cases to further guide coding.
- Use simple risk assessment techniques to help focus testing efforts.
- Use the "Power of Three" when requirements aren't clear or opinions vary.
- Focus on completing one story at a time.
- Collaborate closely with programmers so that testing and coding are integrated.
- Tests that critique the product are part of development.
- Keep customers in the loop throughout the iteration; let them review early and often.
- Everyone on the team can work on testing tasks.

- Testers can facilitate communication between the customer team and development team.
- Determine what the best "bug fixing" choice for your team is, but a good goal is to aim to have no bugs by release time.
- Add new automated tests to the regression suite and schedule it to run often enough to provide adequate feedback.
- Manual exploratory testing helps find missing requirements after all the application has been coded.
- Collaborate with other experts to get the resources and infrastructure needed to complete testing.
- Consider what metrics you need during the iteration; progress and defect metrics are two examples.

## Chapter 19

WRAP UP THE ITERATION

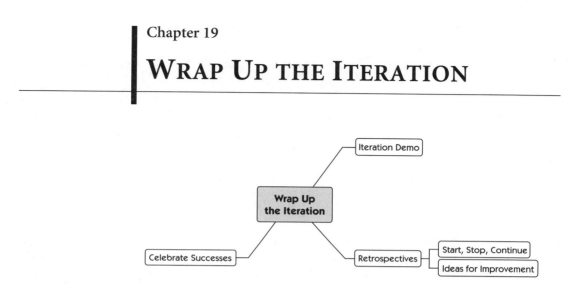

We've completed an iteration. What do testers do as the team wraps up this iteration and prepares for the next? We like to focus on how we and the rest of our team can improve and deliver a better product next time.

ITERATION DEMO

One of the pleasures of agile development is the chance to show completed stories to customers at the end of each iteration. Customers get to see a real, live, working application. They get to ask questions and give feedback. Everyone involved in the project, from both the business and technical sides, gets to enjoy a sense of accomplishment.

On Lisa's team, the testers conduct the iteration review. Among all the team members, they've usually worked on the most stories. They have a natural role as information providers, and they have a good idea what the customers need to know about the new functionality. Having testers show off the deliverables is a common practice, although there is no hard and fast rule. The business experts on the team are a good choice for conducting the demo too, because they have the best understanding of how the software meets the business needs and they'll feel greater ownership of the product. The Scrum-Master, a programmer, or a business analyst could demonstrate the new features and often does. Janet encourages rotating this honor.

Listening to the Customers

Pierre Veragen explains how his team uses iteration demonstrations.

"We shut up and listen to our customers. It's all about the chemistry of the group's presentation. Somehow, sharing the moment brings brains together—we look at things from a different perspective. The event gives birth to ideas and concepts. Some die as the next person speaks; some live on and become that great idea that differentiates the product."

The demo is a chance to show off the new stories, but the feedback customers provide is the biggest reason to do them.

Anyone may note the comments made by customers as they participate in the demo, but testers are good candidates. They may notice previously undetected inconsistencies as the demo progresses. As questions come up, customers might decide they want to change something minor, such as help text, or something bigger, such as how a feature behaves. Minor changes can usually be made into tasks and dealt with in the next iteration, but some changes are big enough to turn into stories to plan into future releases.

Iteration demos (called sprint reviews in the Scrum world) are a super opportunity to get everyone talking and thinking about the application. Take advantage of it. Review meetings are usually short and can be under half an hour. If there's time left over after demonstrating new stories, ask customers if they've experienced any problems with the previous release that they haven't reported. Do they have any general concerns, do they need help understanding how to use a feature, or have any new issues arisen? Of course, you can talk to customers anytime, but having most of the stakeholders in the room with the development team can lead to interesting ideas.

RETROSPECTIVES

Agile development means continually improving the way you work, and retrospectives are an excellent place to start identifying what and how you can do better. We recommend taking time at the end of each iteration and release cycle to look back and talk about what went well, what didn't, and what you might like to try in the next iteration. There are different approaches for conducting retrospective sessions. No matter what approach you use, it's key that each team member feels safe, everyone is respected, and there's no finger-pointing or blame.

The whole idea is to make the process better, one baby step at a time.

Start, Stop, Continue

One common exercise used in iteration retrospectives is "start, stop, continue." The team asks itself: "What went well during this past iteration? What happened that shouldn't happen again? What can we start doing to help with things that didn't go well?" Each team member can suggest things to start doing to improve, things to stop doing that weren't working, and things that are helping that should be continued. A facilitator or ScrumMaster lists them on a whiteboard or big piece of paper. Post them in a location where everyone can read them again during the iteration. Figure 19-1 shows a "stop, start, and continue" retrospective in progress. The ScrumMaster (standing) is writing stop, start, and continue suggestions on the big piece of paper on the story board.

Agile Retrospectives: Making Good Teams Great [2006] has imaginative ideas for making retrospectives more productive (see the bibliography).

Some teams start this process ahead of time. All team members write "start," "stop," and "continue" items on sticky notes, and then during the retrospective meeting they put the stickies on the board and group them by topic. "Start, stop, continue" is just one example of the terms you might use. Some other ideas are: "Things that went well," "Things to improve," "Enjoyable," "Frustrating," and "To Try." Use whatever names that work for you. It can be

Figure 19-1 A retrospective in progress. Used with permission of Mike Thomas. Copyright 2008.

hard to remember the past two weeks, much less an entire release, if that's what your retrospective covers. Research different creative approaches to reflecting on your team's experiences.

Here's a sample "stop, start, continue" list from Lisa's team:

Start:

- Sending out next sprint's stories to us earlier.
- Don't do lazy, single-record processing. Think of every service call as a remote call.
- Communicate any database changes to everyone.

Stop:

- Accepting stories without complete requirements.

Continue:

- Running FitNesse tests for the code you're working on.
- Documenting what came up in meeting or informal discussions.
- Communicating better with each other.
- Showing mock-ups early.
- Doing FitNesse driven development.

If the list of "start, stop, continue" items is long, it's a good idea to choose one or two to focus on for the new iteration. To prioritize the items, give each team member "n" votes they can assign to items. The ten people on Lisa's team each get three votes, and they can apply them all to one item if they feel that's most important, or they can vote for two or three different items. The items with the most votes are noted as the focus items. Janet has had success with this way of prioritizing as well.

In addition to "start, stop, continue" items, the team may simply write task cards for actions to be undertaken the next iteration. For example, if the ongoing build is too slow, write a card to "get ongoing build under ten minutes."

In the next iteration, take some time to look at the one or two focus items you wanted to improve. At the end of that iteration, take a checkpoint to see if you improved. If not, ask why. Should you try something different? Is it still important? It could be it has dropped in importance or really wasn't important in the big picture. If you thought you improved on a problem area and it resurfaces, you'll have to decide to do something about it or else quit talking about it.

We've found that retrospectives are a simple and highly effective way for teams to identify and address issues. The retrospective meeting is a perfect opportunity to raise testing-related issues. Bring up the issues in an objective, non-blaming way. The team can discuss each problem, what might be causing it, and write down some ideas to fix it.

Ideas for Improvements

Let's take a look at some of those items that made it onto the list for improvement. Too many times, a team will identify really big issues but never follow up and actually do something about them. For example, maybe a lot of unit-level bugs are discovered after the programmers have claimed coding was complete.

The team may decide the programmers aren't covering enough code with unit tests. They might write an action item to run the code coverage tool before they check in new code, or start writing a "unit tests" task card for each story to make sure they're completed. Perhaps the team didn't finish all the test automation tasks before the iteration ended. As they discuss the problem, the team finds that the initial executable tests were too complex, and they need to focus on writing and automating a simple test first, or pair for a better test design. Make sure the action items are concrete.

Agile teams try to solve their own problems and set guidelines to help themselves improve. Action items aimed at one problem may help with others. When Lisa's team had trouble finishing stories and getting them tested during each iteration, it came up with various rules over the course of a few retrospectives:

- Finish high-level test cases for all stories by the fourth day of the iteration.
- Deliver one story to test by the fourth day of the iteration.
- Focus on finishing one story at a time.
- 100% of features must be checked in by close of business on the next-to-last day of the iteration.

These rules did more than help the team finish testing tasks. They facilitated a flow and rhythm that helped the team work at a steady, sustainable pace over the course of each iteration.

Begin the next retrospective meeting by reviewing the action items to see what items were beneficial. Lisa's team puts happy, sad, or neutral faces next to items to denote whether the team tried them and found them successful. The team should figure out the reasons behind any sad faces. Were some items simply forgotten? Did time constraints keep the team from trying a new activity? Did it just seem to be less of a good idea later? These discussions might lead to changing the improvement item or evolving it into a new one.

When the actions for improvement become a habit to the team, they no longer need to be written on the "stop, start, and continue" list. "Start" items that work well may be moved to the "Continue" column. Some ideas don't work, or prove to be unnecessary, and those can also be taken off the list for the next iteration.

Refer to your ideas for improvement and action items during the iteration. Post them in a location (on a wall or online) where everyone sees them often. Lisa's team sometimes goes through the list during a mid-iteration stand-up meeting. If you think of new improvement ideas during the iteration, write them down, possibly even on the existing list, so you won't forget for the next iteration.

It's a good idea to keep track of things that get in your way throughout the iteration. Keep an impediment backlog on some big visible chart. Talk about the impediments in each iteration, and write task cards or take action to eliminate them.

See the bibliography for good resources for lean development practices.

An Approach to Process Improvement

Rafael Santos, VP of Software Development and Chief ScrumMaster at Ultimate Software, and Jason Holzer, the Chief PSR (Performance, Security, Reliability) Architect, explained to us that their teams found retrospectives that used the "stop, start, and continue" model ineffective. They made "stop, start, and continue" lists, but those didn't provide enough focus to address issues.

Instead, the ScrumMaster kept an impediment backlog, and the team found that worked better than retrospectives. Impediments may be related to testing or tools.

They also do value stream mapping to find the biggest "wait time," and use the "five whys" from Toyota to understand which impediment is the biggest or which constraint needs to be addressed.

One example shared was that in a team with three programmers and one tester, the biggest problem was a testing bottleneck. Rafael asked the team what the tester does and wrote those items on a whiteboard. Then he asked the programmers which of those things on the board they couldn't do. There was only one item they felt they couldn't handle. This helped the programmers

> understand how everyone on the development team, not only the testers, could be responsible for testing tasks. This was a highly effective exercise.
>
> Creative approaches like this help new agile teams tackle difficult testing challenges. Retrospectives are a good environment for experimenting.

Use retrospectives as an opportunity to raise testing-related issues and get the whole team thinking about possible solutions. We've been pleasantly surprised with the innovative ideas that come out of an entire team focusing on how to improve the way it works.

CELEBRATE SUCCESSES

Agile development practices tend to moderate the highs and lows that exist in more traditional or chaotic processes. If your waterfall team finally manages to push a release out the door after a year-long cycle ending in a two-month stressful fix-and-test cycle, everyone may be ready to celebrate the event with a big party—or they might just collapse for a couple of weeks. Agile teams that release every two weeks tend to stay in their normal coding and testing groove, starting on the next set of stories after drawing just enough breath to hold an iteration review and retrospective. This is nice, but you know what they say about all work and no play.

Make sure your team takes at least a little time to pat itself on the back and recognize its achievements. Even small successes deserve a reward. Enjoyment is a vital agile value, and a little motivation helps your team continue on its successful path. For some reason, this can be hard to do. Many agile teams have trouble taking time to celebrate success. Sometimes you're eager to get going with the next iteration and don't take time to congratulate yourselves on the previous accomplishments.

Lisa's team ends an iteration every other Thursday and conducts its retrospective, iteration review, and release the following day. After their meetings conclude, they usually engage in something they call "Friday Fun." This sometimes consists of playing a silly trivia or board game, going out for a drink, or playing a round of miniature golf. Getting a chance to relax and have a good laugh has a team-building side benefit.

For bigger milestones, such as a big release or achieving a test coverage goal, the whole company has a party to celebrate, bringing in catered food or going out to a restaurant on Friday afternoon. This is a nice reward and recognizes for everyone on both the business and technical teams.

If yours is a new agile team, motivate yourselves by rewarding small accomplishments. Cheer the rising number of unit tests passing in each build. Oooh and aaah over the chart showing actual burn down matching the projected burn down. Ring a bell when the broken unit tests in the build are fixed (okay, that one might be annoying, but recognize it in some way.)

Celebrate your individual successes, too. Congratulate your coworker for completing the project's first performance test baseline. Give your DBA a gold star for implementing a production back-up system. Give yourself a treat for solving that hard test-automation problem. Bring cookies to your next meeting with the customers. Recognize the programmer who gave you a JavaScript harness that sped up testing of some GUI validations. Use your imagination.

The Shout-Out Shoebox

We love the celebration idea we got from Megan Sumrell, an agile trainer and coach. She shared this with an agile testing Open Space session at Agile 2007.

> Celebrating accomplishments is something I am pretty passionate about on teams. On a recent project, we implemented the Shout-Out Shoebox. I took an old shoebox and decorated it. Then, I just cut a slit in the top of the lid so people could put their shout-outs in the box. The box is open to the entire team during the course of the sprint.
>
> Anytime team members want to give a "shout-out" to another team member, they can write it on a card and put it in the box. They can range from someone helping you with a difficult task to someone going above and beyond the call of duty. If you have distributed team members, encourage them to email their shout-outs to your ScrumMaster who can then put them in the box as well.
>
> At the end of our demo, someone from the team gets up and reads all of the cards out of the box. This is even better if you have other stakeholders at your demo. That way, folks on your team are getting public recognition for their work in front of a larger audience. You can also include small give-aways for folks, too.

It may be a cliché, but little things can mean a lot. The Shout-Out Shoebox is a great way to recognize the value different team members contribute.

Taking time to celebrate successes lets your team take a step back, get a fresh perspective, and renew its energy so it can keep improving your product. Give team members a chance to appreciate each other's contributions. Don't fall into a routine where everyone has their head down working all the time.

In agile development, we get a chance to stop and get a new perspective at the end of each short iteration. We can make minor course corrections, decide to try out a new test tool, think of better ways to elicit examples from customers, or identify the need for a particular type of testing expertise.

SUMMARY

- In this chapter, we looked at some activities to wrap up the iteration or release.
- The iteration review is an excellent opportunity to get feedback and input from the customer team.
- Retrospectives are a critical practice to help your team improve.
- Look at all areas where the team can improve, but focus on one or two at a time.
- Find a way to keep improvement items in mind during the iteration.
- Celebrate both big and small successes, and recognize the contributions from different roles and activities.
- Take advantage of the opportunity after each iteration to identify testing-related obstacles, and think of ways to overcome them.

Chapter 20

SUCCESSFUL DELIVERY

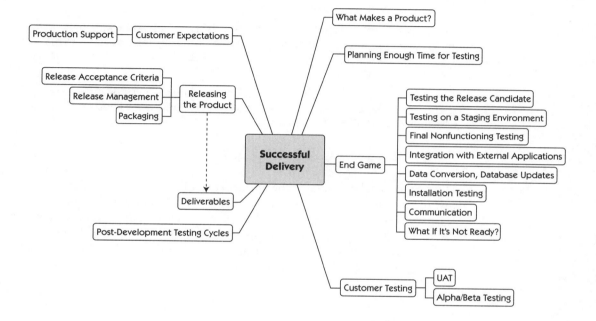

In this chapter, we share what you as a tester can do to help your team and your organization successfully deliver a high-quality product. The same process and tools can be used for shrink-wrapped products, customized solutions, or internal development products. Agile testers can make unique contributions that help both the customer and developer team define and produce the value that the business needs.

WHAT MAKES A PRODUCT?

Many of the books on agile development talk about the actual development cycle but neglect to talk about what makes a product and what it takes to successfully deliver that product. It's not enough to just code, test, and say it's done. It's like buying something from a store: If there is great service to go with the purchase, how much more likely are you to go back and buy there again?

I was talking to my friend, Ron, who buys and sells coins. Over the years he has developed a very good reputation in the industry and has turned away prospective clients because he is so busy.

When I asked him his secret, he said, "It's not a secret. I just work with my customers to make them feel comfortable and establish a trusting relationship with them. In the end, both I and my customer need to be happy with the deal. It only takes one unhappy customer to break my reputation."

Agile teams can learn from Ron's experience. If we treat our customers with respect and deliver a product they are happy with, we will have a good relationship with them, hopefully for many years.

—Janet

Our goal is to deliver value to the business in a timely manner. We don't want just to meet requirements but also to delight our customers. Before we release, we want to make sure all of the deliverables are ready and polished up appropriately. Hopefully, you started planning early to meet not only the code requirements but to plan for training, documentation, and everything that goes into making a high-value product.

Fit and Finish

Coni Tartaglia, a software test manager with Primavera Systems, Inc., explains "fit and finish" deliverables.

It is helpful to have a "Fit and Finish" checklist. Sometimes fit and finish items aren't ready to be included in the product until close to the end. It may be necessary to rebuild parts of the product to include items such as new artwork, license or legal agreements, digital signatures for executables, copyright dates, trademarks, and logos.

It is helpful to assemble these during the last full development iteration and incorporate them into the product while continuous integration build cycles are running so that extra builds are not needed later.

Business value is the goal of agile development. This can include lots beyond the production code. Teams need to plan for all aspects of product delivery.

Imagine yourself in the middle of getting your release ready for production. You've just finished your last iteration and are wrapping up your last story test. Your automated regression suite has been running on every new build, or at least on every nightly build. What you do now will depend on how disciplined your process has been. If you've been keeping to the "zero tolerance" for bugs, you're probably in pretty good shape.

If you're one of those teams that thinks you can leave bugs until the end to fix, you're probably not in such good shape and may need to introduce an iteration for "hardening" or bug fixes. We don't recommend this, but if your team has a lot of outstanding bugs that have been introduced during the development cycle, you need to get those addressed before you go into the end game. We find that new teams tend to fall into this trap.

In addition, there are lots of varied components to any release, some in the software, some not. You have customers who need to install and learn to use the new features. Think about all those elements that are critical to a successful release, because it's time to wrap up all those loose ends and hone your product.

Bob Galen, an agile coach and end-game expert, observes that agile development may not have seeped into every organizational nook and cranny. He notes, "Agile testers can serve as a conduit or facilitator when it comes to physical delivery of the software."

PLANNING ENOUGH TIME FOR TESTING

Because testing and coding are part of one process in agile development, we'd prefer not to make special plans for extra testing time, but in real life we might need some extra time.

Most teams accumulate some technical debt, despite the best intentions, especially if they're working with legacy code. To maintain velocity, your team may need to plan a refactoring iteration at regular intervals to add tests, upgrade tools, and reduce technical debt. Lisa's team conducts a refactoring sprint about every six months. While the business doesn't usually receive any direct benefits at the end of a refactoring sprint, the business experts understand that these special sprints result in better test coverage, a solid base for future development, reduced technical debt, and a higher overall team velocity.

Some teams resort to "hardening" iterations, where they spend time only finding and fixing bugs, and they don't introduce any new functionality. This is a last resort for keeping the application and its infrastructure solid. New teams may need an extra iteration to complete testing tasks, and if so, they budget time for that in the release plan.

Use retrospectives and other process improvement practices to learn ways to integrate testing and coding so that the code produced in each iteration is production-ready. When that goal is achieved, work to ensure that a stable build that could be released to production is available every day. Lisa's team members thought that this was an unattainable goal in the days when they struggled to get any stable build before release, but it was only a couple of years before almost every build was release-worthy.

When your build is stable, you are ready to enter the "End Game."

THE END GAME

What is the end game? We've heard people call the time right before delivery many things, but the "end game" seems to fit best. It's the time when the team applies the finishing touches to the product. You're dotting your i's and crossing your t's. It's the last stretch before the delivery finish line. It's not meant to be a bug-fix cycle, because you shouldn't have any outstanding bugs by then, but that doesn't mean you might not have one or two to fix.

You might have groups in your organization that you didn't involve in your earlier planning. Now it's time to work closely with the folks that administer the staging and production environments, the configuration managers, the database administrators outside of your team, and everyone who plays a role in moving the software from development to staging and production. If you weren't working with them early this time, consider talking to these folks during your next release planning sessions, and keep in touch with them throughout the development cycle.

Bob Galen tells us that the testers on his team have partnered with the operations group that manages the staging and production environments. Because the operations group is remote, it finds that having guidance from the agile team is particularly valuable.

There are always system-level tests that can't be automated, or are not worth automating. More often than not, your staging environment is the only place where you can do some system-level integration tests or system-level load and stress testing. We suggest that you allot some time after development for these types of finishing tasks. Don't code right up to the end.

Plan as much time for the end game as you need. Janet has found that the length of time needed for the end game varies with the maturity of the team and the size of the application. It may be that only one day is needed to finish the extra tasks, but it may be one week or sometimes as much as a whole two-week iteration. The team from the example used in Chapter 12, "Summary of Testing Quadrants," scheduled two weeks, because it was a complex system that required a fair bit of setup and system testing.

Lisa's Story

When I worked on a team developing applications for a client, we had to follow the client's release schedule. Testing with other parts of the larger system was only possible during certain two-week windows, every six or eight weeks. Our team completed two or three iterations, finishing all of the stories for each as if they were releasing each iteration.

Then we entered a testing window where we could coordinate system testing with other development teams, assist the client with UAT, and plan the actual release. This constituted our end game.

—Lisa

If you have a large organization, you might have ten or fifteen teams developing software for individual products or for separate areas of functionality for the same application. These areas or products may all need to release together, so an integrated end game is necessary. This does not mean that you leave the integration until the very end. Coordination with the other teams will be critical all along your development cycle, and if you have a test integration system, we recommend that you be sure that you have tried to integrate long before the end game.

You also may have considerations beyond your team, for example, working with software delivered by external teams at the enterprise level.

Use this end-game time to do some final exploratory testing. Step back and look at the whole system and do some end-to-end scenarios. Such testing will confirm that the application is working correctly, give you added confidence in the product, and provide information for the next iteration or release.

Testing the Release Candidate

We recommend that the automated regression testing be done against every release candidate. If you're following our recommendation to run automated regression tests continually on each new build, or at least daily, you've already done this. If some of your regression tests are manual, you'll need to plan time for those or they might not get done. A risk assessment based on changes made to each build will determine what tests need to be run if there is more than one release candidate.

Test on a Staging Environment

Whether you are using traditional or agile development processes, a staging environment that mimics production is vital for final testing before release, as well as for testing the release process itself. As part of the end game, your application should be deployed to staging just like you would deploy it to production, or as your customers would on their environments. In many organizations that Janet has seen, the staging environment is usually shared among multiple projects, and the deployment must be scheduled as part of the release planning. Consider ahead of time how to handle dependencies, integrating with other teams using the staging environment, and working with external third parties. It might feel like "traditional" test planning, but you might be dealing with teams that haven't embraced agile development.

Although agile promotes continuous integration, it is often difficult to integrate with third-party products or other applications outside your project's control. Staging environments can have better controls so that external applications may connect and have access to third-party test environments. Staging environments can also be used for load and performance testing, mock deploys, fail-over testing, and manual regression tests and exploratory functional testing. There are always configuration differences between environments so your staging environment is a good place to test these.

Final Nonfunctional Testing

Load testing should be scheduled throughout the project on specific pieces of the application that you are developing. If your staging environment is in high demand, you may not be able to do full system load testing until the end game.

By this time, you should be able to do long-running reliability tests on all product functionality. Check for crashes and degradation of performance with normal load. When done at release time, it should be a final confirmation only.

Fault tolerance and recovery testing is best done on your staging environment as well, because test environments usually don't have the necessary setup. For these same reasons, you may only be able to test certain aspects of security. One example is https, a secure http connection through encrypted secure sockets. Some organizations may choose to have the necessary certificates on their staging environment only. Other examples are clustering or data replication. Make sure you involve all parties who need to be included in this testing.

Integration with External Applications

Your team may be agile, but other product teams in your organization, or third parties your team works with, may not be.

Janet's Story

In one organization that I worked with, the third-party partner that approved credit cards had a test account that could be used, but it was only accessible from the staging environment.

To test during development, test stubs were created to return specified results depending on the credit card number used. However, this wasn't sufficient because the third party sometimes changed functionality on its end that we weren't aware of. Testing with the actual third party was critical to the success of the project, and it is a key part of the end game.

—Janet

Coordinate well in advance with other product teams or outside partners that have products that need to integrate with your product. If you have identified these risks early and done as much up-front testing as possible, the testing done during the end game should be final verification only. However, there are always last-minute surprises, so you may need to be prepared to make changes to your application.

Tools like simulators and mock objects used for testing during development can help alleviate some of the risks, but the sooner you can test with external applications, the lower the risk.

Data Conversion and Database Updates

As we are developing an application, we change fields, add columns in the database, or remove obsolete ones. Different teams tackle this in different ways. Some teams re-create the database with each new build. This works for new applications, because there is no existing data. However, after an application exists in production and has associated data, this approach won't work.

An application needs to consider the data that is part of the product. As with so much in agile development, a joint effort by database experts, programmers, and testers on the team is required to ensure successful release of database changes. Janet has seen a couple of different tactics for dealing with data conversion and backward compatibility. Database scripts can be created by the developers or database administrators as the team makes changes. These scripts become part of the build and are continually tested. Another option is for the team to run "diffs" on the database after all of the database changes have been made.

If you're a tester, ask your database administrator/developer to help your team ensure that schemas are kept consistent among the production, testing, and staging environments. Find a way to guarantee that all changes made in the test environments will be done in the staging and production environments during release. Keep the schemas matching (except for the new changes still under development) in terms of column names, triggers, constraints, indices, and other components. The same discipline applied to coding and testing also should be applied to database development and maintenance.

Lisa's Story

We recently had a bug released to production because some of the test schemas, including the one used by regression tests, were missing a constraint. Without the constraint in place, the code didn't fail. This triggered an effort to make sure the exact same update scripts get run against each schema to make changes for a given release.

It turned out that different test schemas had small differences, such as old columns still remaining in some or columns in different order in different schemas, so it wasn't possible to run the same script in every environment. Our database administrator led a major effort to re-create all of the test schemas to be perfectly compatible with production. He creates one script in each iteration with all necessary database changes and runs that same script in the staging and production environment when we release. This seems simple, but it's easy to miss subtle differences when you're focused on delivering new features.

—Lisa

Automating data migrations enhances your ability to test them and reduces the chance for human error. Native database tools such as SQL, stored procedures, data import tools such as SQL*Loader and bcp, shell scripts, and Windows command files can be used for automation because they can be cloned and altered easily.

No matter how the database update and conversion scripts are created or maintained, they need to be tested. One of the best ways to ensure all of the changes have been captured in the update scripts is to use the customer's data if it is available. Customers have a habit of using the application in weird and wonderful ways, and the data is not always as clean as we would like it. If the development team cleans up the database and puts extra restrictions on a column, the application on the customer's site might blow up as soon as a query touches a piece of data that does not match the new restrictions. You need to make sure that any changes you've made are still compatible with existing data.

Lisa's Story

My team uses the staging environment to test the database update scripts. After the scripts are run, we do manual testing to verify that all changes and data conversions completed correctly. Some of our GUI test scripts cover a subset of regression scenarios. This gives us confidence about releasing to production, where our ability to test is more limited.

—Lisa

When planning a data conversion, think about data cleanup as part of the mitigation strategy. You have the opportunity to take the data that was entered in some of the "weird and wonderful" ways we mentioned before and massage or manipulate it so it conforms to the new constraints. This type of job can take a long time to do but is often very worthwhile in terms of maintaining data integrity.

Not everyone can do a good enough simulation of production data in the staging environment. If a customer's data is not available, a mitigation strategy is to have a UAT at the customer site. Another way to mitigate risk is to try to avoid large-scale updates and release in smaller stages. Develop new functionality in parallel with the old functionality and use a system property to "turn on" one or the other. The old functionality can continue to work in production until the new functionality is complete. Meanwhile, testing can be done on the new code at each iteration. New columns and tables can be added to production tables without affecting the old code so that the data migration or conversion for the final release is minimized.

Installation Testing

Organizations often have a separate team that deploys to production or creates the product set. These team members should have the opportunity to practice the deployment exactly as they would for production. If they use the deployment to staging as their proving ground, they can work out any of the problems long before they release to the customer.

Testing product installations can also mean testing various installations of shrink-wrapped products to different operating systems or hardware. How does the product behave? Does it do what is expected? How long will the system need to be down for installation? Can we deploy without taking an outage? Can we make the user experience as pleasant as possible?

Janet's Story

I had an experience a while ago that was not so pleasant, and it led me to wish that someone had tested and fixed the issue before I found it. I bought a new laptop and wanted to transfer my license for one of my applications to the new computer. It came with a trial version of the same application, so the transfer should have been easy, but the new PC did not recognize the product key—it kept saying it was invalid. I called the support desk and after a bit of diagnostics, I was informed they were considered different products, so the key wouldn't work.

Two more hours of support time, and the issue was fixed. The trial version had to be removed, an old version had to be reinstalled, the key had to be reentered, and all updates since the original purchase had to be uploaded. How much easier would it have been for the development team to test that scenario and offer the customer an informative message saying, "The trial version is not compatible with your product key." A message such as that would have let me figure out the problem and solve it myself rather than taking the support person's time.

—Janet

Take the time you need to determine what your requirements are for testing installation. It will be worth it in the end if you satisfy your customers.

Communication

Constant communication between different development team members is always important, but it's especially critical as we wrap up the release. Have extra stand-up meetings, if needed, to make sure everything is ready for the release. Write cards for release tasks if there's any chance some step might be forgotten.

Lisa's Story

My team releases after each iteration. We usually have a quick stand-up on the last afternoon of the sprint to touch base and identify any loose ends. Before the team had a lot of practice with releases, we wrote release task cards such as "run database update script in staging" and "verify database updates in production."

With more experience at deploying, we no longer need those cards unless we have a new team member who might need an extra reminder. It never hurts to have cards for release tasks, though.

—Lisa

Reminders of tasks, whether they are in a full implementation plan or just written on task cards as Lisa's team does, are often necessary. On simple implementations, a whiteboard works well.

What If It's Not Ready?

By constantly tracking progress in many forms, such as builds, regression test suites, story boards, and burndown charts, a team usually knows well in advance when it's in trouble on a release. There's time to drop stories and readjust. Still, last-minute disasters can happen. What if the build machine breaks on the last day of the iteration? What if the test database crashes so that final testing can't be completed? What if a showstopper bug isn't detected until final functional testing?

We strongly advise against adding extra days to an iteration, because it will eat into the next iteration or release development. An experienced team might be flexible enough to do this, but it can derail a new team. Still, desperate times call for desperate measures. If you release every two weeks, you may simply be able to skip doing the actual release, budget time into the next iteration to correct the problems and finish up, and release on the next scheduled date. If testing tasks are being put off or ignored and the release goes ahead, bring up this issue with the team. Did the testing needs change, or is the team taking a chance and sacrificing quality to meet a deadline? The team should cut the release scope if the delivery date is fixed and in jeopardy.

If your release cycle is longer, more like three months, you should know in advance if your release is in jeopardy. You probably have planned an end game of at least two weeks, which will just be for final validation. When you have a longer release cycle, you have more time to determine what you should do, whether it's dropping functionality or changing the schedule.

If your organization requires certain functionality to be released on a fixed day and last-minute glitches threaten the release, evaluate your alternatives. See if you can continue on your same development cycle but delay the release itself for a day or a week. Maybe the offending piece of code can be backed out temporarily and a patch done later. The customers have the ultimate say in what will work for the business.

On the rare occasions when our team has faced the problem of last-minute show-stoppers, we've used different approaches according to the situation. If there's nothing critical that has to be released right now, we sometimes skip the release and release two iterations' worth on the next release day. If something critical has to go in, we delay the release a day or two. Sometimes we can go ahead and release what we have and do a patch release the next day. On one occasion, we decided to have a special one-week iteration to correct the problems, release, and then go back to the normal two-week iteration schedule.

After more than four years of practicing agile development, we have a stable build almost 100% of the time, and we feel confident about being able to release whenever it's necessary. We needed a lot of discipline and continual improvement to our process in order to feel that a more flexible approach could work for us. It's also nice to be able to release a valuable bit of functionality early, if we can. What we've worked hard to avoid is falling into a death spiral where we can never release on schedule and we're always playing catch-up.

Don't beat yourself up if you can't release on time. Your team is doing its best. Do spend time analyzing why you got behind schedule, or over-committed, and take action to keep it from happening again.

—Lisa

Work to prevent a "no go" situation with good planning, close collaboration, driving coding with tests, and testing as you code. If your tracking shows the release could be in jeopardy, remove the functionality that can't be finished, if possible. If something bad and unexpected happens, don't panic. Involve the whole team and the customer team, and brainstorm about the best solution.

CUSTOMER TESTING

There are a couple of different ways in which to involve your customers to get their approval or feedback. User Acceptance Testing can be fairly formal, with sign-offs from the business. It signifies acceptance of a release. Alpha or beta testing is a way to get feedback on a product you are looking to release but which is not quite ready.

UAT

User Acceptance Testing (UAT) is important in large customized applications as well as internal applications. It's performed by all affected business departments to verify usability of the system and to confirm existing and new (emphasis on new) business functionality of the system. Your customers are the ones who have to live with the application, so they need to make sure it works on their system and with their data.

In previous chapters we've often talked about getting the customers involved early, but at those times, the testing is done on specific features under development. UAT is usually done after the team decides the quality is good enough to release. Sometimes though, the timeline dictates the release cycle. If that is the case, then try moving the UAT cycle up to run parallel with your end game. The application should be stable enough so that your team could deploy to the customer's test system at the same time as they deploy to staging.

Janet's Story

In one team I joined, the customers were very picky. In fact, the pickiest I had ever seen. They always asked for a full week of UAT just to be sure they had the time to test it all. They had prepared test cases and checked them all, including all the content, both in English and in French. Showstopper bugs included spelling errors such as a missing accent in the French content. Over time, as they gained more confidence in our releases and found fewer and fewer errors, they relaxed their demands but still wanted a week, just in case they couldn't get to it right away. Their business group was very busy.

One release came that pushed the timeline. We were being held to the release date but couldn't get all the functionality in and leave two weeks for the end game. We talked with the business users and we decided to decrease the end game to one week; the business users would perform their UAT while the project team finished up their system testing and cleanup. The only reason we were able to do this was because of the trust the customer had in our team and the consistency of our releases.

The good news was that, once again, the UAT found no issues that could not wait until the next release.

—Janet

Figure 20-1 shows an example timeline with a normal UAT at the end of the release cycle. The team starts working on the next release, doing release planning, and starts the first iteration with all team members ready to go.

Work with customers so that they understand the process, their role, and what is expected of them. If the UAT is not smooth, then the chances are there will be a high level of support needed. An experienced customer test team may have defined test cases, but most often its testing is ad hoc. Customers may approach their testing as if they were doing their daily job but will probably focus on the new functionality. This is an opportunity to observe how people

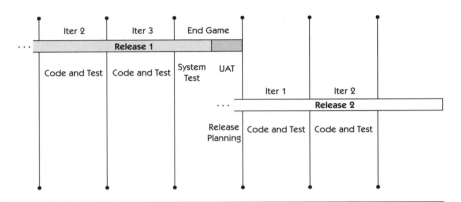

Figure 20-1 Release timeline with UAT

use the system and to get feedback from them on what works well and what improvements would help them.

Testers can provide support to the customers who are doing the UAT by reviewing tests run and defects logged, and by tracking defects to completion. Both of us have found it helpful to provide customers involved in doing UAT with a report of all of the testing done during development, along with the results. That helps them decide where to focus their own testing.

Alpha/Beta Testing

If you are an organization that distributes software to a large customer base, you may not have a formal UAT. You are much more likely to incorporate alpha or beta testing. Your team will want to get feedback on new features from your real customers, and this is one mechanism for doing so. Alpha testing is early distribution of new versions of software. Because there are likely to be some major bugs, you need to pick your customers wisely. If you choose this method of customer feedback, make sure your customers understand their role. Alpha testing is to get feedback on the features—not to report bugs.

Beta testing is closer to UAT. It is expected that the release is fairly stable and can actually be used. It may not be "ready for prime time" for most customers, but many customers may feel the new features are worth the risk. Customers should understand that it is not a formal release and that you are asking them to test your product and report bugs.

As a tester, it is important to understand how customers view the product, because it may affect how you test. Alpha and beta testing may be the only time you get to interact with end users, so take advantage of the chance to learn how well the product meets their needs.

POST-DEVELOPMENT TESTING CYCLES

If you work in a large organization or are developing a component of a large, complex system, you may need to budget time for testing after development is complete. Sometimes the UAT testing, or the test coordination, isn't as smooth as it could be, so the timeline stretches out. Test environments that include test versions of all production systems may only be available for small, scheduled windows of time. You may need to coordinate test sessions with teams working on other applications that interact with yours. Whatever the reason, you need extra testing time that does not include the whole development team.

Lisa's Story

I worked on a team developing components of both internal and external applications for a large telecom client. We could only get access to the complete test environment at scheduled intervals. Releases were also tightly scheduled.

The development team worked in two-week iterations. It could release to the test environment only after every third iteration. At that time, there was a two-week system integration and user acceptance test cycle, followed by the release.

Someone from my team needed to direct the post-development testing phase. Meanwhile, the developers were starting a new iteration with new features, and they needed a tester to help with that effort.

The team had to make a special effort to make sure someone in the tester role followed each release from start to finish. For example, I worked from start to finish on release 1. Shauna took over the tester role as the team started work on the first iteration of release 2, while I was coordinating system testing and UAT on release 1. Shauna stayed as primary tester for release 2, while I assumed that role for release 3.

—Lisa

Figure 20-2 shows an example timeline where the UAT was extended. This could happen for any number of reasons, and the issue may not always be UAT. Most of the team is ready to start working on the next release, but often

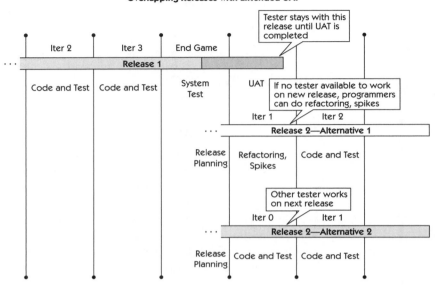

Figure 20-2   Release timeline—alternative approach with extended UAT

a tester is still working with customers, completing final testing. Sometimes a programmer will be involved as well. There are a couple of options. If the team is large enough, you can probably start the next release while a couple of team members work with the existing release (Release 2—Alternative 2 in Figure 20-2). If you have a small team, you may need to consider an Iteration 0 with programmers doing refactoring or spikes (experiments) on new functionality so that the tester working with the customer does not get left behind (Release 2—Alternative 1 in Figure 20-2).

Be creative in dealing with circumstances imposed on your team by the realities of your project. While plans rarely work as expected, planning ahead can still help you make sure the right people are in place to deliver the product in a timely manner.

DELIVERABLES

In the first section of this chapter we talked about what makes a product. The answer to this will actually depend on the audience: Who is accepting the product, and what are their expectations?

If your customers need to meet SOX (Sarbanes-Oxley)compliance requirements, there will be certain deliverables that are required. For example, one customer Janet has worked with felt test results should be thoroughly documented, and made test results one of their SOX compliance measurement points, while a different customer didn't measure test results at all. Work with compliance and audit personnel to identify reporting needs as you begin a project.

How much documentation is enough? Janet always asks two questions before answering that question: "Who is it for?" and "What are they using it for?" If there are no adequate answers to those questions, then consider whether the documentation is really needed.

Deliverables are not always for the end customer, and they aren't always in the form of software. There are many internal customers, such as the production support team members. What will they need to make their job easier? Workflow diagrams can help them understand new features. They would probably like to know if there are work-arounds in place so they can help customers through problems.

Janet often gets asked about test coverage of code, usually by management. How much of the application is being tested by the unit tests or regression tests? The problem is that the number by itself is just a number, and there are so many reasons why it might be high or low. Also, code coverage doesn't tell you about features that might have been missed, for which no code exists yet. The audience for a deliverable such as code coverage should not be management, but the team itself. It can be used to see what areas of the code are not being tested.

Training could be considered a deliverable as well. Many applications require customized training sessions for customers. Others may only need online help or a user manual. Training could determine the success of your product, so it's important to consider. Lisa's team often writes task cards for either a tester or the product owner to make sure training materials and sessions are arranged. Some people may feel training isn't the job of testers or anyone else on the development team. However, agile teams aim to work as closely as possible with the business. Testers often have the domain expertise to be able to at least identify training that might be needed for new or updated features. Even if training isn't the tester's responsibility, she can raise the issue if the business isn't planning training sessions.

Many agile teams have technical writers as part of the team that write online help or electronic forms of documentation. One application even included training videos to help get started, and different members of the team were the trainers. It is the responsibility of the team to create a successful product.

Nonsoftware Deliverables

Coni Tartaglia, software test manager at Primavera Systems, Inc., reflects on what has worked for her team in delivering items that aren't code but are necessary for a successful release.

> Aside from the software, what is the team delivering? It is helpful to have a conversation with the people outside of the development team who may be concerned with this question. Groups such as Legal, Product Marketing, Training, and Customer Support will want to contribute to the list of deliverables.
>
> After there is agreement on what is being delivered, assembly of the components can begin, and the Release Management function can provide confirmation of the delivery through execution of a release checklist. If the release is an update to an existing product, testers can check the deliverables from previous releases to ensure nothing critical is left out of the update package. Deliverables can include legal notices, documentation, translations, and third-party software that are provided as a courtesy to the customers.

Agile teams are delivering value, not just software. We work together with the customer team to improve all aspects of the product.

There are no hard and fast rules to what should be delivered with the product. Think of deliverables as something that adds value to your product. Who should be the recipient of the deliverable, and when does it make the most sense to deliver it?

RELEASING THE PRODUCT

When we talk about releasing the product, we mean making it available to the customer in whatever format that may take. Your organization might have a website that gets updated or a custom application that is delivered to a few large customers. Maybe the product is shrink-wrapped and delivered to millions of PCs around the world, or downloaded off the Internet.

Release Acceptance Criteria

How do you know when you're done? Acceptance criteria are a traditional way of defining when to accept the product. Performance criteria may have to be met. We capture these for each story at the start of each iteration, and we may also specify them for larger feature sets when we begin a theme or epic. Customers may set quality criteria such as a certain percentage of code covered by automated tests, or that certain tests must pass. Line items such as having zero critical bugs, or zero bugs with serious impact to the system, are often part of the release criteria. The customers need to decide how they'll know when there's enough value in the product. Testers can help them define release criteria that accomplish their goals.

Agile teams work to attain the spirit of the quality goals, not just the letter. They don't downgrade the severity of bugs to medium so they can say they achieved the criterion of no high-severity bugs. Instead, they frequently look at bug trends and think of ways to ensure that high-severity bugs don't occur in production.

Your quality level should be negotiated with your customer up front so that there are no unpleasant surprises. The acceptance tests your team and your customers defined, using real examples, should serve as milestones for progress toward release. If your customer has a very low tolerance for bugs, and 100% of those acceptance tests must be passing, your iteration velocity should take that into consideration. If new features are more important than bug fixes, well, maybe you will be shipping with bugs.

A Tale of Multitiered "Doneness"

Bob Galen, agile coach and author of *Software Endgames*, explains how his teams define release acceptance criteria and evaluate whether they've been met.

> I've joined several new agile teams over the past few years, and I've seen a common pattern within those teams. My current team does a wonderful job of establishing criteria at a user story or feature level—basically defining acceptance criteria. We've worked hard at refining our acceptance criteria. Initially they were developed from the Product Owners' perspective, and often they were quite ambiguous and ill-defined. The testers decided they could really assist the customers in refining their tests to be much more relevant, clear, and testable. That collaboration proved to be a significant win at the story level, and the Product Owners really valued the engagement and help.

> Quite often the testers would also automate the user story acceptance tests, running them during each sprint but also demonstrating overall acceptance during the sprint review.

One problem we had, though, was getting this same level of clarity for "doneness" at a story level to extend beyond the individual stories. We found that often, when we approached the end of a Sprint or the end game of a release, we would have open expectations of what the team was supposed to accomplish within the sprint. For example, we would deliver stories that were thoroughly tested "in the small"; that is, the functionality of those stories was tested but the stories were not integrated into our staging environment for broader testing. That wasn't part of our "understanding," but external stakeholders had that expectation of the teams' deliverables.

The way the teams solved this problem was to look at our criteria as a multitiered set of guiding goals that wrap each phase, if you will, of agile development. An example of this is shown in Table 20-1.

Defining doneness at these individual levels has proven to work for our teams and has significantly improved our ability to quantify and meet all of our various customer expectations. Keep in mind that there is a connection among all of the criteria, so defining at one level really helps define the others. We often start at the Release Criteria level and work our way "backwards."

Agile development doesn't work if stories, iterations, or releases aren't "done." "Doneness" includes testing, and testing is often the thing that gets postponed when time is tight. Make sure your success criteria at every level includes all of the necessary testing to guide and validate development.

Table 20-1   Different Levels of Doneness

Activity	Criteria	Example
Basic Team Work Products	Doneness criteria	Pairing or pair inspections of code prior to check-in, or to development, execution, and passing of unit tests
User Story Level	Acceptance tests	Development of FitNesse-based acceptance tests with the customer AND their successful execution and passing
Sprint or Iteration Level	Doneness criteria	Defining a Sprint Goal that clarifies the feature development and all external dependencies associated with a sprint
Release Level	Release criteria	Defining a broad set of conditions (artifacts, testing activities or coverage levels, results/metrics, collaboration with other groups, meeting compliance levels, etc.) that, if met, would mean the release could occur

Each project, each team, each business is unique. Agile teams work with the business experts to decide when they're ready to deliver software to production. If the release deadline is set in stone, the business will have to modify scope. If there's enough flexibility to release when the software has enough value, the teams can decide when the quality criteria have been met and the software can go to production.

Challenging Release Candidate Builds

Coni Tartaglia's team uses a checklist to evaluate each release candidate build. The checklist might specify that the release candidate build:

- Includes all features that provide business value for the release, including artwork, logos, legal agreements, and documentation
- Meets all build acceptance criteria
- Has proof that all agreed-upon tests (acceptance, integration, regression, nonfunctional, UAT) have passed
- Has no open defect reports

Coni's team challenges the software they might ship with a final set of inspections and agreed-upon "release acceptance tests," or "RATS." She explains:

> The key phrase is "agreed-upon tests." By agreeing on the tests in advance, the scope for the release checklist is well defined. Include system-level, end-to-end tests in the RATS, and select from the compatibility roster tests, which will really challenge the release candidate build. Performance tests can also be included in RATs. Agree in advance on the content of the automation suites as well as a subset of manual tests for each RAT.

> Agree in advance which tests will be repeated if a RAT succeeds in causing the failure of a release candidate build. If the software has survived several iterations of continuously run automated regression tests, passing these final challenges should be a breeze.

Defining acceptance criteria is ultimately up to the customers. Testers are in a unique position to help the customer and development teams agree on the criteria that optimize product quality.

Traditional software development works in long time frames, with deadlines set far in advance and hurdles to clear from one phase to the next. Agile development lets us produce quality software in small increments and release as necessary. The development and customer teams can work closely to define and decide what to release and when. Testers can play a critical role in this goal-setting process.

Release Management

Many organizations have a release management team, but if you don't, someone still does the work. Many times in a small organization it is the QA manager who fulfills this role. The person leading the release may hold a release readiness meeting with the stakeholders to evaluate readiness.

A release readiness checklist is a great tool to use to walk through what is important to your team. The intention of this checklist is to help the team objectively determine what was completed and identify the risks associated with not completing a task.

For example, if training is not required because the changes made to the product were transparent to the end user, then the risk is low. However, if there were significant changes to the process for how a new user is created in the system, the risk would be very high to the production support or help teams, and may warrant a delay. The needs of all stakeholders must be considered.

Release notes are important for any product release. The formality of these depends on the audience. If your product is aimed at developers, then a "read me" text file is probably fine. In other cases, you may want to make them more formal. Whatever the media, they should address the needs of the audience. Don't provide a lot of added information that isn't needed.

When Janet gets a new release, one of the first things she does is check the version and all of the components. "Did I get what they said they gave me? Are there special instructions I need to consider before installing, such as dependencies or upgrade scripts?" Those are good simple questions to answer in release notes. Other things to include are the new features that the customer should look for.

Release notes should give special consideration to components that aren't part of what your development team delivered, such as a help file or user manuals prepared by a different team. Sometimes old release notes get left on the release media, which may or may not be useful to the end user. Consider what is right for your team and your application.

Packaging

We've talked a lot about continual integration. We tend to take it for granted and forget what good configuration management means. "Build once, deploy multiple times" is part of what gives us confidence when we release. We know that the build we tested in staging is the same build that the customer tested in UAT and is the build we release to production. This is critical for a successful release.

If the product is intended for an external customer, the installation should be easy, because the installation may be the first look at the product that customer has. Know your audience and its tolerance level for errors. How will the product be delivered? For example, if it is to be downloaded off the Internet, then it should be a simple download and install. If it is a huge enterprise system, then maybe your organization needs to send a support person with the product to help with the install.

CUSTOMER EXPECTATIONS

Before we spring new software on our customers, we'd better be certain they are ready for it. We must be sure they know what new functionality to expect and that they have some means to deal with problems that arise.

Production Support

Many organizations have a production or operations support team that maintains the code and supports customers after it's in production. If your company has a production support team, that group is your first customer. Make it your partner as well. Production support teams receive defect reports and enhancement requests from the customers, and they can work with your team to identify high-risk areas.

Very often the production support team is the team that accepts the release from the development team. If your organization has this type of hand-off, it is important that your development team works closely with the production support team to make it a smooth transition. Make sure the production support team understands how to use the system's log files and the messaging and monitoring systems in order to keep track of operations and identify problems quickly.

Understand Impact to Business

Every time a deployment to production requires an outage, the product is unavailable to your customer. If your product is a website, this may be a huge impact. If your product is an independent product to be downloaded onto a PC, the impact is low. Agile teams release frequently to maximize value to the business, and small releases have a lower risk of a large negative impact. It's common sense to work with the business to time releases for time periods that minimize disruption. Automate and streamline deployment processes as much as possible to keep downtime windows small. A quick deployment process is also helpful during development in short iterations where we may deploy a dozen times in one day.

International Considerations

Markus Gärtner, an "agile affected" testing group lead, explains his team's approach to timing its releases:

> We build telecommunications software for mobiles, so we usually install our software at night, when no one is likely to make calls. This might be during our office hours, when we're handling a customer in Australia, but usually it is during our nighttime.
>
> My colleagues who do the actual installation—there are three within our team—are most likely to appear late during next day's office hours because we don't have a separate group for these tasks.

As businesses and development teams become more global, release timing gets more complicated. Fortunately, production configurations can make releases easier. If your production environment has multiple application servers, you may be able to bring them down one at a time for release without disrupting users.

New releases should be as transparent as possible to the customer. The fewer emergency releases or patches required after a release, the more confidence your customer will have in both the product and the development team.

Learn from each release and take actions to make the next one go more smoothly. Get all roles, such as system and database administrators, involved in the planning. Evaluate each release and think of ways to improve the next one.

Summary

This chapter covered the following points:

- Successful delivery of a product includes more than just the application you are building. Plan the non-software deliverables such as documentation, legal notices, and training.
- The end game is an opportunity to put the spit and polish, the final finishing touches, on your product.

- Other groups may be responsible for environments, tools, and other components of the end game and release. Coordinate with them ahead of time.
- Be sure to test database update scripts, data conversions, and other parts of the installation.
- UAT is an opportunity for customers to test against their data and to build their confidence in the product.
- Budget time for extra cycles as needed, such as post-development cycles to coordinate testing with outside parties.
- Establish release acceptance criteria during release planning so that you can know when you're ready to release.
- Testers often are involved in managing releases and testing the packaging.
- When releasing the product, consider the whole package—what the customer needs and expects.
- Learn from each release, and adapt to improve your processes.

Part VI

SUMMARY

In Chapter 21, "Key Success Factors," we pull things together and summarize the agile approach to testing.

Chapter 21

KEY SUCCESS FACTORS

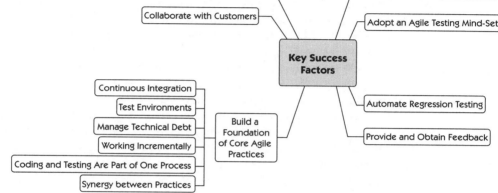

Having traveled through an iteration and beyond, following an agile tester as she engages in many activities, we can now pick out some key factors that help testers succeed on agile teams and help agile teams succeed at delivering a high-quality product. We think agile testers have something special to offer. "Agile-infected" testers learn how to apply agile practices and principles to help their whole team produce a better product. "Test-infected" programmers on agile teams learn how to use testing to produce better work. Lines between roles are blurred, but that's a good thing. Everyone is focused on quality.

We have gleaned some critical testing guidelines for agile teams and testers from our own trial and error as well as from teams with which we've worked. These guidelines are built on the agile testing matrix, on our experience of learning to overcome cultural and organizational obstacles, our adventures in performing the tester role on agile teams, and our experience of figuring out how best to use test automation. We like lucky numbers, so in this chapter we present seven key factors that help an agile tester succeed.

We asked a small group of people who were reviewing some of our chapters to suggest the order in which to present these success factors. The results varied quite a bit, although many (but not all) agreed on the top two. Pick the success factor that will give you the biggest return on investment, and start working on it today.

Success Factor 1: Use the Whole-Team Approach

When the whole development team takes responsibility for testing and quality, you have a large variety of skill sets and experience levels taking on whatever testing issues might arrive. Test automation isn't a big problem to a group of skilled programmers. When testing is a team priority, and anyone can sign up for testing tasks, the team designs testable code.

Making testers truly part of the development team means giving them the support and training they need to adapt to the fast pace of agile development. They have time to acquire new skills in order to collaborate closely with members of both the development and customer teams.

If you manage an agile team, use the suggestions in Part II, "Organizational Challenges," to help your team adopt the whole-team approach. Remember that quality, not speed, is the goal of agile development. Your team needs testers to help customers clarify requirements, turn those into tests that guide development, and provide a unique viewpoint that will promote delivery of a solid product. Make sure the testers can transfer their skills and expertise to the rest of the team. Make sure they aren't pigeonholed in a role such as only doing manual testing. Make sure that when they ask for help (which may require considerable courage on their part), their team members give it. The reverse is true, too; a tester should step up whenever someone needs assistance that they can provide.

See Chapter 2, "Ten Principles for Agile Testers," for an example of how the "Power of Three" works.

If you're a tester on an agile team, and there are planning meetings and design discussions happening that don't include you, or the business users are struggling to define their stories and requirements alone, it's time to get up and go talk to the rest of the team. Sit with the programmers, invite yourself to meetings, and propose trying the "Power of Three" by involving a tester, a programmer, and a business expert. Be useful, giving feedback and helping the customers provide examples. Make your problems the team's problems, and make their problems yours. Ask your teammates to adopt a whole-team approach.

Success Factor 2: Adopt an Agile Testing Mind-Set

In Chapter 2, "Ten Principles for Agile Testers," we cautioned agile testers to lose any "Quality Police" mind-set they might have brought with them. You're on an agile team now, where programmers test and testers do whatever they can think of to help the team deliver the best possible product. As we emphasized in Chapter 2, an agile testing attitude is proactive, creative, open to new ideas, and willing to take on any task. The agile tester constantly hones her craft, is always ready to collaborate, trusts her instincts, and is passionate about helping the team and the business succeed.

We don't mean that you should put on your Super Tester cape and go protect the world from bugs. There's no room for big egos on agile teams. Your teammates share your passion for quality. Focus on the team's goals and do what you can to help everyone do their best work.

Use agile principles and values to guide you. Always try the simplest approach to meeting a testing need. Be courageous in seeking help and experimenting with new ideas. Focus on delivering value. Communicate as directly and as often as possible. Be flexible in responding to change. Remember that agile development is people-centric, and that we should all enjoy our work. When in doubt, go back to the values and principles to decide what to do.

See Chapter 2, "Ten Principles for Agile Testers," for more about the agile testing mindset.

An important component of the agile testing mind-set is the drive to continually find better ways to work. A successful agile tester constantly polishes her craft. Read good books, blogs, and articles to get new ideas and skills. Attend local user group meetings. Participate in mailing list discussions to get feedback on problems or new ideas. If your company won't pay for you to attend a good conference, put what you've learned into an experience report to exchange for a free conference registration. Giving back to your testing and agile development communities will help you, too.

Experiment with new practices, tools, and techniques. Encourage your team to try new approaches. Short iterations are ideally suited to experimentation. You might fail, but it'll be fast, and you can try something else.

If you manage agile testers or an agile team, give them time to learn and provide support for the training they need. Remove obstacles so that they can do their best work.

When you're faced with problems that impact testing, bring those problems to the team. Ask the team to brainstorm ways to overcome these obstacles. Retrospectives are one place to talk about issues and how to resolve them. Keep an impediment backlog and address one or two in every iteration. Use big visible charts, or their virtual equivalents, to ensure that everyone is aware of problems that arise and that everyone can track the progress of coding and testing.

SUCCESS FACTOR 3: AUTOMATE REGRESSION TESTING

Can an agile team succeed with no test automation? Maybe, but the successful teams that we know rely on automated regression tests. As we've said often in this book, if you're spending all your time doing manual regression testing, you'll never have time for the important exploratory testing that will ferret out the damaging behaviors lurking in the code.

Agile development uses tests to guide development. In order to write code to make a test pass, you need a quick and easy way to run the test. Without the short feedback cycle and safety net regression that suites provide, your team will soon become mired in technical debt, with a growing defect queue and ever-slowing velocity.

Automating regression tests is a team effort. The whole team should choose appropriate tools for each type of test. Thinking about tests up front will let programmers design code for ease of test automation. Use the Agile Testing Quadrants and test automation pyramid to help you automate different types of tests effectively.

Remember to start simply. You'll be surprised at how much value some basic automated smoke tests or automated unit tests can provide.

Test automation is a team effort. It's also hard, at least at first. There's often a big "hump of pain" to overcome. If you manage a development or testing team, make sure you're providing enough support in the form of time, training, and motivation. If you're a tester on a team with no automation, and the programmers are too frantic trying to write production code to stop and think about testing, you have a big challenge ahead of you. Experiment with different ways of getting support from management and from team members to start some tiny automation effort.

See Part II for more on the Agile Testing Quadrants.

See Chapter 14, "Automation Strategy," for more on the test automation pyramid.

See the bibliography for resources on promoting change.

SUCCESS FACTOR 4: PROVIDE AND OBTAIN FEEDBACK

Feedback is a core agile value. The short iterations of agile are designed to provide constant feedback in order to keep the team on track. Testers are in a unique position to help provide feedback in the form of automated test results, discoveries made during exploratory testing, and observations of actual users of the system.

Agile Is All about Feedback

Bret Pettichord, CTO of WatirCraft and co-author of *Lessons Learned in Software Testing*, shared these thoughts on the importance of feedback to agile development.

Agile methods allow your team to get feedback regarding the software you are building. That's the point. The feedback works on several levels. Pair programming gives developers instant feedback on their code. Stories represent units of work where testers and analysts can give feedback to developers. Iteration releases facilitate feedback from outside the team. Most agile practices are valuable because they create feedback loops that allow teams to adapt.

A lot of teams adopt Agile with a grab-bag approach without quite realizing the point of the practices. They pair-program without discussion or changing drivers. They send code to QA that the testers can't test because the story boundaries are arbitrary; they can't tell whether they found a bug or just the end of the story. Iterations become schedule milestones rather than real opportunities to improve alignment and adjust objectives.

The reason Agile teams can do with less planning is because feedback allows you to make sure that you are on course. If you don't have meaningful feedback, then you're not agile. You're just in a new form of chaos.

On my last project, we defined our stories so that they made sense to everyone on the team. Our analysts, testers, and developers could all understand and review individual stories. But we found that we had to create a larger grouping, which we called features, to facilitate meaningful review from outside our team. We made sure all the stories in a feature were complete before soliciting feedback from outside the team.

Being able to give and receive meaningful feedback is often a challenge for people. Yet it is crucial to success with Agile.

Agile teams get into terrible binds when executives or clients hand them a list of requirements at the start, tell them to use Agile (because it's faster), and then don't want to participate in the feedback process.

Agile isn't faster all by itself. Agile is only a benefit in a world that acknowledges the value of adapting. And that adaptability needs to go all the way to whoever is funding the project. It is not enough for the team to be agile. The sponsors need to be agile too. Are all of the requirements really required? Do we know exactly what the software needs to look like from the start?

> Agile is faster because feedback allows you to find and focus on the most valuable features. If you are certain you know what needs to be built, don't use Agile. If you don't have time to gather and act on feedback from customers, then don't use Agile. If you are sure that everyone understands exactly what needs to be done from the start, then don't use Agile.
>
> Agile practices build a technical and organizational infrastructure to facilitate getting and acting on feedback. If you aren't going to adapt to feedback, then this infrastructure is waste that will only slow you down.
>
> To us, the value of agile development isn't that it's faster but that it delivers enough value quickly enough to help the business grow and succeed. Testers play a key role in providing the feedback that allows that to happen.

Testers need feedback too. How do you know that you have the right examples of desired behavior from the customers? How do you know if the test cases you wrote reflected these examples correctly? Can the programmers understand what to code by looking at the examples you've captured and the tests you've created?

One of the most valuable skills you can learn is how to ask for feedback on your own work. Ask the programmers if they get enough information to understand requirements and whether that information guides their coding. Ask customers if they feel their quality criteria are being met. Take time in both the iteration planning meetings and retrospectives to talk about these issues and suggest ways to improve.

SUCCESS FACTOR 5: BUILD A FOUNDATION OF CORE PRACTICES

An old saying in the testing business is, "You can't test quality into the product." This is, of course, true of agile development as well. We feel you can't deliver high-quality software without following some fundamental practices. While we think of these as agile practices, they've been around longer than the term "agile development," and they're simply core practices of successful software development.

Continuous Integration

Every development team needs source code management and continuous integration to be successful. You can't test effectively if you don't know exactly what you're testing, and you can't test at all if you have no code you can deploy. All team members need to check in their work at least once a day. Every integration must be verified by an automated build that includes tests to provide rapid feedback about the state of the software.

See the bibliography for more information about continuous integration.

Implementing a continuous integration process should be one of the first priorities of any software development team. If your team doesn't have at least a daily verified build, stop what you're doing and get one started. It's that important. It doesn't have to be perfect to start with. If you have a huge system to integrate, it's definitely more challenging. In general, though, it's not that difficult. There's a plethora of outstanding tools, both open source and commercial, available for this purpose.

Test Environments

You can't test productively without a test environment that you control. You need to know what build is deployed, what database schema is being used, whether anyone else is updating that schema, and what other processes are running on the machine.

Hardware is getting less expensive all the time, and more open source software is available that can be used for test environments. Your team must make the investment so that you can effectively conduct automated and manual exploratory tests quickly and efficiently. If there's a problem with the test environment, speak up and let it be a problem for the team to solve creatively.

Manage Technical Debt

Even good software development teams, feeling time pressure, neglect refactoring or resort to quick fixes and hacks to solve a problem quickly. As the code becomes more confusing and hard to maintain, more bugs creep in, and it doesn't take long before the team's velocity is consumed by bug fixes and trying to make sense out of the code in order to add new features. Your team must constantly evaluate the amount of technical debt dragging it down and work on reducing and preventing it.

People often say, "Our management won't give us time to do things right, we don't have time to refactor, and we're under tight deadlines." However, it's not hard to make a clear business case showing what growing technical debt is costing the company. There are many ways to measure code and defect rates that can translate technical debt into its impact on the bottom line. Merely pointing to your decreasing velocity may be enough. Businesses need their software development teams to remain consistently productive. They may have to reduce the scope of their desired features in order to allow enough time for good, test-guided code design and good practices such as continual small refactoring.

Good coverage from automated regression tests is key to minimizing technical debt. If these are lacking, budget time in each iteration to build up the automated tests, plan a "refactoring iteration" to upgrade or add necessary tools, and write tests and do major refactoring efforts. In every iteration, take the time to guide code with tests, refactor the code you're touching as needed, and add automated tests where they're missing. Increase your estimates to account for this work. In the long run, the team will be able to go much faster.

Working Incrementally

One reason agile teams are able to create a quality product is that they work on a small scale. Stories represent a few days of work, and each story may be broken into several thin slices or steel threads and built step-by-step. This allows testing each small piece and then incrementally testing as the pieces are put together.

If your team members are tempted to take on a large chunk of functionality at once, encourage them to look at a stepwise approach. Ask questions: "What's the central business value in this story? What's the most basic path through this piece of code? What would come next?" Suggest writing task cards to code and test the small pieces, get a proof of concept for your design, and confirm your test and test automation strategy.

Read more about small chunks and thin slices in Chapter 8, "Business-Facing Tests that Support the Team."

Coding and Testing Are Part of One Process

People who are new to agile often ask agile testers, "What do you do until all the stories are finished and you can test?" Experienced agile practitioners say, "Testers must be involved throughout the whole iteration, the whole development process. Otherwise it doesn't work."

Testers write tests, based on examples provided by customers, to help programmers understand the story and get started. Tests and examples provide a common language that everyone involved in producing the software understands. Testers and programmers collaborate closely as coding proceeds, and they both also collaborate closely with the customers. Programmers show testers the functionality they've written, and testers show programmers the unexpected behaviors they've found. Testers write more tests as coding proceeds, programmers make them pass, and testers do more exploratory testing to learn whether the right value has been delivered. Each agile iteration consists of dozens of constant, quick, incremental test-code-test-code-test iterations.

When this collaboration and feedback cycle is disturbed, and testing is separated from development, bad things happen. If a story is tested in the iteration after which it was coded and bugs are found, the programmer has to stop working on the new story, remember how the code worked for the last iteration's story, fix it, and wait for someone to test the fix. There are few facts in software development, but we know for sure that bugs are cheaper to fix the sooner they're found.

Read more about coding and testing in Chapter 18, "Coding and Testing."

When coding is constantly guided by tests, and testing happens alongside coding, we're much more likely to achieve the behavior and provide the value that the customer wanted. Testing is a team responsibility. If your team doesn't share this view, ask everyone to think about their focus on quality, their desire to deliver the best possible product, and what steps they can take to ensure that the team achieves its goals.

Synergy between Practices

A single agile development practice such as continuous integration can make a difference, but the combination of multiple agile practices is greater than the sum of the parts. Test-driven design, collective code ownership, and continuous integration together deliver rapid feedback, continually improving code design and the ability to deliver business value quickly. Automating tests is good, but using automated tests to drive development, followed up by exploratory testing to detect gaps or weaknesses, is many levels of magnitude better.

Some practices don't work well in isolation. Refactoring is impossible without automated tests. It's possible to do small releases in a mini-waterfall fashion and avoid all benefits of agile development. If your on-site customer isn't empowered to make decisions, her value to the team is limited.

Agile practices were designed to complement each other. Take time to understand the purpose of each one, consider what is needed to take full advantage of each practice, and make thoughtful decisions about what works for your team.

SUCCESS FACTOR 6: COLLABORATE WITH CUSTOMERS

Some of the greatest value that testers contribute to agile teams is helping customers clarify and prioritize requirements, illustrating the requirements with concrete examples of desired behavior and user scenarios, and turning those examples into executable tests. Testers speak the domain language of the business and the technical language of the development team. We make good facilitators and translators.

Never get in the way of direct communication between programmers and customers. Do encourage as much direct communication as possible. Use the "Power of Three." When requirements are missed or misunderstood, a customer, programmer, and tester need to work together to get questions answered. Get the customers talking in front of a whiteboard or its virtual equivalent as often as necessary. If customers are scattered around the campus, the country, or the globe, use every tool you can find to enhance communication and collaboration. Teleconferences, instant messages, and wikis aren't an ideal replacement for face-to-face conversation, but they beat sending emails or not talking at all.

SUCCESS FACTOR 7: LOOK AT THE BIG PICTURE

This is a generalization, of course, but we've found that testers tend to look at the big picture, and usually from a customer point of view. Programmers usually have to focus on delivering the story they're working on now, and while they may be using tests to guide them, they have to focus on the technical implementation of the requirements.

This big-picture viewpoint is a huge contribution to the team. Test-driven development, done well, delivers solid code that may, in isolation, be free of defects. What if that new feature causes some apparently unrelated part of the application to break? Someone has to consider the impact to the larger system and bring that to the team's attention. What if we've overlooked some little detail that will irritate the customers? The new UI may be flawlessly coded, but if the background color makes the text hard to read, that's what the end user's going to notice.

Part III explains how to use the Agile Testing Quadrants.

Use the Agile Testing Quadrants as a guide to help you plan testing that will cover all the angles. Use the test pyramid idea to ensure good ROI from your test automation. Guiding development with tests helps make sure you don't miss something big, but it's not perfect. Use exploratory testing to learn more about how the application should work, and what direction your testing needs to take. Make your test environments as similar as possible to production, using data that reflects the real world. Be diligent about re-creating a production-style situation for activities such as load testing.

It's easy for everyone on the team to narrowly focus only on the task or story at hand. That's a drawback of working on small chunks of functionality at a time. Help your team take a step back now and then to evaluate how your current stories fit into the grand scheme of the business. Keep asking yourselves how you can do a better job of delivering real value.

SUMMARY

Testing and quality are the responsibility of the whole team, but testers bring a special viewpoint and unique skills. As a tester, your passion for delivering a product that delights your customers will carry you through the frustrations you and your team may encounter. Don't be afraid to be an agent for continual improvement. Let agile principles and values guide you as you work with the customer and development teams, adding value throughout each iteration.

In this concluding chapter, we looked at seven key factors for successful agile testing:

1. Use the whole-team approach.
2. Adopt an agile testing mind-set.
3. Automate regression testing.
4. Provide and obtain feedback.
5. Build a foundation of core practices.
6. Collaborate with customers.
7. Look at the big picture.

GLOSSARY

This glossary contains the authors' definitions of terms used throughout this book.

Acceptance Test Acceptance tests are tests that define the business value each story must deliver. They may verify functional requirements or nonfunctional requirements such as performance or reliability. Although they are used to help guide development, it is at a higher level than the unit-level tests used for code design in test-driven development. Acceptance test is a broad term that may include both business-facing and technology-facing tests.

Application programming interface (API) APIs enable other software to invoke some piece of functionality. The API may consist of functions, procedures, or classes that support requests made by other programs.

Build A build is the process of converting source code into a deployable artifact that can be installed to run the application. The term "build" also refers to the deployable artifact.

Component A component is a larger part of the overall system that may be separately deployable. For example, on the Windows platform, dynamic linked libraries (DLLs) are used as components, Java Archives (JAR files) are components on the Java platform, and a service-oriented architecture (SOA) uses Web Services as components.

Component Test A component test verifies a component's behavior. Component tests help with component design by testing interactions between objects.

Conditions of Satisfaction Conditions of satisfaction, also called satisfaction conditions or conditions of business satisfaction, are key assumptions and decisions made by the customer team to define the desired behavior of the code delivered for a given story. Conditions of satisfaction are criteria by which the outcome of a story can be measured. They evolve during conversations with the customer about high-level acceptance criteria for each story. Discussing conditions of satisfaction helps identify risky assumptions and increases the team's confidence in writing and correctly estimating all the tasks to complete the story.

Context-Driven Testing Context-driven testing follows seven principles, the first being that the value of any practice depends on its context. Every new project and every new application may require different ways of approaching a project. All seven practices can be found on the website www.context-driven-testing.com/.

Customer Team The customer team identifies and prioritizes the features needed by the business. In Scrum, these features become epics or themes, which are further broken into stories and comprise the product backlog. Customer teams include all stakeholders outside of the development team, such as business experts, subject-matter experts, and end users. Testers and developers work closely with the customer team to specify examples of desired behavior for each story and turn those examples into tests to guide development.

Customer Test A customer test verifies the behavior of a slice or piece of functionality that is visible to the customer and related directly back to a story or feature. The terms "business-facing test" and "customer-facing test" refer to the same type of test as customer test.

Development Team The development team is the technical team that produces the software requested by the customer team. Everyone involved in delivering software is a developer, including programmers, testers, database experts, system administrators, technical writers, architects, usability experts, and analysts. This development team works together to produce the software and deliver value to the business, whether they are a co-located team or a virtual team.

Epic An epic is a piece of functionality, or feature, described by the customer and is an item on the product backlog. An epic is broken up into related stories that are then sized and estimated. Some teams use the term "theme" instead of epic.

Exploratory Testing Exploratory testing is interactive testing that combines test design with test execution and focuses on learning about the application.

See Chapter 10, "Business-Facing Tests that Critique the Product," for an extensive definition of exploratory testing.

Fake Object A fake object replaces the functionality of the depended-on component with a simpler implementation. It emulates the behavior of the real depended-on component but is easier to use for testing purposes.

Feature A feature is a piece of functionality described by the customer and is an item on the product backlog. A feature is broken up into related stories that are then sized and estimated. In agile development, the terms "epic" or "theme" are often used in place of "feature."

Functional Test Functional tests verify the system's expected behavior given a set of inputs and/or actions.

Greenfield Greenfield projects are new application development projects starting from scratch with no existing code base. There are no constraints, so development teams have many options open to them.

Integrated Development Environment (IDE) An Integrated Development Environment, or IDE, is a set of tools that support programming and testing. It usually includes an editor, compiler or intepreter debugger, refactoring capabilities, and build automation tools. IDEs usually enable integration with a source code control system and provide language-specific support to help with code design.

Iteration An iteration is a short development cycle, generally from one to four weeks, at the end of which production-ready code can potentially be delivered. Several iterations, each one the same length, may be needed to deliver an entire theme or epic. Some teams actually release the code to production each iteration, but even if the code isn't released, it is ready for release.

Java Messaging Service (JMS) The Java Messaging Service (JMS) API is a messaging standard that enables application components based on the Java 2 Platform, Enterprise Edition (J2EE) to create, send, receive, and read messages.

Legacy System A legacy system is one that does not have any (or few) automated regression tests. Introducing changes in legacy code, or refactoring it, might be risky because there are no tests to catch unintended changes in system behavior.

Multipurpose Internet Mail Extensions (MIME) Multipurpose Internet Mail Extensions, or MIME, extend the format of Internet mail to enable non-textual messages, multipart message bodies, and non-US-ASCII textual messages and headers.

Mock Object A mock object simulates the responses of an existing object. It helps with designing and testing interactions between objects, replacing a real component so that a test can verify its indirect outputs.

Product Backlog Product Backlog is a Scrum term for the prioritized master list of all functionality desired in the product. This backlog grows over time as the organization thinks of new features they may need.

Product Owner Product Owner is a Scrum term for the person responsible for prioritizing the product backlog, or stories. He or she is typically someone from a marketing role or a key business expert involved with development.

Quality Assurance (QA) Team Quality Assurance, or QA, can be defined as actions taken to ensure compliance with a quality standard. In software development, the term "QA Team" is often used to refer to the team that does software testing. Test teams (see *Test Team*) provide stakeholders with information related to the quality of the software product. They perform activities to learn how the system under test should behave and verify that it behaves as expected. In agile development, these activities are fully integrated with development activities. Testers are often part of the development team along with everyone else involved in developing the software.

Production Code Production code is the code for the system that is, or will be, used in production, as distinguished from the code that is written to test it. Test code invokes or operates on production code to verify its behavior.

Refactoring Refactoring is changing code, without changing its functionality, to make it more maintainable, easier to read, easier to test, or easier to extend.

Regression Test A regression test verifies that the behavior of the system under test hasn't changed. Regression tests are usually written as unit tests to drive coding or acceptance tests to define desired system behavior. Once the tests pass, they become part of a regression test suite, to guard against unintended changes being introduced. Regression tests should be automated to ensure continual feedback.

Release Candidate A release candidate is a version or build of the product that can potentially be released to production. The release candidate may undergo further testing or be augmented with documentation or other materials.

Return on Investment (ROI) Return on investment, or ROI, is a term borrowed from the world of financial investments and is a measure of the efficiency of an investment. ROI can be calculated in different ways, but it's basically the difference between the gain from an investment and the cost of that investment, divided by the cost of that investment. In testing, ROI is the benefit gained from a testing activity such as automating a test, weighed against the cost of producing and maintaining that test or activity.

SOAP SOAP is a protocol for exchanging XML-based messages over networks, normally using HTTP/HTTPS. It forms the foundation layer of the web services protocol stack, providing a basic messaging framework upon which abstract layers can be built. A common SOAP messaging pattern is the Remote Procedure Call (RPC) pattern, in which the client network node sends a request message to the server node, and the server immediately sends a response to the client.

Story A user story is a short description of functionality told from the perspective of the user that is valuable to either the user or the customer team. Stories are traditionally written on index cards. The card typically contains a one-line description of the feature. For example, "As a shopper, I can put items in my shopping cart so that I can check out with them later" is a story. Cards are only useable in combination with subsequent conversations between the customer team and the development team and some verification that the story has been implemented through writing and running tests.

Story Test A story test defines expected behavior for the code to be delivered by the story. Story tests may be business-facing, specifying the functional requirements, or technology-facing, such as security or performance tests. These tests are used to guide development as well as to verify the delivered code. Most agile practitioners use the term "story test" synonymously with "acceptance test," although the term "acceptance test" might be used for tests that verify behavior at a higher level than one story.

Story Board The story board, also called the task board, is used to track the work the team does during an iteration. Task cards, which may be color-coordinated for the type of task, are written for each story. These cards, along with a visual cue of some kind, provide an easy mechanism for seeing the current status of an iteration's progress. It may use columns or different colored stickers on cards for different states such as "To do," "Work in Progress," "Verify," and "Done." The story board might be a physical board on a wall or a virtual online board.

Task Tasks are pieces of work needed to finish a story. A task might be action needed to implement a small piece of a story, or it might be for building a bit of infrastructure, or testing that encompasses more than one story. Generally it should represent a day or less of work.

Technical Debt Ward Cunningham first introduced this metaphor. When a team produces software without using good practices such as TDD, continuous integration, and refactoring, it may incur technical debt. Like financial debt, technical debt accrues interest that will cost the team more at a later date. Sometimes this debt may be worthwhile, such as to take advantage of a sudden business opportunity. Usually, though, technical debt compounds and slows the team's velocity. Less and less business value can be produced in each iteration because the code lacks a safety net of automated regression tests or has become difficult to understand and maintain.

Test Double A test double is any object or component that's installed in place of the real component for the express purpose of running a test. Test doubles include dummy objects, mock objects, test stubs, and fake objects.

Test-Driven Development (TDD) In test-driven development, the programmer writes and automates a small unit test before writing the small piece of code that will make the test pass. The production code is made to work one test at a time.

Test-First Development In test-first development, tests are written in advance of the corresponding production code, but the code is not necessarily made to work one test at a time. Customer or story tests may be used in test-first development as well as unit tests.

Test Stub A test stub is an object that replaces a real component needed by the system under test with a test-specific object that feeds desired indirect inputs into the system under test. This enables the test to verify logic independently of the other components.

Test Team A test team performs activities that help define and subsequently verify the desired behavior of the system under test. The test team provides information to the stakeholders about the external quality of the system, the risks that may be present, and potential risk mitigation strategies. In agile development, these activities are fully integrated with development activities. Testers are often part of the development team along with everyone else involved in developing the software.

Tester A tester provides information to stakeholders about the software being developed. A tester helps customers define functional and nonfunctional requirements and quality criteria, and helps turn these into tests that guide development and verify desired behavior. Testers perform a wide variety of activities related to delivering high-quality software, such as test automation and exploratory testing. In agile development, everyone on the development team performs testing activities. Team members who identify themselves as testers work closely with other members of both the developer and customer teams.

Theme A theme is the same as an epic or feature. It is a piece of functionality described by the customer and placed in the product backlog to be broken up into stories that are sized and estimated.

Unit Test A unit test verifies the behavior of a small part of the overall system. It may be as small as a single object or method that is a consequence of one or more design decisions.

Velocity A development team's velocity is the amount of value it delivers in each iteration, measured in story points, ideal days, or hours. Generally, only completed stories are included in the velocity. Velocity is helpful to the business in planning for future features and releases. Agile teams use their velocity for the previous iteration to help determine the amount of work they can take on in the next iteration.

Web Service Description Language (WSDL) Web Service Description Language (WDSL) is an XML format for describing network services as a set of endpoints operating on messages containing either document-oriented or procedure-oriented information.

BIBLIOGRAPHY

BOOKS, ARTICLES, PAPERS, AND BLOG POSTINGS

Agile Alliance. "Principles Behind the Agile Manifesto," www.agilemanifesto
.org/principles.html, 2001.

Alles, Micah, David Crosby, Carl Erickson, Brian Harleton, Michael Marsiglia, Greg Pattison, and Curt Stienstra. "Presenter First: Organizing Complex GUI Applications for Test-Driven Development," Agile 2006, Minneapolis, MN, July 2006.

Ambler, Scott. *Agile Database Techniques: Effective Strategies for the Agile Software Developer*, Wiley, 2003.

Astels, David. *Test-Driven Development: A Practical Guide*, Prentice Hall, 2003.

Bach, James. "Exploratory Testing Explained," www.satisfice.com/articles/et-article.pdf, 2003.

Bach, Jonathan. "Session-Based Test Management," Software Testing and Quality Engineering Magazine, November, 2000, www.satisfice.com/articles/sbtm.pdf.

Beck, Kent. *Extreme Programming Explained: Embrace Change*, Addison-Wesley, 2000.

Beck, Kent, and Andres, Cynthia. *Extreme Programming Explained: Embrace Change. 2nd Edition*, Addison-Wesley, 2004.

Berczuk, Stephen and Brad Appleton. *Software Configuration Management Patterns: Effective Teamwork, Practical Integration*, Addison-Wesley, 2003.

Bolton, Michael. "Testing Without a Map," Better Software, January 2005, www.developsense.com/articles/Testing%20Without%20A%20Map.pdf.

Bos, Erik and Christ Vriens. "An Agile CMM," in Extreme Programming and Agile Methods–XP/Agile Universe 2004, 4th Conference on Extreme Programming and Agile Methods, Calgary, Canada, August 15–18, 2004, Proceedings, ed. Carmen Zannier, Hakan Erdogmus, Lowell Lindstrom, pp. 129–138, Springer, 2004.

Boutelle, Jonathan. "Usability Testing for Agile Development," www .jonathanboutelle.com/mt/archives/2005/08/usability_testi_1.html, 2005.

Brown, Titus. "The (Lack of) Testing Death Spiral," http://ivory.idyll.org/blog/mar-08/software-quality-death-spiral.html, 2008.

Buwalda, Hans. "Soap Opera Testing," Better Software Magazine, February 2004, www.logigear.com/resources/articles_lg/soap_opera_testing.asp.

Clark, Mike. *Pragmatic Project Automation: How to Build, Deploy and Monitor Java Apps*, The Pragmatic Programmers, 2004.

Cohn, Mike. *User Stories Applied for Agile Software Development*, Addison-Wesley, 2004.

Cohn, Mike. *Agile Estimating and Planning*, Prentice Hall, 2005.

Crispin, Lisa and Tip House. *Testing Extreme Programming*, Addison-Wesley 2002.

Crispin, Lisa. Articles "Hiring an Agile Tester," "An Agile Tool Selection Strategy for Web Testing Tools," "Driving Software Quality: How Test-Driven Development Impacts Software Quality," http://lisa.crispin.home.att.net.

DeMarco, Tom and Timothy Lister. *Managing Risk on Software Projects*, Dorset House, 2003.

Derby, Esther and Larsen, Diana. *Agile Retrospectives: Making Good Teams Great*, Pragmatic Bookshelf, 2006.

Derby, Esther and Rothman, Johanna. *Behind Closed Doors: Secrets of Great Management*, Pragmatic Bookshelf, 2006.

De Souza, Ken. "A tester in developer's clothes" blog, http://kendesouza .blogspot.com.

Dustin, Elfriede, Chris Wysopal, Lucas Nelson, and Dino Dia Zovi. *The Art of Software Security Testing: Identifying Software Security Flaws*, Symantec Press, 2006.

Dustin, Elfriede. "Teamwork Tackles the Quality Goal," *Software Test & Performance*, Volume 2, Issue 200, March 2005.

Duvall, Paul, Steve Matyas, and Andrew Glover. *Continuous Integration: Improving Software Quality and Reducing Risk*, Addison-Wesley, 2007.

Eckstein, Jutta. *Agile Software Development in the Large: Diving Into the Deep*, Dorset House, 2004.

Evans, Eric. *Domain-Driven Design: Tackling Complexity in the Heart of Software*, Addison-Wesley, 2003.

Feathers, Michael. *Working Effectively with Legacy Code*, Prentice Hall, 2004.

Freeman, Steve and Nat Pryce. "Mock Objects," www.mockobjects.com.

Fowler, Martin. "Continuous Integration," http://martinfowler.com/articles/ continuousIntegration.html, 2006.

Fowler, Martin. "StranglerApplication," www.martinfowler.com/bliki/ StranglerApplication.html, 2004.

Fowler, Martin, "TechnicalDebt," http://martinfowler.com/bliki/ TechnicalDebt.html, 2003.

Gårtner, Markus, personal communication, 2008. For more interesting information, visit his blog at: http://blog.shino.de.

Galen, Robert. *Software Endgames: Eliminating Defects, Controlling Change, and the Countdown to On-Time Delivery*, Dorset House, 2005.

Ghiorghiu, Grig. "Performance vs. load vs. stress testing," http:// agiletesting.blogspot.com/2005/02/performance-vs-load-vs-stress-testing.html, 2005.

Ghirghiu, Grig. "Agile Testing" blog, http://agiletesting.blogspot.com.

Hagar, Jon. Software Testing Papers, www.swtesting.com/hagar_papers_index.html.

Hendrickson, Elisabeth. "Tester Developers, Developer Testers," http://testobsessed.com/2007/01/17/tester-developers-developer-testers/, 2007.

Hendrickson, Elisabeth. "Test Heuristics Cheat Sheet," http://testobsessed.com/wordpress/wp-content/uploads/2007/02/testheuristicscheatsheetv1.pdf, 2007.

Hendrickson, Elisabeth. "Agile-Friendly Test Automation Tools/Frameworks," http://testobsessed.com/2008/04/29/agile-friendly-test-automation-toolsframeworks, 2008.

Highsmith, Jim. *Agile Project Management: Creating Innovative Products*, Addison-Wesley, 2004.

Hunt, Andrew and David Thomas. *The Pragmatic Programmer: From Journeyman to Master*, Addison-Wesley, 1999.

Kaner, Cem, James Bach, and Bret Pettichord. *Lessons Learned in Software Testing*, Wiley, 2001.

Kerth, Norman. *Project Retrospectives: A Handbook for Team Reviews*, Dorset House, 2001.

Kniberg, Henrik. "How to Catch Up on Test Automation," http://blog.crisp.se/henrikkniberg/2008/01/03/1199386980000.html, 2008.

Kniberg, Henrik. *Scrum and XP from the Trenches*, Lulu.com, 2007.

Koenig, Dierk, Andrew Glover, Paul King, Guillaume Laforge, and Jon Skeet. *Groovy in Action*, Manning Publications, 2007.

Kohl, Jonathan. "Man and Machine," *Better Software* magazine, December 2007.

Kohl, Jonathan. Blog and articles, www.kohl.ca/.

Louvion, Christophe. Blog, www.runningagile.com.

Manns, Mary Lynn and Linda Rising. *Fearless Change: Patterns for Introducing New Ideas*, Addison-Wesley, 2004.

Marick, Brian. *Everyday Scripting with Ruby: For Teams, Testers and You*, Pragmatic Bookshelf, 2007.

Marick, Brian, "My Agile Testing Project," www.exampler.com/old-blog/ 2003/ 08/21/, 2003.

Marick, Brian. "An Alternative to Business-Facing TDD," www.exampler .com/ blog/category/aa-ftt, 2008.

Marick, Brian. Blog and articles on agile testing, http://exampler.com.

Marcano, Antony. Blog, www.testingreflections.com.

Meszaros, Gerard. *XUnit Test Patterns: Refactoring Test Code*, Addison-Wesley, 2007.

Meszaros, Gerard and Janice Aston. "Adding Usability Testing to an Agile Project," Agile 2006, Minneapolis, MN, 2006, http://papers.gerardmeszaros .com/AgileUsabilityPaper.pdf.

Meszaros, Gerard, Ralph Bohnet, and Jennitta Andrea. "Agile Regression Testing Using Record & Playback," XP/Agile Universe 2003, New Orleans, LA, 2003, http://agileregressiontestpaper.gerardmeszaros.com.

Meszaros, Gerard. "Using Storyotypes to Split Bloated XP Stories," http:// storyotypespaper.gerardmeszaros.com.

Mugridge, Rick and Ward Cunningham. *Fit for Developing Software: Framework for Integrated Tests*, Prentice Hall, 2005.

Newkirk, James and Alexei Vorontsov. *Test-Driven Development in Microsoft .NET*, Microsoft Professional, 2004.

Nielsen, Jakob. "Time Budgets for Usability Sessions," www.useit.com/ alertbox/usability_sessions.html, 2005.

North, Dan. "Introducing BDD," http://dannorth.net/introducing-bdd, 2006.

Patterson, Kerry, Joseph Gernny, Ben McMillan, Al Switzler and Stephen R. Covey. *Crucial Conversations: Tools for Talking when the Stakes are High*, McGraw-Hill, 2002.

Patton, Jeff. "Test Software Before You Code," StickyMinds.com, August 2006, www.stickyminds.com/sitewide.asp?Function=edetail&ObjectType=COL&ObjectId=11104.

Patton, Jeff. "Holistic Agile Product Design and Development," www.agileproductdesign.com/blog/agile_product_development.html, 2006.

Pols, Andy. "The Perfect Customer," www.pols.co.uk/archives/category/testing, 2008.

Pettichord, Bret. "Homebrew Test Automation," www.io.com/~wazmo/papers/homebrew_test_automation_200409.pdf, 2004.

Pettichord, Bret. "Seven Steps to Test Automation Success," www.io .com/~wazmo/papers/seven_steps.html, 2001.

Poppendieck, Mary and Tom Poppendieck. *Implementing Lean Software Development: From Concept to Cash*, Addison-Wesley, 2006.

Poppendieck, Mary and Tom Poppendieck. *Lean Software Development: An Agile Toolkit*, Addison-Wesley, 2003.

Rainsberger, J. B. *JUnit Recipes: Practical Methods for Programmer Testing*, Manning Publications, 2004.

Rasmusson, Jonathan. "Introducing XP into Greenfield Projects: Lessons Learned," IEEE Software, 2003, http://rasmusson.files.wordpress.com/2008/01/s3021.pdf.

Robbins, Stephen and Tim Judge. *Essentials of Organizational Behavior, 9th Edition*, Prentice Hall, 2007.

Schwaber, Ken. *Agile Project Management with Scrum*, Microsoft Press, 2004.

Shore, James and Shane Warden. *The Art of Agile Development*, O'Reilly Media, 2007.

Soni, Mukesh. "Defect Prevention: Reducing Costs and Enhancing Quality," iSixSigma, http://software.isixsigma.com/library/content/c060719b.asp.

Sumrell, Megan. "'Shout-Out' Shoebox – Boosting Team Morale," http://megansumrell.wordpress.com/2007/08/27/shout-out-shoebox-boosting-team-morale, 2007.

Sutherland, Jeff, Carsten Ruseng Jakobsen, and Kent Johnson. "Scrum and CMMI Level 5: The Magic Potion for Code Warriors," Agile 2007, Washington, DC, 2007, http://jeffsutherland.com/scrum/Sutherland-ScrumCMMI6pages.pdf.

Tabaka, Jean. *Collaboration Explained: Facilitation Skills for Software Project Leaders*, Addison-Wesley, 2006.

Thomas, Mike. "Strangling Legacy Code," *Better Software* magazine, October 2005, http://samoht.com/wiki_downloads/StranglingLegacyCodeArticle.pdf.

Tholfsen, Mike. "The Rise of the Customer Champions," STAREAST, May 7–9, 2008.

Voris, John. ADEPT AS400 Displays for External Prototyping and Testing, www.AdeptTesting.org.

Wake, Bill. "XP Radar Chart," http://xp123.com/xplor/xp0012b/index.shtml, 2001.

Wilson-Welsh, Patrick and Lisa Crispin, "Flipping the Triangle: Paths to Best, Least-Cost Automated Testing", Agile 2008, 2008, http://patrickwilsonwelsh.com/wp-content/uploads/2008/08/flipping-the-triangle.pdf.

Vriens, Christ. "Certifying for CMM Level 2 and ISO9001 with XP@Scrum," in ADC 2003: Proceedings of the Agile Development Conference, 25–28 June 2003, Salt Lake City, UT, USA, 120–124, IEEE, 2003.

TOOL REFERENCES

Abbot Java GUI Test Framework, http://abbot.sourceforge.net/doc/overview.shtml.

Adzik, Gojko. DbFit: Test-driven Database Development, http://gojko.net/fitnesse/dbfit/.

Faught, Danny. "Test Tools List," http://testingfaqs.org, 2008.

Canoo WebTest, Open Source Tool for Automated Testing of Web Applications, http://webtest.canoo.com.

easyb, Behavior Driven Development Framework for the Java Platform, www.easyb.org/.

Fit, Framework for Integrated Test, http://fit.c2.com.

JUnit, Resources for Test-Driven Development, www.junit.org.

JUnitPerf, JUnit Test Decorators for Performance and Scalability Testing, http://clarkware.com/software/JUnitPerf.html.

FitNesse, Fully Integrated Standalone Wiki and Acceptance Testing Framework, www.fitnesse.org.

Hower, Rick, Software QA and Testing Tools Info, www.softwareqatest.com/qattls1.html.

NUnit, Unit-testing Framework for .NET Languages, http://nunit.org/index.php.

Open Source Software Testing Tools, News and Discussion. www.opensourcetesting.org/.

RpgUnit, RPG Regression Testing Framework, www.RPGunit.org.

Selenium, Web Application Testing System, http://seleniumhq.org/.

soapUI, Web Services Testing Tool, www.soapui.org.

Source Configuration Management, http://better-scm.berlios.de.

Subversion, Open Source Version Control System, http://subversion.tigris.org/.

Unit Testing Frameworks. http://en.wikipedia.org/wiki/List_of_unit_testing_frameworks.

Watir, Web Application Testing in Ruby, www.watir.com.

INDEX

A

Abbot GUI test tool, 127

Acceptance tests. *See also* Business-facing tests
definition, 501
Remote Data Monitoring system example, 245
UAT (user acceptance testing) compared with, 130

Ad hoc testing, 198

Adaptability, skills and, 39–40

ADEPT (AS400 Displays for External Prototyping and Testing), 117–118

Advance clarity
customers speaking with one voice, 373–374
determining story size, 375–376
gathering all viewpoints regarding requirements, 374–375
overview of, 140–142, 373

Advance preparation
downside of, 373
how much needed, 372–373

Agile development
Agile manifesto and, 3–4
barriers to. *See* Barriers to adopting agile development
team orientation of, 6

Agile Estimating and Planning (Cohn), 331, 332

Agile manifesto
people focus, 30
statement of, 4
value statements in, 21

Agile principles. *See* Principles, for agile testers

Agile testers. *See also* Testers
agile testing mind-set, 482–483
definition, 4
giving all team members equal weight, 31
hiring, 67–69
what they are, 19–20

Agile testing
definition, 6
as mind-set, 20–21
what we mean, 4–7

Agile values, 3–4

Alcea's FIT IssueTrack, 84

Alpha tests, 466–467

ant, 284
as build tool, 126
continual builds and, 175, 291

AnthillPro, 126

ANTS Profiler Pro, 234

Apache JMeter. *See* JMeter

API-layer functional test tools, 168–170
Fit and FitNesse, 168–170
overview of, 168
testing web Services, 170

API testing
automating, 282
overview of, 205–206

APIs (application programming interfaces), 501

Appleton, Brad, 124

Application under test (AUT), 246